LUNATICS AND LOVERS

LUNATICS
AND
LOVERS

A Tribute to the Giddy
and Glittering Era of the
Screen's "Screwball" and
Romantic Comedies

TED SENNETT

ARLINGTON HOUSE   *New Rochelle, N.Y.*

Library of Congress Catalog Card Number 73–10709

MANUFACTURED IN THE UNITED STATES OF AMERICA

Library of Congress Cataloging in Publication Data

Sennett, Ted.
  Lunatics and lovers.

  Bibliography: p.
  1. Comedy films.   2. Moving-pictures—United
States.   I.   Title.
PN1995.9.C55S4   791.43'0909'17   73–10709
ISBN 0–87000–196–5

*For my mother
and my father,
with gratitude
and love*

CONTENTS

ACKNOWLEDGMENTS   9

CHAPTER ONE: A WORLD OF LUNATICS AND LOVERS   13

CHAPTER TWO: THE CINDERELLA SYNDROME   20

CHAPTER THREE: WIFE, HUSBAND, FRIEND, SECRETARY   52

CHAPTER FOUR: POOR LITTLE RICH GIRLS (AND BOYS)   90

CHAPTER FIVE: LAMB BITES WOLF   116

CHAPTER SIX: BATS IN THEIR BELFRY   142

CHAPTER SEVEN: THE THIN MAN, TOPPER, AND FRIENDS   163

CHAPTER EIGHT: BOSS-LADIES AND OTHER LIBERATED TYPES   197

CHAPTER NINE: THE AMAZING MR. STURGES   225

CHAPTER TEN: STAGE TO SCREEN   256

POSTSCRIPT   289

APPENDIX I: THE PLAYERS   290

APPENDIX II: THE DIRECTORS   311

APPENDIX III: THE WRITERS   320

FILMOGRAPHY   327

BIBLIOGRAPHY   355

INDEX   357

ACKNOWLEDGMENTS

I should like to thank the wonderfully cooperative people at Columbia Pictures for permitting me to screen a number of Columbia comedies. My thanks also to Films, Incorporated for films in their collection.

I should also like to thank the following for their help in obtaining photographs: Jerry Vermilye, Movie Star News, Gene Andrewski, Columbia Pictures, and Movie Poster Service.

Above all, I am grateful to my wife Roxane for her patience, encouragement—and faith.

LUNATICS AND LOVERS

A WORLD OF LUNATICS AND LOVERS

Laughter can be mocking. Laughter can be healing. Laughter can reverberate with echoes of despair. And laughter can reassure us that men and women, despite their pretensions and their lofty ideas, still have the capacity to make fools of themselves.

In the 1930s, in a gray and troubled America, the laughter that bubbled up from screen comedy was all of these: it poked fun at our absurdities and eased our tensions, while concealing a deep-rooted hopelessness.

The earliest years of the decade brought very little cause for laughter. Following the Black Thursday of October 24, 1929, the country settled into a grim, joyless, even ugly mood: gangs of desperate farmers assembled to prevent the taking over of their land; shabby men waited in breadlines, all self-respect destroyed by hunger; youngsters, stripped of family ties, haunted the hobo jungles, or drifted aimlessly through the streets.

Not many films of the early thirties confronted the real problems of the Depression head-on. For every film such as *I Am a Fugitive From a Chain Gang* (Warners, 1932) or King Vidor's *Our Daily Bread* (United Artists, 1934), there were dozens in which the numbing poverty and desolation were either handled glancingly or simply ignored. The constant struggle for money was implicit in the breezy Warners comedies in which James Cagney, the sly, conniving urban animal, sought to outsmart the system, or in the lavish musical films about penniless performers or bankrupt producers working to "put on a show." The desperate surrender to expediency was suggested in the parade of tear-streaked dramas about "fallen" women—Barbara

Stanwyck, Ruth Chatterton, *et al.*—who turned to prostitution or took up with nasty but generous gangsters. Nowhere could the Depression be found in the "high society" dramas and comedies of indiscretions among the rich, and even the cheery effusions of Shirley Temple urged Americans to simply laugh and sing their troubles away.

For the movies, bad times may have been an illusion—yet much of the film comedy of that early period had a sour taste, an edge of hostility and scorn. The Marx Brothers tumbled into films from the stage, bringing their anarchic view of society, their wildly mocking attitudes toward man's pomposity and stupidity. While audiences roared at their antics, the brothers thumbed their noses at war, education, romance, and just plain people. In his hilarious films, W. C. Fields betrayed a contempt that actually went beyond children and dogs to include all humanity. Mae West's sinuous walk and suggestive little moans of pleasure laughed derisively at sex.

As times improved and the country began to overcome its lethargy, the mood changed gradually to one of hope and promise. Shaking the dust from their clothes and the cobwebs from their minds, people started to rebuild their lives and to insist that the conditions that had kept them mired in hopelessness be alleviated or destroyed. A growing desire to topple old and outmoded institutions brought workers into rebellion against management, or found minorities resisting majority rule. It was a time of slow, painful, and sometimes exhilarating rebirth.

By the mid-thirties, the evolving optimism began to affect the comedies that flowed from the Hollywood studios. Certain biases persisted: to be rich and idle was to be a target for contempt. Poverty had its compensations. Love was more important than a bank account. But attitudes were changing, and the comedies began to center, not on grotesque figures with painted moustaches or rag-mop hair or bulbous noses, but on identifiable people, foolish, scatterbrained, and laughably fallible, but also good-natured, honest, and likeable. A spoiled heiress could be forced to take to the road and not only learn humility but find romance as well. A poor girl could suddenly acquire a sable coat and a rich boyfriend (though a poor one was even nicer). Husbands and wives could banter merrily, even while investigating a homicide. They all seemed to be saying: If nothing makes sense in a crisis-ridden, dangerous world, then why behave sensibly? Why not confront life's problems—a broken love affair, a crumbling marriage, a murder—with cheerful impudence and occasionally a wide streak of lunacy?

And so, as film comedy softened around the edges, a new genre was born, one that persisted through the thirties, then changed form and direction in the forties. It was dubbed the "screwball" comedy.

To alleviate the frustrations and bitter disappointments of the time, the screwball comedies brought nervous explosions of slapstick and occasional touches of asperity. But essentially their tone was only gently mocking—the idle rich bore the brunt of the attack—and reassuring. With good will and honest intentions, management could not only sit down with labor but they could become fast friends, sharing a common bond of decency and concern. The country was in deep trouble, but love was still possible, and family ties were stronger than ever. The remedy was laughter, and John Sullivan voiced it much later in Preston Sturges' 1941 film, *Sullivan's Travels:* "There's a lot to be said for making people laugh! It isn't much, but it's better than nothing in this cockeyed caravan!"

The foremost exponent of this brand of optimism had good reason to feel this way. Director Frank Capra was the son of resilient Italian immigrants who had struggled for survival in the early years of the century. Aggressive, determined, and believing strongly in his own ability, he had joined the budding film industry in California. For a while he worked for producer Hal Roach and then for the innovative "King of Comedy," Mack Sennett, turning out gags, plots and pieces of slapstick "business" for the films churned out by the Sennett studio. After directing several of "baby-face" comic Harry Langdon's most successful movies, he joined Harry Cohn at Columbia Pictures on "Poverty Row," where he sought to direct films that could reflect his own buoyant feelings about America.

His early films at Columbia were a curious lot: they included *Platinum Blonde* (1931), a comedy titled to capitalize on Jean Harlow's appearance in a featured role; *American Madness* (1932), an offbeat drama about a bank president (Walter Huston) with severe business and marital problems; and *The Bitter Tea of General Yen* (1933), an exotic and rather self-conscious drama about an interracial romance. Then the quintessential Capra emerged when he directed veteran stage star May Robson in *Lady for a Day* (1933), a sentimental Damon Runyon story about "Apple Annie," a whisky-soaked old derelict who is transformed into a society matron by her friends for the benefit of her homecoming daughter. Performed zestfully by a cast that included Warren William, Glenda Farrell, and Guy Kibbee, it assured Capra's position as a director of popular entertainment.

It was Capra's next film, *It Happened One Night* (1934), a comedy that began life as a much-maligned orphan, which firmly established Capra's style and launched the genre of screwball comedy. Its beginnings as a Samuel Hopkins Adams story, "Night Bus," its cursory dismissal by producers, studio lackeys, and stars (turning down the film, Capra has said, was becoming a trend), have been fully recorded. The film's special, durable charm, and the warmly agreeable performances by reluctant leads Claudette Colbert and Clark Gable, are discussed elsewhere in this book. Despite an inauspicious start, *It Happened One Night* spurred the development of a body of films that gave a human dimension to film comedy and expressed the daffy, endearing quality of its lunatic fringe.

Luckily, Frank Capra was not the only director who could offer the freewheeling approach essential for screwball comedy. A number of his contemporaries had enjoyed a similar apprenticeship in the silent era, learning to strengthen their sense of comic timing, their ability to handle rough-house slapstick, by working with the masters. Leo McCarey, who directed *Duck Soup* (1933), *Ruggles of Red Gap* (1935), and *The Awful Truth* (1937), had been employed as a gag writer and had directed Laurel and Hardy films for Hal Roach. (One of the comedies was *Battle of the Century*, which featured astonishing variations on the standard pie-throwing routine.) George Stevens, who directed *Woman of the Year* (1942), *The Talk of the Town* (1942), and *The More the Merrier* (1943), had also worked for Hal Roach in various capacities. Gregory La Cava, whose *My Man Godfrey* (1936) was one of the funniest films of the thirties, had directed such mid-twenties farces as *Womanhandled* (1926) and *Say It Again* (1926), both starring young Richard Dix. Director Wesley Ruggles, whose credits include *The Gilded Lily* (1935) and *True Confession* (1937), was originally one of Mack Sennett's Keystone Kops and had directed silent films with blunt titles: *Beware of Widows* (1927), *The Fourflusher* (1928), etc.

Many screenwriters of the period were also capable of turning out the bright banter, the insouciant, irreverent, tongue-in-cheek dialogue that helped to keep these comedies afloat. Frank Capra had his favorite scenarist, Robert Riskin, who was clearly in tune with Capra's requirement for combining humor with folksiness. Other writers, such as Norman Krasna, George Seaton, Claude Binyon, Charles Brackett and Billy Wilder, Virginia Van Upp, and the Epstein brothers, Julius and Philip, kept the comic situations spinning merrily from living room to bedroom, from New York penthouse to small-town porch. Sometimes they ran out of breath or out of inventive devices, but the pace was always swift and the results were often hugely entertaining.

Above all there were the performers, the actors and actresses with diverse backgrounds and experience, who brought a matchless elegance and style to these films. Moving gracefully through their lines, even when the lines were less than witty, they expressed a variety of moods—romantic, vindictive, irrepressible, petulant—in a manner that was paradoxically civilized and demented, as if behaving irrationally was the only rational thing one could do under trying circumstances.

The actresses, in particular, were a breed apart. Carole Lombard appeared in a number of silent films, often as one of Mack Sennett's bathing beauties, and then made over twenty films for Paramount in the early thirties. In 1934, cast opposite John Barrymore in *20th Century* as a volatile stage star, she revealed a comic ability that bolstered and brightened many films until her death in 1942. Jean Arthur was a Wampas Baby Star in 1929 and a conventional heroine in early sound films, until producers noted that her inimitable voice could express joy, exasperation, or any number of moods and emotions. After appearing in *The Whole Town's Talking* (1935) and *Mr. Deeds Goes to Town* (1936), she was a popular star.

There were other actresses who could play screwball comedy expertly. Myrna Loy was featured in a number of silent films that drew on her vaguely Oriental name and appearance, and she was a serviceable actress in the early thirties. Then, as Nora Charles, she traded quips with detective husband William Powell in *The Thin Man* (1934) and made marriage freshly attractive rather than relentlessly boring. Irene Dunne emerged from heavy films (*Back Street,* 1932; *Magnificent Obsession,* 1935), as well as elaborate operettas such as *Show Boat* (1936), to portray witty, womanly heroines in *Theodora Goes Wild* (1936), *The Awful Truth* (1937), and other movies. Claudette Colbert starred in over twenty films before agreeing to take the historic bus ride with Clark Gable, thus launching a new career as one of the screen's best comediennes. Katharine Hepburn was dubbed "box-office poison" by film exhibitors, her gift for playing comedy buried under yards of crinoline or soggy scripts. Happily, *Bringing Up Baby* (1938), *Holiday* (1938), and *The Philadelphia Story* (1940), all first-rate comedies, restored her to lasting favor with audiences.

Many actors also proved adept at capturing the mood and spirit of screwball or romantic comedy. Cary Grant made his debut as Thelma Todd's husband in *This Is the Night* (1932), then went on to play rather wooden leading men opposite Mae West, Marlene Dietrich, Jean Harlow, and other flamboyant actresses of the period. His cool, suave, lightly mocking manner was finally put to good use in *Topper* (1937) and *The Awful Truth* (1937), and his dashingly handsome and debonair presence kept him a durable film star for many years. William Powell had enjoyed a long career in silent films and had appeared in dozens of sound films when MGM cast him as detective Nick Charles opposite Myrna Loy and gave full rein to his inimitably wry delivery of lines. Fred MacMurray's earnest, "nice-guy" manner played well against the sophisticated, tongue-in-cheek attitudes of his leading ladies, who included Claudette Colbert, Rosalind Russell, and Madeleine Carroll. From his debut in *So This Is College* (1929) until his retirement from acting in 1950, Robert Montgomery often starred in romantic comedies that called for little more than quizzical looks and an elegantly ironic manner. (His two best performances, however, were as the sly murderer in *Night Must Fall,* 1937, and as the amiable prizefighter in *Here Comes Mr. Jordan,* 1941.) Other actors who seemed at ease playing lunatics and/or lovers included Melvyn Douglas, Ray Milland, David Niven, and Franchot Tone.

Aside from the stars, there were players who appeared regularly in the screwball comedies, adding a welcome note of eccentricity or a pronounced touch of absurdity to the proceedings. Often they were friends or confidantes to the hero or heroine: Edward Everett Horton, fretting endlessly over some dilemma or crisis, permitting his worried face to lapse occasionally into a self-satisfied smirk; Eve Arden dispensing acid like wine to the fools she was obliged to tolerate; Robert Benchley, forever genial, hopeful, and vague; Franklin Pangborn, on the verge of collapse as circumstances conspire to confound him; Helen Broderick, looking with cynical eye on the antics of her friends and relatives; Eugene Pallette, all bombast and bluster; and many other richly gifted comedy performers.

The screwball comedies continued into the forties, entertaining audiences with their humorous and sometimes witty approach to love, marriage, and other of life's staples. Yet something had vanished from the genre, making many of the films a little more forced, a little more mechanical than their predecessors, as if the atmosphere in which the thirties comedies had thrived could no longer be sustained. Most of the popular stars were still active and a few, such as Katharine Hepburn, were finding their stride again after years of neglect. But the air of strain was still evident. Pauline Kael has stated it well:

By the end of the thirties, the jokes had soured. The comedies of the forties were heavy and pushy, straining for humor, and the comic impulse was misplaced or lost; they came out of a different atmosphere, a different *feeling*. The comic spirit of the thirties had been happily self-critical about America, the happiness born of the knowledge that in no other country were movies so free to be self-critical. It was the comedy of a country that didn't yet hate itself.*

Still, the early forties produced their share of superior comedies—the Hepburn-Tracy films and *The More the Merrier* (1943), for example—and they deserve a place in this book.

It is time now to roll the cameras and to restore in memory a special group of delightful movies which critic Otis Ferguson described as "pictures with a styling, a speed, and lightness and frequency of absurd surprise that combined sight, sound, motion, and recognition into something like music."

"Something like music." The phrase is apt. And the overture begins.

*Pauline Kael, *The Citizen Kane Book* (Boston: Atlantic Monthly Press/Little Brown, 1971), p. 25.

CHAPTER TWO

THE CINDERELLA SYNDROME

"Hard-boiled Hannah was going to fall in love with a bankroll. You can't run away from love!"—Carole Lombard in *Hands Across the Table*

"Every Cinderella has her midnight."—Claudette Colbert in *Midnight*

In the bleak years of the Depression, life for the working girl offered few enticements—and fewer prospects for change. A new shade of Tangee Lipstick. A round of contract bridge with girlfriends. A weekly visit with Amos 'n Andy and the "Kingfish." And the not very reassuring certainty that the next day, the next month, would bring more of the same.

But of course there was always the movies where, for a few coins, a girl could project herself easily into Hollywood's manufactured dreamworld. In the darkened theatre, she could pretend that her cold-water flat was a bitter memory, replaced by a "swell" Park Avenue apartment or a "nifty" mansion on Long Island, courtesy of some young, dashing, and conspicuously available millionaire. She could pretend that her dull job as a stenographer or salesgirl was ended—that some cold-eyed "bozo" with a mysterious air of danger about him would sweep her into the deliciously corrupt underground world hinted at in the newspaper headlines. For an hour or two, she could be Cinderella in pursuit of her Prince Charming—and Prince Charming might carry a billfold—or a revolver.

In the early thirties, with life at its grimmest, Cinderella's search for her Prince was no laughing matter, and her single-minded drive for wealth and excitement often ended with the loss of her freedom or her virtue or even both. In a succession of tawdry melodramas, Hollywood was telling that girl in the audience: Follow your dream of luxury and romance, but more likely than not it will turn to ashes or dust. Go after that handsome young man in the tuxedo but chances are he will lead you to ruin and disgrace. For the girl in the audience, it was exhilarating to accompany Loretta Young or Constance Bennett into a moneyed world. And, oh, so comforting to learn that she would be better off exactly where she was.

And, so the screen gave her what she wanted: Loretta Young in Warners' *They Call It Sin* (1932), following an engaged millionaire (David Manners) to the "big city" and falsely confessing to a murder to save the young doctor (George Brent) she really loves; or in MGM's *Midnight Mary* (1933), becoming innocently involved in a life of crime and killing a nasty crook (Ricardo Cortez) to save the young man (Franchot Tone) she really loves. There were many variations and many other heroines—Barbara Stanwyck, Kay Francis, Ruth Chatterton, *et al.*—but the essential theme was the same: Cinderella tarnished by taking up with the wrong Prince Charming. The titles told the story: *Bought* (Warners, 1931), *Compromised* (Warners, 1931), *Shopworn* (Columbia, 1932), and Fox's *She Wanted a Millionaire* (1932), which had beauty-contest winner Joan Bennett marrying a vicious millionaire (James Kirkwood) but ending up with a loyal locomotive engineer (Spencer Tracy).

In these early years, there were few films that took a comic approach to this theme; the girls in the audience clearly preferred raw emotion laced with a generous dose of melodrama. In *Sinners in the Sun* (Paramount, 1932), Carole Lombard wore a procession of gowns as a fashion model who sets her sights on a wealthy married man (Walter Byron), only to settle down with a garage mechanic (Chester Morris). In MGM's *Red-Headed Woman* (1932), Jean Harlow blithely went the route of the avaricious Cinderella as a stenographer who lures her rich boss to the altar, to her bitter regret. (This time she finds true love with his chauffeur.)

As the moviegoer learned to relax and live a little more comfortably with his economic plight, the screen began to find some humor in the spectacle of the poor Depression Cinderella edging her determined and occasionally even innocent way into high society. Writers who had formerly required their heroines to face the torments of hell in affluent sin recognized that the same girls could pursue, find, and even enjoy great wealth and remain untarnished. Of course if they wanted to keep their audiences, they had to make certain that their shopgirls, waitresses, and homeless waifs ended the film not with the dapper playboy in tails but with the Prince Charming in overalls or

THE GOOD FAIRY (1935). Lawyer Herbert Marshall courts innocent Margaret Sullavan.

THE GILDED LILY (1935). Claudette Colbert with her titled suitor, Ray Milland.

a ten-dollar suit. By the unwritten film code of the thirties, the heroine could dream of a large bank account, but she had to learn to live with a small or nonexistent one. And be happy about it as well. (One acceptable variation: the poor Prince could turn out to be a rich Prince, incognito. This, of course, gave the girl the best of both worlds.)

By 1935, the screen was clearly ready for a more lighthearted look at Cinderella than the sex-and-sin melodramas of the very early thirties offered. Though heiress Ellen Andrews was no depressed girl of the streets, her romance with reporter Peter Warne in Columbia's *It Happened One Night* the year before had created a new climate for film comedy in which recognizable people behaved in ways that resembled actual life. The Capra film may have spawned a great many runaway heiresses in the next few years, but it also reaffirmed that comedy could develop naturally in commonplace surroundings—a cross-country bus, a motel—that there could be hearty and healthy laughter as well as wracking sobs in relationships between the sexes.

An even stronger influence for changing the image of the suffering Cinderella was the emergence of the gold-digger, predatory and proud of it, blonde and blunt, who had only one pervading goal: to snare a rich sucker. In films such as the Warners' *Gold Diggers* series and *The Greeks Had a Word for Them* (1932), she flirted, ogled, and finagled her way into the heart and bank account of some unwary millionaire. "It's so hard to be good under the capitalistic system," says Glenda Farrell in *Gold Diggers of 1937*, as she draws a bead on wealthy Victor Moore, and obviously she is feeling no remorse or pangs of guilt. If *It Happened One Night* brought film comedy down to a more comfortable level, the gold-digging girls gave it an honestly earthy touch that made it possible to laugh at working girls on the prowl for moneyed men. Together, they gave film comedy a new direction, and a new, untarnished, totally disarming Cinderella far removed from the sin-soaked heroine of *Midnight Mary*.

Fortunately, actresses were available who could embody this new-style Cinderella and bring to their roles the proper mixture of sophistication and ingenuousness. For years Jean Arthur had been playing conventional heroines in films as varied as *The New Adventures of Dr. Fu Manchu* (1930) and *The Virtuous Husband* (1931). Claudette Colbert had been Maurice Chevalier's leading lady in *The Big Pond* (1930) and the wicked Empress Poppaea in Cecil B. DeMille's *The Sign of the Cross* (1932). Carole Lombard had gone from the Mack Sennett chorus line to suffering-heroine roles in *I Take This Woman* (1931), *No Man of Her*

Own (1932), and other films. Now the moment had come for them to develop their comic skills in a memorable series of diverting Cinderella comedies.

In 1935, no less than eight comedy films released during the year involved a wistful or determined heroine dreaming of and finding (if only temporarily) a life steeped in luxury on the arm of her Prince. For the secretary down to her last pair of nylons, or the housewife surrounded by squalling children and unpayable bills, it was a very good year—for moviegoing.

First on the scene was Margaret Sullavan, who early in February appeared in Universal's *The Good Fairy*, directed by William Wyler and adapted from Ferenc Molnar's play by Preston Sturges (before he joined Paramount as a staff writer). As Luisa Ginglebusher, an innocent maid who becomes involved with an amorous millionaire (Frank Morgan), a protective waiter (Reginald Owen), and a cynical lawyer (Herbert Marshall), Sullavan brought her distinctive throaty voice and a somewhat lugubrious air that clashed with the delicate fantasy of the Molnar play. (This was her third film, made after *Little Man, What Now?* [Universal, 1934], in which she gave a luminous performance as a young bride in Depression-ridden Germany.) Gamely sprinting through the role that Helen Hayes had played on the stage in 1931, she went from orphan to movie usherette to imaginary "wife" during the course of the comedy. The critics agreed that the best performance in the film was given by Frank Morgan as the wealthy man who decides to lavish money on Luisa's nonexistent "husband." In the stage version, this role was played by Walter Connolly, whose later career in films included several choleric millionaires. (*The Good Fairy* was remade in 1947 as *I'll Be Yours*, with Deanna Durbin in the Sullavan role.)

Later the same month, Claudette Colbert turned up in Paramount's *The Gilded Lily*, returning to comedy after two wildly disparate performances as the Queen of the Nile in *Cleopatra* (Paramount, 1934) and as a mother beset with emotional problems in *Imitation of Life* (Universal, 1934). With an amiable but not very witty script by Claude Binyon from a story by Melville Baker and Jack Kirkland, *The Gilded Lily* offered Colbert as a stenographer who suddenly finds herself something of a celebrity when she turns down the proposal of a wealthy young nobleman (Ray Milland). Dubbed "The 'No' Girl" by the press, she is alarmed by the publicity and annoyed at her reporter boyfriend (Fred MacMurray in his first major role), who wrote the original story out of pique. When she is booked into a

THE GIRL FROM 10TH AVENUE (1935). Tenement girl (Bette Davis) and dissolute playboy (Ian Hunter).

HANDS ACROSS THE TABLE (1935). Ex-millionaire Ted Drew (Fred MacMurray) shares apartment with manicurist Regi Allen (Carole Lombard).

nightclub as a singing attraction, she wins over the audience by her blunt ingenuousness and becomes a sensation. (The headlines read: "NO" GIRL STARTLES BROADWAY! "NO" GIRL SHOCKS NEWPORT! "NO" GIRL FOILS JEWEL THIEF!) To nobody's surprise, she finally returns to the arms of her boyfriend after an abortive fling with the nobleman; who evidently admires her status as a celebrity more than her womanly charms.

A slight, fairly engaging comedy directed by Wesley Ruggles, *The Gilded Lily* depended for most of its appeal on Claudette Colbert, who was already working to perfect her ability to handle comic dialogue. Sulking at a nightclub table about her notoriety, she manages to give a fine edge to a line like "I'll drink Scotch, hair tonic, or rat poison." Her best sequence comes with her singing debut. After a series of hopeless voice lessons from that definitive demented Russian, Leonid Kinskey, she appears in an outlandish costume at the nightclub. "I fell like a fancy porch swing!" she announces to the audience. She begins to sing, falters, then decides to tell the truth: "I'm just a freak!" She makes a clumsy attempt to dance, then tries to sing again but keeps forgetting the words. ("That has to be right," she mutters, "It rhymes.") Of course the audience finds all this diverting and she enjoys rapturous applause.

Typical of the thirties film heroine, she rushes back to down-to-earth MacMurray after some unsatisfactory high living. "I'm going home to sit on a bench and eat popcorn!" she cries to her baffled nobleman. And sure enough, her loyal beau is waiting for her in the park. He (smiling as he munches popcorn): "Boy, this is what I call living!" She: "Take off your shoes and kiss me!" Once again the proletarian princess returns to her roots.

The late spring and summer of 1935 brought two entries from Warner Brothers in which a poor but winsome heroine encountered, respectively, fortune and fame, and ended up happily with her Prince. In *The Girl From 10th Avenue*, Bette Davis played Miriam Brady, a spirited tenement girl who marries dissolute playboy Geoffrey Sherwood (Ian Hunter) and finds herself playing the reforming society wife. With the tenacity and firm-mindedness of most Depression heroines, she not only succeeds in making him a useful citizen but prevents his old girlfriend (Katharine Alexander) from winning him back. Directed by Alfred E. Green from a screenplay by Charles Kenyon, it was a mild affair, sparked only by Colin Clive's performance as Miss Alexander's cuckolded husband and by the always welcome presence of Alison Skipworth as a crusty old lady.

Late in the summer, Marion Davies turned up in *Page Miss Glory*—her first film after a year's retirement—playing Loretta, a chambermaid who becomes America's movie sweetheart on a ruse: she resembles the composite photograph of Garbo, Harlow, Dietrich, and Kay Francis assembled by three conspirators for a radio contest. Inevitably, all the glitter and glamour of her new star status is meaningless to her without the love of famous aviator Bingo Nelson (Dick Powell), whom she worships secretly. And just as inevitably, she wins him over after many noisy, farce-heavy incidents and a few songs. Delmer Daves and Robert Lord's adaptation of a Joseph Schrank–Philip Dunning play was not notable for wit or originality but the film boasted a first-rate cast from the Warners stock company: Pat O'Brien, Frank McHugh, Mary Astor, Patsy Kelly, Allen Jenkins, Barton MacLane, and Lyle Talbot.

In the fall, Fox released one of the most pleasing films in the year's Cinderella cycle, a comedy called *The Gay Deception*. This had Frances Dee as a stenographer from the West who wins $5,000 in a lottery and sets herself up as a lady of means at the Waldorf-Plaza Hotel. There she is pursued by Francis Lederer as an exuberant and amorous bellhop who is actually a prince. The familiar situations were given some bright satiric touches in the screenplay by Stephen Avery and Don Hartman—swank hotel ritual is given a few friendly jabs—and director William Wyler, in his second bout that year with romantic comedy, kept the proceedings moving smoothly with the help of a cast that included Alan Mowbray, Akim Tamiroff, Benita Hume, and Ferdinand Gottschalk. (The ubiquitous Luis Alberni appeared briefly but hilariously as a waiter who breaks up a fashionable banquet by accusing the prince of stealing his shirt.) Francis Lederer, in his fourth American film, gave a good account of himself as the bellhop-prince, and Frances Dee made a sprightly heroine, particularly in one scene where she gradually gives way to tears as she nibbles at a biscuit.

A few weeks later, Paramount released *Hands Across the Table*, a highly adroit entry in the poor-girl-seeks-rich-husband series. Under Mitchell Leisen's direction—it was his sixth film and first comedy—it brought together Carole Lombard, in her best comedy role since *Twentieth Century* (1934), as Regi Allen, a manicurist with money on her mind; Fred MacMurray as Ted Drew, a poverty-stricken ex-millionaire about to marry an heiress for security; and Ralph Bellamy as Macklyn, a wealthy aviator consigned to a wheelchair, who is much taken with Regi. Produced under the personal guidance of Ernst

Lubitsch, whose famous "touch" was more than fleetingly evident, the film boasted a consistently funny screenplay by Norman Krasna, Vincent Lawrence, and Herbert Fields and an air of amiable irreverence that seldom faltered. (Mitchell Leisen claims that Dorothy Parker wrote one line of the script, but he has never mentioned which line.)

The film begins with Lombard's single-minded pursuit of MacMurray, whom she believes to be rich and unattached. She meets him playing "indoor" hopscotch in a hotel corridor. Succeeding in getting to his room, ostensibly to give him a manicure, she proceeds to nervously draw blood from his fingertips. (He: "Stabbed in the cuticle. What a way to die! If you think I should draw ether—.") She tries to engage him in conversation about polo, the rich man's sport, but this doesn't work. "What position do you play?" he asks her when she claims to be "mad about polo." "I play chess myself," he confesses. "I don't even *like* horses."

By the time she learns that he has no money—his father was wiped out in the Crash—and, what is worse, that he is engaged to marry "the daughter of the Pineapple King," it is too late to get him out of her life. Reluctantly, she takes him on as a boarder in one-half of her apartment. ("I'm practically a married man. I'll be no trouble.") His presence sparks several of the funniest scenes in the film. When one of Regi's suitors (William Demarest) comes to call, Ted frightens him off by pretending to be her irate husband, discovering her in a liaison with another man. As he pretends to beat her behind a closed door, the suitor flees in terror and tumbles down the stairs. In another scene, one of the most uproarious in thirties comedy, Ted places a telephone call to his fiancée Vivian Snowden (Astrid Allwyn), supposedly from Bermuda where she thinks he has gone for a vacation. His attempts to engage in conversation with Vivian while Regi plays a dim-witted "long-distance operator" constantly interrupting them with nasal directives, and Regi and Ted's efforts to restrain their giggling hysterics, make for delightful comedy.

A few of the scenes in *Hands Across the Table* contain glimmers of the Lubitsch combination of charm and sexuality. As Regi and Ted become increasingly fond of each other, their nighttime banter becomes less acerbic. Sleepless in the living room, Ted tumbles out of bed and awakens Regi. Playfully, he asks her to tuck him in, which she does. He tells her: "You're as good as my mother was. Mother used to kiss me goodnight." She replies: "I'm *almost* as good as your mother was." In another nighttime encounter, they talk together in a warm, rueful mood. They are trying to cling to their determination

THE BRIDE COMES HOME (1935). A glum romantic triangle: Fred MacMurray, Claudette Colbert, Robert Young.

I MET HIM IN PARIS (1937). On the ski slopes with Robert Young, Claudette Colbert, and Melvyn Douglas.

to marry for money. "There's a hundred million miles between us," he tells her. She urges him to marry Vivian, so that he won't have to "scratch for a living in a world you know nothing about." But their faces are wistful and softly focused in the moonlight.

Of course, in true thirties fashion, Regi realizes that she cannot accept the marriage proposal of her wealthy, doting suitor, even though it's what she has always claimed to want. "Hard-boiled Hannah was going to fall in love with a bankroll!" she sobs. "You can't run away from love!" Ted also confesses to Vivian that he loves Regi. "I'm in love with a manicurist," he tells her, warming the hearts of all the girls in the audience who aren't heiresses. But when they meet again, they begin to bicker as usual, until Macklyn stops them: "Shut up, the both of you!" he shouts. "It *is* love that counts." Again, money takes second place to romance.

As Regi, Lombard gives her characteristically winning performance, which combines the proper amounts of vulnerability and impudence. MacMurray is genial as Ted, whether trying to help Regi with the cooking ("Where's the zipper on the eggplant?") or explaining Regi's effect on him to Macklyn. ("She ruined my life. She has me looking for a job.") The stars get good support from Bellamy, Astrid Allwyn, and Ruth Donnelly as Regi's supervisor, who gives her the wrong advice about polo. ("Tell him how you just *love* polo. That's always safe.")

The final Cinderella comedy of 1935 brought back Claudette Colbert in a frail jape inexplicably entitled *The Bride Comes Home*. (She is never a bride during the course of the film and she never comes home, either.) Here Colbert played Jeanette Desmereau, an heiress made poor by the Crash ("I'm practically flat broke, not including the silverware"), who is pursued by two men, one rich (Robert Young) and one not (Fred MacMurray). This was virtually the entire plot—the *New York Times* critic remarked that "its story is so thin as to be very nearly non-existent"—but it was played with some finesse, particularly by William Collier, Sr. as Colbert's sensible father. Featuring the standard number of triangular quarrels, recriminations, and romantic musings—of course Colbert chooses the poor suitor—the Claude Binyon screenplay skips along lightly and unmemorably, under Wesley Ruggles' direction. It gains momentum only at the climax in one hilarious scene featuring "slow-burn" artist Edgar Kennedy. As a harassed justice of the peace whose flowery marriage ceremony ("uncharted sea of life") is continually interrupted, he progresses from mild annoyance to towering rage ("I demand quiet during this ceremony!"), ending in a frenzy that almost demolishes the scenery.

It is one of two bright moments in a sluggish romantic comedy. The other involves Donald Meek as another justice of the peace, this one timid, who finds himself caught in the middle of a quarreling couple he is supposed to marry.

The year 1936 brought no new additions to the Cinderella cycle but there were two the following year. Claudette Colbert appeared in Paramount's *I Met Him in Paris,* once again directed by Wesley Ruggles in yet another screenplay by Claude Binyon. Here she was Kay Denham, an independent-minded girl with a stuffy fiancé (Lee Bowman), who decides to stage a "one-woman rebellion against everything that's sweet and conventional." Her "rebellion" takes the form of leaving her job in a department store and going to Paris. There she is hotly pursued by Gene Anders (Robert Young), a secretly married playboy, while his best friend, playwright George Potter (Melvyn Douglas), acts as a disapproving chaperone. All three go off to Switzerland for several rounds of arguments, recriminations, and winter sports. (These scenes were filmed in Idaho's Sun Valley.) Inevitably, George's interest in Kay becomes more than protective and they end up being married despite his glum and serious-minded attitude.

This time Claude Binyon's script was surprisingly devoid of solid humor and the result was a conventional and not especially amusing triangle comedy. Colbert, Douglas, and Young are proficient, as always, but there is not one memorable or truly comic sequence in the film, as it moves predictably from situation to situation. Much of the humor depends on the ineptitude of the principals at winter sports —they go tobogganing and Gene falls off as they start; Kay narrowly escapes disaster when she falls in the path of a careening bobsled; they all have trouble on skis and skates. Once again Cinderella is offered a life of luxury—Gene proposes marriage after his wife agrees to a divorce—but she settles for George's honest virtues. "I want security," she tells Gene. "You're as irresponsible as a two-month-old kitten."

Inexplicably, the film was warmly received by the critics, with Frank S. Nugent in the *New York Times* calling it "the brightest comedy of the year—a gay, urbane, and witty show." It had, he thought, "the cleverest script of the season." The film was even listed among his selections for the best of the year, though he "hesitated long" over *Nothing Sacred* and *True Confession.*

Later in 1937, Paramount released *Easy Living,* one of the most enjoyable and representative Cinderella comedies of the thirties. With a bright script by Preston Sturges, still three years away from

EASY LIVING (1937). Ray Milland caught up with a hapless customer in a comic riot in the Automat.

his auspicious debut as writer-director with *The Great McGinty*, the film combined elements of the Cinderella story—a poor working girl suddenly finds herself surrounded by ostentatious wealth—with typically thirties situations—her motives and actions are subject to misunderstanding, and her down-on-his-luck Prince Charming turns out to be a millionaire's son.

In the formula Cinderella comedy, the heroine, by means of dogged persistence somewhat short of the blatant single-mindedness of the gold-diggers, usually falls headlong into the lap of luxury. In the clever switch of *Easy Living*, luxury falls *literally* into the heroine's lap when a sable coat is tossed from a rooftop by an irate millionaire and lands on her as she rides by in a bus. Mary Smith (Jean Arthur) is innocently minding her business, unaware that at that very moment irascible banker J. B. Ball (Edward Arnold) is venting his fury on the extravagances of his family and staff. (His chef is using too much butter, and his son John has bought a foreign car.) Confronted by his wife's $58,000 sable coat, he pursues her to the roof, pulls it out of her hands, and heaves it over the side in a rage. Enter Mary Smith at this propitious time, as girl meets coat. (A turbaned Indian aboard the bus cries "Kismet!")

From this improbable coincidence, *Easy Living* spins a gossamer but highly amusing plot line. After a noisy set-to with his chef, who leaves shouting "You dirty capitalist!," J. B. Ball sees Mary trying to return the coat to its proper owner. He encourages her to accept it as a gift and offers to take the perplexed girl home in his car. Telling him of her meager income as a staff member of the magazine *Boy's Constant Companion*, Mary provokes him to a generosity he never feels for his family, and he insists on buying her a sable hat for her sable coat. The store's proprietor is a nervously twittering Franklin Pangborn, who immediately misunderstands their relationship and telephones his friend Louis Louis (Luis Alberni) to announce that J. B. Ball has a "mistress." Louis, it appears, owns a hotel on which Ball is foreclosing, and he has an inspired idea: Make Ball's "mistress" a guest of the hotel, and Bell would never *dare* to foreclose!

In a matter of days, Mary, puzzled and bemused in the style that only Jean Arthur could manage so attractively, finds herself living in the hotel's Imperial Suite. (She was under the impression that she had been summoned by telegram for a job interview.) The scene in which she races through the suite's extravagant rooms, gasping at the undreamed-of luxury, expresses the wish-fulfillment of every girl in the audience, who, like Mary, had to break her piggy bank for living expenses. "A nice place to flop!" Mary cries, as she falls upon the giant bed. She is baffled when Louis asks her to mention the hotel to someone named J. B. Ball, but she agrees graciously.

The film's best-known scene takes place shortly afterwards as Mary, still broke despite her lavish new surroundings, finds her way to an Automat. Here she meets young John Ball (Ray Milland), working as a busboy to prove to his father that he can support himself instead of living off "charity." When he tries to get some food for Mary without paying, he is spotted and a policeman tries to arrest him. In the ensuing fight, a switch is pulled that opens all the food slots simultaneously. The result is bedlam, and one of the most hilarious slapstick scenes of the thirties, as well as an early example of Preston Sturges' gift for lunatic farce. As the customers clamor to seize the suddenly free food, a delirious tramp is constantly thwarted in his attempts to fill up a tray. Finally, he sprinkles pepper liberally about the premises, gets everyone to sneeze, and piles up *several* trays with edibles. Of course he is knocked down in a crescendo of falling crockery. Mary and John flee to her hotel, where they are both puzzled: he by her luxurious apartment and she by his name, which is similar to the one mentioned by Louis. (Naturally, he pretends to be jobless.)

From this point the comic confusion is compounded, as Mary's innocent friendship with J. B. Ball and her growing affection for his son generate a variety of complications. At the same time that the elder Ball is unwarily sparking a scandal by his attentions to Mary—he meets her at the hotel and insists on her joining him for a lavish supper—the younger Ball, still pretending to be penniless, is attracted to Mary and pleased by her concern. One charming scene has them scanning the papers for a job for John, only to have them doze off together on the floor. Mary wakes up abruptly and smiles happily at her sleeping partner-in-poverty.

The balance of the comedy centers on the chaos resulting from a stock tip given by young Ball, which everyone believes comes from his father. (The mistake stems from Mary's quoting the wrong "Mr. Ball.") With Ball Enterprises near bankruptcy and J. B. Ball threatened with divorce by his incensed wife, the script develops a comic frenzy that again suggests the later work of Sturges. As Mrs. Ball (Mary Nash) descends on his office like an avenging fury, Ball's associates are trying frantically to avert ruin. (One man appears to be forever on his way from the barber, his face covered with lather and a hot towel around his neck.)

When the bedlam subsides, all misunderstandings are smoothed over in expected fashion. John returns to his father's fold to help him

IT'S ALL YOURS (1938). Charles Waldron tries to keep playboy Francis Lederer from leaping at secretary Madeleine Carroll.

THREE LOVES HAS NANCY (1938). Nancy (Janet Gaynor) with two of her loves: Robert Montgomery and Franchot Tone.

out of his dilemma. Mrs. Ball forgives her husband. J. B. Ball learns the source of his predicament. And Mary Smith, thirties Cinderella, has not only enjoyed a touch of notoriety but will clearly continue to enjoy "easy living" with the young millionaire she has unwittingly found. Truly an encouraging tale for Depression-weary maidens, and an expert comedy of the era.

The year 1938 passed with only a few screen Cinderellas making fairly perfunctory appearances. There was Columbia's *It's All Yours,* in which Madeleine Carroll played a loyal secretary who inherits her millionaire boss' fortune, to the anger of his playboy nephew (Francis Lederer). Of course she loves him secretly and plots to make him fall in love with her. The comedy was stolen by Mischa Auer as a frenetic baron but the material, under Elliott Nugent's direction, was fragile. There was also MGM's *Three Loves Has Nancy,* directed by Richard Thorpe from a screenplay by Bella and Samuel Spewack, George Oppenheimer, and David Hertz. Four writers had labored to bring forth a slender fable about a young Southern girl (Janet Gaynor, not quite so young any longer and in her next-to-last role before retirement), who must choose between a successful writer (Robert Montgomery) and a publisher (Franchot Tone).

The first Cinderella comedy to appear in 1939 was not only one of the best of the group but came closest to matching the original tale of the hapless duck who becomes a beautiful swan for one glamorous evening. This was Paramount's *Midnight,* released in the spring. Under the direction of Mitchell Leisen, who had helped to make *Hands Across the Table* and *Easy Living* two of the most diverting comedies of the period, it was a witty and charming film that boasted a sparkling screenplay by Charles Brackett and Billy Wilder (from a story by Edwin Justus Mayer and Franz Schulz) and a cast of farceurs including Claudette Colbert, Don Ameche, John Barrymore, Mary Astor, Francis Lederer, and Rex O'Malley.

The story's Cinderella is named Eve, an American nightclub singer who arrives one rainy night in Paris without money or luggage and wearing only an evening gown. She meets and is befriended by a volatile taxi-driver named Tibor Czerny (Don Ameche). At dinner she tells him about her chequered past, particularly about being offered a bribe by the mother of an English lord. "Didn't you throw her out?" Tibor asks. "How could I," she replies, "with my hands full of money?" When she realizes that Tibor is getting entirely too serious—he offers to have her sleep at his place—she leaves quickly.

Anxious to get out of the rain, Eve finds herself an unexpected guest at a chic musicale, where a shrill soprano and a frenzied piano-

MIDNIGHT (1939). Don Ameche is tended by Claudette Colbert. John Barrymore holds the ice.

BACHELOR MOTHER (1939). "Swedish" girl Ginger Rogers tells off David Niven's society girlfriend, June Wilkins.

player are holding forth at the behest of the hostess (Hedda Hopper). Almost spotted as a fraud, she is watched surreptitiously by Georges Flammarion (John Barrymore), a wealthy gentleman with a frivolous, cheating wife Helene (Mary Astor). Introducing herself as the rich Baroness Czerny, Eve gets into a bridge game with Helene, her current boyfriend Jacques (Francis Lederer), and a society hanger-on named Marcel (Rex O'Malley). (Marcel claims to be a "telephone worshipper." Each night he looks at the phone and prays someone will call him.) Eve's presence interests Jacques as much as it irritates Helene.

Shortly afterwards, much to her amazement, Eve suddenly finds herself in possession of a pocketbook filled with money and a luxurious room at the Ritz Hotel. And in the morning she is told that her baggage has arrived and her car is below with a chauffeur waiting! The mystery is solved when Georges Flammarion arrives to explain his "deal." (He had guessed at her dress size: "I've always had a weakness for size twelve.") He will set Eve up as the Baroness Czerny, paying all expenses, if she will agree to steal Jacques from his wife. She consents readily and even appears to have a head start when flowers arrive from Jacques with a card reading, "Hosannas to the high gods for bringing us together." (Georges' comment: "I should resent that. To my wife he only wrote: 'So glad we met.' ")

Eve's campaign gets under way at a dress shop where she meets Helene and Jacques and promptly spirits Jacques away, to Helene's vast annoyance. In a short time, Jacques confesses to Helene that he has fallen in love with Eve. (Eve's remark to Georges on Jacques' speedy courtship: "He ought to have his brakes relined.") Georges' plan appears to be working until Marcel, in league with Helene, uncovers Eve's old luggage and brings it to the house. "Let's have a glorious scandal!" he cries, believing he has the key to Eve's true identity. Eve realizes that her glamorous life as "Baroness Czerny" will be over soon. "Every Cinderella has her midnight," she says, glumly.

But she hasn't reckoned with the *real* Czerny, who has been organizing his fellow cab-drivers in a frantic search for Eve and has finally learned that she is a guest of the Flammarions. To everyone's astonishment, particularly Eve's, he turns up at the house to be reunited with his "wife," fully dressed as the "Baron Czerny." Alone with Eve, he tells her that he loves her. But she is adamant in the tradition of thirties Cinderellas: she refuses to be poor like her parents, constantly quarreling over a lack of money. Jacques is the man she's been waiting for all her life.

From this point, *Midnight* moves into high gear as the screenplay develops a few delightful variations on the familiar theme. While Eve is still allowing Jacques to believe that he is in the running despite her "husband," Czerny pulls a ruse: he announces that their three-year-old daughter "Francie" is seriously ill with the measles and requires her mother's presence at once. Trying to outmaneuver him, Eve pretends to call Budapest and speak with her "mother-in-law" and poor, ill "Francie." On the other end of the line, Georges plays both roles. As the imaginary three-year-old, Barrymore is hilarious in his best flamboyant manner, telling Eve that he is really suffering from "alcoholic poisoning." Eve is almost caught in her ruse when it is revealed that the house telephone is out of order. Quickly she invents an excuse: she was only pretending to call to humor Czerny, who is either eccentric or insane. They really have no daughter. When Czerny turns up as a taxi-driver, everyone is convinced he is demented and their cheerful disbelief provokes him to fury and finally to a violent quarrel with Eve. There is only one recourse: Eve and Czerny must appear to get a divorce, even if there is no marriage!

The film's climax is one of those courtroom scenes so popular during this period, but here performed with enormous relish by the entire cast, with Monty Woolley on hand as an acidulous judge. Eve and Czerny claim that they were truly married—in Shanghai—but their records were destroyed in a fire. Eve is claiming "mental cruelty." "Oh, *that* again," the judge mutters. Czerny struck her, she claims, to which the judge counters: "It's permissible for a wife to be beaten, as long as she's struck not more than nine times with an instrument not larger than a broomstick."

Brought together to the "reconciliation" room, Eve and Czerny are not making any progress until Czerny suddenly decides to become "insane" again. He insists vociferously that he must shave on the spot. Now the judge insists that he cannot grant a divorce as long as one party is deranged. "Go home with your unfortunate husband," he tells Eve. Finally won over, Eve agrees to be reconciled. But she and Czerny startle the judge by announcing that they are now going off to get married.

Acted with finesse by the principal players—Barrymore is a total joy and Mary Astor is especially good as his wife—*Midnight* is an effervescent farce that suggests the films of Ernst Lubitsch in its high polish and brittle style.*

A few months after *Midnight,* Ginger Rogers came on the scene in

---

*It was poorly remade in 1945 by Paramount as *Masquerade in Mexico*, with Dorothy Lamour, Arturo de Cordova, Patric Knowles, and Ann Dvorak in the Colbert-Ameche-Barrymore-Astor roles. Mitchell Leisen again directed, but it was a hopelessly botched affair.

RKO's *Bachelor Mother,* playing a department-store salesgirl who finds herself saddled with a deserted baby and ends up winning the boss' son. Having started to break away from her popular image as Fred Astaire's dancing partner, she appeared to be an ideal choice to play sensible, slightly acidulous working-girl Cinderellas. The previous year she had played opposite James Stewart in *Vivacious Lady* as a nightclub singer who marries a professor of botany, and opposite Douglas Fairbanks, Jr. in *Having Wonderful Time* as a girl who finds romance at a summer camp. In both she was pertly appealing, although the latter film gave her little chance to shine and diluted much of the humor of the Arthur Kober stage play.

In *Bachelor Mother,* under Garson Kanin's direction, she was even better, giving warmth and freshness to a conventional role. Norman Krasna's script was helpful, too, adding a number of wryly amusing touches to an improbable situation. Lighthearted at a time when unwed motherhood was still a subject for tragedy in most films, it brought together Polly Parrish (Rogers), forced to keep a baby in her apartment when everyone refuses to believe it isn't hers, with David Merlin (David Niven), playboy son of the owner of Merlin's Department Store, who is incensed at Polly's heartlessness at "deserting" her baby at a foundling home. His attitude softens, of course, when he falls in love with Polly, and he is even willing to accept the "paternity" foisted upon him by his own father.

Much of the humor in the early part of this ingratiating comedy stems from Niven's fury at Rogers' seemingly coldblooded behavior. When she leaves the baby at his home after he has generously had the foundling home return it to her, he pursues her indignantly to a dance hall, where she has gone with her obnoxious boyfriend Freddie (Frank Albertson). Trying to reach Polly, he drags a hostess across the dance floor, only to be thrown out unceremoniously. (A nice late-Depression touch occurs here. Polly and Freddie win first prize in the dance contest—a loving cup—and they are terribly glum. They wanted the second prize—cash.) Equally funny is the scene in which David tries to return a broken toy duck to the exchange department of his own department store. Faced with smug disbelief by the clerk, he gets angrier and angrier, until he can only whine: "I want a new duck!" Thinking he is either a crackpot or a thief, Freddie, in his new job of assistant floorwalker, tackles him and is sent back to the stock room. "You have disgraced the toy department," his boss tells him.

Rogers and Niven play well together, and even their scenes with the baby are charming. In one, he insists on reading instructions from a book on baby care, which tells Polly to "place oatmeal on a piece of gauze and rub it into the baby's navel." (It turns out the pages were stuck together.) In another scene, he brings Polly to a nightclub, dressed, Cinderella-style, in clothes from Merlin's Department Store, and tells his snobbish society friends that she is Swedish and can't speak a word of English. As they are leaving, David asks his jealously glowering ex-girlfriend how she likes Polly. "She's all right for a filly," the girl remarks. "I'd rather go stag." To which Polly remarks, in clearly enunciated English: "You could, too, with those shoulders."

The film also draws much of its appeal from the presence of the unfailing Charles Coburn as Niven's father, John Merlin. Unshakably convinced that the baby is his grandson, he is incensed by David's denial: "Don't be a cad, sir. He looks exactly like me!" Told that the baby's name is John, he says, "Thanks for *that*, anyhow." The film's best scene occurs in his office, to which all the characters converge in a desperate attempt to prove that someone other than David— *anyone* other than David—is the child's father. The elder Merlin is triumphantly clear on his attitude: "I don't care who the father is," he shouts, "*I'm* the grandfather!" Even at the close of the film, when David, in love with Polly, decides to "confess" being the father, the old man feels vindicated. He tells his son: "Those are the truest words you've said today!"

Several months after *Bachelor Mother*, Ginger Rogers was starring in another RKO comedy, *Fifth Avenue Girl*, again playing a luckless girl who becomes involved with a wealthy old man and his playboy son. But the resemblance to *Bachelor Mother* went no further than that. This time the script was by Allan Scott, whose view of the human race (and particularly its richest representatives) was apparently more jaundiced than Norman Krasna's, surprisingly so for a film produced as late as 1939.* And it was directed by Gregory La Cava, whose deft handling of *My Man Godfrey* in 1936 had revealed a skill with tart, sophisticated, screwball comedy, whereas Garson Kanin's forte was comedy leavened with "warmth" and sentiment.

Not that *Fifth Avenue Girl* could truly be termed tart or sophisticated. It did, however, have a nicely malicious edge that cut deeper

---

*Allan Scott's previous screenplays showed no evidence of this bias. With various collaborators, he had written the scenarios for the best of the Fred Astaire–Ginger Rogers musicals, including *Top Hat, Swing Time, Follow the Fleet,* and *Shall We Dance?*

FIFTH AVENUE GIRL (1939). Mary Gray (Ginger Rogers) enjoys a ride with millionaire Alfred Borden (Walter Connolly).

LUCKY PARTNERS (1940). Explaining the situation to Judge Harry Davenport: Ronald Colman, Ginger Rogers, Jack Carson.

than many other films as it told of the predicament of Mary Gray (Rogers), who finds herself lodged in the Fifth Avenue home of an unhappy millionaire (Walter Connolly) with an eccentric and unappreciative family. Bristling with the true thirties girl's contempt for rich folks (she calls them "cadavers" who look like "a lot of wax dummies who've had an overdose of dill pickles"), she still learns to set things right for the Borden family—and even carries off the Borden son into marriage. Yet another case of thirties ambiguity.

The film begins with the elder Borden, dejected at being ignored on his birthday, meeting Mary in the park. She is hungry and jobless —"I could jump in the seal pond. Maybe somebody would throw me a fish"—and responds readily to his invitation to celebrate his birthday with him. He pours out his problems to a sympathetic Mary: his son is a polo-playing nincompoop. His daughter is in love with his Communist chauffeur. And his wife has taken a gigolo. To ease his woes, he goes on a drunken bender and wakes up the next morning with a black eye and a front-page story in the newspaper. Mary had brought him home, but now her one evening as Cinderella is over. "I've had a beautiful evening," she tells him. "I've been out in society and I've got a wonderful headline. I couldn't be happier. But I've really got to be running along." Borden responds with a speech that epitomizes a prevalent attitude of the thirties, admittedly making a rather late showing in 1939, that wealth is a burden and a detriment to enjoyment:

> I know you don't like the rich, but I'm really not a capitalist. I'm a victim of the capitalistic system, Mary. All right—I didn't want all this. Is it my fault that I invented a pump? All I ever wanted in life was to have some fun and a family. I haven't got a family and I haven't had any fun—until last night.

Mary stays on, of course, and the rest of the film is concerned with her getting the Borden family to appreciate the head of their household, while she reluctantly falls in love with Tim Borden (Tim Holt). Mary's cure for the ills of the Bordens is a mixture of common sense, thirties variety ("I guess rich people are only poor people with money"), blunt honesty, and coercion. She intimidates Tim into taking charge of his father's business. She precipitates a fight between daughter Katharine and her Communist boyfriend to expose the emptiness of his beliefs. ("You haven't enough courage to be a capitalist yourself, so you try to drag everyone else down to where you are.")* And she convinces a chastened Mrs. Borden (Verree Teasdale) that she can win back her husband by giving him the simple thing he loved best when they were poor and living in a three-room apartment: namely, beef stew. The scene in which she proudly serves him the stew while he pretends to be disappointed with Mary has great charm. ("All young people today are very, very irresponsible," he murmurs as she ladles out the stew to his satisfaction.)

The film ends with Borden facing a happy retirement ("I was chained to a pump for twenty-five years and that's long enough") and pretending to "denounce" Mary for disrupting his household. He accuses her of being a wicked, conniving woman, a gold-digger. But Mary, unable to play-act any longer, flees in tears, only to be followed by Tim Borden, who loves her. Presumably she won't mind being married to a young "cadaver" or "wax dummy." Or as she remarked earlier in the film: "I've got my claws in plush and I like the feel of it."

Ginger Rogers appeared in yet another Cinderella comedy of a sort the following year. In RKO's *Lucky Partners* (1940), she played Jean Fenton, a modest bookstore clerk engaged to an insurance salesman (Jack Carson), who has a sudden streak of luck when she meets artist David Grant (Ronald Colman). When they win some money on a shared sweepstakes ticket, David makes one of the least likely proposals in the history of screen comedy: he offers to take her on a "strictly impersonal" honeymoon, so that she can enjoy life before settling into a mundane marriage. For reasons known only to the authors of the screenplay (Allan Scott and John Van Druten, from a story by Sacha Guitry), Jean accepts his proposal and they are soon living in adjoining rooms of a Niagara Falls hotel. Naturally, she suspects his motives, which are pure (this, after all, was 1940), her angry fiancé pursues them to the hotel, and the entire foolish business ends up in the favorite haunt of comedy in that era: the courtroom, presided over by Judge Harry Davenport. By this time, the weary audience knows well before Jean that she really loves David. (David, inciden-

---

*The screenplay is very careful to treat the Communist chauffeur with derision, to prevent having its frequent "digs" at the rich interpreted as subversive. He speaks pompously to everyone—"The nocturnal meanderings of the upper class do not interest me"—and he is forever threatening revolution. But in the end he turns up in a fedora and announces that he is opening a repair shop. ("I shall never forget my proletariat beginnings.") The film mocks the rich but, like many thirties films, it is really on their side.

tally, turns out to be a famous artist who dropped out of society three years earlier.)

Lacking the charm of *Bachelor Mother* or the tart flavor of *Fifth Avenue Girl, Lucky Partners* is Ginger Rogers' weakest film of the period. Unbecomingly brunette, she gives a strained performance marked by an excess of intense frowning. Ronald Colman is equally uneasy, forcing his trademarked debonair manner to the breaking point. Lewis Milestone directed this feeble effort.

By the start of the forties, the theme of the poor girl pushing—or stumbling—her way into a life of luxury had become fairly worn. Except for RKO's amusing *Tom, Dick and Harry* (1941), which had Ginger Rogers rejecting a rich suitor for an auto mechanic, the few films that pursued the theme were not especially notable. In the summer of 1940, Olivia de Havilland appeared in a Warners comedy, *My Love Came Back,* as a prize-winning violinist who is secretly sponsored by a wealthy old man (Charles Winninger), with the usual misunderstandings. It was a lighthearted affair, directed by Curtis Bernhardt, with a genial supporting cast that included Eddie Albert, Spring Byington, Jane Wyman, and S. Z. Sakall. The following year, Joan Bennett starred with Franchot Tone in Columbia's *She Knew All the Answers,* as a simpleminded girl pursued by a playboy (John Hubbard) to the disapproval of the playboy's stuffy guardian (Tone). Of course the guardian finds himself unbending with the girl, sharing popcorn on a Coney Island carousel and turning "all too human." This predictable situation was routinely directed by Richard Wallace.

Paramount's contribution to the cycle in 1941 was *New York Town,* directed by Charles Vidor from a screenplay by Lewis Meltzer and an original story by Jo Swerling. This had Mary Martin as a penniless, homeless waif from Vermont taken under the protective wing of sidewalk photographer Fred MacMurray, who urges her to find a rich husband. She settles on wealthy young Robert Preston but only after MacMurray obtusely refuses to admit that he loves her. The film moved along pleasantly and rather foolishly under Vidor's aimless direction—that same year he had done much better by an entirely different film, Columbia's *Ladies in Retirement*—but it benefited from the amusing supporting performances of Akim Tamiroff as a Polish painter anxiously seeking American citizenship, Lynne Overman as a legless beggar, and Eric Blore, as Preston's butler, forever being bitten by the household dachshund. The film reached its nadir, how-

Upper left:

SHE KNEW ALL THE ANSWERS (1941). Joan Bennett models her coat for Eve Arden and Franchot Tone.

Upper right:

NEW YORK TOWN (1941). Mary Martin and her benefactors: Lynne Overman, Fred MacMurray, and Akim Tamiroff.

Below:

TOM, DICK, AND HARRY (1941). Janie (Ginger Rogers) and her poor but carefree suitor Harry (Burgess Meredith).

ever, in an inane radio quiz scene, which had Mary Martin responding to such questions as "Who wrote Benjamin Franklin's autobiography?" to the admiring cheers of a studio audience.*

The most popular of the Cinderella comedies that year was *Tom, Dick and Harry,* which reunited Ginger Rogers with Garson Kanin, her director for *Bachelor Mother.* (In the interim Kanin had directed the hilarious *My Favorite Wife.*) Blending the standard trappings of romantic comedy with some touches of mildly satirical fantasy, the Paul Jarrico screenplay involved Rogers as Janie, an incurably romantic, incessantly dreaming telephone operator with three suitors: Tom (George Murphy), an aggressive car salesman; Dick (Alan Marshal), a dashing millionaire, and Harry (Burgess Meredith), an easy-going car mechanic.

A good part of the film is devoted to Janie's nighttime fantasies as she envisions married life with each of her suitors. In a final fantasy, she imagines herself married to all three, with husbands-in-triplicate leaving for work, taking a group shower, and preparing for bed together. Her decision is in Hollywood's best storybook tradition: Tom's "get-ahead" attitude is admirable but much too unromantic. ("Maybe he gets promoted too much," Janie remarks.) Dick is merely the embodiment of wish-fulfillment and not a real person. She settles on Harry, the "laissez-faire" idealist, simply because she hears bells whenever they kiss. Poor but happy, Janie and Harry ride off on his motorcycle.

The film has its amusing moments, but most of the humor is soured by Ginger Rogers' surprisingly unconvincing and charmless performance as Janie. Forcing her voice into a querulous whine and pouting dreamily and incessantly, she makes the character appear feebleminded rather than winsome. The other cast members are much better, particularly Burgess Meredith in an amiable performance as Harry and Lenore Lonergan as Janie's realistic-minded young sister. Phil Silvers also contributes a funny bit as an ice cream vendor in Lover's Lane.

Of course the screen Cinderella never really expired after 1940: she merely lowered her sights. The working girl of the thirties who had dreamed of capturing a millionaire found herself too busy, too caught up in the rush of events, to concentrate on money matters. During the war years especially, the millionaires vanished, to be

---

*Preston Sturges directed a few days of retakes on this film after Charles Vidor was forced to leave because of other obligations. He received no credit.

replaced by princes in uniform and mysteriously dashing men involved in "government" affairs.

In wartime, Washington was where the "action" was, and many film comedies dealt with conscientious women who spent as much time fighting for living space as they did searching for men. In RKO's *Government Girl* (1943), Olivia de Havilland coped gamely with crowded quarters in the nation's capital, and with a frustrated longing for her boss, a "dollar-a-year" man played by Sonny Tufts. Paramount's *Standing Room Only* (1944) found Paulette Goddard and Fred MacMurray resorting to a drastic measure to beat the Washington housing shortage: they take jobs as servants. Here, the fun was as thin as the situation was improbable, but Roland Young and Edward Arnold lent able assistance.

By far the most successful of the "wartime Washington" Cinderella tales was George Stevens' *The More the Merrier* (Columbia, 1943). This nimble comedy starred Jean Arthur as Connie Milligan, a pert working girl who, much against her will, finds herself renting half of her apartment to elderly Benjamin Dingle (Charles Coburn), a "retired, well-to-do millionaire" by his own description, in Washington on business. Unable to find a place to stay, Mr. Dingle simply turns away the competition for Connie's apartment and moves in. (His favorite dictum is: "Damn the torpedoes! Full steam ahead!") Later, when Mr. Dingle rents out half of *his* half of the apartment to Joe Carter (Joel McCrea), an Army sergeant in Washington on special duty, there are many complications, some of them romantic, all of them amusing.

Four writers—Richard Flournoy, Lewis R. Foster, Robert Russell, and Frank Ross—were assigned to *The More the Merrier*, but in this case too many hands did not create confusion but a witty and inventive script. From the moment Mr. Dingle receives Connie's minute-by-minute morning schedule and asks: "Do we do all this on railroad time or Eastern war time?" it is clear that the film will move smoothly to a satisfying conclusion. Their first attempt at carrying out the schedule results in bedlam, and one of the comedy's funniest sequences. Mr. Dingle finds himself locked out of the apartment and is forced to knock frantically on Connie's window to attract her attention. In a matter of minutes, he tries vainly to remove his bathrobe while clutching a hot coffee pot, pours most of the coffee into the water in the bathtub, and makes his bed with his pants still in it!

When Joe Carter takes over half of Mr. Dingle's space, the old gentleman immediately sees a good prospect for Connie, though she

THE MORE THE MERRIER (1943). Mr. Dingle (Charles Coburn) and Connie (Jean Arthur) try to work out Connie's morning schedule.

is already engaged to a pompous government official named Charles
J. Pendergast (Richard Gaines). (Connie approves of him because
he's forty-two—"a safe, sane age.") However, she is irate at having
another man in her apartment. (She hears Joe making odd, seal-like
noises in the shower.) But she finally relents—for a one-week "trial"
period. At any rate, Joe seems safe enough—he professes to have
little interest in women.

One of the movie's most felicitous scenes occurs on the roof of
Connie's house, where Connie, Joe, and Mr. Dingle are sharing the
Sunday paper. Joe and Dingle are reading the comics. "You should
read the columnists," she tells them reprovingly. "Are they funny?"
Joe asks. Connie replies: "Sometimes. But no pictures." Mr. Dingle,
who has met Charles J. Pendergast at a symposium on housing,
blithely describes the Pendergast "baby" of the future: "The baby
arrived fifteen minutes before schedule. So Mr. Pendergast refused
delivery." But their brief idyll is ended shortly afterwards when Connie comes upon Mr. Dingle reading her diary and tearfully asks him
to leave with Joe the next day. In the morning, Mr. Dingle is gone
but Joe, conciliatory and obviously attractive to Connie, is permitted
to stay.

Though he is no longer sharing the apartment, Mr. Dingle is still
determined to play an aging Cupid and skillfully manages to get
Connie away from Pendergast and alone with Joe. In a well-remembered scene on the front steps, Joe loses his disinterest in women and
becomes very amorous with Connie, who makes an hilarious attempt
to ignore his kissing of her neck and shoulder. Desperately, she talks
about her engagement ring and her fondness for Pendergast. "He's
so considerate," she murmurs. "A girl gets to appreciate the more
mature (Joe kisses her throat) viewpoint . . ." Later, in the apartment,
they have a split-frame conversation which ends in their confessing
their love for each other. Yet Joe is scheduled to leave Washington
the next day.

Romantic comedy now turns into raucous farce as the FBI abruptly
turns up at the apartment to take Joe into custody. In a rash moment,
Joe had frightened off a jittery neighbor boy by claiming he was a
Japanese spy, and the boy had reported him to the officials. In the
confusion at the police station, Messrs. Dingle and Pendergast turn
up, but apparently Pendergast is more shocked at Joe's sharing the
apartment with Connie than at the charges against him. Dingle hardly
helps matters by claiming falsely that he's always lived in the hotel.
When the entire story is picked up by a reporter and threatens to

make scandalous headlines, Pendergast is distraught, seeing his future in ruins. The only solution, he maintains, is for Connie to marry Joe quickly and get an annulment afterwards. By this time Connie finds Pendergast's attitude hateful. "For twenty-two months," she cries, "I've been engaged to a career." She calls him "Mr. Smug."

Glumly, Connie and Joe go ahead with the plan and return just as glumly to the apartment. But their depression lasts only a short time as the couple, prodded not too gently by Mr. Dingle, fall into each other's arms, ready to make their marriage more than a convenience. And Mr. Dingle leads his cronies in a joyous chorus of "Damn the torpedoes! Full steam ahead!"

As Connie, Jean Arthur has one of her best roles and her winsome manner gives the character great appeal. Joel McCrea is his familiar placid but likeable self, but the film belongs almost entirely to Charles Coburn, who won the year's Academy Award for Best Supporting Actor as the amiable Benjamin Dingle. The film itself was extremely popular, winning an Academy Award nomination for Best Picture and a Best Actress nomination for Jean Arthur. It was also selected by *New York Times* critic Bosley Crowther as one of the ten best films of 1943. (Twenty-three years later, it was remade as *Walk, Don't Run*, with Cary Grant in Coburn's role and Samantha Eggar and Jim Hutton in the Arthur-McCrea parts. Color was added and the setting was changed to Tokyo during the Olympic games.)

In the years following the war and into the fifties, the screen Cinderella turned up intermittently in various guises—as *Sabrina* (Paramount, 1954), the starry-eyed chauffeur's daughter (Audrey Hepburn) who finds unexpected romance with a tycoon (Humphrey Bogart); as a showgirl (Marilyn Monroe) in London who is wooed by a prince (Laurence Olivier) in *The Prince and the Showgirl* (Warners, 1957), and even under her original name in MGM's *The Glass Slipper* (1955), portrayed by Leslie Caron.

Their earlier counterparts—Jean Arthur with sable coat, Claudette Colbert stranded in Paris, Ginger Rogers dreaming of wealth—may have lacked the glitter supplied by Technicolor. And they were certainly more realistic, more mercenary Cinderellas. But they adorned a series of film comedies that retain much of their sparkle and provide an entertaining view of a vanished time when Cinderella's coach was a Cadillac and her Prince worked on Wall Street.

CHAPTER THREE

WIFE, HUSBAND, FRIEND, SECRETARY

"Marriage is a beautiful thing."—Lawyer to Irene Dunne in *The Awful Truth*

"Shut your big mouth."—Irene Dunne to lawyer in *The Awful Truth*

Until Nick and Nora Charles came merrily into view in *The Thin Man* (1934) and showed that ordinary—or reasonably ordinary—husbands and wives could enjoy living, eating, and even sleeping together, marriage on the screen was often depicted as a stately charade enacted by aristocratic people in posh surroundings. Flirtations by wandering husbands were carried out and usually observed by jealous wives at lavish dinner parties. Accusations of infidelity were made across lengthy dinner tables, while discreet servants parceled out uneaten food. Mammoth bedrooms contained widely separated twin beds, and marital kisses and embraces were either chaste or simply not shown. "Other men" and "other women" were wicked or seductive, but errant spouses and wives almost invariably returned to home and hearth, however cavernous and chilly.

In the early sound years, both comedies and dramas observed this view of the marital state, and in drama particularly, there were such popular actresses as Ruth Chatterton, Kay Francis, and Ann Harding who could play elegantly unhappy wives. Paramount's *Tomorrow and Tomorrow* (1932), from Philip Barry's play, offered Ruth Chatterton as a restless wife who has a child by a Viennese brain surgeon (Paul Lukas) but stays with her husband (Robert Ames). Samuel Goldwyn's *Cynara* (1932), directed by King Vidor, starred Kay Francis as a wife whose philandering husband (Ronald Colman) has a tragic affair with a shopgirl (Phyllis Barry). In RKO's *The Right to Romance* (1933), Ann

Harding played a dedicated surgeon whose marriage to dashing aviator Robert Young is a failure. Marriage in these and other dramas was tolerable at its best, doomed at its worst, and usually lugubrious.

Even most marital comedies of the early thirties presented few recognizable, relaxed, everyday views of marriage. Married couples were too busy exchanging harmless flirtations with other couples, husbands were too busy deciding between legal wives and office wives, mates were too busy accusing each other of flagrant infidelities to exchange cheerful quips or simple words of affection. Sex was relegated to meaningful glances, or ardent embraces that conveyed no real ardor. The Hays Office decreed that in bedroom scenes even between married couples, at least one of the partners must keep his or her feet firmly on the ground.

Then William Powell, dryly urbane, and Myrna Loy, quizzical and charming, came on the scene in *The Thin Man* and a refreshing new note entered the screen's idea of marriage. Though the film was actually a murder mystery (and, as such, will be discussed in a later chapter), it drew its fame and popularity from the husband-and-wife banter of Powell as a suave detective and Loy as his sophisticated and loving wife. There was little doubt that the Charleses derived a great deal of pleasure out of living together and that their relationship was not confined to meals, parties, and solving murders. Nora enters a scene accompanied by their dog, Asta. "I like lanky brunettes with wicked jaws," Nick exclaims, eyes gleaming. In the midst of thickening plot complications, Nora cries: "Oh, Nicky, I love you. Because you know such lovely people." *The Thin Man* showed something new to the movies: a marital state that was more fun than bachelorhood, a state in which simply living together as man and wife was a daily adventure with blissful rewards.

Nick and Nora Charles may have set a new pace for movie marriage but it was not until 1937 that a comedy film—and a new comedy team —took that image a few steps further into the realm of pure marital farce. (*The Thin Man* had been primarily a mystery film, not a comedy.) This was Columbia's *The Awful Truth*, which defined marriage as a reasonable relationship between two often unreasonable people. Hardly a new property, it had been filmed twice before—in 1925 and 1929*—and the original play by Arthur Richman had been produced as far back as 1922 with Ina Claire in the leading role. Now

---

*It was remade again in 1953 as *Let's Do It Again*, with Jane Wyman and Ray Milland. Color and a few songs were added, but the film was not successful.

Columbia decided to shake the dust from this reliable tale and refurbish it for the lengthening parade of screwball comedies.

To direct the new version, studio head Harry Cohn selected Leo McCarey, whose triumphs at Paramount had included such varied films as *Duck Soup* (1933), *Belle of the Nineties* (1934), *Ruggles of Red Gap* (1935), and, most recently, a small but moving drama of old age entitled *Make Way for Tomorrow* (1937). After rejecting a screenplay by Dwight Taylor, McCarey assigned the job to Viña Delmar, who had written *Make Way for Tomorrow* and whose only previous connection with sophisticated comedy was as co-author of the original story of *Hands Across the Table* (1935).

For the leading roles, the studio chose Irene Dunne and Cary Grant, though both were reportedly unhappy about the assignments. Irene Dunne had enjoyed a successful but unremarkable career in a series of romantic, tear-jerking dramas and in several adaptations of Jerome Kern stage musicals. Twice, in *Back Street* (Universal, 1932) and *If I Were Free* (RKO, 1934), she was a woman hopelessly in love with a married man. She was especially charming as Magnolia in the 1936 version of *Show Boat*. Her only previous noteworthy comedy, *Theodora Goes Wild*, had been produced the year before *The Awful Truth* by Columbia. Cary Grant had also been on the scene for some years—*The Awful Truth* was his twenty-eighth movie—playing conventional romantic leads opposite the screen's most flamboyant ladies: Mae West in *She Done Him Wrong* (Paramount, 1933) and *I'm No Angel* (Paramount, 1933), Marlene Dietrich in *Blonde Venus* (Paramount, 1932), Tallulah Bankhead in *Devil and the Deep* (Paramount, 1932), and Jean Harlow in *Suzy* (MGM, 1936). In most of these films, he was debonair and handsome but easily overshadowed by his costars. Then came *The Awful Truth* and both stars were launched in new careers as two of the screen's most accomplished comedy performers.

The premise of *The Awful Truth* is simple. Lucy and Jerry Warriner are a divorced couple who, despite all their vociferous protests, still love each other. They constantly thwart each other's attempts to build new lives apart and are eventually reunited. Around this small idea the film builds a large amount of hilarity, combining a clever script, fast-paced direction by McCarey, and, above all, the infectious good humor and charm of the leading players.

The film is replete with sly touches. Lucy and Jerry's big quarrel —he has protested her staying out all night with Armand Duvalle (Alexander D'Arcy), a French singing teacher; she realizes he has

THE AWFUL TRUTH (1937). Irene Dunne tries to hide her visitor's hat from ex-husband Cary Grant.

been lying about his trip to Florida—is photographed through the baffled eyes of their dog, Mr. Smith. Lucy's lawyer tries to convince her to "think it over." "Marriage is a beautiful thing," he tells her. "Shut your big mouth," she says, smiling through clenched teeth. At the divorce hearing, Mr. Smith is treated as a child who is given in custody to his mother. "I ought to be able to see the dog twice a month," Jerry complains.

With the arrival of new people in their lives, the comedy takes a freshly amusing turn. Jerry pretends to take up briefly with Dixiebelle Lee (Joyce Compton), a nightclub singer who does a rendition of "Gone With the Wind" in which her skirt is lifted by blowers. And Lucy becomes engaged to Daniel Leeson (Ralph Bellamy), an earnest but not-too-bright Oklahoma oil millionaire with a battle-axe mother (Esther Dale). Trying to win Lucy back, Jerry makes a great pretense of defending her innocence in the matter of Armand Duvalle to Leeson and his mother. (Lucy is "as pure as the driven snow," he tells them, but he keeps his fingers crossed.) In a hilarious scene, he hides behind the door in Lucy's apartment while she tries to keep Leeson from entering. Jerry keeps tickling her as she talks, reducing her to uncontrollable laughter.

Grant also shines in a funny episode in which he attends a recital given by Lucy. After a noisy entrance, he proceeds to fall off his chair while Lucy looks on in numb embarrassment. But later, in her apartment, she confesses to Armand that she still loves Jerry, despite his disreputable habits. At this point, a scene follows that is a model for playing farce deftly. Jerry shows up to apologize, forcing Lucy to hide Armand in her bedroom. Whereupon Leeson and his mother appear, causing Lucy to hide Jerry in the bedroom with Armand. A noisy fight ensues behind the closed doors of the bedroom while the Leesons listen in astonishment. Jerry and Armand dash out of the room in wild disarray as Lucy's Aunt Patsy (Cecil Cunningham) comments: "They forgot to touch second."

The film's funniest, best-remembered scene comes after Jerry's divorce from Lucy is final, and he becomes engaged to socialite Barbara Vance (Molly Lamont). At a party in the Vance house, with friends and family of Barbara's milling about, Lucy suddenly appears, trailing yards of chiffon and pretending to be Jerry's Southern "sister." Her first comment to Barbara leaves Jerry aghast: "I never would have known you from *his* description." Affectionately, she calls him "Jerry the Nipper," and creates a nasty scene when she pretends to have lost her purse. "Don't anybody leave this room!" she cries.

WIFE, DOCTOR AND NURSE (1937). Dr. Warner Baxter cautions wife Loretta Young about her injured arm. Nurse Claire Du Brey looks on.

SECOND HONEYMOON (1937). Loretta Young converses with ex-husband Tyrone Power, while Claire Trevor listens.

To cap her performance, she does a song for the guests: Dixiebelle Lee's memorable version of "Gone With the Wind," complete with uplifted skirt.

Jerry is appalled, but by this time, the film's outcome is inevitable. Lucy is clearly determined to win him back and works out a series of manipulations (even wrecking their car) so that they are forced to stay together. In a clever final touch, the camera focuses on two tiny boy-and-girl figures in a clock, each of which emerges and then returns to a separate little house. The clock strikes, the figures appear, and the boy suddenly veers off his course and goes off with the girl into her house. The End.

As in so many comedies of the period, the lines and situations, comic in themselves, are given an extra measure of enjoyment by the performances. The charm and urbanity that Grant projects as Jerry, combined with Dunne's womanly grace and slightly tongue-in-cheek attitude, make *The Awful Truth* a special delight. Their support, especially by Cecil Cunningham as wry Aunt Patsy, is also good.

There were a few other marital comedies released in 1937 but none matched the ebullience and wit of *The Awful Truth*. (Leo McCarey won an Academy Award as Best Director, and there were nominations for the film itself and for Irene Dunne as Best Actress.) Fox's *Wife, Doctor and Nurse,* written by Kathryn Scola, Darrell Ware, and Lamar Trotti and directed by Walter Lang, revealed its entire plot line in its title —Doctor Warner Baxter was suspected by wife Loretta Young of dalliance with nurse Virginia Bruce. But it was pleasantly acted and it featured an unusual (for Hollywood) ending which suggested that the doctor could keep both wife and nurse and settle into a kind of domestic, semiprofessional *ménage à trois.* Also from Fox, *Second Honeymoon* had two of the same writers as *Wife, Doctor and Nurse*— Kathryn Scola and Darrell Ware—and the same director, Walter Lang, but it was not as enjoyable. This comedy starred Tyrone Power as a wealthy man-about-town working to win back ex-wife Loretta Young, who has married conservative tycoon Lyle Talbot. The plot line was its only resemblance to *The Awful Truth,* although a game cast that included Stuart Erwin, Claire Trevor, and Marjorie Weaver, tried to make something amusing out of the tired material.

A minor but pleasant marital comedy of 1937 was MGM's *Live, Love and Learn,* directed by George Fitzmaurice. This starred Rosalind Russell as a rich girl who marries Greenwich Village artist Robert Montgomery, whose picturesque "garret" shows any artist how to live well while starving. As expected, she leaves him in tears when he

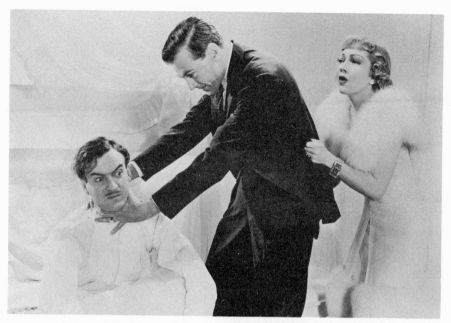

BLUEBEARD'S EIGHTH WIFE (1938). Claudette Colbert tries to keep Gary Cooper from strangling David Niven.

WIFE, HUSBAND AND FRIEND (1939) Warner Baxter gives a firm push to Helen Westley.

becomes obnoxiously successful, but he learns humility after art critic Monty Woolley attacks his paintings. The principal virtue of the movie was the presence of Robert Benchley as a whimsical friend of the couple. (Mickey Rooney also appeared briefly as a neighborhood urchin.)

The one fairly notable comedy of marriage released in 1938 was Ernst Lubitsch's *Bluebeard's Eighth Wife.* In this stylish but slightly stale and attentuated romance, Gary Cooper played Michael Brandon, a forthright, much-married millionaire who meets Nicole de Loiselle (Claudette Colbert), daughter of an impoverished French aristocrat (Edward Everett Horton) on the Riviera. (They meet in a department store in a classically "cute" fashion: he insists on purchasing only the tops of a pair of pajamas; she agrees to buy only the bottoms.) He pursues her tenaciously, but with a brisk businesslike manner that annoys Nicole and she turns down his proposal of marriage. (Her father is upset: "To say 'no' to a man like that—a man who wasn't even hit by the Depression!")

Actually, of course, Nicole loves Michael and before long she changes her mind and agrees to marry him. But then she learns that she is the eighth in an extended line of Brandon wives (six divorces, one death), and not wishing to become another casualty, her attitude changes to one of cool calculation. She will marry him only if he agrees to a premarriage settlement: if they are divorced, he will pay her $100,000 a year for the rest of her life. Michael balks at the idea but finally consents when a determined Nicole tells him that her price "is going up every minute."

At this point, the plot takes a curious and unconvincing turn that permits Lubitsch to stage several of his lightly "risqué" situations. Ostensibly, Nicole loves Michael and wants to remain his wife. Yet for reasons not made clear in the screenplay, she opts for the financial settlement and proceeds to drive Michael into a divorce by firmly insisting on remaining—in the movie euphemism of the time—"kiss-less." While he fumes in frustration, she keeps him coolly at arm's length, seeing him only on occasion, as a sort of pleasant but hardly intimate acquaintance. While she reads *Live Alone and Like It,* he buys *The Taming of the Shrew,* but his aggressive tactics fail. (She hits back.) In one of the film's most amusing scenes, he attempts to seduce her by plying her with drink but, aware of his tactics, she consumes a dish of onions, the food he finds most offensive of all.

As he becomes angrier and more frustrated, they battle their way across Europe ("The pigeons in Venice are still frightened," she tells him), but she refuses to give in. In a series of maneuvers which become increasingly tiresome, they attempt to outsmart each other, but Nicole invariably gets the upper hand. Finally, his tenacity broken, Michael agrees to a divorce and collapses with a nervous breakdown. In the inevitable "turning of the tables," Nicole, now wealthy, realizes that she loves Michael and becomes the ardent pursuer. She tracks him down in a sanatorium near Paris, where they are reconciled. (Cooper plays this scene in a straitjacket, posing the question of why Hollywood, for a number of years, treated mental disorder as a subject for hilarity.)

The Charles Brackett–Billy Wilder screenplay is not nearly as witty or sparkling as their subsequent collaborations on *Midnight* (1939) and *Ninotchka* (1939), but it has amusing moments, contributed mostly by such veteran performers as Edward Everett Horton as Nicole's money-minded father, Elizabeth Patterson as the crusty family matriarch, Herman Bing as a harried detective, and Warren Hymer as a rough-hewn professional "corespondent" in divorce cases. Only David Niven is badly miscast as Nicole's obsequious, mild-mannered suitor. As the amorous millionaire, Gary Cooper appears uncomfortable in a role he played with greater success nineteen years later in Billy Wilder's very Lubitsch-like comedy, *Love in the Afternoon* (1957). Lubitsch's direction maintains the sardonic, sophisticated air characteristic of his films, but there is also more than a slight mustiness about this "naughty" farce.

The year 1939 was also a fairly slim one for marital farce. Fox's *Wife, Husband and Friend* was a likeable comedy about a wife (Loretta Young) with ambitions to become a great singer and her husband (Warner Baxter), who discovers that *he* is the member of the family endowed with a magnificent voice. The not-so-friendly rivalry between them is compounded by the presence of a blonde soprano (Binnie Barnes) who would like to give the husband's voice to the world while claiming his person for her own. (The film was remade by Fox in 1949 as *Everybody Does It*, with Paul Douglas, Celeste Holm, and Linda Darnell in the Baxter-Young-Barnes roles.) Another Fox comedy that year was *Daytime Wife*, a tedious affair directed by Gregory Ratoff from a screenplay by Art Arthur and Robert Harari. Here, sixteen-year-old Linda Darnell, in her second film, played wife to Tyrone Power, rebelling against his neglect and innocent peccadillos by taking a job as secretary to his best friend. The cast included Warren William, Wendy Barrie, and the ubiquitous Binnie Barnes.

Walter Wanger's *Eternally Yours*, directed by Tay Garnett, was a moderately amusing entry that starred David Niven as a successful magician and Loretta Young as his wife, weary of all the prestidigita-

DAYTIME WIFE (1939). Tyrone Power is sleepily indifferent to young wife
Linda Darnell.

ETERNALLY YOURS (1939). Loretta Young assists husband David Niven in his
magician's act.

tion and anxious to retire to a Connecticut farm. When he is reluctant to settle down, she leaves him and he pursues her across the globe, recapturing her before she can marry the wrong man (Broderick Crawford).* The film was only mild fun but it had the distinction of being the first feature film to be tied in with the New York World's Fair. The finale found Niven parachuting over the Lagoon of Nations and falling into a Flushing swamp.

The first marital comedy of the year 1940 was another entry from Fox cryptically entitled *He Married His Wife*. It took no less than four writers—Sam Hellman, Darrell Ware, Lynn Starling, and, surprisingly, John O'Hara—to concoct the tale of a light-headed divorcee (Nancy Kelly) who cannot choose between two eager suitors—Lyle Talbot and Cesar Romero—and ends up remarrying her horse-loving, alimony-hating ex-husband, played by Joel McCrea. The proceedings, directed by Roy Del Ruth, gained some comic momentum from Roland Young, droll as always as McCrea's lawyer, and the marvelous Mary Boland as her usual scatterbrained matron.

In the spring Columbia released *Too Many Husbands*, which brought together director Wesley Ruggles and scriptwriter Claude Binyon for their ninth collaboration. Based on a play by W. Somerset Maugham, the film was yet another version of the familiar "Enoch Arden" theme: the newly married woman confronted by the unexpected return of her "dead" first husband. Here, Vicky Lowndes (Jean Arthur), recently married to her late husband Bill's best friend, Henry (Melvyn Douglas), is shocked to discover that Bill (Fred MacMurray) has not drowned after all and has come back to claim his wife.

The idea has obvious comic possibilities that the script and the direction fail to realize, despite valiant playing by the leads. The expected jokes are there: Henry refuses to go to the airport to meet Bill. "I thought I married a man!" Vicky protests. "*Two* men!" her father (Harry Davenport) retorts. Or Bill, appalled by the situation, cries: "My best friend! My own wife!" and claims that he feels like "an unwanted corpse at a party." But spinning about a single joke, the film's comic invention begins to wear thin after the first fifteen minutes, and the acting becomes noticeably desperate.

Most of the film is given over to the two men's determined pursuit

*Three years later, in Columbia's *Bedtime Story*, Miss Young was leaving Fredric March for the very same reason. March refused to retire from the theatre, and she divorced him. Apparently, she never gave up.

TOO MANY HUSBANDS (1940). A ticklish situation for Jean Arthur and her two husbands, Fred MacMurray and Melvyn Douglas. Harry Davenport is an anxious observer.

HE MARRIED HIS WIFE (1940). Nancy Kelly gets an attentive kiss from Cesar Romero. Looking on: Joel McCrea, Roland Young, and Lyle Talbot.

of their wife. Consigned to the guest room until the dilemma can be resolved, both men try to get at Vicky, with Henry even pawing her amorously in a narrow clothes closet. Bill also plays at being romantic, though he is still fretting at his predicament: "This is the night I dreamed about while I starved on berries and fish!" One of the film's few genuinely funny scenes comes when Henry steals into Vicky's room to deliver an impassioned speech, only to discover that he is talking to his father-in-law. Through all this, Vicky's reaction combines dismay with pleasure: "This is awful but I love it!" she tells her father.

With slim possibilities for developing the situation, *Too Many Husbands* settles for noisy farce, and the results are negligible. While Vicky tries to make up her mind, Bill and Henry engage in childish antics for her benefit. Bill shows that he can leap nimbly over chairs; Henry demonstrates that he can spell long words. They draw lots for her, and when Bill loses, he suspects Henry of cheating and ransacks the living room looking for Henry's "winning" slip of paper. (He turns out to be right.) The bickering continues endlessly—at one point both men pretend to be cold and indifferent to Vicky—and their plight even becomes a nationwide story. ("DOUBLE WIFE FACES JUDGE!" a banner headline reads.) Finally, they end up together in a nightclub, with both men dancing simultaneously with "their" wife. The film concludes with the suggestion that Vicky, curiously enchanted with the idea of having two husbands, will somehow keep their relationship going!

Jean Arthur and Fred MacMurray are passable in their roles, but Melvyn Douglas is obviously ill at ease as Henry, his well-developed instinct for comedy confounded by having to play a shrill, whimpering, and decidedly unpleasant character. But the principals get good support from Harry Davenport as the rational father who tells his two sons-in-law: "I hope the loser will have the decency to join the Foreign Legion," and from Melville Cooper as the butler in the Lowndes household. One of the film's best moments comes when Cooper hears about the two husbands and drops a tray of dishes with a clatter. "I guess I'm a bit old-fashioned," he murmurs apologetically. He is also a pleasure to watch as he dresses Henry for dinner. "The tie is so important," he asserts. "It either makes or breaks." But neither Davenport nor Cooper can save this tame comedy. (In 1955 it was remade by Columbia as *Three for the Show,* a heavy-handed color musical with Betty Grable, Jack Lemmon, and Marge and Gower Champion in the leading roles.)

Several months after *Too Many Husbands,* RKO released a marital comedy that virtually duplicated the plot, only reversing the sexes. This time, however, the Enoch Arden theme proved successful, and the film restored a hearty measure of wit and style to the genre. This was *My Favorite Wife,* directed by Garson Kanin from a screenplay by Samuel and Bella Spewack. The plot was familiar: Nick (Cary Grant) marries a svelte brunette, Bianca (Gail Patrick), believing that his first wife, Ellen (Irene Dunne), had died in a shipwreck. To his astonishment and dismay, she returns from her watery grave not only very much alive and anxious to return to her wifely ways but highly secretive about her years on a desert island with a muscular Adonis (Randolph Scott).

Here was a tried-and-true situation, but all parties concerned managed to turn it into one of the year's most festive films. As the beleaguered husband, Cary Grant gives one of his best comedy performances. His shock at seeing his "dead" wife from inside a closing elevator, his sprinting from hotel room to hotel room to the dismay of the clerk (Donald MacBride in another of his irate characterizations), his desperate attempts to avoid bedding down his new bride, these and many other moments are handled by Grant with finesse. Irene Dunne is equally fine as his wife, bringing her satirical air and touches of tenderness to the role.

Inevitably, the double-wife situation must be resolved in the courtroom. This leads to a riotously funny scene stolen entirely by Granville Bates as an addled and acid-tongued judge. "Where did you go to school?" he asks Grant balefully. "Harvard," Grant replies. A meaningful pause, a lift of the eyebrows, and the judge states casually, "I'm a Yale man myself."*

Another successful attempt at marital farce appeared later that year in MGM's *I Love You Again.* Here, under the direction of W. S. Van Dyke, William Powell played George Carey, a suave confidence man who discovers that for nine years, suffering from amnesia, he has lived an entirely different life in Haberville, Pennsylvania, as a dull and pompous man named Larry Wilson. Returning to his true identity after a blow on the head, he finds himself confronted with a beautiful but bored and unhappy wife (Myrna Loy) he has never met. Determined to walk off with his alter ego's bank account (and ulti-

---

*The film was remade by Fox in 1963 as *Move Over, Darling,* with Doris Day, James Garner, and Polly Bergen in the Dunne-Grant-Patrick roles. The studio had started filming it as *Something's Got to Give,* with Marilyn Monroe and Dean Martin, but the production was halted by Monroe's death.

MY FAVORITE WIFE (1940). Irene Dunne meets her children (Scotty Beckett and Mary Lou Harrington) after a long separation. Looking on: Ann Shoemaker, Gail Patrick, and Cary Grant.

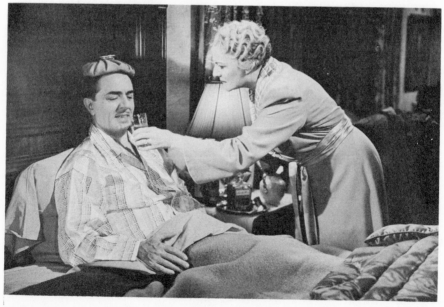

I LOVE YOU AGAIN (1940). Nella Walker nurses her ailing son-in-law, William Powell.

mately his wife as well), he decides to impersonate Larry—with the expected comic results.

The story's credits listed six writers—screenplay by Charles Lederer, George Oppenheimer, and Harry Kurnitz, from a story by Leon Gordon and Maurine Watkins, based on a novel by Octavus Roy Cohen—but in this case too many cooks stirred up a savory broth. Powell was vastly comic as the con man–turned–respectable citizen who has to cope with a troop of Boy Rangers, Larry's penchant for taxidermy, and other unpleasant surprises. Myrna Loy matched him every step of the way as the wife with deep-seated animosity for her irritating husband. "You've turned my head," Powell tells her gallantly, attempting to court her again. To which she replies in her best acid tones, "I've often wished I could turn your head–on a spit over a slow fire."

Other husband-wife comedies released throughout 1940 lacked the comic inventiveness of *My Favorite Wife* and *I Love You Again*, though a few were agreeable enough. And all of them lacked the sparkle of the Grant-Dunne, Powell-Loy teams. Hal Roach's *Turnabout*, adapted from Thorne Smith's novel, was the weakest of the lot, devoid not only of inventiveness and sparkle but taste as well. A labored fantasy about a husband and wife who reverse their biological status, it offered the spectacle of Carole Landis, stridently masculine and bellowing in a deep bass voice, and John Hubbard, falsetto-voiced and hand on hip, mincing about his home and office. Despite a strong cast that included Adolphe Menjou, Mary Astor, Verree Teasdale, Franklin Pangborn, Marjorie Main, and Donald Meek, the low level of the humor was painfully apparent throughout.

No Time for Comedy, released in the fall, was Warners' version of S. N. Behrman's stage comedy in which Katharine Cornell had starred as the skeptical actress-wife of a successful playwright who suddenly decides that his comedies are too frivolous for the times. On screen the role went to Rosalind Russell, for once neither brittle nor domineering, as she set about wresting her husband (James Stewart) from the clutches of a foolish patroness of the arts (Genevieve Tobin), who was seeing him through his "serious" period. The play was adapted by the busy Epstein brothers, Julius and Philip, who kept it light and pleasing throughout. Once again, the best performances came from the supporting cast, particularly Genevieve Tobin and Charles Ruggles as her bemused and patient husband. The film's theme—that comedy has a rightful place in this troubled world—was repeated much more emphatically the following year by Preston Sturges in his "dark" comedy, *Sullivan's Travels*.

Rosalind Russell turned up again in Universal's *Hired Wife*, this time playing in her familiar style as a crisply efficient executive secretary in a cement company—she refers to herself dryly as "Little Annie Cement"—who consents to an "in-name-only" marriage to her boss (Brian Aherne) for business reasons. Naturally she schemes to turn it into a true marriage by eliminating the competition, mainly a gold-digging blonde model (Virginia Bruce), and by convincing her "husband" that she can be much more than a secretary to him. When her plans go awry and she finds herself losing ground rapidly, she persuades a penniless friend (John Carroll) to impersonate a South American millionaire bent on marrying the model. Following a few unlikely complications, she gets her man (Obligatory line: "Why don't we stop kidding ourselves?")

The Richard Connell–Gladys Lehman screenplay is breezy if not witty and the situations are pleasantly foolish under William A. Seiter's indulgent direction, but whatever sparkle the film has comes from Rosalind Russell, in fine fettle despite having to cope with such lines as "I'm only substituting for the woman you really wanted." Few actresses could manage to look as attractive while forced to play the aggressive, pile-driving businesswoman. The *New York Times* review of the film praised her "magnificent self-possession, her ability to fling a barbed retort," and "her vast superiority over lesser females in matters requiring maneuver." She is helped by Brian Aherne's assured performance as the husband and by Robert Benchley in his characteristic role of the bemused friend. But the movie really belongs to her.

Rosalind Russell's excursions into marital comedy continued into 1941 with two films, Columbia's *This Thing Called Love* and MGM's *The Feminine Touch*. *This Thing Called Love* was a rarity for its time, one of the few Hollywood films to take a passing stab at "adult" or "risqué" material. Derived from a 1928 play by Edwin Burke and a 1929 film version, it implied and even demonstrated that married couples could seek and even enjoy an active sex life. In some films there were glimmers that a man and his wife were not always quarreling in elegant drawing rooms or exchanging witticisms across twin beds. But few comedies ventured into the bedroom for anything more than a chaste kiss. In *This Thing Called Love*, Melvyn Douglas' unrelenting attempt to seduce his "kissless" bride was, for 1941, a source of titillation for naïve audiences. (Curiously, the film opened at New York City's family emporium, the Radio City Music Hall.)

Aside from its "bold" approach to sex, *This Thing Called Love* was a sporadically funny comedy directed by Alexander Hall. Its fragile

TURNABOUT (1940). John Hubbard and Mary Astor.

NO TIME FOR COMEDY (1940). At a theatre rehearsal: Allyn Joslyn, James Stewart, Rosalind Russell, and Clarence Kolb.

HIRED WIFE (1940). Rosalind Russell introduces friend John Carroll to model Virginia Bruce. Brian Aherne watches.

THIS THING CALLED LOVE (1941). A reunion at the train station: Rosalind Russell, Melvyn Douglas, Allyn Joslyn, Binnie Barnes, and dog.

plot was built on an improbable premise: Ann Winters (Rosalind Russell), an insurance company executive, is about to marry wealthy miner and explorer Tice Collins (Melvyn Douglas). She decides arbitrarily that they will have a three-month "trial marriage" to determine whether they are really compatible. There will be no sexual relations during these months. (She tells her sister: "Somebody has to do the pioneering," to which the sister replies: "Bet he doesn't want to be Daniel Boone.") Tice's reaction is predictable: shock and anger—"That's the most fantastic thing I've ever heard of!"—followed by grudging approval. They are married, although Tice confides to his attorney Harry (Allyn Joslyn) that Ann has "a shoulder that would make dry ice feel like a bed-warmer."

Of course Tice is nothing less than dauntless and most of the film deals with his increasingly desperate attempts to lure Ann into his bed. In a long comic scene, he draws on soft music, a raging fire, and a comfortable sofa for romantic props, only to discover Ann's booklet, *A Practical Solution to the Marriage Problem*, under a pillow. Grimly, he lifts the little plastic man from their wedding cake and retires for the night, pausing only to call Harry and tell him: "You stink!" He even places the statue of a Mexican god of plenty and fertility in their living room, but when Ann remains aloof, he tells the statue: "You're a fraud. You couldn't make spinach grow in the garden of Eden." Finally, Harry persuades him to give a lavish dinner party for Julio Diestro (Lee J. Cobb), the South American millionaire from whom Tice wants to borrow a million dollars for a new mine. Harry's idea: invite all the guests to stay over and Ann will be forced into your bedroom.

Unfortunately, the dinner party turns out to be a comic disaster replete with misunderstandings, tense feelings, and nearly open warfare. Somehow Diestro, head of a populous family, gets the impression that Ann is pregnant, and their conversation causes some confusion and embarrassment. "Does your doctor believe in exercise?" he asks her. Bewildered but game, Ann replies: "I think so. He rides in the park every morning." Each time the conversation takes a dangerous turn, Tice proposes a loud toast and bursts into a chorus of "America, the Beautiful."

But the worst is yet to come. Trying to get rid of Ann's amorous boss, who has turned up at the party, Tice joins with Harry to stage a fake fire in their bathroom, complete with noisy outcries and simulated fire-fighting. Instead, they are discovered by the bewildered Diestros. Later, Tice finds himself innocently in a bedroom with

Harry's secretary Charlotte (Binnie Barnes), whose gown has just been ripped off by Harry's fiercely jealous wife. Of course they are found by Ann and the Diestros. "Shame!" Ann cries. "And me about to become a mother!" In the seduction of his "kissless" bride, Tice is scoring zero.

From this point, despite energetic performances by Russell and Douglas, the film moves steadily downhill. Ann decides to end the "plan," only to be confounded by a nervously twitching and scratching husband. It appears that he has a bad case of poison oak, caught in an innocent encounter in the woods with Charlotte—and he is naturally reluctant to tell Ann. After many similar complications, all unconvincing and none more than mildly amusing, Ann and Tice finally get together. (Ann slides her hand through Tice's bedroom door, holding the statue of the god of plenty and fertility.)

The Feminine Touch, Rosalind Russell's second husband-wife comedy for 1941, was only slightly better. Under the direction of W. S. Van Dyke, she played the wife of a pompous professor (Don Ameche, in his only film for MGM), who has written a tome on the evils of jealousy. On a trip to New York City, Russell teaches her teacher husband some of the unwritten laws of movie matrimony: that a wife finds it flattering to have a jealous husband—and that a wife does not necessarily object to caveman tactics now and again. Professor Ameche ends up discarding his theories of jealousy by leveling a punch at an overzealous gentleman (Van Heflin) who has designs on this wife. The patly amusing screenplay by George Oppenheimer, Edmund L. Hartmann, and Ogden Nash offered no surprises but the support by Heflin, Kay Francis, and Donald Meek was helpful.

Early in 1941, RKO released a comedy that had one (and only one) surprise: it was directed by Alfred Hitchcock, whose views of marriage until then had been more menacing than mirthful. Drawing on none of the familiar techniques he used for suspense melodrama, Hitchcock led Carole Lombard and Robert Montgomery, two of the screen's most attractive comic performers, though *Mr. and Mrs. Smith,* Norman Krasna's sprightly screenplay about a married couple's discovery that they were never legally wed. Inevitably, the husband is forced to pursue and win his "wife" all over again, and just as inevitably he succeeds despite every obstacle.

The film begins on a high note. Anne and David Smith, making up after one of their numerous arguments, have just completed three days locked in their bedroom to the admiration and amazement of

THE FEMININE TOUCH (1941). The eternal quadrangle: Don Ameche, Rosalind Russell, Van Heflin, and Kay Francis.

MR. AND MRS. SMITH (1941) The Smiths (Carole Lombard and Robert Montgomery) at home.

their servants. But then they learn that their marriage is not legal and the complications begin to mount. Irate that David is apparently considering *not* remarrying her, Anne tosses him out of the house and falls into the waiting arms of David's law partner, Jeff (Gene Raymond trying—and failing—to gain some laughs as an earnest and intensely respectable bore).

Whatever amusement the film may have is certainly due to the professional skills of the leading players, whose handling of the stock situations is a lesson in comedy acting. Montgomery is very funny in his desperate attempt to punch himself in the nose and induce a nose bleed. (In a nightclub with a repulsive "date" for the evening, he has spotted Anne and is anxious to arouse her sympathy.) Lombard is equally hilarious in a Lake Placid cabin that just happens to be adjacent to Montgomery's. Trying to make her estranged husband believe that she is being attacked by an amorous Jeff, she launches a one-woman display of shrieks and protests accompanied by much furniture-banging. There are a few other bright spots: Anne and Jeff finding themselves trapped together on the famous Parachute Ride at the 1940 World's Fair in New York City; David deliberately shocking Jeff's conservative Southern parents (Lucile Watson and Philip Merivale) about his relationship with Anne—they are unaware of the "marriage"—and Jeff's fixed-smile, glassy-eyed tipsiness after only two drinks, although Gene Raymond ineptly plays a scene Gig Young would have carried off with style.

Lombard, as always, is a delight to watch, whether fuming over her husband's patronizing remark, "You're a great kid," or shaving him when he is supposed to be unconscious and frostbitten from the Lake Placid cold (of course he is faking), or finally surrendering to him with little squeals of joy.

Other marital comedies through the spring and summer of 1941 included no gems but a few managed to wring some laughs from isolated pieces of comic business. MGM's *Come Live With Me*, directed listlessly by Clarence Brown, involved Hedy Lamarr, beautiful but a dull actress, as a refugee who evades deportation by marrying—in name only—a young writer (James Stewart). Not too surprisingly, they manage to fall in love. Universal's *Model Wife* reunited Joan Blondell and Dick Powell as a secretly married couple—they work for a company that prohibits employing married girls. Here the only compensations were named Charlie Ruggles, Ruth Donnelly, and Lucile Watson. Ernst Lubitsch's *That Uncertain Feeling* was not very good but Donald Ogden Stewart's screenplay about a battling couple

(Merle Oberon and Melvyn Douglas) contained a sharply observed dinner party scene in which most of the guests are vociferous Hungarians. Burgess Meredith also contributed a hilarious performance as a boorish and demented pianist who strikes the wife's fancy.

The best of the group was MGM's *Love Crazy*, not because of its screenplay by William Ludwig, Charles Lederer, and David Hertz, nor its direction by Jack Conway, though all hands were slickly professional. This antic piece, about a husband who pretends to be ferociously insane in order to keep his wife from starting divorce proceedings, enjoyed the presence of William Powell and Myrna Loy in their tenth film together. Powell was in especially fine form as the wronged husband who is forced to confront a lunacy commission, escape from an asylum, and impersonate an elderly matron before winning back his coolly stubborn wife (Loy). He was particularly funny "freeing" his feet from his shoes in the manner of Lincoln freeing the slaves.

The fall crop of marital comedies included several winners and quite a few losers. Columbia's *Our Wife* was a mild trifle directed by John Stahl in which the romance between a tippling composer (Melvyn Douglas) and a lady scientist (Ruth Hussey) is thwarted by the composer's scheming ex-wife (Ellen Drew). Charles Coburn brightened the proceedings to some degree. Ruth Hussey also turned up in MGM's *Married Bachelor* as the wife of a man (Robert Young) who pretends to be the unmarried author of a book of marital advice. Here, the familiar situations were given some gloss by the Dore Schary script (from a story by Manuel Seff) and by the performances of Sam Levene and Sheldon Leonard as Runyonesque characters.

One comedy, Universal's *Appointment for Love,* promised more than it delivered. It offered Charles Boyer dispensing all of his Gallic charm and Margaret Sullavan in one of her infrequent comedy roles in a screenplay by Bruce Manning and Felix Jackson. The director was William A. Seiter, who had a respectable track record in comedy (*If You Could Only Cook,* 1935; *Three Blind Mice,* 1938; *Hired Wife,* 1941). Yet somehow the tale of a marriage between a debonair playwright and a clinical, unemotional doctor fell short of its mark. When the doctor expresses her "scientific" attitude toward marriage—she studiously refuses to be jealous and insists on separate apartments to keep their marriage "perfect"—there is little doubt that she will eventually succumb to her baffled husband's sexual blandishments. The humor becomes strained as husband and wife veer in separate directions, trying frantically to induce jealous feelings in each other.

MODEL WIFE (1941). Dick Powell is clearly annoyed with wife Joan Blondell.

THAT UNCERTAIN FEELING (1941). In deep conversation: Burgess Meredith, Merle Oberon, and her husband Melvyn Douglas.

LOVE CRAZY (1941). Myrna Loy and William Powell have come to a parting of the ways.

MARRIED BACHELOR (1941). Robert Young tries to explain the situation to wife Ruth Hussey.

APPOINTMENT FOR LOVE (1941). Playwright Charles Boyer courts Dr. Margaret Sullavan. Nurse Virginia Brissac looks on.

YOU BELONG TO ME (1941). Playboy Henry Fonda helps his doctor-wife Barbara Stanwyck with her dress.

Only one exchange has any humor. The husband, convinced that he has married a "monster," tries to explain his predicament to his producer (Eugene Pallette):

> *Andre:* My wife eats breakfast at seven in the morning—ham—eggs —oatmeal—then walks to work—one mile. If I'm dressed, she's going to let me walk with her. What can I do?
> *Hastings:* Shoot her.
> *Andre:* I love her.
> *Hastings:* Then shoot yourself.

Boyer and Sullavan try to invest their roles with some semblance of life but they are defeated by the script. Only Rita Johnson, sinking her teeth into still another "other-woman" role, and Gus Schilling, as a totally confused elevator operator, contribute to the limited fun.

Another lady physician appeared at the same time in Columbia's *You Belong to Me,* directed by Wesley Ruggles. Here, Barbara Stanwyck played Dr. Helen Hunt, formidably efficient yet romantically vulnerable. The screenplay by Claude Binyon,* from a story by Dalton Trumbo, dealt with her marriage to a wealthy playboy, Peter Kirk (Henry Fonda), who takes on an unreasoning jealousy about her male patients. From this idea, the film develops a number of moderately funny complications. Some of the lines are felicitous, as when Stanwyck, irked at a hotel clerk's comment that she didn't register as a doctor, remarks: "As a girl scout, I won three merit badges but I didn't mention it on the register." A few of the situations draw laughs, as when Peter storms into her office where she is examining a male patient and knocks him down.

Several things, however, conspire to defeat the film. One is Fonda's behavior, which is so asinine and childish that any sensible audience response can only be irritation rather than laughter. ("I'll bear the scar of this the rest of my life," he says when Helen leaves on an emergency call.) Another shortcoming is the absence of the kind of juicy character roles that often made these films diverting. The cast includes Ruth Donnelly, Melville Cooper, and Jack Norton (sober for a change), but they have very little to do.

The film's most serious flaw is its dated attitude towards the idle rich. By 1941, it was no longer persuasive to suggest that being rich brought only unhappiness and being *idle* and rich was virtually a

*His eleventh and last collaboration with director Ruggles.

crime, or conversely, that living in near-poverty was ideal and romantic. Yet Helen is deliriously happy when she learns that Peter has taken a job as a clerk in a department store—she'll have "a husband with pride and twenty bucks a week"—and after a few setbacks, she is even *more* pleased when he gives up most of his money to buy a hospital. (Her joy at their upcoming poverty may be somewhat influenced by her appointment as the hospital's chief of staff.)

Even more curiously dated is the attitude of the department-store workers towards Peter. Recognized by a few of the employees, he is treated in surly fashion as a "no-good millionaire." A delegation of workers (led, incidentally, by Larry Parks five years before he played Al Jolson) reports him to the management and accuses him of "stealing the job" of someone who really needs the work. Their vindictiveness seems very much of the thirties, though Peter's immediate response is not. "Why should a few million dollars keep me from having a chance like everyone else?" he asks, questioning the movie-induced Depression myth that money was a handicap impeding fulfillment. But of course he reverts in the end to true Mr. Deeds form by giving up his fortune.

Another comedy of marriage released late that year was Paramount's *Skylark*, adapted by Allan Scott from Samson Raphaelson's novel and play. Here, Claudette Colbert appeared in the role Gertrude Lawrence had played on the stage, as Lydia Kenyon, a neglected wife who left her business-minded husband to enjoy a skylarking life with another, more romantically inclined man. The husband, a disagreeable and disreputable type, was played by Ray Milland and the lover, arch and patronizing, was Brian Aherne.

A pleasant entry in the series of comedies, *Skylark* succeeded in working up a reasonable amount of entertainment due chiefly to Colbert's effective way with a line and to the presence in the cast of two splendid troupers, Walter Abel and Binnie Barnes. As the husband's perennially tipsy confidante, Abel was a delight, and Miss Barnes was even better as the nasty wife of the husband's boss. "I've been coveting and coveting your cook," she tells Colbert, and the message is very clear indeed. Later, she and Colbert have a fine time hurling invective at each other in a showdown scene. (Colbert cheerfully calls her a "greedy, scheming cow.")

Colbert is given one funny scene (reminiscent of a Lucille Ball television routine) in which she has all kinds of farcical troubles aboard a storm-tossed yacht. She tries to make coffee on a tilted stove, falls down the galley stairs, confronts a very dead fish in the

SKYLARK (1941). Claudette Colbert and her business-minded husband, Ray Milland.

TWO-FACED WOMAN (1942). Melvyn Douglas is captivated by Greta Garbo's imaginary twin sister.

refrigerator, and ends up in tears, calling for her ex-husband.* Most of the time, her dilemma in the film is hardly earth-shaking, since she is forced to choose between a husband who thinks nothing of lying outrageously to keep her from leaving him and a lover who is given to such coy remarks as "I could show you the moon, lady," and "Why can't we walk out on the world?"

At the start of 1942, MGM released two films that marked a low point—and a high point—in their attempts at marital comedy. The low point, *Two-Faced Woman,* was one of the greatest disappointments of the film year, considering its credentials. Three years earlier, Greta Garbo had made her first venture into comedy with *Ninotchka,* under the assured helm of Ernst Lubitsch (the ads read: "Garbo laughs!"), and the result was a sparkling film in which Garbo was totally captivating as a grim Communist maiden who unbends in Paris. In 1940, director George Cukor guided Katharine Hepburn through one of her most brilliant performances as the willful society girl in the film version of Philip Barry's *The Philadelphia Story.* For *Two-Faced Woman,* the studio brought Garbo and Cukor together, added Melvyn Douglas as leading man (repeating from *Ninotchka*) and presented them with a screenplay by S. N. Behrman (no apprentice at comedy), Salka Viertel, and George Oppenheimer.

The result was a disaster, a muddled and foolish comedy in which Garbo appeared to great disadvantage. (It was her last film.) Badly costumed (her clothes looked like hand-me-downs from an MGM rummage sale) and visibly straining to appear effervescent, she played ski instructor Karin Borg, who marries publisher Larry Blake (Douglas) and then pretends to be her own sexy, animated twin sister "Katherine" when she fears she is losing him to an old rival (Constance Bennett). The script is totally devoid of wit or surprise, leaning heavily on vaguely suggestive situations in which Larry apparently** attempts to seduce his "sister-in-law" to Karin's chagrin and consternation. Garbo's attempts to play the alluring "Katherine" are embarrassing to behold, becoming most painful when she is called

---

*This scene also works well because it is one of the few in the film that doesn't have a patently artificial setting. The Kenyons live in a wildly extravagant home, early forties style, and one scene in a theatre has the principals staring intently into space at what appears to be an empty stage. Also, there is a subway scene which shows an underground unrecognizable to any New Yorker.

**A viewer can only say "apparently" because there is evidence that a scene was forcibly inserted at the insistence of the Legion of Decency in which Douglas recognizes Garbo's ruse and says aloud: "Two can play at this game." Yet in later scenes he seems to be unaware of the ruse. It is all very confusing.

upon to dance the torrid "Chica Choca" in a nightclub. A long scene with Douglas has her tantalizing him with arms outstretched as she sprawls on the sofa and then murmuring "Not yet" at regular intervals. (Finally, when she says "Come, come," naturally he says "Not yet.")

Garbo is plainly awful, but she gets very little help from a surprisingly good supporting cast. Roland Young is lost as Douglas' partner who is enchanted by "Katherine," as is Ruth Gordon as a knowing secretary. As Griselda Vaughn, Douglas's ex-girlfriend, Constance Bennet contributes the only enjoyable moments, confronting Karin at one point with baleful eye and muttering: "You made me lose my poise. For that I will never forgive you." She elicits one of the film's few laughs when, after a scene in a powder room with the irrepressible "Katherine," she emits a solitary shriek at her reflection in the mirror, to the astonishment of the other ladies.

Happily for MGM (and for the filmgoing public), a high point in screen comedy appeared shortly after *Two-Faced Woman*. To follow Katharine Hepburn's success in *The Philadelphia Story*, the studio selected an original screenplay by Ring Lardner, Jr. and Michael Kanin that preserved her "Philadelphia" image as the independent-minded woman who is vulnerable to romance after all. In *Woman of the Year*, she played Tess Harding, renowned and aggressive political columnist who falls in love with and marries Sam Craig, a rugged sports columnist for the same newspaper. As Sam, the studio cast Spencer Tracy—his last previous role as *Dr. Jekyll and Mr. Hyde* was somewhat different—thus launching one of the most durable and affectionately remembered teams in motion pictures. Under George Stevens' expert and only occasionally slack direction—he can seldom resist a few touches of easy sentiment—the movie was an enormous success.

The stars were to make wittier films in later years but this first venture is a deft and winning comedy in which the two play off each other with ease and obvious delight. Basically, the Academy Award-winning screenplay by Lardner and Kanin works over the familiar "boss-lady" idea: the brilliant, brittle, sophisticated woman of the world who discovers that love is more important than politics or fame. But the exceptionally bright dialogue and amusing situations, played in high style, carry the film to a triumph.

The "feud" between Tess and Sam that starts the film is short-lived but immediately diverting. He calls her the "Calamity Jane of the fast international set" and remarks "I understand she doesn't like to talk to anybody who hasn't signed a non-aggression pact." Tess counters

WOMAN OF THE YEAR (1942). Sports writer Sam Craig (Spencer Tracy) and political columnist Tess Harding (Katharine Hepburn) fall in love.

by mocking the game of baseball, provoking the memorable comment by one of Sam's cronies (Roscoe Karns): "Women should be kept illiterate and clean, like canaries." But soon the two meet in their publisher's office and are instantly attracted to each other.

The vast bridge between their worlds is demonstrated in the next few sequences. Sam takes Tess to a baseball game, where her efforts to understand the game (and her wide-brimmed hat) cause all kinds of comic difficulties. Later, Sam learns that his pursuit of Tess will only get him into embarrassing situations. At a party in her apartment, he is discomfited by a babel of tongues—one turbaned Indian can only answer "Yes" to his every remark—and shortly afterwards he finds himself onstage as the only male at a crowded women's meeting called to honor Tess' aunt, Ellen Whitcomb (Fay Bainter). Here, Tracy's attempts to extricate himself from the scene are uproarious, ending with a slight, neatly executed curtsy as he leaves the stage.

When Sam and Tess realize they are in love, the film takes on a special glow. The scene in which he proposes to her with great difficulty is filmed entirely in loving close-up, the camera staying on her sharp features and his rugged Irish face as a kind of comment on their contrasting backgrounds and inclinations. Yet they are married —in a small town in North Carolina—with Sam in striped pants surrounded by people of the town as Tess's VIP father (Minor Watson) drives up with a police escort. After the ceremony, Sam is left forlornly alone with the baffled justice of the peace.

Their marriage places Tess' hectic life, filled with thunderclaps of impending world disaster and imminent international crises, against Sam's life of sports games and Runyonesque characters. On their wedding night, a defecting scientist friend of Tess' turns up, along with his noisy Hungarian compatriots, and Sam retaliates by inviting a cluster of his bar friends, led by bartender Pinkie Peters (William Bendix in his film debut). Sam and Tess can only sit together morosely at the edge of their bed until the crowd leaves.

From this inauspicious beginning, the situation becomes steadily worse, as Sam is forced to contend with Tess' feverish activities—at one point he is required to make eggs for her and her secretary, Gerald—and Tess' humanitarian instincts, which cause her to take a Greek refugee boy into their home. When she is named Woman of the Year, Sam refuses to attend the banquet in her honor and insists on staying home with the boy. "The outstanding woman of the year isn't a woman at all!" he tells her. "I thought we had a perfect

WOMAN OF THE YEAR (1942). Sam marries Tess. At either side: Fay Bainter and Minor Watson.

BEDTIME STORY (1942). Actress Loretta Young decides to end her marriage to playwright Fredric March.

marriage," she says querulously. Sam is adamant: "It wasn't perfect or a marriage."

Eventually, Tess learns to soften her stance, especially when her Aunt Ellen decides to marry Tess' widowed father after a lifetime of spinsterhood. "Success is no fun if you're alone," Ellen tells her, voicing a familiar theme of the thirties and forties, "I'm tired of winning prizes. They're cold comfort." Tess hurries home to Sam to demonstrate her wifely ways in the kitchen. In the film's funniest scene, she tries to prepare his breakfast. Sam watches in silent amazement as Tess struggles with elusive eggs, overboiling coffee, waffles that rise almost to the ceiling, and toast that pops up frenetically. "Why can't you be Tess Harding Craig?" he asks his battered bride. And clearly, from now on she will be. Yet she still has a schedule to meet. According to Gerald, she is late for her appointment to launch a ship. Sam leaves Tess to speak to Gerald. A thunderous crash of dishes and cutlery and Sam returns. "I just launched Gerald," he says, embracing Tess.

Except for a few stretches in which the film slows down to turn sentimental—can Hepburn ever resist a crying scene?—*Woman of the Year* is a delightful film that demonstrates the kind of rare film magic that turns filmgoers into film buffs: the give-and-take of two players who know how to blend their contrasting moods and effects into a matchless unity of performance. (Hepburn was nominated for an "Oscar.")

Aside from Warners' amusing but rather broad version of *The Male Animal*, the James Thurber–Elliott Nugent stage comedy about a beleaguered college professor and his wife, the balance of 1942 produced no marital comedy that came within even hailing distance of *Woman of the Year*. Paramount's *Are Husbands Necessary?*, directed by Norman Taurog, was a silly affair which had Betty Field as Ray Milland's dim-witted wife who insists on meddling in his career and almost loses him to old flame Patricia Morison. The *New York Times* pronounced the film "an anachronism."

Columbia's *Bedtime Story*, directed by Alexander Hall from a screenplay by Richard Flournoy, was not appreciably better, but it had a few funny moments. Loretta Young played a beautiful if unlikely stage star who divorces her playwright husband Fredric March when he refuses to retire with her from the theatre. The plot revolved about his many ruses to win her back and get her to play the leading role in his newest play. The leads were at a loss to cope with the flat dialogue but the supporting cast was good: Robert Benchley as the standard best friend, Allyn Joslyn as a stuffy banker, and Eve Arden as an actress. One scene was genuinely laugh-provoking: to divert his ex-wife from her honeymoon with her new husband (Joslyn), March has all the hotel personnel—plumbers, electricians, exterminators, bellboys, even a group of drunken conventioneers—converge on the wedding suite. The resulting bedlam was reminiscent of the Marx Brothers' mayhem in the stateroom scene of *A Night at the Opera*, but it was funny, nevertheless.

Marital comedies continued on the screen, of course, until the present day, changing very little until the sixties, when the concept of the wife as a loving, dutiful, vulnerable creature, subject only to her husband's whims, began to disappear, and the idea of marriage as little more than a series of mild tiffs and misunderstandings, followed by blissful reconciliation, became virtually obsolete. The wives of *Too Many Husbands, I Love You Again,* and *The Feminine Touch* would never recognize the wives of *Bob and Carol and Ted and Alice* (1969). The battling couple of *The Awful Truth* would probably be shocked by the bluntness and acerbity of the married squabblers in *Divorce American Style* (1967). Twenty-five years later, the ladies of *Appointment for Love, You Belong to Me,* and *Woman of the Year* would probably think twice before giving up their professional careers for any mere man.

The husbands and wives of the comedies of the thirties and forties may have lived in a marital "never-never land." But while it may not have been the ideal land to live in, it was great fun to visit.

CHAPTER FOUR

POOR LITTLE RICH GIRLS (AND BOYS)

"You're the spoiled brat of a rich father!"—Clark Gable to Claudette Colbert in *It Happened One Night*

"You've never had an idea in your life. You've done nothing all your life except give parties, each one sillier than the rest."—Claude Gillingwater to Madeleine Carroll in *Cafe Society*

"You glamour girls are a drug on the market."—James Cagney to Bette Davis in *The Bride Came C.O.D.*

It lasted only one week at New York's Radio City Music Hall. The *New York Daily News*, on a rating scale of one to four stars, gave it two-and-a-half stars. Its leading man was forced into making the film as punishment and considered the assignment offensive. Its leading lady insisted on double her usual salary to appear in it and thought it was the worst film she had ever made. Even before filming began, studio executives condemned it as "froth" and "trivia" with no "suspense" or "heart."

The film was *It Happened One Night* (1934), the Columbia comedy that won all five major Academy Awards in its year,* gave remarkable impetus to the careers of stars Clark Gable and Claudette Colbert, and—most important of all—had an enormous impact on the direction of humor on the screen. For once, the simple story of romance between a spoiled heiress and an earthy reporter did not take place in a mammoth drawing room but on a night bus to New York. Its principal character was not a pouting debutante wallowing in her wealth but a charming, albeit spoiled and headstrong rich girl who

*Best Picture, Best Actress, Best Actor, Best Director, Best Writer.

could thumb a ride, dunk a doughnut, and fall for a plain-speaking man who didn't wear undershirts. And she was surrounded this time —not by butlers, earls, and dowagers, but by ordinary "little" people. Despite some (but not all) of the critics,* the studio executives, and the unhappy stars, filmgoers took it to their hearts, and *It Happened One Night* was a resounding success and a classic example of Hollywood's inability to judge the value of its own material.

Viewed nearly four decades later, *It Happened One Night* dates surprisingly little. It is still a blithe and engaging comedy in which the people are recognizable and the situations deftly handled in the Robert Riskin screenplay and in Frank Capra's direction. From the moment heiress Ellie Andrews (Colbert) leaps off her father's yacht, where he is holding her prisoner to keep her from marrying fortune-hunter King Westley (Jameson Thomas), the comedy spins along at a brisk pace. On the bus to New York, Ellie meets reporter Peter Warne (Gable) by falling into his lap. "Next time you drop in," he tells her, breaking into the quizzical Gable grin, "bring your folks." When he finally realizes who she is and offers to help in exchange for her exclusive story, she tries to give him money. He is offended: "You're the spoiled brat of a rich father! The only way you can get anything is to buy it. Ever hear of the word 'humility'?" he asks her. But he wires his editor that he has found the runaway heiress and will get her story.

When they are forced to share a cabin in an auto camp after a bridge is washed out, Peter resorts to unusual measures to keep them apart. He divides the room by stringing a blanket along a clothes line. "Behold the walls of Jericho. Maybe not as thick as the ones that Joshua blew down with his trumpet, but a lot safer. You see, I have no trumpet." He undresses, chattering all the time (and incidentally striking a blow at the manufacturers of undershirts with his bare chest), until Ellie decides to follow suit. She flings her undergarments on the blanket. "Do you mind taking those things off the walls of Jericho?" he asks. "It's tough enough as it is."

The dialogue in this first intimate scene is especially felicitous. Ellie asks his name:

Peter: Who, me? Why, I'm the whippoorwill that cries in the night. I'm the soft morning breeze that caresses your lovely face.

*The *New York Times* liked the film—the review said it was "blessed with bright dialogue" and praised Colbert's "engaging and lively performance."

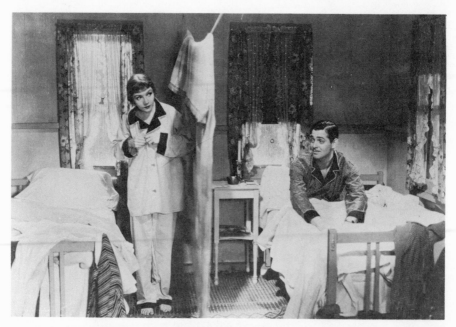

IT HAPPENED ONE NIGHT (1934). Heiress Ellie Andrews (Claudette Colbert), reporter Peter Warne (Clark Gable), and "the walls of Jericho."

LOVE ON THE RUN (1936). Wealthy Sally Parker (Joan Crawford) and foreign correspondent Michael Anthony (Clark Gable).

Ellie: You've got a name, haven't you?
Peter: Yeah, I got a name. Peter Warne.
Ellie: Peter Warne. I don't like it.
Peter: Don't let it bother you. You're giving it back in the morning.
Ellie: Pleased to meet you, Mr. Warne . . .
Peter: The pleasure is all mine.

Their cross-country trek to elude the police (and for Peter—to keep the story exclusive) is filled with scenes that are now part of movie lore: Peter teaching Ellie how to dunk a doughnut ("Dunking's an art. Don't let it soak so long. A dip and plop, into your mouth."); Peter and Ellie pretending to be a battling married couple when the police stop at their cabin; Peter frightening off a prying, obnoxious salesman (Roscoe Karns as Shapeley—"Shapeley's the name—and that's the way I like 'em!"); and Peter's attempt to carry Ellie across a stream. They quarrel over the nature of a "piggy-backer."

Peter: To be a "piggy-backer" it takes complete relaxation—a warm heart—and a loving nature.
Ellie: And rich people have none of these qualifications, I suppose.
Peter: Not a one.

The film's best-remembered scene occurs when Peter tries to explain the subtle technique of hitch-hiking to Ellie. ("Number one is a short, jerky movement—that shows independence. Number two is a wider movement—a smile goes with that one.") When he fails to stop a car, Ellie merely lifts her skirt above the knees, pretending to fix her garter, and a car screeches to a halt.* Peter is chagrined: "Why didn't you take all your clothes off? You could have stopped *forty* cars." Her retort: "We didn't *need* forty cars."

Inevitably, in spite of their bickering, Ellie and Peter realize they are in love. But a rift occurs when Peter leaves her during the night to prod some money from his irate editor. (Movie newspaper editors are always irate.) When Ellie wakes up alone, she believes he has deserted her and hurries home to her father and King Westley. After further misunderstandings and confusion, Ellie finds herself marching down the aisle to marry Westley. But her father has spoken to Peter and knows that the reporter truly loves his errant daughter. "You don't want to be married to a mug like Westley," he tells her

---

*Frank Capra has written that Colbert was reluctant to show her leg until he tried to get a shapely chorus girl to double for her in the shot.

in a whisper. "I can buy *him* off for a pot of gold, and you can make an old man happy, and you wouldn't do so bad for yourself." At the altar Ellie turns and flees into a waiting car. Later, at an auto camp, the owner and his wife discuss the newlyweds who have just arrived. The wife says that she brought them a rope and a blanket, and her husband is puzzled by their request for a trumpet. To the sound of a trumpet blast, the film ends.

Gable and Colbert have been justifiably praised over the years for their performances, he a romantic playing at being a cynic and she a vulnerable girl pretending to be sophisticated.* They are both fine, but Walter Connolly is equally good as Ellie's father, loving his incorrigible daughter and trying to keep his exasperation under control. He is delightful in the first scene as he tries to break her hunger strike by overreacting enthusiastically to a tray of aromatic food, and also in the final scene, in which he enthusiastically settles accounts with King Westley. ("Hello, my would-be ex-son-in-law. I've sent you a check for a hundred thousand.")

In 1956, Columbia remade *It Happened One Night* as *You Can't Run Away From It*, adding Technicolor and several mediocre songs. Under actor Dick Powell's direction, June Allyson played Ellie, Jack Lemmon was Peter, and Charles Bickford played Ellie's father. Some of the bright original dialogue was retained but much more was changed to accommodate June Allyson's simpering sentimentality, and the result was negligible.

Inevitably, the amazing success of *It Happened One Night* prompted other studios to attempt carbon copies of the original, or to draw on certain elements of the plot and build new situations around them. For the rest of the thirties and even into the forties, the screen was overrun with willful heiresses fleeing stuffy marriages, or rich young men and women mingling incognito with the common folk to learn humility and understanding, and—more often than not—finding true love in the bargain. True to the movies' unwritten code of the Depression years, film after film mocked and castigated the silly self-indulgence of the idle rich and sought to prove that lasting romance could be found in a cold water flat more easily than a Park Avenue mansion. Ambivalently, of course, the same films inspired filmgoers' envy by showing glamorous people, dressed to the nines, moving through lavish settings.

*The role of Ellie had been turned down by Myrna Loy (Capra's first choice), Margaret Sullavan, Miriam Hopkins, and Constance Bennett. And Robert Montgomery rejected the role of Peter.

LOVE IS NEWS (1937). Tyrone Power, Pauline Moore, Dudley Digges, and Loretta Young in a cheerful moment.

THERE GOES MY HEART (1938). Another reporter (Fredric March), another heiress (Virginia Bruce).

Some of the offspring of *It Happened One Night* were virtually twins. The gambit of the spoiled heiress tangling with a cheeky newspaper man turned up in MGM's *Libeled Lady* (1936), in which editor Spencer Tracy tried to thwart a libel suit brought against the paper by angry heiress Myrna Loy; MGM's *Love on the Run* (1936), which has W. S. Van Dyke directing Joan Crawford as a wealthy girl balking at marriage to a prince and Clark Gable as a foreign correspondent who helps her flee across Europe; and Fox's *Love Is News* (1937), a featherweight farce starring Loretta Young as a rich girl who fights back at reporter Tyrone Power's nasty stories about her by announcing her "engagement" to him. Don Ameche appeared as an improbable city editor in this comedy, with George Sanders, Dudley Digges, and the amusing Slim Summerville in support.* The most blatant imitation of *It Happened One Night* came in 1938—a Hal Roach comedy called *There Goes My Heart* offered Virginia Bruce as the headstrong heiress who leaps off her family yacht and meets reporter Fredric March. It was no surprise that he learns her true identity while falling in love with her.

By 1939 the "headstrong-heiress-meets-scornful-reporter" plot had run its course, and Paramount's *Cafe Society* was only a feeble echo of the original. In this Virginia Van Upp screenplay, Madeleine Carroll played party-mad, irresponsible heiress Chris West, who marries gullible ship's reporter Chick O'Bannon (Fred MacMurray) to win a bet she had made with gossip columnist Sonny DeWitt (Allyn Joslyn). She had bet $1,000 that she could still get her name in his column after years of publicity for her antics. To her chagrin, she spoils her own trick by falling in love with Chick and after the requisite number of spats and disagreements, they live happily (and richly) ever after.

Though Madeleine Carroll and Fred MacMurray were pleasant as usual (they co-starred again later that year in *Honeymoon in Bali*), the film was thin and sluggish. Like RKO's *Fifth Avenue Girl*, it had an unusually large number of nasty remarks about the idle rich and their frivolous life-style. "Cafe society!" says Chick's singer girlfriend Belle (Shirley Ross), "I'd rather read about the zoo!" "Cafe society!" says Chick to Chris, "If you'd die tomorrow, they'd have to hire half your pallbearers!" He calls her an "elegant meringue." Even Chris' affluent grandfather (Claude Gillingwater) berates her: "You've

---

* *Love Is News* was remade by Fox in 1948 as *That Wonderful Urge*, with Tyrone Power repeating his original role. Gene Tierney played the heiress.

CAFE SOCIETY (1939). On ship's deck, heiress Madeleine Carroll dances with Don Alvarado, but has eyes for reporter Fred MacMurray.

THE COWBOY AND THE LADY (1938). Cowboy Gary Cooper castigates wife Merle Oberon and her rich friends. At her side: Berton Churchill.

never had an idea in your life. You've done nothing all your life except give parties, each one sillier than the rest." And when Sonny DeWitt tells Chick that he can attend his monster party for Chris and "see cafe society in the raw," Chick remarks: "Medium rare will do."*

Of these heiress-newsman confrontations, *Libeled Lady* was by far the best and was, in fact, one of the most successful comedies of the thirties. (It was nominated for an Academy Award as Best Picture.) The screenplay by Maurine Watkins, Howard Emmett Rogers, and George Oppenheimer, under Jack Conway's sure-footed direction, had Myrna Loy as heiress Connie Allenbury, determined to carry out a $5,000,000 libel suit against the *Evening Star* for printing a false story about her stealing someone's husband. Complications ensue when the *Star's* enterprising editor Warren Haggerty (Spencer Tracy) schemes to thwart Connie by making her appear to be a *genuine* "husband-stealer." For his scheme he enlists the services of Bill Chandler (William Powell), a master at breaking tough libel cases, and his own long-suffering fiancée, Gladys (Jean Harlow). (We first meet her as she storms into Haggerty's office in her bridal gown, shouting "For two years, I've played second fiddle to this newspaper!") Haggerty persuades dubious Gladys to marry Bill "in name only" and then play the outraged wife when Bill takes up romantically with Connie Allenbury.

Around this situation, *Libeled Lady* spins a surprising amount of fast-paced merriment. One of the funniest scenes occurs early in the film when Bill and Gladys are married by a justice of the peace. She gives husband Bill a light peck on the cheek—and then proceeds to kiss "best man" Warren passionately. "An old friend," Bill says to the astonished justice and, as the two prolong their kiss, "a *very* old friend." Shortly afterwards, the newlyweds are required to fake an emotional parting when Bill is called to London on business. (Connie will be on the boat.) Gladys grumbles at being left alone. "You can sew and listen to the radio," Warren tells her. To which Bill adds: "Maybe you can learn to read."

Bill's pursuit of Connie is marked by a number of wry exchanges in the nimble Powell-Loy manner—naturally she must first believe he is a fortune-hunter, and just as naturally he must pretend to be

---

*A salute in passing should be made to veteran actress Jessie Ralph's too-brief appearance in this film as Sonny DeWitt's tough-minded old mother. She sits in a nightclub, working on a hook rug with an image of Sonny at its center. "I can't wait to get it finished," she says, "so I can walk on it!"

LIBELED LADY (1936). Gladys (Jean Harlow), her fiancé (Spencer Tracy), and her husband-to-be (William Powell) meet for the wedding.

annoyed by her too-fragile, rich girl attitudes. His determination to score points with Connie and her father leads him to take up Mr. Allenbury's favorite pastime, trout-fishing, and to the film's single most hilarious sequence. After taking some instruction from the redoubtable E. E. Clive ("follow the natural spring of the rod"), with Clive pretending to be a tree and using Gladys as a boulder, Bill is finally forced to impress the Allenburys with his skill at trout-fishing. Of course the experience is comically disastrous. He wanders into the stream with the instruction book in his hand, is completely submerged, chases after the book downstream, and gets his face caught in a fish net. Somehow he manages to hook a huge trout to his own and the Allenburys' amazement.

As Bill falls genuinely in love with Connie, he balks at Haggerty's scheme, though the editor insists that he see it through. (Gladys: "You'd make your crippled grandmother do a fan dance.") Connie is becoming equally fond of Bill and is on the verge of dropping the libel suit at Bill's advice. But an unexpected complication occurs when Gladys develops an increasingly warm feeling for her new husband, which sends Haggerty into a fit of irate jealousy. ("She may be his wife," he says, "but she's engaged to me!") But he is not so jealous that he cannot use her feeling to provoke her into action against her "cheating" husband. The film's climax has Haggerty and a fuming Gladys in full pursuit of Connie and Bill, who have gone off to be married. By the time they reach the scene, the marriage has taken place. "It's arson!" Gladys cries, the personification of the outraged wife confronting a bigamous husband. Coolly, Bill sideswipes her protest by claiming that her former divorce in Mexico was declared illegal; that is, their marriage is illegal. A fight ensues, which ends with the two couples pairing off exactly as they were intended from the start.

The plot, of course, is totally inane, and yet the film sustains its brightness for most of the way, buoyed by a first-rate cast: William Powell, suave, dry, and elegantly right as Bill; Myrna Loy, charming and likeable as Connie; Spencer Tracy, ingratiating as Haggerty; and —best of all—Jean Harlow at her most inimitable as Gladys. Brash, vulgar, and very funny, she makes expert use of her nasal voice and blunt sexiness as in few of her other films. Only watch the fleeting look of mockery that passes across her face when Myrna Loy, urging her to give up her husband, says "You can't build love on hate or marriage on spite!" For Gladys, hate and spite are quite satisfying emotions. (*Libeled Lady* was remade by MGM in 1946 as *Easy to Wed,* with Van Johnson, Esther Williams, Lucille Ball, and Keenan Wynn in the Powell-Loy-Harlow-Tracy roles.)

A favorite device for the "rich boy–rich girl" comedies, also echoing *It Happened One Night,* was placing the protagonist incognito in unfamiliar surroundings and having him/her learn first hand about "the real world": the world of tourist camps and motels and servants' quarters. Or discovering the simple pleasures of rural life as opposed to the empty glamour of the big city (a standard movie myth).

The most persistent ploy of these "incognito" comedies was the heiress-disguised-as-maid, or the playboy-disguised-as-butler. In Fox's *Servants' Entrance* (1934), Janet Gaynor played a rich girl about to lose her money to the Depression, who hires out as a servant girl and promptly falls in love with the family chauffeur (Lew Ayres). A very minor RKO comedy, *Maid's Night Out* (1938), presented Joan Fontaine as an heiress who pretends to be her own maid and gets caught up in witless complications. Samuel Goldwyn's *The Cowboy and the Lady* (1938) offered Merle Oberon as the daughter of a presidential candidate who elopes impulsively with a rodeo cowboy (Gary Cooper) who thinks she is a maid in her own household.

The latter comedy, blandly directed by H. C. Potter, lacked sparkle and wit—the comic highlight was a spirited rendition of "A-Tisket, A-Tasket" by elderly Harry Davenport—but once again it featured an unusually vitriolic attitude toward the rich. In a climactic scene, Cooper, bitter at his new wife's rejection of his way of life, bursts in on dinner at her Palm Beach home and castigates the guests. He attacks her "smart-aleck" friends, urges them to "go out and learn what people think and feel." "I'd like to invite you all to the ranch," he shouts, clearly convinced that a session with the cows and horses will turn them from their frivolous ways. Later, Oberon's father, obsessed with his candidacy until this point, appears at the ranch, properly remorseful. "People should get off their high horses," he tells Cooper. And of course Oberon has settled into the ranch kitchen, the loving wife submissive to her husband's will. (Inexplicably the movie won an Academy Award for Best Sound Recording.)

One of the better incognito comedies of the thirties was Columbia's *If You Could Only Cook* (1935), brightly directed by William A. Seiter. The screenplay by Howard J. Green and Gertrude Purcell (from a story by F. Hugh Herbert) centered on Herbert Marshall as automobile tycoon Jim Buchanan. Exasperated by his dull-witted board of directors and his nasty fiancée, he flees to the park where he meets jobless Joan Hawthorne (Jean Arthur). Thinking he is also

IF YOU COULD ONLY COOK (1935). Joan Hawthorne (Jean Arthur) and Jim Buchanan (Herbert Marshall) take jobs as cook and butler.

THE MOON'S OUR HOME (1936). In a New England boarding house: Laura Hope Crews, Margaret Hamilton, incognito actress Margaret Sullavan, and new husband Henry Fonda. (Note the newspaper headline: "Where's Cherry Chester?")

down on his luck, she persuades him to join her in accepting jobs as cook and butler in the home of Mike Rossini (Leo Carrillo), a retired racketeer and active gourmet. ("My stomach lives for good things.") Joan gets the job by passing Rossini's stringent "garlic test"—she uses only "the ghost of a shadow of garlic." There are predictable complications when Joan and Jim must pretend to be married, but then a fresh touch is added when they both begin to *believe* it—Jim is indignant at Rossini's attentions to his "wife" and Joan is convinced he is "pussy-footing around" with other women, though he is actually stealing to his office at night to recover his plans for a revolutionary automobile.

The plot thickens (and, in fact, becomes rather lumpy) when Joan takes the plans to a rival company, thinking they are the work of her very own designing genius "Jim Burns." When they are recognized as Buchanan's, she is arrested as a confidence woman. Thinking she has deserted him, Jim returns to his fiancée and Joan, learning his true identity, is angry and mortified. Enter the *deus ex machina* in the form of Rossini, who has his gang abduct Jim from his wedding and bring him to his house to marry Joan. After the obligatory amount of grumbling, the two are reunited.

The film draws its considerable charm from the amiable playing of the cast—even Herbert Marshall is reasonably animated—and from a number of amusing scenes. One of the best has Jim practicing how to "buttle" with his own butler. "It's all a simple masquerade," the butler tells him, but "you must know your master like a book." "Do you think I'm out of my mind?" Jim asks. "I'm hoping for the best, sir," is the butler's proper reply. Another well-played scene has Joan and Jim discovering that they love each other as they wax enthusiastic over Jim's new car model. Imagine, he tells her, having a car "to carry you long the open road with your hair streaming across your adorable brow!" The film's funniest sequence is its wild climax, with Rossini's mob spiriting Jim out of the chapel at gunpoint, while the wedding party watches in astonishment, hands in the air. The hoods are pursued by the police, who only want them to remove the tin cans from the rear of their car. In a riotous moment, Rossini's chief henchman "Flash" (Lionel Stander) and another gang member are forced to play the newly married couple, embracing happily in the back of the limousine.

Jean Arthur and Herbert Marshall are pleasing in the leading roles, but Leo Carrillo is even more delightful as the food-loving racketeer. Best of all is Lionel Stander, inimitable as the dour and ever-suspicious Flash, troubled by Joan and Jim's "marriage." ("If she was your wife, would *you* sleep on the porch?") He also worries about Joan's experience in the kitchen. ("If her hands ever did dishwashing before, I'm an embroidery designer.")

One of the popular variations of the incognito plot dealt with the temperamental stage or screen star who disguises herself as a "commoner" to escape her deliriously demanding public. Universal's *It Happened in New York* (1935) centered on film idol Vania Nardi (Gertrude Michael), who tries to "get away from it all" and becomes involved with a taxi-driver (Lyle Talbot) and jewel thieves in New York. Hailed as "a gay and rollicking comedy" by the *New York Times*, it was directed by Alan Crosland, who had contributed to movie history by directing *Don Juan* (1926), the first film to have a musical score synchronized with the action, and *The Jazz Singer* (1927), the first film with sound sequences. In RKO's comedy *In Person* (1935), Ginger Rogers played movie star Carol Corliss, who puts on a wig, spectacles, and false teeth and flees from her overeager fans to a rural retreat, where she meets George Brent. Here the paper-thin screenplay was bolstered by several songs from Oscar Levant and Dorothy Fields.

The Moon's Our Home (1936) was Paramount's contribution to this cycle, and one of the year's most ingratiating comedies. Derived from a Faith Baldwin story, the screenplay by Isabel Dawn and Boyce DeGaw (with added dialogue by Dorothy Parker and Alan Campbell) concerned tempestuous screen star Cherry Chester (Margaret Sullavan), who retreats into anonymity under her true name, Sarah Brown, and impulsively marries travel writer Tony Amberton (Henry Fonda). The story takes several improbable turns after their disastrous wedding night—he is violently allergic to her perfume and she assumes he is repelled by *her*—but after a few setbacks and a long, noisy, and rather foolish denouement, the two are happily reuinted.

Despite the screenplay's conspicuous lack of sense or reason, *The Moon's Our Home* succeeds in being genuinely amusing. The early scenes offer a lightly malicious look at the headstrong movie star in full bloom—Cherry gives an interview to a Hedda Hopperish reporter in which she describes marriage as a ski-jump, "swift, reckless!" (Her companion, Beulah Bondi, comments that she would settle for "a nice job as a night nurse in a psychiatric ward.") And Sullavan and Fonda are extremely likeable as "two free people with the world behind them" who somehow manage to quarrel incessantly at the same time that they confess their love for each other. He proposes and she protests, "We'll fight every day." "We'll make up every night," he replies. "I'll leave you constantly," she warns. "I'll always find you," he counters. One of the film's best scenes is the wedding ceremony, with the couple quarreling and punctuating their quarrel with cries of "I do!" and "I certainly do!", which the deaf justice of the peace takes to be answers to the wedding vows.

Margaret Sullavan is radiant as Cherry Chester, though her wistful, throaty voice is somewhat at odds with the character, and Henry Fonda is familiarly appealing as Tony. But the film's most delightful moments are contributed by Margaret Hamilton as the owner of a New England boarding house. Blunt as always, she introduces one of her boarders as a lady who has had "three nervous breakdowns." She shows Sullavan to her room, which is covered in flowered wallpaper. "This is the Rose Room," she remarks. "We call it that on account of the roses." The funniest scene finds her putting on the flimsy nightgown given to her by Cherry. Primping ludicrously in front of the mirror, she is discovered by her bewildered husband.

When the screen's rich girls and boys weren't away from their familiar society haunts learning to live as "ordinary people," they were discovering tolerance, humility, and (of course) true love in other ways. Examples abound in the thirties. In Columbia's *She Couldn't Take It* (1935), directed by Tay Garnett from a screenplay by Oliver H. P. Garrett, Joan Bennett played a giddy, irresponsible debutante who is "tamed" by gunman George Raft, hired by her dying father (Walter Connolly) to administer his estate and teach his family some manners. Only Connolly, expiring too early in the film, helped to relieve the general tedium. In Paramount's *Spendthrift* (1936), derived from a story by Eric Hatch, Raoul Walsh directed Henry Fonda as a profligate playboy who loses his money, takes a job as a radio sports announcer, and marries the stableman's daughter (Pat Paterson). One heiress, played by Brenda Joyce in Fox's *Public Deb No. 1* (1940), even fell prey to the lure of communism, only to be set back on the democratic path by waiter George Murphy.

One variation on the theme came in Columbia's screen version of Philip Barry's stage comedy, *Holiday* (1938), first filmed by RKO-Pathé in 1930, with Ann Harding, Robert Ames, and Mary Astor. Here the rich girl, played by Doris Nolan, is snobbish and intolerant in the prescribed manner, certain of her place in "society," and anxious for her about-to-be husband (Cary Grant) to join her in the safe, untroubled world of the rich. The switch comes when she loses her fiancé permanently to her sister (Katharine Hepburn), a charm-

SHE COULDN'T TAKE IT (1935). Debutante Joan Bennett with gangsters Wallace Ford and Lloyd Nolan.

HOLIDAY (1938). Johnny Case (Cary Grant) meets his fiancée's wealthy father (Henry Kolker). Between them: his prospective sister-in-law Linda (Katharine Hepburn).

ingly straightforward free spirit with none of the hang-ups of her class. Here, the snobbish debutante is not "tamed," only dropped for good.

As directed by George Cukor from an adaptation of the play by Donald Ogden Stewart and Sidney Buchman, *Holiday* is an enjoyably witty and sparkling film. Once again, the mindless accumulation of wealth at the expense of happiness, good cheer, and other virtues is roundly criticized. Johnny Case (Grant) is the film's central character, an amiable young man with one pervading goal: to make a lot of money quickly and then take an extended "holiday" to learn who he is and where he fits in. Engaged to his "perfect playmate" Julia Seaton (Nolan), he is shocked to discover that she is not only fabulously wealthy but that she has no use for his dreams or his plans. Disillusioned and unhappy, he turns to Julia's enchanting sister Linda (Hepburn), who tells him as soon as they meet that she "can't decide whether to be Joan of Arc, Florence Nightingale, or John L. Lewis." Linda informs him that the Seton house is "haunted by ghosts wearing stuffed shirts and mink-lined ties" and urges him not to get caught up in "a reverence for riches."

Johnny's interview with his conservative prospective father-in-law (Henry Kolker), with Linda happily present, further convinces him that he is all wrong for the Seton household. (Linda asks her father: "Would you like me to hide under the sofa and take shorthand notes?") Mr. Seton is profoundly startled by Johnny's ideas. "There's a strange new spirit in the world today," he tells him. "A spirit of revolt. I don't understand it—and I don't like it." Yet he gives his reluctant consent to Julia and Johnny's marriage.

At a lavish New Year's Eve party given for Julia at her father's insistence, Linda pointedly refuses to attend, preferring to stay in the family playroom with the "real" people, including Johnny's eccentric friends Nick and Susan Potter (Edward Everett Horton and Jean Dixon)* and her perennially drunk young brother Ned (Lew Ayres), whose remarks are tinged with bitterness. ("Mother tried to be a Seton. Then she gave up and died.") Ultimately, Johnny turns up, too. Elated, he tells them that the money he has been expecting is finally on its way and he can go on his long holiday with Julia. They are interrupted by Mr. Seton, who orders Linda to some down to the party. In tears, she tells him: "This room is my home—the only home

---

*In the 1928 stage version, Nick Potter was originally played by Donald Ogden Stewart, co-author of the screenplay.

THE PHILADELPHIA STORY (1940). Tracy Lord (Katharine Hepburn) converses with ex-husband C. K. Dexter Haven (Cary Grant). Listening in: her sister (Virginia Weidler) and mother (Mary Nash).

THE BRIDE CAME C.O.D. (1941). Pilot James Cagney and runaway heiress Bette Davis talk with old miner Harry Davenport.

I've got." Following an angry scene with Julia, in which she insists that "there's nothing more exciting than making money," Johnny turns to Linda and they kiss tenderly as the New Year comes in.

Johnny vanishes for a while and then returns to announce that he is sailing for Europe and wants Julia to come with him. She refuses adamantly, despite Linda's urgings. And Mr. Seton backs her up, convinced that Johnny's attitude is "un-American." Ned, sensing that Linda loves Johnny very much, tells her that she has "twice the looks, twice the brains" of Julia. Johnny returns to take the job in the Seton bank, only to discover that Mr. Seton has tried to arrange the entire honeymoon trip. Unable to tolerate the situation any longer, Johnny finally rebels and goes off, telling Julia: "I love feeling free inside better than I love you." Realizing that Julia no longer loves him, Linda proposes to strengthen Johnny's belief in himself:

> I've got all the faith in the world in Johnny. Whatever he does is
> all right with me. If he wants to sit on his tail, he can sit on his tail.
> If he wants to come back and sell peanuts, Lord how I'll believe
> in those peanuts!

Though its brittle style is dated, *Holiday* remains one of the best comedies of the thirties, notable for its bright dialogue, which brims along at a lively pace, and for the performance of Katharine Hepburn in a role eminently suited to her style. Whether telling Johnny with tongue in cheek that "Chase has such a sweet banking sound," or tremulously telling him: "There's a conspiracy against you and me, child," she projected the image of the emancipated, rebellious young woman with enormous flair. (She had been understudy to Hope Williams in the 1928 stage production.) Cary Grant is also good as Johnny, and Edward Everett Horton and Jean Dixon are especially delightful as the Potters.

The year after *Holiday* was released, Hepburn returned to Broadway to star with Joseph Cotten and Van Heflin in Philip Barry's comedy, *The Philadelphia Story*. It was a major triumph, and after a long run she was signed by MGM to appear in the film version. In her first film for the studio, her radiant performance launched her in a new film career that has thrived to the present day.

Released in 1940, *The Philadelphia Story* is still one of the most glittering, most silken, of screen comedies, and if its view of the idle rich is far kinder than any film of the thirties (even the rich can learn love and humility), it is couched in witty terms, and the idle rich never had a lovelier representative than Hepburn. She plays Tracy Lord, a cold, brittle, selfish Main Line heiress who, during the few days preceding her impending second marriage, discovers that she can have "an understanding heart," and that she really loves her first husband, C. K. Dexter Haven (Cary Grant in the role Joseph Cotten played on the stage).

The early scenes, on the day before Tracy's marriage to stuffy George Kittredge (John Howard), quickly set the plot spinning, as Tracy plays the disdainful "goddess" for the benefit of various people: her mother (Mary Nash)—"Tracy sets exceptionally high standards for herself"—her father (John Halliday), who calls her a "perennial spinster"; Dexter, who refers to her as "a married maiden with no regard for human frailty"; and especially Mike Connor (James Stewart in the Van Heflin stage role), a reporter for *Spy* magazine who is covering the wedding. Undaunted by everyone's disapproval, Tracy remains coolly contemptuous. Mike tells her he comes from South Bend. "Sounds like dancing," she tells him. He is "Mike" to his friends. "Of whom you have many, I am sure," she remarks with icy hauteur.

The thawing of Tracy begins at a party that evening, when she is finally alone with Mike after both have done some heavy drinking. In a scene of vast romantic charm, they dance together in the moonlight at the edge of the Lord pool. "There's a magnificence in you, Tracy," he tells her. "You're lit from within. You're the golden girl, full of life and warmth and delight." Later that night Mike, singing an off-key version of "Over the Rainbow," carries a tipsily happy Tracy over his shoulder, only to be confronted by Dexter and a thoroughly shocked George. Tracy greets them all cheerfully, turning *sotto voce* for George. "How art the mighty fallen!" Dexter declares.

In the inevitable morning after, Tracy can barely face the light and she is troubled about the events of the evening. But she is also feeling much more human and mellow. With Dexter, she talks about their boat *True Love*, conveying wistfully an image of love lost but not forgotten. She also gets a note from George, testily saying goodbye. (He shows up later, highly apologetic, but by then it is too late.) As the wedding approaches, Tracy is in need of a substitute groom. Mike volunteers, but she turns him down. Instead, Dexter dictates her speech to the assembled guests, presenting himself, the husband-who-was, as the husband-to-be. Tracy, radiantly happy, confides to her father that she feels "like a human being."

In a role tailored snugly to her special gifts (as well as her eccentricities), Hepburn is marvelous, expressing a grace and elegance that she matched only in a few of her films with Spencer Tracy. Others in the cast are fine: James Stewart in his Academy Award–winning performance as Mike (the award probably given for his long drunk scene); Ruth Hussey, also nominated for her performance as Liz, the caustic photographer who loves Mike ("Here," she says, handing him a handkerchief after his first encounter with Tracy, "wipe the spit out of your eye."); Virginia Weidler as Tracy's sister Dinah (the sight of her dancing on tiptoes as she sings a chorus of "Lydia the Tattooed Lady" is thoroughly risible); and Roland Young as the lecherous Uncle Willie, compulsively pinching every female rear in sight.*

By the early forties, heiresses—especially runaway heiresses—were anachronisms not likely to provoke much laughter in movie audiences. RKO's *Cross Country Romance* (1940), a direct descendant of *It Happened One Night,* had rich girl Wendy Barrie fleeing an unwanted marriage and hiding out in the trailer of poor boy Gene Raymond. An even more direct descendant of the Capra film was Warners' *The Bride Came C.O.D.* (1941), which offered the surprising view of Bette Davis, free for once from her lugubrious dramas, as heiress Joan Winfield. True to form, she fled from her irate father (Eugene Pallette), who was opposed to her marrying a bandleader (Jack Carson), only to end up in the arms of pilot Steve Collins (James Cagney), originally hired by her father to bring her back home.

Unfortunately, Davis' excursion into comedy (at one point she fell into a bed of cactus) was a labored affair that neither of the stars, working frenetically, could make more than mildly amusing. Davis, particularly, attacked all her lines as if she were back in *Dark Victory,* doomed to blindness and death, and Cagney, pugnacious and irritable, was not exactly right for romantic comedy. In a script by Philip and Julius Epstein that was devoid of wit, only one word was memorable—Davis' cry of "Mustard!" when she kisses Cagney and realizes he has been eating a sandwich outside the abandoned mine in which they are presumably "trapped." Otherwise *The Bride Came C.O.D.* was merely a last gasp of a fading genre.**

One of the brightest, funniest "madcap-heiress" comedies of the

---

*The film also received four other Academy Award nominations: for Best Picture, Best Actress (Hepburn), Best Director (George Cukor), and Best Screenplay (Donald Ogden Stewart). Of these only Stewart won the award. In 1956 the film was remade as *High Society,* a passably entertaining Technicolor musical, with Bing Crosby, Grace Kelly, Frank Sinatra, and Celeste Holm in the Grant-Hepburn-Stewart-Hussey roles.

**But apparently not *the* last gasp. *You Gotta Stay Happy,* a 1948 comedy from Universal-International, involved Joan Fontaine as heiress Dee Dee Dillwood, who flees from a stuffy bridegroom into the arms of flyer Marvin Payne (James Stewart). H. C. Potter directed a Karl Tunberg screenplay.

thirties achieved a distinction all its own, and deserves to be discussed separately. This was RKO's *Bringing Up Baby* (1938), directed by Howard Hawks from a screenplay by Dudley Nichols and Hagar Wilde. (Miss Wilde wrote the original story.) It brought together Cary Grant and Katharine Hepburn in the first of their felicitous teamings: Grant fresh from his expert performance in *The Awful Truth,* and Hepburn in her last film for the studio before venturing to Columbia for *Holiday* and then MGM.

One of the distinctions of *Bringing Up Baby* is that its heiress, Susan Vance (Hepburn), is *not* running away from either a mismatched or loveless marriage. She is merely a dizzy and impulsive rich girl who encounters and finally snares a serious (and engaged) young archaeologist (Grant). They meet on the golf links, where Susan keeps insisting that everything of David's belongs to her: his golf ball and even his car. She causes a series of accidents that embarrass him in front of the attorney he is trying to impress. (He wants the attorney's client, Mrs. Random, to endow a museum, not knowing that Mrs. Random is Susan's Aunt Elizabeth). Later, in a nightclub, David is again mortified by Susan when she tears her dress down the back, and he is forced to walk behind her to conceal the tear.

Clearly, David has met a formidable obstacle to peace and stability in the irrepressible Susan. ("Our relationship," he tells her, "has been a series of misadventures.") This relationship takes a surprising turn when he meets Susan's newest companion, a large but gentle leopard named "Baby." Susan badgers him into taking Baby to her aunt's home in Connecticut. On their way, one of the film's most hilarious sequences takes place when David's car hits a wagon filled with chickens, ducks, and a pair of swans. Knee-deep in livestock, David learns that Baby can only be controlled by a soothing chorus of "I Can't Give You Anything But Love."

David's plight worsens by leaps and bounds (Baby's leaps and his bounds) when they finally arrive at the farmhouse. Forced to remove his clothes, he puts on Susan's fluffy robe, muttering "Of all the conceited, spoiled little scatterbrains," only to be confronted by Susan's startled aunt (May Robson). "Why are you wearing a robe?" she asks, reasonably. "Because I just went gay all of a sudden!" he tells her. Susan fails to clarify the situation when she tells her aunt that David is the only man she has ever loved. When David learns that Aunt Elizabeth is the client whose money he craves, he is flabbergasted and swears Susan to secrecy.

From this point, *Bringing Up Baby* veers from insanity into lunacy,

BRINGING UP BABY (1938). A disgruntled Cary Grant is forced to explain why he is wearing a woman's robe. His audience includes Katharine Hepburn and May Robson.

with no pause to catch its breath. A rare and valuable dinosaur bone just received by David is spirited away by Susan's dog George, and David and Susan are obliged to rush about the grounds following the dog as he digs hole after hole. (They find boots and other objects but no bone. "Couldn't you go back and find another?" Susan asks David.) This is followed by a mad dinner party attended by Aunt Elizabeth's friend Major Applegate (Charlie Ruggles), a big-game hunter only too eager to tell about his African adventures. David keeps leaving the table to look for the bone. "Why are you stalking about like Hamlet's ghost?" Aunt Elizabeth asks him.

Then the final dilemma: Baby has broken loose! Major Applegate hears Baby's growlings and insists it's a loon. "There aren't any leopards in Connecticut," he claims, adding a querulous "Are there?" A drunk stableman (Barry Fitzgerald) spots Baby and swears off liquor. And Susan and David, in a scene of consummate hilarity, join in the leopard hunt, romping through the woods to a chorus of "I Can't Give You Anything But Love." One riotous moment has David stepping into a stream Susan insists is shallow and becoming completely submerged with the first step.

As if all this weren't enough, the confusion is compounded when another leopard, this one vicious, escapes from the local circus and is, of course, confused with the gentle Baby. Major Applegate faces the snarling leopard and can only think to murmur: "Here, kitty, kitty. Puss, puss." Susan and David come upon Baby on the roof of a neighbor's house but when they try to explain, they are taken to jail. In jail, they are soon joined by Aunt Elizabeth and Major Applegate, when the major tells the constable (wonderfully played by Walter Catlett) that he's been "hunting leopards." Susan manages to escape by confusing the constable with a wild story about her being a gun moll—"Swingin' Gate Susie"—and that they are all members of the "Leopard Gang." David, she tells him, is "Jerry the Nipper."* Susan finds the vicious leopard, thinking it is Baby and David leads it blithely into a cell.

Afterwards, David, no longer engaged and busily assembling his dinosaur, claims to be annoyed with Susan when she brings him the missing bone. But he is soon admitting that he had the best day of his life, and that he loves her. When they try to embrace, the dinosaur crumbles and is completely demolished!

*A curious aside: In *The Awful Truth*, released a year earlier, Irene Dunne, trying to confound her ex-husband (Cary Grant) by impersonating his Southern "sister," refers to him as "Jerry the Nipper." But in this case, the character's name *is* Jerry.

In its merry, unrelenting pace, its ability to draw laughs by topping one incongruous situation with another, *Bringing Up Baby* is one of the treasures of the genre. Hepburn may have given more polished performances but none more engaging, and Grant, though perhaps not exactly the model of a timid archaeologist, is also in fine fettle. The supporting players are splendid, especially Charlie Ruggles as the befuddled Major Applegate and May Robson as the crusty Aunt Elizabeth. Astonished when a leopard actually returns his own cry, the major exclaims "A mating call!" "Don't be rude," Aunt Elizabeth retorts. Even Baby joins in the spirit of this entertaining film.

Susan Vance may fill a special niche among madcap heiresses but she is surely followed closely by Ellie Andrews or Connie Allenbury or Tracy Lord. Rich and scatterbrained, incorrigible and inconsequential, they disappeared from the movie scene a long time ago, along with incognito millionaires and actresses. But for a while these delightfully daft people made filmgoing a pleasure.

Chapter Five

LAMB BITES WOLF

"All famous people aren't big people."—Gary Cooper in *Mr. Deeds Goes to Town*

In a crowded courtroom, a modest, deeply troubled young man named Longfellow Deeds, tuba-player, writer of greeting card verse, and accidental millionaire, is the central figure at a sanity hearing. A venal lawyer has testified about his irrational antics: his feeding doughnuts to horses, his playing the tuba at unlikely moments, and especially his desire to create "social unrest" by giving away all his money to the nation's poor. Two elderly ladies from his hometown of Mandrake Falls have asserted on the witness stand that Longfellow is known to be "pixilated," a word aptly coined by the ladies themselves. Totally beaten and depressed, Deeds has surrendered to apathy and is even willing to be committed to an institution for treatment.

Then his friends rally to his cause. The girl who loves him, though she had written newspaper articles mocking him, tells the judge that Longfellow is "honest, sincere, good." The farmers he has offered to help rise in unison to sing his praises. Roused by their loyalty and affection, Deeds finally speaks at length in his own defense. He has only wanted to give away his money to help people—the money is simply "messing up" his life. And he points out, quietly but firmly, that others in the courtroom are as eccentric as he is. The judge is an "*o*-filler," obsessed with darkening the circles in his *o*'s. The court psychiatrist is a compulsive "doodler." ("Doodling" hereupon became part of American slang.) And when the two hometown ladies are summoned back to the stand, they admit that *everybody* is "pixilated," even the judge. (Of course *they* are excluded.) To the cheering spectators, the judge announces that Longfellow Deeds is "not only sane, but the sanest man who ever walked into this courtroom!" Deeds is the hero of the day, free to enjoy his happy, uncomplicated life.

This scene, of course, is the climax of *Mr. Deeds Goes to Town,* Frank Capra's 1936 comedy produced by Columbia. In depicting the triumph of one small, insignificant, if slightly daft, man over the forces of corruption and selfishness, it represented one of the screen's fondest delusions of the thirties: that a "lamb" could bite a "wolf" and get away with it, if his heart is in the right place. The scene in *Mr. Deeds* epitomized the comforting idea that the greedy men in striped suits, the shysters, the tycoons, the bosses, were no match for small-town folk who thrived on—and were strengthened by—the homespun virtues. Frank Capra himself expressed the theme of the film in his autobiography: "A simple, honest man, driven into a corner by predatory sophisticates, can, if he will, reach deep down into his God-given resources and come up with necessary handfuls of courage, wit, and love to triumph over his environment." "Longfellow Deeds," Capra said, "was the living symbol of the deep rebellion in every human heart—a growing resentment against being compartmentalized."*

This was a theme that was to be sounded many times and in many different forms throughout the decade and beyond, but it was never so felicitously, if naively, expressed as in *Mr. Deeds Goes to Town.* If its solution to the weighty problems of the Depression was more than slightly simplistic, it nevertheless stated its point of view with considerable charm. Given a firm footing by Gary Cooper's convincing embodiment of Longfellow Deeds, and by Jean Arthur's winsome playing of the heroine—it was her first really important role—the Robert Riskin screenplay managed to make the hero's plight amusing and rather touching. And Frank Capra's expert direction tied it all up into an attractive package. He reports that many film professionals, including Josef von Sternberg and B. P. Schulberg, warned him against having his hero behave like an idiot by turning down millions of dollars, or having him accused of insanity. Capra persevered and made the film.

The early scenes introducing Longfellow Deeds are wry spoofs of the cynical "show-me" attitudes of "big-city" types vs. the easygoing ways of "small-town" folk. Crooked lawyer Cedar (Douglas Dumb-

*Frank Capra, *The Name Above the Title* (New York: Macmillan, 1971), p. 186.

rille), accompanied by press agent "Corny" Cobb (Lionel Stander), arrives in Mandrake Falls to tell Longfellow about his huge inheritance from his uncle Martin. An unenlightening conversation with a laconic railroad station agent leads them to the Deeds house, where the young man's reaction to his sudden wealth is to continue playing his tuba. "I don't need it," he announces to the astonishment of Cedar and Cobb. Later, at a jubilant town send-off in his honor, he is discovered playing the tuba in the town band!

His first days in New York are made up of a series of encounters with greedy types all seeking his money. He throws out a lawyer who claims to represent his late uncle's common-law wife. He refuses to give money to an opera group which has made him chairman of the board (If the opera is losing money, "there must be something wrong.") And he democratically refuses to allow his butler (Raymond Walburn) to help him on with his trousers. Corny Cobb is delighted with Deeds' behavior: "Lamb bites wolf! Beautiful!" he exclaims as Deeds locks his bodyguards in a room and proceeds to go out into the rain. There, he meets Babe Bennett (Jean Arthur), a reporter assigned to get a series of exclusive stories on Deeds, who wins his sympathy by pretending to be a starving lady in distress.

At a restaurant with Babe, Deeds tangles with a group of local literary figures who take pleasure in making fun of him. (They include Walter Catlett in a brief but memorable appearance as a tipsy poet named Morrow.) When Deeds realizes he is being kidded, he states: "All famous people aren't big people," and proceeds to knock them down. "What a magnificent deflation of smugness!" Morrow cries, as the fight rages around him. Afterwards, Babe's story reports on all of Deeds' unorthodox activities, dubbing him the "Cinderella Man." Unaware, Deeds continues to see Babe, taking her with him on his sojourns about the city. (At Grant's Tomb, where his impassioned patriotic remarks are reminiscent of Jefferson Smith's emotional outbursts in Washington three years later, one begins to suspect that von Sternberg and Schulberg may have been right after all.)

As Deeds becomes increasingly baffled and disturbed by the behavior of the people he meets ("They work so hard at living, they forget how to live"), Babe is falling in love with him—her own small-town roots are surfacing again—and she worries about crucifying him with stories about his escapades. In one charming scene in the park, he amuses her by improvising a chorus of "Swanee River" on a makeshift drum. In another, he insists on demonstrating the delights of raising an echo in a large house to his startled butler and domestic staff. For Babe, these eccentricities are trivial compared with his basic "goodness."

When Longfellow finally learns the truth about Babe, he is wretchedly unhappy and plans to leave for Mandrake Falls. But then, in a moment that smacks of easy contrivance, a desperately impoverished farmer (John Wray) suddenly appears on the scene to denounce Deeds. While his family is starving and he is forced to stand on breadlines, Deeds has the audacity to feed doughnuts to a horse. Calling Deeds a "money-grabbing hick," he threatens him with a gun but is restrained and bursts into tears. Deeply moved, Deeds decides to give all his money to form a farm cooperative for downtrodden farmers. In a scene that now seems painfully naive, Deeds is confronted by a mass of wretched faces that suddenly turn grateful as he buys lunches for them all. "We think you're swell," they tell him. But of course he is taken into custody and charged with being insane. Deeds is bewildered by the accusation: "Just because I want to give my money to people who need it!" But he is vindicated and triumphant at the sanity hearing. He is also reconciled with Babe.

Longfellow Deeds may have scored a gratifying triumph over the forces of cynicism and corruption but despite Corny Cobb's admiration, he was not the first movie "lamb" to bite a "wolf" and escape being devoured. In 1934, Harold Lloyd appeared in Fox's *The Cat's Paw*, one of his little-remembered sound comedies, which, like *Deeds*, was adapted from a story by Clarence Budington Kelland. He played Ezekiel Cobb, a timid soul who returns to his hometown from China and is set up as a "dummy" mayor by crooked politicians. Largely by bumbling accident, he manages to rid the town of graft and to sweep away the dishonest officials. Una Merkel played the girl who comes to love and understand him, and the cast included such expert "con men" as Alan Dinehart and Grant Mitchell. Sam Taylor, who had directed some of Lloyd's most famous silent films, was on hand again to keep things moving.

In a switch from his gangster roles, Edward G. Robinson also preceded Longfellow Deeds in John Ford's comedy for Columbia, *The Whole Town's Talking* (1935). As meek Arthur Ferguson Jones, Robinson succeeded in becoming a national hero by routing a vicious killer and his gang. Considering that he had established his screen reputation as nasty thug Caesar Enrico Bandello in *Little Caesar,* it came as no surprise that he also doubled as the vicious killer in the film.

One of the oddest and most interesting comedies of the period,

The Whole Town's Talking centers on Jones, a plodding, mild-mannered, and invariably punctual clerk (Robinson), who has been intimidated for years by his boss, Mr. Seaver, delightfully played by Etienne Girardot. Unfortunately, Jones happens to look exactly like "Killer" Mannion, Public Enemy No. 1, who has just escaped from prison. Mistaken for Mannion by a nervous little man (Donald Meek), Jones becomes the bewildered victim of a public uproar and is taken into custody by the police. The head of his company, Mr. Carpenter (Paul Harvey), refuses to identify him as Jones, while Mannion's terrified arch-enemy, "Slugs" (Edward Brophy), insists he *is* Mannion. Jones' only friend is Miss Clark (Jean Arthur), the flippant little clerk he secretly loves, but she makes matters worse by gaily playing the tough "gun moll" for the benefit of the police. Jones is freed and given a police letter identifying him as Jones, but only after Mannion robs a bank while the clerk is still in custody.

Now Jones is a celebrity in the office, lionized by everyone, including (to his amazement) Messrs. Carpenter and Seaver. Made bold by their attention—he even works up the courage to kiss Miss Clark—Jones agrees to lend his name to a newspaper series, "The Man Who Looks Like Mannion." But then his nightmare begins: arriving home that night, he finds the real Killer Mannion (Robinson again) waiting for him, snarling his contempt and forcing Jones to hand over his police letter so that he can move freely about the streets during the night and commit his crimes.

Terrified, Jones becomes Mannion's virtual prisoner, unable to tell anyone about the ruse. When Jones' bylined article appears calling Mannion "a moron with false courage," Mannion is incensed and insists on relating his true story to Jones for the paper. The articles arouse the curiosity of the Department of Justice—how could Jones know so many details of the escape?—and even Miss Clark grows suspicious at Jones' behavior when she visits him at his apartment. (She is puzzled because Jones has never been so amorous—actually, she is being kissed by Mannion.)

In the confusion that follows, Mannion deliberately gets himself arrested as Jones, but only for the purpose of seeking out and killing Slugs in prison. Knifing Slugs in the prison yard, he succeeds in breaking out and returns to hold Jones as his hostage. In a wild climax, Jones finally summons up all his wavering courage and traps the entire gang. Now a *true* hero, Jones receives the $25,000 reward for the killer's capture, as well as the hand of Miss Clark.

Baldly stated, the plot of *The Whole Town's Talking* is something less

MR. DEEDS GOES TO TOWN (1936). Longfellow Deeds (Gary Cooper) relaxes in the park with Babe Bennett (Jean Arthur).

THE WHOLE TOWN'S TALKING (1935). Meek Arthur Ferguson Jones (Edward G. Robinson) is chastised for lateness by his boss, Mr. Seaver (Etienne Girardot).

than hilarious and in fact, for all the incidents satirizing the standard gangster melodramas of the period, this is a singularly "dark" comedy. Though Robert Riskin, Frank Capra's favorite scenarist, wrote the screenplay with Jo Swerling (from a story by W. R. Burnett), the film is some distance from Capra's sentimental, "warmhearted," and lightly satirical films. A number of sequences are more cynical and nasty than any Capra would have attempted, and much of the humor is surprisingly harsh: the brutal way in which the police interrogate Jones until he is near collapse; their willingness to toss Jones into prison, though they know he's the wrong man; and especially (in a bizarre sequence) the coldblooded manner in which the timid Jones sets up the murder of Mannion by his own men. One scene—the stabbing of Slugs in the prison courtyard—is as chillingly realistic as any scene out of the Cagney-Robinson crime thrillers of the early thirties. The presence of a familiar group of comedy players —Donald Meek, Etienne Girardot, Edward Brophy, *et al.*—does little to allay the uneasy feeling generated by this curious film.

Robinson is expert in his double role, playing Mannion in his trademarked "Little Caesar" style and making Arthur Ferguson Jones a convincing "lamb." In one scene, he finds that he lacks the courage to hold a gun on the sleeping Mannion, and Mannion, waking up abruptly and seizing the gun, sneers: "You're afraid of me— asleep or awake." Jean Arthur is also good in one of her best roles before her triumph in *Mr. Deeds Goes to Town.*

Throughout the thirties, the theme of lamb biting wolf, of David defeating Goliath and Jack outwitting the giant, remained a popular and—to a depressed public—comforting theme. The villains included an assortment of liars, braggarts, and thieves, but they were invariably routed or reformed by the pure and noble (though meek) hero.

One of the more unlikely but likeable of these heroes of the period was a very proper, very efficient British butler named Marmaduke Ruggles. In Paramount's *Ruggles of Red Gap* (1935), the first sound version of Harry Leon Wilson's famous story, Ruggles (Charles Laughton) is won in a poker game by the vulgar, newly rich Americans, the Flouds (Mary Boland and Charlie Ruggles). Unhappily transplanted to the American West, Ruggles comes up against the spirit of free enterprise and equality—and likes it. He courts a widow (ZaSu Pitts), is mistaken by the community of Red Gap for an English duke, and, after a few setbacks, becomes the proprietor of a successful restaurant.

RUGGLES OF RED GAP (1935). A turn-of-the-century portrait featuring (left to right) Charles Laughton, ZaSu Pitts, Charlie Ruggles, Mary Boland, Roland Young, Leila Hyams, Lucien Littlefield, and Maude Eburne.

Directed at a leisurely pace by Leo McCarey (surely he found this assignment a welcome oasis of calm and quiet after coping with the Marx Brothers and W. C. Fields), *Ruggles of Red Gap* includes many highlights still fondly recalled by filmgoers. Certainly the most notable is Laughton's affecting recitation of the Gettysburg Address as the camera pans across the awestricken faces of barflies and cowhands. Ruggles' drinking bout with Egbert Floud; his sedate courtship of Mrs. Judson, climaxed by a sudden urge to kiss her ("I coarsely gave way to the brute in me"); and the opening of his restaurant, at which everyone (including Ruggles) joins in a chorus of "For He's a Jolly Good Fellow"—these are other memorable moments.

The movie is dominated by Laughton's impeccable and even rather restrained performance as the triumphant Ruggles, but Mary Boland and Charlie Ruggles make the Flouds hilarious embodiments of the vulgar *nouveaux riches*. (Effie Floud on acquiring a butler: "He'll give us joy de vive." Or commenting on her husband's unstylish clothing: "Even the moths wouldn't eat these.") Ruggles is a complete joy as a simple man startled to find himself in high society and forced to wear spats for the first time. As Egbert's salty, outspoken mother, Maude Eburne contributes a very funny vignette, as does Roland Young as the Earl of Burnstead, Ruggles' original master. (In 1950 the movie was retailored as *Fancy Pants* to suit the measurements of Bob Hope.)

Other timid types were played by actors who, unlike Laughton, were usually cast to the mold. In MGM's *Baby Face Harrington* (1935), Charles Butterworth of the woebegone mien was cast as Willie Harrington, a diffident soul with a disgruntled wife (Una Merkel), who becomes embroiled with police and gangsters when he mislays some money from his insurance policy. The Nunnally Johnson–Edwin H. Knopf screenplay was fairly ramshackle material but it had one grotesquely funny sequence. Held prisoner in a barn by some gangsters, Willie reads that his wife is going to divorce him and decides to hang himself. He is discovered by Rocky (Nat Pendleton), one of the hoods, who offers to help him with the knot. Talking, the two discover that they are members of the same "Junior Woodmen" lodge and enjoy a happy, back-slapping reunion. Demonstrating his superior knowledge of knots to Willie, Rocky manages to tie a rope around his own waist. The police burst into the barn, arresting Rocky (who is his own captive) and his fellow hoods. Willie the failure is now a national hero.

Another familiar movie Milquetoast was Joe E. Brown, who turned up regularly in a series of Warner Brothers (and later Columbia) farces (*Elmer the Great*, 1933; *Alibi Ike*, 1935; *Earthworm Tractors*, 1935, etc.) in which he played an amiable, wide-mouthed boob who usually emerged unscathed from one slapstick disaster after another. And in 1936, Harold Lloyd made another of his rare appearances in sound comedy as the hero of Paramount's *The Milky Way*. Under Leo McCarey's direction, he played a timid milkman who is deluded into believing he is a top-ranking prizefighter. With slippery Adolphe Menjou as his manager and sardonic Lionel Stander as his ice cream-loving trainer, Lloyd is clearly a lamb being led to the slaughter, but in the tradition of his silent comedies, he manages to win the championship through a combination of simple, dogged persistence and extraordinary luck. (After his first knockout, he announces: "You know, I'd have sworn I missed him.") The screenplay by Grover Jones, Frank Butler, and Richard Connell (from the play by Lynn Root and Harry Clork) included a few broadly comic scenes, particularly one set aboard a train in which Menjou, an insomniac, desperately tries to sleep over the deafening uproar all around him. (Newly titled *The Kid from Brooklyn*, the film was remade by Samuel Goldwyn in 1946 as a vehicle for Danny Kaye.)

Occasionally the innocent person who outfoxed the knowing rascals was a wide-eyed damsel. In MGM's *Times Square Lady* (1935), Virginia Bruce portrayed a winsome girl who comes to New York to claim the inheritance left by her father and finds herself in a den of thieves. In a situation strikingly similar to *Mr. Deeds Goes to Town*, a shady lawyer (Henry Kolker) tries to bilk her of her fortune with the aid of a band of ruffians. Assisted by a romantic nightclub host (Robert Taylor) and a group of warm-hearted Broadway types, including Nat Pendleton, Isabel Jewell, and Pinky Tomlin, she succeeds in routing the enemy. Virginia Bruce pouted prettily and George B. Seitz directed with a fairly light touch.

Certainly one of the slyest and most appealing small-town girls to set the "big-city" world on its ear was Hazel Flagg, heroine of the wickedly satirical comedy *Nothing Sacred* (Selznick-International, 1937). A blowtorch attack on human gullibility and slobbering sentimentality, the Ben Hecht scenario cast Carole Lombard as Hazel, a Vermont lass whose doctor (Thomas Mitchell) wrongly diagnoses a fatal case of radium poisoning. Her tale reaches the ear of Wally Cook (Fredric March), a reporter on the *Morning Star*, who sees Hazel as a once-in-a-lifetime chance to boost his paper's circulation and

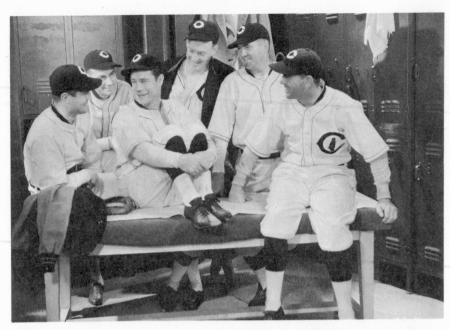

ALIBI IKE (1935). Joe E. Brown is surrounded by his admiring teammates.

THE MILKY WAY (1936). Insomniac Adolphe Menjou is prevented from sleeping by Harold Lloyd.

restore him to favor with the paper's apoplectic publisher, Stone (Walter Connolly). To get a long-coveted trip to New York City, Hazel persuades the doctor to keep her true condition a secret.

Wally's campaign to boost Hazel as a tragic heroine succeeds admirably, and she soon has the entire country weeping over her fate. A parade is held in her honor, and she is given the key to the city by the mayor. Her presence in a nightclub casts a lachrymose pall over everyone. Even a wrestling match is halted to observe a few minutes of silence for poor Hazel. ("For good clean fun, there's nothing like a wake," Wally remarks. "Oh, please, let's not talk shop," says Hazel.) Ultimately, however, her "sponsors" learn that she is as healthy as anyone, and they fear the bubble will burst. But Hazel, in love with Wally and unwilling to destroy his reputation, agrees to stage a "suicide." As a state-wide holiday is declared on the day of her "funeral," Hazel sails away to happiness with Wally.

In his acrid screenplay, Ben Hecht truly holds "nothing sacred" as he proceeds to thumb his nose at many a revered American tenet: the sweet gentility of small-town life (Wally arrives in Hazel's town and is treated in nasty or surly fashion by everyone, including a small boy who rushes from behind a fence to bite his leg); the ethics of the medical profession (Hazel's Dr. Downer is an incompetent rogue); the public responsibility of journalism (Wally and Stone gleefully manipulate the feelings of their readers). The relatively brief (75-minute) production, filmed in Technicolor, moves swiftly under William Wellman's direction, and the cast performs ably. Lombard and March have a climactic fight scene that is as funny as it is violent, ending with March knocking Lombard out with a well-aimed blow at the chin, and Walter Connolly, always expert at depicting towering rages, gives one of his best performances. (At one point he threatens to take Wally's heart out and "stuff it—like an olive!") Others in the cast included Sig Rumann, Maxie Rosenbloom, Margaret Hamilton, and Monty Woolley.*

In 1939, Frank Capra returned to the mood of *Mr. Deeds Goes to Town* with another film that celebrated the right of "ordinary" people to oppose and defeat graft and corruption in high places. He had become wildly enthusiastic about a story concerning a naive and

---

*Hazel Flagg subsequently had an odd career in show business. In 1953, she was played by Helen Gallagher in a stage musical version called *Hazel Flagg*. And in 1954, Paramount remade the story as *Living It Up*, a shaky vehicle for Jerry Lewis, here named Homer, with Janet Leigh playing the reporter, still called Wally Cook, and Dean Martin as the doctor.

idealistic young senator who is attacked and nearly consumed by the Washington wolves but emerges triumphant. It appealed not only to his strongly patriotic instincts but to his well-developed awareness of the ingredients for an effective screen story. With writer Sidney Buchman and his entire crew, he traveled to Washington to visit and photograph the city's monuments and points of interest, to soak up the atmosphere of this "godhead of freedom," and to learn about Senate procedures. To his mind, the film was going to be "a ringing statement of America's democratic ideals." Time and care were devoted to casting, although the leads were set from the beginning. Capra has written: "Jimmy Stewart and Jean Arthur were a made-to-order natural team—the simon-pure idealist, and the cynical, fed-up-with-politics Washington secretary with a dormant heart of gold."* Claude Rains was signed to play the sadly corrupt "White Knight," Senator Joseph Paine, and Edward Arnold was cast in a crucial role as powerful political boss Joseph Taylor.

The film was *Mr. Smith Goes to Washington,* one of Capra's greatest successes with the critics and the public: a movie as naive and idealistic as its hero, and with as much simple emotional appeal as well. With a view of the workings of government that seemed to have been taken from a primer for backward grade-school children, with scenes that alternated between homespun humor and tear-inducing bathos, *Mr. Smith Goes to Washington* was clearly another large helping of Capra-corn. Yet it also had his proven skill for seasoning his corn well and making it palatable even for more refined tastes, and it remains one of the most enjoyable movies of the period.

The film begins with the death of a senator, and the rallying of the state's all-power forces to choose a successor. The widely admired senior senator (Rains) and the governor (Guy Kibbee), a bumbling idiot named Hopper, are under the thumb of boss Taylor (Arnold), who insists on a nonentity for the vacant senatorial seat. On the advice of his many children, Governor Hopper ignores Taylor's wishes and appoints young Jefferson Smith (Stewart), earnest, sweet-natured, and not overly bright. Senator Paine, who was a close friend of Jeff's noble father, begins to see Jeff as a good choice: "A young patriot turned loose in our nation's capital—I can handle him."

Jeff's first words are at the banquet in his honor, and they suggest immediately the trouble he is certain to have: "I can't help feeling that there's been a big mistake made somehow." But he goes to

*Capra, *op. cit.,* p. 261.

Washington, armed with his ideals, where he promptly causes consternation by vanishing to gawk at the sights. As the camera tours
Washington with Jeff, the viewer can sense Capra's own pride and
awe. Oddly, the scene that is most excruciating—Jeff's visit to the
Lincoln Memorial, where he watches a small boy read the inscription
to his grandfather—is the one Capra claims to have witnessed himself. Watching the boy reading the Second Inaugural Address, Capra
has written, sounded "so eloquent, so moving, so powerful" that it
became his single justification for making the film.

A welcome note of wry cynicism is introduced with the character
of Saunders (Jean Arthur), Jeff's secretary, who begins by laughing
at him ("What is he—animal, vegetable, or mineral?") and ends by
loving him. She watches in amused disbelief as Jeff is made the
innocent dupe in an interview with reporters and becomes a laugh-
ing-stock in the newspapers. Though Jeff responds in the same direct
fashion as Longfellow Deeds—he seeks out the offending reporters
and knocks them down—he is still scorned by the press as an "honor-
ary stooge." When Senator Paine, to keep him out of mischief, suggests that he introduce a bill, Jeff decides to present a bill for a badly
needed boys' camp in his state. Though Saunders tries to discourage
him, Jeff is fired by the idea—"Liberty is too precious a thing to be
buried in books"—and with Saunders' help, he spends the night
working out his bill.

But now the seeds of Jeff's downfall have been planted. The site
he has chosen for his camp is also the site for a dam sponsored by
Taylor and his henchmen: a project buried in an impending bill that
is nothing more than a model for government corruption. Now Jeff
must be stopped for good. While Saunders watches with increasing
hopelessness, Taylor marshals his forces to "get" Jeff. Saunders
urges Jeff to leave ("This is no place for you—you're half-way decent"), and in a long scene expertly played by Jean Arthur, she tipsily
and desperately tells him about the dam.

But the steamroller cannot be stopped, and Taylor is adamant
about destroying Jeff, despite Senator Paine's conscience-stricken
waverings. (In one meeting of Taylor's cronies, everyone is smoking
a cigar, which indicates either Capra's simplistic notion of political
hangers-on, or his lightly satirical comment on their uniformity.) As
Jeff reacts with shock, confusion, and finally bitter disillusion, he is
badgered, lied about, and shunned by Paine and other senators in a
well-organized plan to "frame" him. (The principal charge is that he
owns the land on which he wanted to build his boys' camp.) These

NOTHING SACRED (1937). An antic moment shared by Sig Rumann, Charles Winninger, and poor "dying" Carole Lombard.

MR. SMITH GOES TO WASHINGTON (1939). New Senator Jefferson Smith (James Stewart) and his cynical secretary Saunders (Jean Arthur).

scenes have a brutal power showing Capra's ability to handle scenes devoid of sticky sentimentality.

Now Jeff is preparing to leave Washington, but Saunders finds him at the Lincoln Memorial and urges him not to quit. Firmly, she states the film's central theme: that men like Jeff strengthen the country by their "plain, decent, common, every-day rightness." She coaches him in a risky plan to take over the Senate floor with a filibuster and prove his innocence of the charges against him. In the film's most famous scene, Jeff, exhausted, desperate, and on the verge of crumbling, keeps himself talking for many hours, cheered by Saunders in the gallery and by the tacit support of the Vice President. (In this role Harry Carey gives a performance that consists mainly of sly smiles and gavel-banging, but he is somehow memorable.) As Saunders tearfully shrieks: "Stop, Jeff, stop!" he collapses in defeat. But his defeat becomes victory when Senator Paine, overcome with guilt and self-hatred, tries to shoot himself. Now Jeff is a hero again, enthusiastically surrounded by the faithful.

This scene may be a calculated crowd-pleaser but it is also exciting to watch, a stunning combination of "rightness" in setting and dialogue, in Stewart's intense performance—he was nominated for an Academy Award but lost to Robert Donat in *Goodbye, Mr. Chips*—and in Capra's sure-footed direction. Capra himself has described it well: "Gutty ideals, the words of Lincoln, the wit of Jean Arthur, plus a one-man filibuster, and the conscience of the White Knight—all drive relentlessly toward an emotion-packed climax."*

With its irresistible blending of comedy, "lamb-bites-wolf" sentiment, and flag-waving patriotism, *Mr. Smith Goes to Washington* was immensely popular, although Capra has reported on its tumultuous premiere in Washington on October 16, 1939. At a special, highly publicized showing of the film sponsored by the Washington Press Club, Capra drew the wrath of many prominent figures who objected to the film for showing that graft could conceivably turn up in the U.S. Senate, or that members of the press could on occasion, on *any* occasion, indulge too freely in drink. (A central character in the film, played engagingly by Thomas Mitchell, is a reporter frequently in a state of mild intoxication.) Capra was in even greater trouble when a wire from Joseph P. Kennedy, then American ambassador in London, urged Columbia to drop the film because it ridiculed democracy and could be construed as anti-American propaganda. Capra persev-

*Capra, *op. cit.*, p. 257.

MR. SMITH GOES TO WASHINGTON (1939). A desperate, disillusioned Jeff Smith, his filibuster crumbling, is challenged by Senator Paine (Claude Rains).

ered, producing ardent testimonials for the film in many newspapers across the country, and Mr. Smith was soon filibustering everywhere. The *New York Times* praised Sidney Buchman's "cogent and workmanlike script," which received an Academy Award, and called the movie "one of the best shows of the year." It was also nominated for an award as Best Picture of the year, but lost inevitably to *Gone With the Wind.*

Although the thirties seemed a propitious time for the lambs to triumph over the wolves, the early forties brought their share of victories to what Hollywood liked to think of condescendingly as "ordinary" people. In MGM's *The Golden Fleecing* (1940), Lew Ayres appeared as mild-mannered insurance agent Henry Twinkle, who inadvertently sells a policy to a mobster with a price on his head and must somehow keep him alive or lose his job. His plight becomes increasingly desperate as he finds himself wanted by both the mob and the police, while his exasperated fiancée (Rita Johnson) simmers in the background. Leslie Fenton directed the screenplay by (surprisingly) S. J. Perelman and his wife Laura, collaborating with Marion Parsonnet. (A similar plot line was used for Danny Kaye's 1963 comedy, *The Man from the Diners' Club.*)

In a 1941 comedy, RKO's *The Devil and Miss Jones,* the wolf and the lamb turned out to be one and the same. Charles Coburn starred as John P. Merrick, the crochety owner of a department store who is anxious to learn why he is so thoroughly disliked by his employees. He joins the staff as a down-on-his-luck codger named "Tom" and ingratiates himself with Mary Jones (Jean Arthur) and her boyfriend Joe (Robert Cummings), who is organizing the employees against Merrick. Since Norman Krasna's original screenplay is a perfect labor-management fairy tale, Merrick becomes a warm-hearted, understanding person who not only saves the store from serious labor troubles but wins the heart of a sweet spinster (Spring Byington).

The film wisely takes full advantage of Charles Coburn's acting skills by making Merrick the central character and relegating the nominal lead, Jean Arthur, to the background. He is delightful as an old man who suddenly finds that he enjoys mixing with the common folk, gets lost at a Coney Island picnic and is jailed as a derelict, and ends up being serenaded with "He's a Jolly Good Fellow" by the very people who were willing to burn him in effigy. Sam Wood directed this pleasant fable at a leisurely pace suitable to the folksy material.

The Magnificent Dope, a 1942 comedy from Twentieth Century–Fox,

THE GOLDEN FLEECING (1940). Cab driver Nat Pendleton accosts insurance agent Lew Ayres, while Virginia Grey looks on.

THE DEVIL AND MISS JONES (1941). Robert Cummings addresses a labor meeting. In the front row: Jean Arthur, Charles Coburn, and Spring Byington.

starred Henry Fonda in another slow-thinking, country-bumpkin portrayal as Tad Page, a yokel who arrives in New York and becomes the butt of a publicity scheme manipulated by con man Dwight Dawson (Don Ameche). As the head of a floundering school created to turn pathetic failures into self-confident successes, Dawson runs a contest to locate the country's most complete failure. The winner is Tad, who not only proceeds to demonstrate that he is actually a very happy and fulfilled man but also manages to convert Dawson's pupils to his easygoing philosophy. ("I haven't any respect for a man who was born lazy; it took me a long time to get where I am.") He also wins Dawson's girlfriend Claire (Lynn Bari). The clever George Seaton screenplay (from a story by Joseph Schrank), briskly directed by Walter Lang, was lightly spiced with satire of the "personality" schools still flourishing thirty years later.

Cary Grant played one of the more fascinating underdogs of the period in Columbia's film, *The Talk of the Town* (1942). As Leopold Dilg, a self-professed anarchist, falsely accused of murder in a New England town, he was clearly cast in the same eccentric mold as Longfellow Deeds. In his *New York Times* review, Bosley Crowther noted the similarities between the two characters: "Both boys have in common the unmerited scorn of society; both have to put up a battle against intolerance and hypocrisy, and both have the obvious advantage of Jean Arthur in their corners."

In the Irwin Shaw–Sidney Buchman screenplay for *The Talk of the Town*, Dilg has been charged with setting a factory fire in which the foreman was killed. Escaping from prison, he is forced to hide out in the home of schoolteacher Nora Shelley (Arthur), which she has rented for the summer to one Professor Michael Lightcap (Ronald Colman). When the professor arrives unexpectedly, Nora tries to keep Dilg's presence a secret, resulting in some close calls and several funny scenes. (Hearing Dilg snore in the middle of the night and thinking it's Nora, the professor remarks: "She must have adenoids.") For his part, Dilg is entirely convinced of the rightness of his behavior—he calls it "a form of self-expression." Dilg's lawyer Sam Yates (Edgar Buchanan) shares the anarchist's good opinion of himself and asks the professor to head a committee to defend Dilg. Professor Lightcap, absorbed in his own research, insists loftily on remaining outside the controversy.

As the days pass, Nora is forced to identify Dilg to the professor as "Joseph," the gardener—and Joseph begins to have lively discussions about the law with his employer. The law, Dilg tells Lightcap,

THE MAGNIFICENT DOPE (1942). Henry Fonda waxes tender with Lynn Bari.

THE TALK OF THE TOWN (1942). An anxious moment for anarchist Leopold Dilg (Cary Grant), housekeeper Nora Shelley (Jean Arthur), and Professor Michael Lightcap (Ronald Colman).

is "a gun pointed at someone's head," and the professor has "no blood in his thinking." Lightcap defends the law, especially when he learns that he will be appointed to the U.S. Supreme Court in the fall. For her part, Nora works desperately to keep the professor from learning Dilg's identity. (In one amusing moment, she sees his photograph on the front page of the newspaper and proceeds to drop the professor's morning eggs directly on top of it.)

Dilg and Lightcap continue to argue about the law, Dilg maintaining that laws should be made out of common sense—out of what people actually *do*—and Lightcap asserting that his way would lead to disorder and violence. But gradually he begins to change his attitude and feel favorably disposed toward Dilg. He becomes angry at the town's corrupt officials, who are controlled by factory-owner Andrew Holmes (Charles Dingle). Also, his own serene and scholarly life is badly shaken when—wearing Dilg's slippers—he is pursued by eager bloodhounds and chased up a tree. Finally, Nora deliberately leads him to a rally where Holmes is arousing the townspeople against Dilg.

When Dilg reveals his true identity to Lightcap the professor feels he should call the police, but Dilg knocks him down and flees. In the resulting fracas, the police question Nora and Lightcap, who surprisingly lies about Dilg. Convinced by this time that Dilg is innocent, Lightcap begins an investigation of his own, tracking down everyone in the case, including the foreman's girlfriend (Glenda Farrell). He learns that the foreman was not killed in the factory fire, that he is not only alive but set the fire himself at Holmes' orders. But now the tables are turned: Dilg wants to surrender to the police, while Lightcap believes that in cases like Dilg's, there might be "extenuating circumstances."

When Dilg is taken by the police, a mob stirred up by Holmes descends on the court, ready to lynch him. At the last minute, Lightcap shows up with the missing foreman and speaks forcefully on Dilg's behalf: "His only crime was that he had courage and spoke his mind." "The law must be engraved into our hearts," he tells them. In a final scene in Washington, Lightcap proudly dons his Supreme Court Justice's robes. Nora, loving and admiring both men, is required to make a choice between them. In the last moment, she chooses Dilg.

If the script's pronouncements on the nature and meaning of the law tend to be somewhat fuzzy and debatable, *The Talk of the Town* is still an exceptionally literate and full-bodied comedy-drama that sags only towards the end of its excessive two-hour length. The three principals play together beautifully under George Stevens' direction, with Ronald Colman outshining the others in a wise, appealing, and (for once) non-pompous performance. His quiet modesty at his sudden fame and prestige, his dawning realization that he needs Nora for more than housekeeping, and his eloquent plea for Dilg's rights as a citizen are all limned gracefully.

In movie lore, the triumph of lambs over wolves is never outmoded, and films throughout the forties celebrated their small victories. Gary Cooper, the original Longfellow Deeds, continued to appear as a series of Deeds-like characters who could be counted on to respond vigorously in a dilemma. In Samuel Goldwyn's *Ball of Fire* (1941), he played sober-sided Professor Bertram Potts—the *New York Times* called him "really just Mr. Deeds with a lot of book learning" —who is engaged in writing an encyclopedia with a number of equally stuffy colleagues. For his article on American slang, he asks for the help of burlesque stripper Sugarpuss O'Shea (Barbara Stanwyck), who moves in with the professors when the police start looking for her. Soon Professor Potts is contending with Sugarpuss' gangster boyfriend Joe Lilac (Dana Andrews), Lilac's thugs, and the police. The professors, like the seven dwarfs defending Snow White, take Sugarpuss to their academic hearts. She, in turn, falls for Professor Potts, who thwarts Lilac and his gang. Directed by Howard Hawks, *Ball of Fire* was a genial comedy, with a first-rate Charles Brackett–Billy Wilder scenario and good performances by Cooper and Stanwyck. (She received an Academy Award nomination for Best Actress.) In 1948, *Ball of Fire* was turned into *A Song Is Born*, a mediocre musical with Danny Kaye in the Cooper role.

In 1945, shyer and more diffident than ever, Cooper starred in RKO's *Along Came Jones*, as an inept cowboy who drifts into a small Western town with his caustic sidekick (William Demarest) and is mistaken for notorious holdup man Monte Jarrad (Dan Duryea). Since gentle Melody Jones is even unable to handle a gun, his position is precarious, but with the help of Jarrad's sympathetic girl Cherry (Loretta Young), who can shoot on target, he not only manages to stay alive but becomes a temporary hero. ("For one hour," he says, "I felt what it feels like to be high-regarded.") Stuart Heisler directed the mildly satirical but entertaining screenplay by Nunnally Johnson.

Other "little people" turned up sporadically in the forties to earn their brief moments of glory. In Columbia's *Mr. Winkle Goes to War*

THE TALK OF THE TOWN (1942). A noisy fracas leaves Cary Grant and Ronald Colman unconscious. Jean Arthur attends Grant; Rex Ingram attends Colman. Police Chief Don Beddoe investigates.

BALL OF FIRE (1941). The professor (Gary Cooper) and the stripper (Barbara Stanwyck).

(1944), Edward G. Robinson, playing his first really meek role since *The Whole Town's Talking,* was henpecked Wilbert Winkle who is drafted into the Army at age forty-four and becomes a stalwart hero in battle with the Japanese. Alfred E. Green directed the predictable story, which featured Ruth Warrick as Winkle's wife and Ted Donaldson as his idolizing juvenile friend. In 1947, Victor Moore, possibly the master at portraying timid, downtrodden types, starred in *It Happened on Fifth Avenue,* directed by Roy Del Ruth, as a tramp who spends his winters in an empty New York mansion and makes the mistake of inviting in other unfortunate drifters. When the owner (Charlie Ruggles) returns, he angrily attempts to toss out the nonpaying guests but of course the old tramp's gentle philosophy prevails and soon the hard-hearted Mr. Moneybags is himself joining the vagabonds, while the tramp enjoys the good life. A sentimental fable out of the Frank Capra school of comedy, *It Happened on Fifth Avenue* relied heavily on the charm of Victor Moore, who had long refined his lumpish presence and pathetic whine into an art. As usual, Charlie Ruggles provided agreeable support.

Over the years, the pattern was the same: the put-upon, laughed-at, "pixilated" people of the world could somehow overthrow the cynical, corrupt, pompous, life-denying wretches who sought to dominate or destroy them. Like love at first sight, like families sworn to eternal devotion, this concept of lambs biting the wolves was a movie tenet much closer to fantasy than reality. Yet, at least for those magical few hours in the darkness, filmgoers could pretend it was real, and that Longfellow Deeds, clutching his beloved tuba, could march forth to vanquish the enemy, side by side with Arthur Ferguson Jones, Jefferson Smith, and all the other movie Milquetoasts.

ALONG CAME JONES (1945). Cowboy Melody Jones (Gary Cooper) awaits the shoot-out.

CHAPTER SIX

BATS IN THEIR BELFRY

"All you need to start an asylum is an empty room and the right kind of people."—Eugene Pallette in *My Man Godfrey*

"Well, Sir, here we are again."—Lionel Barrymore to God in *You Can't Take It With You*

In the darkest days of the thirties, it was a common and comforting belief that families, confronted with adversity and a dwindling bank account, would be drawn closer together. With little money but stiffened backbones and a lot of mutual affection, they could somehow survive. In many despair-wracked homes, the belief may have been mythical or ironic, but the movies, that repository of myth, certainly encouraged it.

But what of the wealthy families during this period? Many films of the Depression years had twitted the feather-brained heiresses who married or ran off with the wrong men and received their comeuppance at the hands of virile, "down-to-earth" types. When these same heiresses were surrounded by families, their parents, siblings, and relatives turned out to be every bit as feather-brained as they: shrill, self-indulgent, and mindless people deserving only of our mocking laughter.

And so many thirties comedies fostered and thrived on a double illusion: that poor families survived on charm, luck, and childlike innocence, while rich families, lacking charm and needing no luck, frittered their time away with games, flirtations, and idle chatter. Poor families may have craved money but found life more cheerful without it. Rich families spent their money on frivolous pursuits but found that it couldn't buy love or happiness. A false dichotomy at best, it faded with the forties and the melding of rich and poor in a common cause. But while it lasted, it formed the foundation for some enjoyable movies.

An early family comedy of the poor-but-lovable species was Paramount's *Three-Cornered Moon* (1933), adapted from Gertrude Tonkonogy's stage play by S. K. Lauren and Ray Harris. It dealt with the Rimplegar family of Brooklyn, presided over by an addled mother (Mary Boland) who invests all their money in a worthless mine. The Rimplegar children are forced to find employment: Elizabeth (Claudette Colbert) goes to work in a shoe factory; Douglas (William Bakewell) strives to be an actor; and Kenneth (Wallace Ford) works at becoming a lawyer. Much of the comedy's footage was devoted to Elizabeth's on-again, off-again romance with a gloomy, would-be novelist (Hardie Albright), and with her falling in love with the family's only boarder, a young doctor (Richard Arlen). Under Elliott Nugent's direction, the antics of the Rimplegars managed to be reasonably amusing. One of the best episodes, the family's search in the newspaper for the results of Kenneth's bar examination, offered a nicely controlled picture of nervous apprehension building up to delirious joy. In the role played on the stage by Ruth Gordon, Claudette Colbert displayed some evidence of the comic finesse she was to reveal the following year in *It Happened One Night*.

Relatives of the zany Rimplegars turned up in surprising numbers the year following *Three-Cornered Moon*. RKO's *We're Rich Again* (1934) repeated the plot device of a family down on its luck and obliged to marry off the daughter to a wealthy young man, while dodging the bill-collectors at the same time. Here the family matriarch, a polo-playing grandmother, was portrayed by the dour-faced Edna May Oliver, and others in the cast were Billie Burke, Buster Crabbe, and Marian Nixon. Another RKO farce, *Down to Their Last Yacht* (1934), told its story in the title: a socialite family reduced to poverty, which somehow retains its yacht and turns it into a chartered boat for the *nouveaux riches*. Mary Boland was on hand again, playing the highly improbable queen of a tropical island on which the yacht is beached, and she was accompanied by Polly Moran, Ned Sparks, Sidney Fox, and Sterling Holloway. This nonsense was directed by Paul Sloane.*

Columbia's *Blind Date* (1934) was a curious entry in the cycle. A

---

*This film was originally written by Lou Brock as a vehicle for Ginger Rogers and Fred Astaire, then beginning their rise to stardom at RKO. Brock was most directly responsible for bringing the team together. The story was rejected by RKO production head Pandro S. Berman in favor of *The Gay Divorcee*, which Berman had seen on the London stage (as *The Gay Divorce*).

conventional Cinderella story (girl must choose between rich and poor suitors), it offered an original twist by having the girl (Ann Sothern) settle on the wealthy playboy (Neil Hamilton) instead of the hard-working owner of a car repair shop (Paul Kelly). It also gave much footage to the girl's dizzy family, consisting of shiftless, jobless Pa (Spencer Charters), practical-minded Ma (Jane Darwell), daughters Ann Sothern and Joan Gale, and a bratty son (Mickey Rooney, who had made his feature debut two years earlier). A neatly turned little film directed by Roy William Neill, *Blind Date* mirrored its time in the dialogue ("Hey, you bozo," "Gee, you're swell," etc.) and in a dance marathon sequence that suggested some of the barbarity of this thirties phenomenon.

One happily eccentric family, the Pembertons, turned up in *Danger —Love at Work* (Fox, 1937), a farce that had its roots in *Three-Cornered Moon* but bore a surprising resemblance to *You Can't Take It With You*, released the following year. The Pembertons consisted of dim-witted Mama (Mary Boland); Papa (Etienne Girardot), whose hobby is stargazing; Herbert (John Carradine), who paints surrealist scenes on window panes; Uncle Alan (Walter Catlett), a very odd stamp collector; obnoxious son Junior (Bennie Bartlett); and daughter Toni (Ann Sothern), who changes boyfriends daily. The plot turned on the appearance among this untidy group of a lawyer (Jack Haley) who wants to obtain their signatures on a document involving the sale of their deceased grandfather's farm. The strenuous proceedings were directed by Otto Preminger (his second American film) from a screenplay by James Edward Grant and Ben Markson.

Certainly the best-remembered comedy of the thirties in which a crackpot family from the lower rungs of society somehow manages to surmount bad times, was Frank Capra's *You Can't Take It With You* (Columbia, 1938), adapted by Robert Riskin from the George S. Kaufman–Moss Hart stage success. (Columbia had bought the play for an at-the-time record price of $200,000.) The play was a merry farce about the Sycamores, a family of carefree, self-indulgent lunatics presided over by a genial old codger with a cordial dislike and disregard for money and employment. The screen version retained much of the offbeat, knockabout comedy of the play, but added a hearty measure of Capra's familiar "little-people" sentiment, his standard device of pitting "ordinary" men and women devoted to the simple pleasures against the nasty, life-denying figures of power. (Capra himself has written that the film was "a golden opportunity to dramatize Love Thy Neighbor in living drama.") The result was

THREE-CORNERED MOON (1933). Displaying various reactions to a newspaper item are Tom Brown, Wallace Ford, Richard Arlen, and Claudette Colbert.

RICH MAN, POOR GIRL (1938). Robert Young meets the family: Sarah Padden, Guy Kibbee, Lana Turner, and Don Castle. Ruth Hussey stands behind him.

a well-liked film, but one that was considerable distance from the original Kaufman-Hart comedy.

Even at the film's beginning, the changes made by Capra and Riskin are evident. The stage's Mr. Kirby, the cantankerous rich man who finds himself reluctantly involved with the Sycamores, is now Capra's favorite big businessman, Edward Arnold, engaged in forming a munitions empire—not the most subtle concept—and, for obscure reasons, buying up all the houses in one area of the city. Only one homeowner refuses to move: Grandpa Vanderhof (Lionel Barrymore), head of the Sycamore family. And when Grandpa comes to Kirby's office, he doesn't even bother to engage in battle with the enemy. He merely walks off with a timid accountant, Mr. Poppins (Donald Meek), whom he invites to stay at his house, where "everybody does exactly what he wants to do."

The screen Sycamores are similar to their stage counterparts: Grandpa, attending commencement exercises for their humorous content and enjoying his snakes and his dart board; Paul Sycamore (Samuel S. Hinds), making fireworks in the cellar; his scatterbrained wife Penny (Spring Byington), writing an inane play—a typewriter had been delivered years before by mistake—and using a kitten as a paperweight; their daughter Essie (Ann Miller), continually toe-dancing, even as she makes candy; Essie's husband Ed (Dub Taylor), who innocently prints inflammatory messages and puts them in Essie's candy; and assorted boarders, servants, and hangers-on. The most "normal" member of the group is daughter Alice (Jean Arthur), in love with rich young Tony Kirby (James Stewart). But Grandpa is the central figure of the family and Riskin's screenplay, no doubt with Capra's approval, gives him a neat little speech on "isms" early in the film, reserving the highest praise, of course, for "Americanism." Grandpa also vows to hold onto his home and never sell out to Kirby.

Occasionally the spoonfuls of romance and sentiment that Riskin pours into his essentially farcical mixture succeed in working to the film's advantage. An early love scene between Alice and Tony is charmingly played by Arthur and Stewart, and Alice's long scene with Grandpa, in which she tells him about Tony and he reminisces about Grandma, is touching and not too cloying. The comedy picks up again when Grandpa is visited by an irate government representative who accuses him of failing to pay his income tax over the years. Grandpa offers to pay about $75: "It's not worth a penny more!" The government man, terrified by the blaring music and the explosion of Paul's firecrackers, flees from this clearly insane household. (On the scene is the matchless Mischa Auer as Essie's demented and eternally hungry Russian ballet teacher—"The Monte Carlo ballet. It *stinks!*")

Once again the script brings in a sequence not in the play: In the park, Tony and Alice ask a group of urchins to teach them the new dance craze, the Big Apple, and Alice somehow gets a sticker on the back of her dress reading "Big Apple, 10¢" on one side and "Nuts" on the other. They go to a nightclub where Tony's father and mother are astonished to see them. Flustered when he notices the sticker on Alice's dress, Tony tries to back her out of the room. They flee into the night after he causes pandemonium by suggesting he spotted a rat. This sequence is undiluted Capra in its combination of condescending to the poor, while confounding the rich.

To its credit the film does repeat (though not verbatim) the key scene of the play, in which the Kirbys arrive at the Sycamore house a day early and are shocked to find the usual relaxed chaos instead of the orderly, well-behaved household Alice had hoped to prepare for them. Penny has turned from playwriting to art and is busy sketching a boarder, Mr. De Pinna (Halliwell Hobbes), who is wearing a toga. Essie, in ballet costume, is performing a wild Hungarian dance. And Alice greets them by sliding down the bannister! Except for the word association game invented by Penny in the stage version, which leads Mrs. Kirby to the brink of an embarrassing confession, the scene retains the original series of comic disasters, which is climaxed when the police arrive to arrest Ed for the messages he placed in Essie's candy—and Paul's fireworks are ignited in a noisy pyrotechnic display.

Everyone is taken off to jail, including the dismayed Kirbys. ("Never a dull moment," says Grandpa. "I always say, never a dull moment.") Here, the comic momentum is again slowed down by a confrontation scene between Kirby and Grandpa, wealth soured by greed facing the "laissez-faire" idealist. Or, as Capra himself put it, "a bankful of money against a houseful of love." "You can't take it with you," Grandpa tells Kirby, "so what good is it?" When Kirby learns that Grandpa is the single holdout tying up his business deal, he explodes in anger, but Grandpa, in a rare show of rage, explodes right back. "You stupid idiot!" he shouts. "Dull-witted fool! You and your jungle and your long claws!" In a quite nasty, vituperative outburst, he calls Kirby a failure as a man, as a human being.

The stage is now set for a typical Capra scene. In the courtroom, Grandpa's neighborhood friends swarm around him, contributing money to pay his $100 fine. A surly Mr. Kirby glowers at everyone,

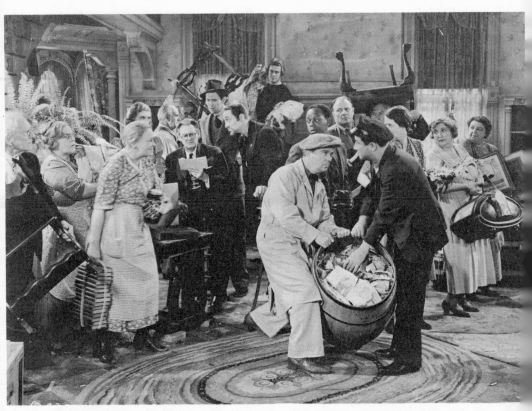

YOU CAN'T TAKE IT WITH YOU (1938). Chaos reigns at the Sycamore house. Visible in the fracas are Lionel Barrymore (reading a letter), James Stewart, Mischa Auer, and Eddie Anderson. In the football helmet: Dub Taylor.

until he finds a harmonica in his pocket. (Earlier in the fatal evening, he had talked about his childhood fondness for the harmonica.) Not content to leave all of the film's speeches to Grandpa, Alice speaks up, rejecting Tony forever and blaming herself tearfully for everything.

The following day, life is at a low ebb for the usually buoyant Sycamores. Alice has left home and Grandpa will sell the house—for a smaller sum than Kirby originally offered. The only glimmer of hope is in Kirby's sad, distracted countenance as he prepares to close his big munitions deal. Once again, as in *Mr. Deeds Goes to Town*, Capra turns to the *deus ex machina* of one hysterical, downtrodden soul speaking some harsh truths to change a crucial point of view. In *Mr. Deeds*, it was the starving farmer castigating Longfellow Deeds; here it is Kirby's desperately ill, destroyed former business partner Ramsey (H. B. Warner) who bitterly confronts him and gasps: "You can't shut out every decent impulse—and survive!" Ramsey collapses and dies.

At the very door of his board room, Kirby suddenly changes his mind and hurries off to the Sycamore house where Alice and Tony have also converged. As Tony tries to change her mind about marrying him, Mr. Kirby appears, contrite and unhappy. "I'm a failure as a father," he tells Tony. Grandpa, of course, is pleased at Kirby's display of abject guilt: "Mr. Kirby, you're beginning to act quite human." In one of the film's most excruciating moments, Grandpa and Kirby join in a duet on the harmonica. The film closes with everyone seated about the dinner table and Grandpa delivering his famous curtain line to God: "Well, Sir, here we are again."

Although most of the Rifkin-Capra intrusions are irritating and serve only to soften further an already soft-headed point of view, the film is enjoyable and likeable, mostly due to the capable cast. No player is cast against type—that would distract from Capra's intention—but they are all good, especially Spring Byington as the lovably daffy mother and Donald Meek as meek Mr. Poppins. "The die is cast!" he cries as he marches off to a new life with Grandpa. (Another sad loss in the stage-to-screen transaction: the character of the soddenly drunk actress, Gay Pennington.)

You Can't Take It With You was phenomenally popular with the critics and the public. The *New York Times* called it "a grand film" that "jumps smack into the list of the year's best," and *Time* magazine hailed it as "the Number 1 cinema comedy of 1938." It received the Academy Award as the Best Picture of the Year, and Frank Capra won

as Best Director. Spring Byington was nominated for Best Supporting Actress but lost to Fay Bainter in *Jezebel*. Otis Ferguson's review
in the *New Republic* (September 21, 1938) was one of the few to pan
the film. Calling it "a dud," he wrote: *"Mr. Deeds* seems to have given
writer and director an idea of themselves as social philosophers
which does them no good. There is an embarrassing amount of space
here given over to the spiritual poverty of riches, the wealth of the
simple heart, the glory and pity of it all."

You Can't Take It With You produced no direct imitations, but several succeeding comedies continued the plot line in which the daughter of a crackpot family settles for conventionality. MGM's *Rich Man,
Poor Girl* (1938), directed by actor Reinhold Schunzel, concerned a
wealthy young man (Robert Young) who falls in love with his secretary (Ruth Hussey) and comes to live with her slightly mad family as
a democratic gesture, only to find that it is not so easy to adjust to
the lower classes. After a few setbacks, rich man marries poor girl.
In addition to Ma and Pa (Sarah Padden and Guy Kibbee), the family
included Lana Turner, in one of her first featured roles, as daughter
Helen, and Lew Ayres as nephew Henry, Hollywood's 1938 concep-
tion of a wild-haired, wild-eyed radical. The screenplay by Joseph A.
Fields and Jerome Chodorov was hardly original, but the *New York
Times* called the movie "a genial and heart-warming little comedy
which crackles and pops so pleasantly that you can hardly hear its
joints creak."

Primrose Path (RKO, 1940) was quite another case. A laundered
version of the 1939 stage play by Robert L. Buckner and Walter Hart,
it still raised eyebrows and sparked protests as it told of the Adamses
of Primrose Path, whose lives have apparently been dedicated from
generation to generation to pursuing the world's oldest profession.
Grannie (Queenie Vassar), though grotesquely rouged and be-
wigged, has retired; good-natured mother Mamie (Marjorie Rambeau), no longer in active employment, is saddled with a gin-swilling
husband (Miles Mander); and precocious daughter Honeybell (Joan
Carroll) is still too young. Only tomboy Ellie May (Ginger Rogers)
seems a possible candidate to carry on the family tradition. But she
proceeds to fall in love and marry a young man (Joel McCrea) who
runs a hamburger stand. Despite some nasty business in which he
learns about the disreputable family background, Ellie May seems
destined to break the mold and settle into respectable housekeeping.
Gregory La Cava directed and co-authored the screenplay with Allan
Scott, who had written La Cava's previous film, *Fifth Avenue Girl*
(1939).

PRIMROSE PATH (1940). Marjorie Rambeau expresses admiration for daughter Ginger Rogers' fur piece.

MURDER, HE SAYS (1945). The daft Jean Heather is playful with Fred MacMurray. Helen Walker looks on, amused.

Comedies such as *You Can't Take It With You* and *Primrose Path* drew their humor from observing families of amiable oddballs. By 1945 a comedy appeared that carried oddity to its ultimate point by dealing farcically with a family of stamped and certified lunatics. This was Paramount's *Murder, He Says*, directed by George Marshall, a comedy that has acquired a reputation (not really deserved) as one of the funniest movies of the forties.

A combination of murder mystery, raucous farce, and broad satire, *Murder, He Says* presented a hillbilly family both bizarre and homicidal, composed of Mamie Johnson (Marjorie Main), a leather-lunged, whip-cracking harridan; her deceptively meek husband (Porter Hall); her feeble-minded twin sons (Peter Whitney), one of whom constantly needs a resounding whack from his mother to cure a crick in his back; a dim-witted niece Elany (Jean Heather), who sings mad little tunes in the style of Hamlet's Ophelia; and Grandma (Mabel Paige), an elderly lady who is dispatched by the family's unique brand of poison. (It causes the victim to glow.) Into their ramshackle house comes earnest insurance agent Pete Marshall (Fred MacMurray), looking for the family's missing gun-moll daughter Bonnie, and a girl (Helen Walker) who pretends to be Bonnie but is actually looking for a treasure buried in the house.

Lou Breslow's screenplay dispenses with logic entirely to offer a series of wild and sometimes hilarious sequences as the family of rampant maniacs proceeds to carry out murderous activities with little regard for anyone's life, least of all each other's. The funniest scene occurs when Mamie serves a dinner heavily spiced with poison (the dishes shine in the dark like deadly Christmas trees), and everyone tries desperately to avoid eating the fatal food by spinning the round table. MacMurray's frantic attempt to unravel the mystery by way of a series of puzzling clues leads him ultimately to the culprit, Porter Hall, and to a funny climax in which the entire family is caught up in a hay-baling machine and trussed up in neat bundles for the police.

Of the many comedies of the Depression years to deal with the antics of upper-class families, none was as successful, or as amusing, as Universal's *My Man Godfrey* (1936). A brightly paced farce sprinkled with social comment, it was written by Morrie Ryskind and Eric Hatch (from Hatch's novel) with a grace and an elegance rare even for this period in film comedy, and directed in high style by Gregory La Cava. Very much a film of its time, it juxtaposed the giddy and

MY MAN GODFREY (1936). Butler Godfrey (William Powell) dispenses advice to his daffy employer, Irene Bullock (Carole Lombard).

fatuous world of fashionable society and the drab, despairing world of the hobo colony, with memorable results.

My Man Godfrey revolves about the rich Bullocks of Park Avenue, composed of (in Godfrey's words) a group of "empty-headed nitwits." Mother Angelica (Alice Brady) is given to adopting "protégés," chattering inanely, and misunderstanding everything said to her. Her daughters are Cornelia (Gail Patrick), frosty and bad-tempered, and Irene (Carole Lombard), a captivating, willful girl determined to have her own way with everyone and usually succeeding. Mr. Bullock himself (Eugene Pallette) is a grumpy Wall Street tycoon whose business is teetering on the edge of ruin. Rounding out this family of scatterbrains is Mrs. Bullock's current protégé, Carlo (Mischa Auer), a wild-eyed scrounger whose talents are confined to filling his stomach and imitating a gorilla.

Into this booby hatch steps Godfrey (William Powell), a wry and somehow fastidious tramp living in a hobo colony at the city dump with his down-and-out cohorts. Godfrey is claimed by Irene as a "forgotten man"—the winning "item" in a society scavenger hunt and brought home to become the latest in a long succession of butlers to the Bullock family. "You're my protégé," she tells him. "My responsibility." With his air of cool authority and his vaguely mysterious background, Godfrey appears a likely person to survive the Bullock insanity. Irene is enchanted by him and even the family cook (Jean Dixon) finds him a romantic figure. His only enemy is Cornelia, irked at losing him to Irene and furious at his rude treatment of her at the city dump.

For a while, Godfrey makes an ideal butler, apparently able to cope with the family's many quirks and antics: as a lark, Irene leads a horse up the front steps of the house and leaves it in the library; Angelica speaks in a language that might be called Pure Nonsense; to amuse everyone, Carlo leaps onto the sofa and makes grotesque King Kong noises, when he isn't crying "Money, money! The Frankenstein monster that destroys souls!" Godfrey is even able to ward off a persistent and infatuated Irene.

But then his secret is revealed: Godfrey is no tramp at all, but a member of the affluent Parke family, a Harvard man who decided to withdraw from society after an abortive romance. To cover his story, an overhelpful friend, Tommy Gray (Alan Mowbray), invents a wife and five children for Godfrey, which leads Irene to impulsively announce her engagement to her longtime suitor, Charlie Van Rumpel (Grady Sutton). No one is more bewildered by all this than Charlie.

Godfrey's contempt for his fellow rich, expressed at several points throughout the film, has a biting edge unmatched by any film until Gregory La Cava's 1939 comedy, *Fifth Avenue Girl.* "The Parkes," he tells Tommy, "were never educated to face life. We've been puppets for ten generations." Later, speaking with Tommy in "Shacktown" at the city dump, he reacts to Tommy's remark that he has "a peculiar sense of humor": "Over here we have some very fashionable apartment houses—over there is a very swanky nightclub, while down here men starve for want of a job. How does that strike your sense of humor?" He enrages Cornelia by calling her "a spoiled child who has grown up in ease and luxury, who always had her own way and whose misdirected energies are so childish that they hardly deserve the comment even of a butler—on his off Thursday."

Cornelia plots to get revenge on Godfrey by placing her diamond necklace under his mattress and calling the police, so that he can be accused of theft. Her plot is foiled, however, when the police can find no necklace in Godfrey's room, despite her prodding. (Godfrey has uncovered and hidden it, recognizing Cornelia's scheme to trap him.)

Later, when the Bullocks return from a long trip to Europe, Irene still insists petulantly that she loves Godfrey—"every place I went, everybody was Godfrey"—and she is determined to wear down his resistance. But Godfrey, still stung by his "bitter experience" with romance, decides that the time has come for him to move on, to place a comfortable distance between himself and temptation. Irene tries extreme measures to hold him—she falls into a dead "faint" which Godfrey recognizes as obviously fake. He places her in a shower stall and turns on the water, but Irene, undaunted, interprets this as a token of his deepest affection. "Godfrey loves me!" she sings exultantly. "Godfrey loves me! He put me in the shower!" Godfrey flees, pausing only to tell Mr. Bullock that he has succeeded in rescuing him from ruin by astutely playing the stock market (using Cornelia's necklace to raise money) and winning back all of Bullock's lost stock.

In an ending of pure Depression fantasy, Godfrey leaves the Bullocks and builds a lavish nightclub on the site of the city dump, where he employs his old hobo friends. ("One thing I discovered," he tells Tommy, "was that the only difference between a derelict and a man was a job.") He also plans to set up housing for his friends for the cold winter months. (He is told that the cost of partitioning the building for at least fifty people will be $5,000, "but that includes steam heat.") Irene appears on the scene, refusing to surrender an inch in her desire to marry Godfrey. "You love me and you know it," she insists. "There's no sense in struggling with a thing when it's got you." From this point, the usually articulate Godfrey has little to say. They are married by the mayor of the city, summoned by Tommy Gray, and Irene's final line is "Stand still, Godfrey, it'll all be over in a minute."

As Godfrey, William Powell uses his wry approach to great advantage, bringing a special assurance to every line. As the highly correct butler, he acts with his tongue placed ever so slightly in his cheek, and his sequences with Carole Lombard are models of charm and sophistication. In one of her best roles, Lombard succeeds admirably in keeping Irene from becoming an irritating nincompoop by virtue of her unparalleled sense of comic timing and the glints of knowing wit that shine through her "rich dumb girl" routine. The other cast members are equally fine: Alice Brady at her most lovably bewildered; Gail Patrick, so enjoyably mean-spirited that her reformation at the end is a letdown; Eugene Pallette at his burly best, and Mischa Auer, striking a memorable comic figure as the "protégé" given to singing *"Otchi tchornia!"* at every opportunity. (Angelica likes the song because "the words are all the same. It makes it so easy to remember. That's probably why the 'Star-Spangled Banner' is so confusing. Nobody seems to know the words.")

My Man Godfrey was followed by a rash of comedies involving rich families in which at least one prominent member could be safely called mad or at least very strange. Samuel Goldwyn's *Woman Chases Man* (1937), directed by John Blystone, was a lightweight farce concerning architect Virginia Travis (Miriam Hopkins), who becomes involved with wealthy, eccentric B. J. Nolan (Charles Winninger) and his conservative-minded son Kenneth (Joel McCrea). She comes to the elder Nolan with architectural plans for his housing development, immodestly called Nolan Heights, but finds that he needs $100,000 to hold off his creditors, money his prudent son refuses to give him. Learning that young Kenneth has a secret weakness for liquor, she succeeds in getting the money by plying him with drinks. By the time the film has run its course, she has also won Kenneth himself. The film's comic highpoint found the leading players, including Broderick Crawford as a butler and Ella Logan as a maid, literally up a tree.*

*The writing credits for this movie are somewhat complicated. The writers are officially cited as Joseph Anthony, Manuel Seff, and David Hertz (from a story by Lynn Root and Frank Fenton), but it was reported that half a dozen other writers contributed to the script. In fact, the *New York Times* review lists the writers as Dorothy Parker, her husband Alan Campbell, and Joe Bigelow.

Upper left:
WOMAN CHASES MAN (1937). The players up a tree: Miriam Hopkins, Joel McCrea, Broderick Crawford, and Ella Logan.

Upper right:
CALL IT A DAY (1937). Frieda Inescort gives a motherly ear to daughter Olivia de Havilland.

Below:
MERRILY WE LIVE (1938). Constance Bennett tries to prevent a fight between Tom Brown and Bonita Granville.

A much more genteel variation of the theme was provided by Warner Brothers in their adaptation of Dodie Smith's 1936 stage comedy, *Call it a Day* (1937). With an impeccable cast that included Ian Hunter, Frieda Inescort, Roland Young, and Peggy Wood, this film recounted the tribulations faced by the well-to-do and rather balmy Hilton family during one long and eventful spring day. The father of the family (Hunter) is embarrassed but flattered to find himself pursued by an amorous actress (Marcia Ralston). Mrs. Hilton (Inescort) has to cope with the persistent attentions of Roland Young. (Alice Brady is his fluttery sister.) The elder Hilton daughter (Olivia de Havilland) is in romantic thrall to a married artist (Walter Woolf King), and son Martin (Peter Willes) is ready to leave home until he meets the pretty girl next door (Anita Louise). Through all these activities, younger Hilton daughter Bonita Granville makes her loquacious comments. Casey Robinson, one of Warners' busiest and most competent writers, was responsible for the screenplay, which was directed in leisurely style by Archie Mayo.

Easily the most blatant imitation of *My Man Godfrey* was Hal Roach's 1938 comedy, *Merrily We Live*. (The first line of Frank S. Nugent's *New York Times* review was: "Hal Roach has taken the livery of *My Man Godfrey* from its closet, has whisked it a bit and lengthened the sleeves to fit Brian Aherne.") In this variation of the original, Aherne, doubling for William Powell, played a writer disguised as a tramp who is adopted by wealthy madcaps named Kilbourne, including a light-headed mother (Billie Burke sitting in for Alice Brady), crotchety father (Clarence Kolb substituting for Eugene Pallette), and irrepressible daughter (Constance Bennett standing in for Carole Lombard). Other family members included brother Tom Brown and bratty young sister Bonita Granville. The Jack Jevne–Eddie Moran screenplay, directed by Norman Z. McLeod, also had the wise and understanding tramp, here named Wade Rawlins, ultimately help the family avoid financial disaster, but it leaned much more heavily on slapstick than its predecessor. The only area in which the film improved on its model was in the casting of the domestic help: Alan Mowbray and Patsy Kelly lent support as the family's butler and cook. Nevertheless, the *Times* review called it "too close for comfort and too loose to be anything but average light entertainment."

One family comedy of special distinction was produced by Selznick International in 1938. *The Young in Heart* discarded the eccentric humor and farcical antics of *You Can't Take It With You* and *My Man Godfrey* to relate a gentle, quietly winning fable about a family of frauds and fortune-hunters who plot to inherit the estate of a rich, lonely old woman and who are themselves converted to respectability. With a graceful and only occasionally treacly screenplay by Paul Osborn (adapted by Charles Bennett from I. A. R. Wylie's novel), and a splendid cast headed by Janet Gaynor, Douglas Fairbanks, Jr., Roland Young, and venerable Minnie Dupree, *The Young in Heart* was captivating entertainment.

The larcenous family includes "Colonel" Anthony Carleton (Young), a retired actor who pretends to have lived and fought in India—he is called "Sahib" by his family; his good-hearted wife Marmy (Billie Burke); son Rick (Fairbanks), charming but indolent; and daughter George-Anne (Gaynor), inclined to wonder about the shady life they lead and attracted to her firm-minded Scots suitor, Duncan MacCrae (Richard Carlson in his film debut). We first meet the Carletons as they are forced by the police to leave the Riviera, where Rick had gotten himself engaged to a senator's daughter. (The girl's parents are played by Lucile Watson and Irvin S. Cobb, too briefly on the scene.) On the train, the Carletons meet wispy old Ellen Fortune (Minnie Dupree), for whose benefit they tell a series of fanciful lies. (Sahib affects a terrible wheeze from being "poisoned" by gas in the war; Marmy pretends to be recovering from a serious "operation.") Delighted with her new friends—she finds them all so "young in heart"—Miss Fortune invites them to stay at her large house.

The Carletons decide on a plan to inherit Miss Fortune's money by pretending to turn respectable—even getting *jobs*—and ingratiating themselves with the old woman so strongly that she will change her will in their favor. After long hesitation—one charming scene has Sahib and Rick watching a building excavation and musing on the possible motives of the workers—the two Carleton men find jobs, Sahib as salesman of a modernistic car called the "Flying Wombat" and Rick with an engineering firm which seems to have a single other employee: Leslie Saunders (Paulette Goddard in her first film after *Modern Times*). On the first day of his job, Sahib parts from Rick in a comically emotional scene: "I'm not good at farewells. Don't be too lonely."

As time passes, Sahib comes to love his job, and is even promoted to sales manager. Rick, falling in love with Leslie, begins to work up an interest in engineering. And George-Anne, still troubled by her family's crooked ways and touched by Miss Fortune's faith in them, begins to look more favorably on Duncan's attentions. (He knows about her background but still wants to marry her.) Miss Fortune,

THE YOUNG IN HEART (1938). Colonel Anthony ("Sahib") Carleton (Roland Young) and his daughter George-Anne (Janet Gaynor).

frightened that the Carletons will leave her, gets George-Anne to promise that they'll stay indefinitely. Even when an old friend (Henry Stephenson) exposes the truth about the Carletons, she retains her faith in them. "How sad," she remarks. "How cruel life must have been to them." She tells him: "I've learned to give complete and unquestioning faith to the people I love."

When Miss Fortune decides to leave her money to the Carletons, they are oddly glum about their triumph. Deeply fond of the old woman, enjoying their new lives as working citizens, they surprise even themselves by rejecting the inheritance. "We don't want it," Sahib announces proudly. "We don't need it." The film ends with a rather absurd round of happy occurrences: After a sudden illness which threatens her life, Miss Fortune recovers and is last seen driving a Flying Wombat at high speed. (In the original version, she died serenely but adverse reaction at a few previews changed the studio's mind.) George-Anne marries Duncan, Rick marries Leslie, and Sahib and Marmy enjoy comfortable respectability.

Though the story is awash in sentimentality, *The Young in Heart* largely avoids mawkishness by means of many warm and humorous touches in the screenplay and the glowing performances of the principals. (Only Janet Gaynor seems somewhat out of place as an artful schemer.) Sahib entering the Flying Wombat showroom to apply for a job, with the knell of doom ringing in his ears; the Carletons playing cards with Miss Fortune, their eyes exchanging glances mixing conspiracy with a touch of shame; George-Anne gleefully realizing that Miss Fortune's love has actually redeemed them ("She saved us! She saved us all!")—these are among the highlights in a pleasing film.

The entire cast is excellent, but the film is dominated by Minnie Dupree as Miss Ellen Fortune. In one of her few film appearances— she had acted on the stage for over fifty years—the elderly actress is luminous and lovely, joyfully welcoming the Carletons into her empty life, or telling them wistfully about her one lost chance at love, or simply reacting to each turn of events with graciousness and equanimity. (She played in only one more film, *Anne of Windy Poplars* in 1940, and died in 1947.) Roland Young deserves special mention for his splendid performance as Sahib, adding an understated note of poignancy to his droll characterization of a self-deluded rogue who is loved and tolerated by his family. (Only watch him murmur "Honored, ma'am, honored," as Miss Fortune gives him an affectionate kiss on the cheek.)

Rich or poor, demented or just slightly eccentric, the families who bellowed and pranced their way through the comedies of the thirties and early forties reflected the prevalent idea that living together could be rewarding or at least entertaining and filled with surprises, despite depressing headlines. In the lexicon of these staunch but pixilated people, "alienation" was an unknown word, and "permissiveness," "sibling rivalry," and "generation gap" were nonexistent concepts. Existing happily in their celluloid world, the Sycamores, the Bullocks, and the Carletons were all myths and shadows, barely acquainted with actuality. But joining them in their ramshackle or well-appointed living rooms was a pleasant moviegoing experience.

CHAPTER SEVEN

THE THIN MAN, TOPPER, AND FRIENDS

"Oh, Nicky, I love you. Because you know such lovely people."—
Myrna Loy to William Powell in *The Thin Man*

"I can learn to live, after all."—Roland Young in *Topper*

In 1934, the casting of William Powell and Myrna Loy as Mr. and Mrs.
Nick Charles in the film version of Dashiell Hammett's mystery novel,
The Thin Man, created no special excitement at MGM. In fact, Louis
B. Mayer was strongly opposed to their playing the roles, until he was
finally persuaded otherwise by director W. S. Van Dyke. Yet *The Thin
Man* launched one of the most popular and best-remembered of
screen teams.

Since the early twenties, William Powell had been a serviceable
leading man, appearing in adventure stories (*Beau Geste*, 1926; *The
Four Feathers*, 1929), frivolous comedies (*She's a Sheik*, 1927; *Feel My
Pulse*, 1928), and romantic dramas—in Warners' *One Way Passage*
(1932), he was a convicted murderer who had a poignant love affair
with fatally ill Kay Francis. He played detective Philo Vance in four
films and starred in a group of largely forgettable films for Warners
between 1931 and 1933. In 1934, he joined MGM, where he first
starred with Clark Gable and Myrna Loy in *Manhattan Melodrama*.
Beginning as an oriental temptress in silent films, Myrna Loy had
been a featured player for a number of years, in films as varied as
Show of Shows (Warners, 1929), *Arrowsmith* (Goldwyn, 1931), and *Love
Me Tonight* (Paramount, 1932). After running the gamut of vamps
and hussies, she began appearing in films for MGM, including *Emma*
(1932), *The Mask of Fu Manchu* (1932), and *Men in White* (1934).
Then she was assigned to co-star with William Powell in a modestly

THE THIN MAN (1934). Nick Charles (William Powell) confronts the "Thin Man's" daughter (Maureen O'Sullivan) with an incriminating weapon.

AFTER THE THIN MAN (1936). Sam Levene questions Myrna Loy while William Powell and James Stewart look on.

budgeted comedy-mystery involving a jaunty detective and his sophisticated wife. It was their second film together, but by no means
their last.

The Thin Man was not the first film to blend murder with mirth, but
in this case a dollop of engagingly frank husband-and-wife banter was
added to the mixture, and the result surprised and pleased filmgoers.
Living in a well-appointed apartment (courtesy of the studio's art
director, Cedric Gibbons) with their frisky dog, Asta, Nick and Nora
were obviously delighted to be married to each other and not at all
taken aback by having to cope with a little homicide in their merry-go-
round existence. When the two are exchanging quips in the Albert
Hackett–Frances Goodrich screenplay, the film sparkles brightly, and
the ostensible plot—a tangle of murder and deception—fades into
the background.

Shorn of the Nick-and-Nora byplay, *The Thin Man* is actually a
routine film, with a confusing and not very interesting story. It revolves largely about a wealthy businessman named Wynant (Edward
Elis) who vanishes mysteriously—the newspapers refer to him as the
"Thin Man"—and whose mistress Julia (Natalie Moorhead) is found
murdered. The web of suspicion catches a number of suspects: Wynant's daughter Dorothy (Maureen O'Sullivan), his son Gilbert (William Henry), his ex-wife (Minna Gombell), her new husband Chris
(Cesar Romero), Joe Morelli, a friend of Julia's (Edward Brophy), and
Wynant's lawyer McCauley (Porter Hall). They are an unsavory lot,
yet Nora can still murmur happily, "Oh, Nick, I love you. Because you
know such lovely people." Nick finally gathers all the suspects together and reveals that the murderer of Julia (and Wynant, too) is
McCauley.

All of this is handled in perfunctory fashion by director W. S. Van
Dyke. Yet the few exchanges between Powell and Loy lingered in the
minds of audiences and critics and turned an ordinary film into a
huge success. Writing in the *New York Times,* Mordaunt Hall called
The Thin Man "an excellent combination of comedy and excitement."
He noted that William Powell was "thoroughly in his element" as
Nick Charles and that Myrna Loy helped "considerably in making this
film an enjoyable entertainment," adding: "She speaks her lines
effectively, frowns charmingly, and is constantly wondering what her
husband's next move will be." (At one point Nick sends her off to visit
Grant's Tomb to keep her out of danger. "How did you like Grant's
Tomb?" he asks her afterwards. "It's lovely," she replies. "I'm having
a copy made for you.")

The popularity of *The Thin Man*—it was nominated for an Academy Award as Best Picture—led inevitably to a sequel from MGM, and late in 1936 the studio released *After the Thin Man*, capitalizing on the original title and causing generations of moviegoers to believe that Nick Charles himself was the title character. Surprisingly, with the same writers and director, *After the Thin Man* was superior to the original. The Nick-and-Nora quips were still present and if the plot was still unconvincing and unnecessarily complicated, it held the interest and even succeeded in working up some suspense. Also, the supporting cast was exceptionally strong: James Stewart, Jessie Ralph, Sam Levene, Joseph Calleia, Elissa Landi, and Penny Singleton (here known as Dorothy McNulty).

This time Nick (with Nora as a charming tagalong) sets out to solve a murder within the bosom of Nora's rich and snobbish family. The victim is the shiftless husband of Nora's cousin Salma (Elissa Landi). Urged by Nora to handle the case, Nick rounds up a group of suspects: a shifty restaurant owner named Dancer (Joseph Calleia); a nightclub singer (Penny Singleton, whose frenetic renditions of two musical numbers, "Smoke Dreams" and "Blow That Horn," are among the film's highlights); Salma's rejected suitor David (James Stewart); and Salma herself.

Nick's sleuthing uncovers the murderer—a highly improbable and hysterical James Stewart—but again the film's principal pleasure is not in watching the mystery unravel but in observing the relationship of Nick and Nora, which is one of love tempered with the slightest edge of malice and mockery. Nora nods to a passing elegant couple. "Who are they?" Nick asks. Nora answers: "You wouldn't know them. They're respectable." Or Nick pauses at the door of the palatial home of Nora's family, muttering incoherently. "What are you saying?" Nora asks. "I'm trying to get all the bad words out of my system," he replies. In one of the film's best scenes, Nick and Nora are about to retire but Nora refuses to let him sleep, suggesting, obliquely and often, that he prepare scrambled eggs for her. Despite the circumstances, even when events turn perilous, they enjoy being together. In the middle of the action, Nick asks her: "Having a good time, Mrs. Charles?" To which she responds: "Couldn't be better."

There were four other *Thin Man* films, but none of them matched the charm and freshness of the first two. *Another Thin Man* (1939), again written by Albert Hackett and Frances Goodrich and directed by W. S. Van Dyke, introduced baby Nicky Jr. (William A. Paulsen) —this time Nora tells *him:* "Your father has such lovely friends"—but

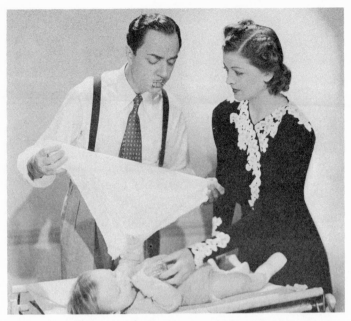

ANOTHER THIN MAN (1939). Nick and Nora fuss over baby Nicky Jr. (William A. Paulsen).

SHADOW OF THE THIN MAN (1941). A tense moment with the Charleses.

it concentrated on Nick's involvement in a fairly dull and nearly incomprehensible murder case. C. Aubrey Smith and Sheldon Leonard were the victims and the suspects included Ruth Hussey, Patric Knowles, and Virginia Grey. One of the film's few good sequences had Nick bantering with Marjorie Main as the ribald owner of a shady boarding house. ("This ain't the YMCA.") *Shadow of the Thin Man* (1941) had new writers—Irving Brecher and Harry Kurnitz—and a new Nick Jr. (Dickie Hall), but the ingredients were largely the same as before. (The *New York Times* reviewer commented that "William Powell still drinks cocktails with an obvious zest that must be worth millions in advertising to the liquor industry.") Here, Nick investigated several racetrack killings and assembled the standard quota of suspects, including Barry Nelson, Donna Reed, Stella Adler and Alan Baxter.

The last two films in the series were rather weak entries. *The Thin Man Goes Home* (1944), with new writers—Robert Riskin and Dwight Taylor—and a new director—Richard Thorpe—found Nick Charles visiting his parents (played by Harry Davenport and Lucile Watson) and uncovering a murdered artist along the way. His trail of detection led to a mysterious couple (Helen Vinson and Leon Ames) and to a local eccentric named Crazy Mary (Anne Revere) who also became a corpse. The Charles' repartee now seemed a little forced, a little tired. The final *Thin Man* film—*Song of the Thin Man* (1947)—employed a battalion of writers—the credits read: "screenplay by Steve Fisher and Nat Perrin, with additional dialogue by James O'Hanlon and Harry Crane, from a story by Stanley Roberts, based on the characters created by Dashiell Hammett"—and the director this time was Edward Buzzell. The result of all this concerted effort was a mildly entertaining film which had Nick and Nora seeking out a murderer in a jazz setting. Nick Charles, Jr. reappeared for this last enterprise, played by MGM's hard-working juvenile actor, Dean Stockwell.

The success of the *Thin Man* films could hardly be ignored by the other studios and throughout the thirties and into the forties a number of mystery comedies appeared in which the husband and wife, dropping quips while picking up clues, managed to solve a crime by the final reel.* The variations in these films were few—often the wife lacked the impudent wit and elegance of Nora Charles—but they were frequently enjoyable.

---

*Nick and Nora outlasted them all, but not on the screen. They starred in a radio series and later, on television, they were played by Peter Lawford and Phyllis Kirk.

THE THIN MAN GOES HOME (1944). Nick and Nora Charles have dinner with Nick's parents (Lucile Watson and Harry Davenport).

SONG OF THE THIN MAN (1947). William Powell and Myrna Loy, accompanied by Keenan Wynn, question hotel clerk Clinton Sundberg.

STAR OF MIDNIGHT (1935). Lawyer Clay Dalzell (William Powell) and his girlfriend (Ginger Rogers) investigate a murder.

THE EX-MRS. BRADFORD (1936). Paula (Jean Arthur), ex-wife of Dr. Bradford (William Powell) comes to see him, to the obvious displeasure of his butler (Eric Blore).

Three of the most obvious imitations were *Remember Last Night?* (Universal, 1935), *Star of Midnight* (RKO, 1935), and *The Ex-Mrs. Bradford* (RKO, 1935). *Remember Last Night?* assembled a group of society madcaps at a Long Island mansion where corpses began to pile up with alarming regularity. The police investigation, led by Edward Arnold, was assisted by Robert Young and Constance Cummings, very Nick-and-Nora-like as a flippant young married couple. This mystery-comedy, which featured the marvelous Ed Brophy as a befuddled detective, was directed by James Whale, whose previous excursions into mystery—*Frankenstein* (1931), *The Invisible Man* (1933), and *Bride of Frankenstein* (1935)—were much more macabre. In reviewing the film in the *New York Times*, André Sennwald pointed out that it betrayed "the influence of *The Thin Man* in its merry attitude toward homicide."

An even more blatant imitation was RKO's *Star of Midnight.* (André Sennwald's review in the *Times* began by noting that the film was "in the tradition of urbane screen homicide originated by *The Thin Man*.") This movie, directed at a fast clip by Stephen Roberts, even had William Powell, as debonair and quizzical and fond of cocktails as ever, playing lawyer Clay Dalzell, who finds himself suspected of murder when a gossip columnist is shot dead in his apartment. He solves the case to the accompaniment of some brisk repartee supplied by Anthony Veiller, Howard J. Green, and Edward Kaufman (from a novel by Arthur Somers Roche). Ginger Rogers co-starred as a girl determined to lure Dalzell into marriage despite his protests, and the cast included Paul Kelly, Ralph Morgan, and Gene Lockhart. Powell, however, dominated the film, playing his role with what the *Times* called "that blend of bored nonchalance and native shrewdness which we found so captivating last year."

Later that year, RKO released *The Ex-Mrs. Bradford,* which offered the same director (Stephen Roberts), one of the same writers (Anthony Veiller), and the same star (William Powell) in still another *Thin Man* offspring. This time Frank S. Nugent's review in the *Times* began by stating: "Behind the entirely metaphoric petticoats of *The Ex-Mrs. Bradford* hides the still nimble figure of *The Thin Man.*" Here, William Powell played Dr. Bradford, a prominent surgeon whose ex-wife Paula (Jean Arthur) is a prolific writer of mystery stories, so obsessed with all aspects of murder and mayhem that she is in a continual state of nervous shock and suspects foul play at every turn. (Reviewing their broken marriage, Bradford tells her: "I spent more time at the morgue than at my office. You and your mysteries were making a wreck out of me.") Together—he reluctantly, and she eagerly—they investigate a series of murders beginning with a jockey's mysterious death during a race. As with *The Thin Man,* the case itself, a tangled affair involving the use of a black widow spider as a murder weapon, is much less diverting than the repartee supplied by Anthony Veiller in his screenplay (from a story by James Edward Grant).

As the couple who battle incessantly but cannot remain apart for long, William Powell and Jean Arthur deliver their flippant lines in high style, especially in a dinner scene at which Paula serves gelatin in a variety of forms. (She is testing a clue, rather than indulging in culinary experiments.) "The ex-Bradfords at home," she sighs, but he is determined to stay aloof. "We're on the verge of getting sentimental," he warns her—in vain. By the time the film ends and they have revealed the murderer in the standard "detective-assembles-suspects" scene, Bradford and Paula have agreed to remarry. As Dr. Bradford's butler, who can barely conceal his annoyance with Paula, Eric Blore contributes a delightful performance. Asked by his employer if he had to use force to get Paula back into her hotel, he answers: "Only in a mild way, and always with tact." James Gleason is also happily on hand as a baffled police detective.

The influence of *The Thin Man* continued into the late thirties and early forties, but no studio was ever able to match the original model in a sustained series of films. MGM itself tried to establish a new husband-and-wife team in detective and rare-book dealer Joel Sloane and his helpful wife Garda, but curiously they cast different actors in the leading roles in each of the three films, neatly canceling the possibility of audience identification. In the first, *Fast Company* (1938), Melvyn Douglas played Joel Sloane to Florence Rice's Garda in an amiable mystery-comedy involving the murder of a bibliophile (George Zucco). The suspects in the Marco Page–Harold Tarshis screenplay (from Mr. Page's novel) included Louis Calhern, Claire Dodd, Shepperd Strudwick, and Douglas Dumbrille. Much was made of Joel Sloane's being shot by the villain in his posterior and required to wear a pneumatic tube for comfort. Edward Buzzell directed the film, which the *Times* called "a brash and amusing detective story of the light-hearted or *Thin Man* school."

In the second film, *Fast and Loose* (1939), Robert Montgomery and Rosalind Russell took over as Joel and Garda Sloane, this time under Edwin L. Marin's direction. The screenplay by Harry Kurnitz concerned some murders committed in connection with a rare Shakespeare manuscript and the Sloanes' hectic and farcical attempts to

FAST COMPANY (1938). Melvyn Douglas and Florence Rice as Joel and Garda Sloane.

FAST AND LOOSE (1939). Rosalind Russell and Robert Montgomery take over as the crime-solving Sloanes.

FAST AND FURIOUS (1939). Beauty-contest winner Gladys Blake, accompanied by promoter Lee Bowman, is greeted by Ann Sothern and Franchot Tone as Garda and Joel Sloane.

THERE'S ALWAYS A WOMAN (1938). A critical moment with Assistant District Attorney Melvyn Douglas, his detective wife Joan Blondell, and her only client, Mary Astor. Observing at left: District Attorney Thurston Hall.

discover the culprit. Assorted suspects and victims included Reginald Owen, Etienne Girardot, Sidney Blackmer, and Ralph Morgan. Once again, some of the humor stemmed from Joel Sloane's being shot in his trousers and forced to wear a pneumatic tube. Despite the repetition of this not especially hilarious joke, the film was praised by the *Times* for its "sense of humor, facile style, and genial performances."

The third Sloane film, *Fast and Furious* (1939) cast Franchot Tone and Ann Sothern as the Sloanes, but by this time some of the freshness had worn off and the shadow of *The Thin Man* was growing fainter. Neither the script by Harry Kurnitz nor the direction by Busby Berkeley—in his first film since leaving Warner Brothers— were of much help. Here the Sloanes become mixed up in a disreputable beauty contest, which leads to murder and mayhem (but no pneumatic tube), all broadly served up. The supporting players included Ruth Hussey, Lee Bowman, Allyn Joslyn, and Mary Beth Hughes.

Columbia also produced two mystery-comedies, *There's Always a Woman* (1938) and *There's That Woman Again* (1939), involving husband-and-wife detective team Bill and Sally Reardon, but neither of them came within hailing distance of *The Thin Man*. In both films, directed by Alexander Hall, Melvyn Douglas played a detective saddled with a well-meaning but bumbling wife (Joan Blondell in the first, Virginia Bruce in the second) who confounds the police and her husband by stumbling onto the solution to a crime.

In *There's Always a Woman,* Bill Reardon leaves his failing detective agency ("no work, no glory, and nothing a year") to return to the district attorney's office, and Sally, eager to prove him wrong, takes over the first case to appear. This happens to be one Mrs. Fraser (Mary Astor, smartly groomed and devious in an arresting trial run of her famous role of Brigid O'Shaughnessy in *The Maltese Falcon*), and soon enough Sally—and the district attorney's office—are involved in a double homicide. In her anxiety to uncover the murderer of Mrs. Fraser's husband, Sally drags Bill into all sorts of embarrassing and dangerous escapades, sprinting madly from nightclubs to penthouse apartments. After a few narrow escapes, she learns that Mrs. Fraser is a villainess who hired a nightclub owner named Shane (Jerome Cowan) to kill her cheating husband, then killed Shane when he demanded more money.

As usual for the genre, the murder case itself offers very little in the way of sense or interest. Unfortunately, the screenplay by Gladys Lehman (from a story by Wilson Collison) contains none of the

THERE'S THAT WOMAN AGAIN (1939). Detective Bill Reardon (Melvyn Douglas) is helped by his scatterbrained wife Sally (Virginia Bruce).

TRUE CONFESSION (1937). Carole Lombard is questioned by detective Edgar Kennedy.

bright repartee between the principals required to keep the film from collapsing. Much of the humor, in fact, has the edge of harshness and nastiness prevalent in comedies of the period. Alone in the Fraser apartment, Sally opens a closet door and Bill's apparently dead body tumbles upon her. His intention, he explains, was only to frighten her into withdrawing from the case. Furious, Sally tells him: "Those widow weeds are hot. I hope I don't lose you in the summertime." Though Joan Blondell plays Sally in her familiar ebullient style, the character's behavior is oddly reprehensible. Publicly accusing one of the murder suspects of threatening the victim's life, she feels no tinge of remorse when she offers to take him on as a client to prove his innocence. Only once in the film does she succeed in drawing laughs: questioned by a group of policemen under glaring lights, she remains cool and cheerful while the policemen disintegrate into exhaustion and hysteria.

Despite the efforts of three writers—Philip Epstein, James Edward Grant, and Ken Englund—the sequel, *There's That Woman Again*, was no better. This time Bill and Sally Reardon are caught up in an investigation of jewel thefts that quickly leads to murder. As Sally, Virginia Bruce lacked Joan Blondell's bouncy, wide-eyed charm, but she fared well enough as the meddlesome wife who insists on getting herself into perilous situations. (At one point she is discovered in a suspect's shower-bath.) Margaret Lindsay, Stanley Ridges, and Gordon Oliver were present and accounted for in the plot, but the movie was only fair fun.

Most of the wives and girlfriends who played sleuth alongside the heroes of these comedy-mysteries were as persistent and as faintly dim-witted as Sally Reardon, making Nora Charles seem the zenith of intelligence and sophistication. One of these was Helen Bartlett as played by Carole Lombard in Paramount's uproarious film, *True Confession* (1937). As wife to dedicated and scrupulously honest young attorney Kenneth Bartlett (Fred MacMurray, with a disfiguring moustache), she is given to lying outrageously when the truth seems dull and commonplace. (Neighbors and tradesmen keep hearing from her that Kenneth is insane, or a drug addict, or dead.) When she suddenly finds herself falsely accused of murdering a lecherous broker, she realizes that nobody will believe her protestation of innocence, least of all her husband. With tongue in cheek, she allows him to enter a plea of "justifiable homicide in defense of chastity."

At a hilarious trial in which Kenneth makes an emotional speech describing Helen's desperate fight to save her virtue, she is acquitted and becomes a national heroine who is asked to write her memoirs. Kenneth acquires admiring new clients, and the Bartletts' future looks bright. Enter Charley (John Barrymore), a scoundrelly barfly who knows the identity of the true killer (his recently deceased brother-in-law) and is not above blackmailing Helen to keep him from telling Kenneth. Nevertheless, Kenneth hears about her deception and leaves her, only to return when she tells him yet another lie—that she is going to have a baby.

As directed zestfully by Wesley Ruggles, the screenplay by Claude Binyon (from a play by Louis Verneuil and Georges Berr) missed few opportunities to draw laughs, but the film's success was due largely to its expert cast. In addition to Carole Lombard as the lie-prone wife —the *New York Times* called her "a tower of comic strength"—the players included Edgar Kennedy as an excitable detective, Lynne Overman as a bartender, and Porter Hall as a cantankerous prosecuting attorney. John Barrymore gave one of his flamboyantly entertaining performances as the antic blackmailer who enjoys blowing up toy balloons. The film was remade by Paramount in 1946 as *Cross My Heart,* with Betty Hutton in the Lombard role. Despite the same scenarist—Claude Binyon, collaborating with Harry Tugend—the film was hardly noticed.

Other scatterbrained heroines with a penchant for involving themselves in crime turned up regularly in comedy-mysteries of the thirties and forties. One slightly offbeat entry in the genre was Paramount's *The Princess Comes Across* (1936), directed by William K. Howard. Starting as a straight romantic comedy set aboard an ocean liner, it veered in midstream into conventional mystery melodrama and sank, unexpectedly, out of sight.

The problem may have been caused by an excess of writers—the credits listed four authors for the screenplay (Walter De Leon, Francis Martin, Frank Butler, and Don Hartman), which was based on a story by Philip MacDonald that had been adapted from a novel by Louis Lucien Rogger. Apparently, too many cooks spoiled this broth, which had promised to be delicious. It began auspiciously with the entrance of Princess Olga (Carole Lombard) onto a ship bound from Le Havre to New York. She arrives in grand style, looking and sounding very much like Garbo—her first word is "Vait"—and accompanied by Lady Gertrude Allwyn, the very model of portly dignity in the person of Alison Skipworth. The princess is scheduled to star in a movie entitled *She Done Him Plenty.*

She finds her suite occupied by bandleader King Mantell (Fred

THE PRINCESS COMES ACROSS (1936). Phony Princess Olga (Carole Lombard) and her companion, Lady Gertrude Allwyn (Alison Skipworth).

ADVENTURE IN MANHATTAN (1936). Jean Arthur helps Joel McCrea foil a bank robbery.

MacMurray) who graciously gives it up to her. Alone with Lady Gertrude, the princess begins to speak in tones that are unmistakably Brooklynese: "I'd like to smack that guy right in the kisser!" Princess Olga, it appears, is a fraud, though King is enchanted with her and insists on serenading her with his concertina.

At this point the stage is set for a typical romantic encounter between a phony princess and a jaunty, potentially amorous bandleader. Yet somehow the plot takes a decidedly noncomic turn when it is announced that an escaped murderer is aboard the ship, shadowy figures are seen skulking about the decks, and dead bodies begin to appear on a regular basis. The first victim is a nasty sort named Darcy (Porter Hall), who is blackmailing King for a prison incident in his past and is also threatening to reveal Olga's true identity as Wanda Nash of Brooklyn. The second victim is German detective Steindorf (Sig Rumann), one of a group of international detectives joining forces to find the murderer. The culprit turns out to be the French detective Lorel (Douglas Dumbrille), who is apprehended by King Mantell.

All this murderous business is more confusing than intriguing, and the details are not very well worked out in the scenario. Only a few tattered remnants of the comedy that might have been come to the surface: the Princess Olga looking mournfully out to sea in her best Garbo style and murmuring: "I never knew there was so much vater in the vorld"; Lady Gertrude, suspicious of King's motives in serenading Olga: "I've never known any good to come from a concertina." Or the same lady telling Olga: "Do you know, it wasn't until I was a married woman that I learned that kings don't sleep with their crowns on?" Of course the film ends with Olga confessing the truth to King—"I gave Hollywood a title and they gave me a contract"—and then revealing her true identity to the press when she realizes that she loves King and might lose him.

Other popular female stars took at least one turn at performing in a comedy-mystery. Jean Arthur appeared in Columbia's *Adventure in Manhattan* (1936) as actress Claire Peyton, who helps ace reporter and crime expert George Melville (Joel McCrea) foil a bank robbery by a sinister master criminal named Andre Berlea (Reginald Owen). A flat and uneasy melodrama laced with heavy-handed comedy, it featured an unintentionally hilarious robbery—the bank is adjacent to a theatre and Berlea's plan is to drill an underground tunnel from the theatre to the bank, with the noise of the drilling obliterated by the sounds of battle in the war play being staged at the theatre!

THE MAD MISS MANTON (1938). Newspaper editor Peter Ames (Henry Fonda) gets the film's best gag.

A NIGHT TO REMEMBER (1942). Nancy and Jeff Troy (Loretta Young and Brian Aherne) work to solve a murder in their Greenwich Village apartment.

Neither competent playing by the cast, which included Thomas Mitchell and Herman Bing, nor brisk direction by Edward Ludwig could keep the Sidney Buchman–Harry Sauber–Jack Kirkland script from seeming other than silly.

Barbara Stanwyck fared somewhat better in RKO's *The Mad Miss Manton* (1938). Under Leigh Jason's direction of a Philip Epstein–Wilson Collison screenplay, she appeared as madcap heiress Melsa Manton, here engaged—not in fleeing from an unwanted marriage —but in solving a double murder. Helped by six of her Social Register girlfriends, all given to a great deal of shrieking and wisecracking, she confounded the police, aroused the sarcasm (and later admiration and love) of a newspaper editor named Peter Ames (Henry Fonda), and ignored death threats to uncover the murderer. Despite a chaotic and untidy plot, the result was a lively farce bolstered by a good cast that included Sam Levene as a dyspeptic police lieutenant irritated by Miss Manton's persistence ("Either your education or your spanking has been neglected"), Hattie McDaniel as a grumbling maid, and Stanley Ridges as an ex-convict of unstable mind. The fun was marred only by another of the uncomfortably cruel scenes prevalent in thirties comedy: To obtain vital information from Melsa, Peter pretends to be dying from a gunshot wound. A tearful, stricken Melsa divulges the information and then becomes furious when she sees through the ruse.

Claudette Colbert took a turn at comedy-mystery in MGM's *It's a Wonderful World* (1939). In this mixture of slapstick and homicide, she played a determined poet who helps detective James Stewart apprehend a double murderer and save the life of a playboy convicted of the crimes. Despite the grim-sounding plot, this was a gag-laden comedy written by Ben Hecht (from a story by Hecht and Herman J. Mankiewicz) and directed at breakneck speed by W. S. Van Dyke. A comic highlight had Stewart impersonating a Boy Scout leader and making a shambles of the job.

Even less of a triumph was scored by Loretta Young in Columbia's *A Night to Remember* (1942), in which she appeared as Nancy Troy, wife to mystery writer Jeff Troy (Brian Aherne). They rent a basement apartment in Greenwich Village to "soak up atmosphere" but are soon involved in shady and perilous events when the body of a man is found in their garden. The Richard Flournoy–Jack Henley screenplay (from a story by Kelley Roos) worked hard at being funny by involving the Troys in a variety of false leads and narrow escapes as Jeff tries to find the murderer himself, but there was little menace

THE AMAZING MR. WILLIAMS (1940). Melvyn Douglas, a policeman obviously on special duty, is admonished by girlfriend Joan Blondell and police captain Clarence Kolb.

THE CAT AND THE CANARY (1939). Paulette Goddard and Bob Hope are greeted by Gale Sondergaard in a mysterious mansion. At right: George Zucco.

and less fun in the proceedings. Loretta Young contributed nothing more than nervous screams and an air of desperation and only Donald MacBride, in his familiar role of an eloquently irate and bewildered policeman, was tolerably amusing.

Only Joan Blondell, already a veteran at this sort of airy nonsense, seemed to be able to relax and enjoy herself in spite of the mayhem around her. In *The Amazing Mr. Williams* (1940), a minor but likeable exercise from Columbia, she played Maxine, whose boyfriend Kenny Williams (Melvyn Douglas) is an industrious detective always getting into scrapes with his captain (the inimitable Clarence Kolb), or with the mayor's office, where Maxine works. When his zeal leads him to getting the wrong person arrested and convicted for robbery and murder, he sets about finding the real culprit, with Maxine's eager help. Another case has him charged with finding the "Phantom Slugger," whose specialty is attacking defenseless women. Kenny is required to pose as a woman to catch the Slugger, which leads to predictable complications.

The Dwight Taylor–Sy Bartlett–Richard Maibaum screenplay and Alexander Hall's direction have little distinction, but the film is fun to watch, due to Blondell's and Douglas' good cheer, and to the presence in the cast of Ed Brophy. As an ingratiating convicted killer on his way to prison manacled to Douglas, he is taken by Douglas on a double date with Blondell to keep her from getting angry at being "stood up" for yet another time. The delight on his dumb but amiable face as he finds himself leading a girl about a dance floor instead of clutching iron bars is a pleasure to behold. Donald MacBride is also on hand, again playing a stupid and furious policeman.

Even radio comedienne Gracie Allen deserted husband and partner George Burns on two occasions to appear in comedy-mysteries. In Paramount's *The Gracie Allen Murder Case* (1939), she played her scatterbrained, malapropism-addicted self, helping none other than detective Philo Vance (Warren William) solve a murder. (She called him "Fido.") Alfred E. Green directed a cast that included Ellen Drew, Kent Taylor, Jerome Cowan, and—yes—Donald MacBride. In 1942 Gracie Allen starred in MGM's film version of Owen Davis' play, *Mr. and Mrs. North,* adding her own touch of lunacy to a plot that had a murder committed in the Norths' Greenwich Village apartment. (Possibly this was the same apartment rented by Nancy and Jeff Troy in *A Night to Remember.*) To accommodate Gracie's inanities, S. K. Lauren's screenplay did minor damage to Richard and Frances Lockridge's original concept of Pamela North, but a cast that included William Post, Jr. (as Gerald North), Felix Bressart, Paul Kelly, and Rose Hobart worked in spirited fashion under Robert B. Sinclair's direction.

Not all the comedy-mysteries of those years were derivations of *The Thin Man*. Several of them took the familiar conventions of the mystery film—the lurking menace, the screams and shots in the night—and remodeled them for the benefit of a popular comedian. RKO's *Super-Sleuth* (1937) was a direct assault on the movie concept of criminology, with Jack Oakie as a simpleminded detective trained in Hollywood's methods of crime detection, who finds himself confounded by a genuine arch-villain known as the "Poison Pen." Naturally he captures the culprit (Eduardo Ciannelli) but not without the aid of Willie Best as a terrified valet and Edgar Kennedy as a movie-struck detective. Ann Sothern played Oakie's exasperated girlfriend in this lively farce directed by Ben Stoloff.

The "old haunted house" mystery was spoofed in two films starring Paramount's rising young comedian, Bob Hope. *The Cat and the Canary* (1939), the third film version of the popular John Willard melodrama—the second, released in 1930, was called *The Cat Creeps*—retained the plot device of gathering a group of people at a creepy old mansion in the swamps for a reading of a will. Paulette Goddard played the frightened heiress whose life is in peril at all times. The gimmicks were all present—the dimming lights, the sliding panels, etc.—but the Walter De Leon–Lynn Starling screenplay added a generous sprinkling of gags for Bob Hope as Miss Goddard's none-too-brave protector. Director Elliott Nugent kept the fun moving at a fast clip. The following year, in *The Ghost Breakers*, Paulette Goddard inherited a castle in Cuba, and again Bob Hope came along to cope with ghostly beings, a buried treasure, and assorted frightening occurrences. This time the Walter De Leon script (from the play, *The Ghost Breaker*, by Paul Dickey and Charles W. Goddard)* gave much footage to Willie Best as yet another terrified valet, including a full quota of racial gags. (In a moment of total darkness, Hope tells him: "You look like a black out in a blackout.") The direction by George Marshall left no gimmick untried, as he moved the cast, including Paul Lukas, Anthony Quinn, and Richard Carlson, through its paces.

In 1941, Red Skelton appeared in his first starring role for MGM in a remake of the 1933 comedy melodrama, *Whistling in the Dark*, directed by S. Sylvan Simon. As a radio criminologist named Wally

---

*Two silent versions of the play were produced—one in 1915 (with H. B. Warner) and one in 1922 (with Wallace Reid). In 1955 it was remade as *Scared Stiff* with Dean Martin and Jerry Lewis.

THE GHOST BREAKERS (1940). Bob Hope finds an uncomfortable hiding place, attended by a wary Paulette Goddard.

WHISTLING IN THE DARK (1941). Red Skelton defends Ann Rutherford from villainous Conrad Veidt.

Benton but known as the "Fox" to his devoted audience, he is kid-napped by a gang of phony clairvoyants who want him to construct the perfect murder. Trapped in a spooky house overrun with sinister types and filled with obligatory sliding panels, he manages to escape, but not before registering various degrees of comic terror. In the role played by Ernest Truex in the 1933 version (repeating his stage performance), Skelton proved to be a likeable knockabout comedian, and he starred in two sequels, *Whistling in Dixie* (1942) and *Whistling in Brooklyn* (1944), both with the same director, S. Sylvan Simon, and the same leading lady, Ann Rutherford. (The resemblance of *Whistling in the Dark* to *The Cat and the Canary* may not have been entirely coincidental—Elliott Nugent, who directed the Hope film, also directed and wrote the screenplay for the 1933 version of *Whistling in the Dark.*)

While comedy-mysteries flourished in the thirties and forties, comedies in which elements of fantasy appeared were much less frequent. Until *Topper* turned up in 1937, the idea of mixing ghostly emanations with worldly laughter had met with relatively little favor from film producers—a notable exception was René Clair's delightful 1936 comedy, *The Ghost Goes West,* in which a Scottish ghost (Robert Donat) follows his castle to America where it has been transported stone by stone.

Then *Topper* appeared in the droll, diffident person of Roland Young and started a modest trend in comedy-fantasy. Thorne Smith's story, adapted for the screen by Jack Jevne, Eric Hatch, and Eddie Moran, dealt with staid, respectable Cosmo Topper, president of a bank, who is troubled, plagued, and finally taken under the wing of George and Marion Kerby (Cary Grant and Constance Bennett), two gay, rich, irresponsible people who happen to be ghosts. Most of the humor, frayed now but fresh and amusing in its day, was sparked by the Kerbys' invisibility and their playful attitude toward their ghostly status.

The contrasting characters of the (pre-ghost) Kerbys and the Toppers are quickly established. Topper is saddled with a nagging wife (Billie Burke) and an officious butler (Alan Mowbray) who keep him regimented at all times. ("We dress now.") Marion Kerby enjoys dancing by herself on nightclub floors, and George Kerby sits at board meetings muttering to himself. "It can't be done," he insists. "What?" a board member asks. Kerby answers: "Writing your name upside down and backwards without stopping."

Then the Kerbys are killed in an auto accident and dematerialize

TOPPER (1937). Topper (Roland Young) and his ghostly friends George and Marion Kerby (Cary Grant and Constance Bennett).

TOPPER RETURNS (1941). Joan Blondell as vivacious ghost Gail Richards.

into cheerful ghosts. Immediately, their task is to teach Cosmo Topper how to live while he's still alive (barely) and they set out to turn his routine existence upside down. (Topper is their "last chance to do a good deed.") In very little time, they have disconcerted everyone with their invisible antics and have convinced Topper that he must break out of his shell. One poignant moment has Topper in the Kerby penthouse, moving his feet in a small dance step and murmuring: "I can learn to live, after all." He becomes noisily drunk, and the sight of Topper, soused, supported on both sides by the invisible Kerbys as they move through the hotel lobby, is one of the film's comic highlights.

There are others: Topper arrested for disorderly conduct and appearing before a startled judge as the Kerbys straighten out his clothing; Mrs. Topper amazed to learn that her husband's irrational behavior has made him attractive to her friends; Marion causing a storm of papers in a bank or creating an uproar in a boutique, or later, wreaking havoc with a house detective (Eugene Pallette). One hilarious scene has George Kerby, anxious to get Topper to return to his wife, moving Topper's chair about a room to everyone's consternation. Topper, of course, is ultimately forgiven by his wife but his outlook on life is much brighter as the Kerbys look down upon him from the roof, satisfied to have done their good deed.

If Norman Z. McLeod's direction is not all it might have been, if there are perhaps one too many ghostly "tricks," the film still retains a great deal of its lighthearted humor, and Grant, Bennett, and especially Roland Young cannot be faulted. After years of playing sin-ridden heroines, Constance Bennett appears delighted to be playing farce, and Cary Grant, only one film away from his triumph in *The Awful Truth,* makes an amiable George Kerby. But Roland Young, past master at conveying shyness that hides more than a trace of hedonism, is the comic heart of the film. He won an Academy Award nomination for Best Supporting Actor.

Young appeared in the two sequels to *Topper,* but neither of them was as amusing as the original. *Topper Takes a Trip* (1939) dropped Cary Grant but had Constance Bennett as Marion Kerby pursuing Topper to Paris where he has gone to get a divorce. Norman Z. McLeod directed again, this time giving much footage to Mister Atlas, the Kerbys' dog, who vanishes and reappears at strategic moments throughout the movie. There were still some laughs in Topper's solo rhumba with an invisible Marion, or in his being chased down a street by an invisible but audible dog, but some of the brightness was gone. On hand again were Billie Burke as Mrs. Topper and Alan Mowbray as the butler Wilkins.

Topper Returns (1941), directed by Roy Del Ruth, dropped Constance Bennett and replaced her with Joan Blondell, but the law of diminishing returns was very much in evidence. This pointless farce had Blondell as Gail Richards, goading poor Topper into tracking down the person who had stabbed her to death in the spooky old Carrington mansion, where she had gone with friend Ann Carrington (Carole Landis). Among the people rushing about the mansion were Billie Burke, repeating her role as Mrs. Topper, Eddie "Rochester" Anderson going through the standard "frightened black" routine as the Toppers' chauffeur, and Donald MacBride as his trademarked furious policeman. Only Joan Blondell's bright way with a quip kept this third *Topper* film from being unendurable.

A rash of *Topper* imitations and derivations appeared throughout the forties, replete with ghostly trappings (disembodied voices, objects moving mysteriously at their own will, etc.) and astonished cast members. Universal's *The Invisible Woman* (1941), with John Barrymore and Virginia Bruce, was an obvious example, a ramshackle attempt to cash in on the *Topper* popularity while exploiting the connection to H. G. Wells' *The Invisible Man* (1934), to which it bore not even the slightest resemblance. A few of the ghostly comedies, however, had merit. MGM's *The Canterville Ghost* (1944), loosely adapted by Edwin Harvey Blum from Oscar Wilde's story, offered Charles Laughton as the ghost of the cowardly Sir Simon de Canterville, doomed to haunt a castle until one of his descendants can perform a heroic deed. This task is carried out by an American soldier (Robert Young) billeted in the castle, who is unaware of his Canterville blood. Director Jules Dassin kept the whimsy reasonably under control, despite Laughton's usual excesses and Margaret O'Brien's self-conscious cuteness as the six-year-old owner of the Canterville castle.

More conventional movie ghosts were played by Lou Costello and Marjorie Reynolds in Universal's *The Time of Their Lives* (1946). As the spirits of pioneer Americans unjustly branded as traitors in the Revolutionary War, they played their ghostly tricks on a group of people stranded overnight in a restored colonial mansion. This time Bud Abbott took a back seat to the ectoplasmic antics. Rex Harrison also appeared as one half of *The Ghost and Mrs. Muir* in Fox's comedy-fantasy of 1947. As the sharp-tongued spirit of a dead sea captain, he materialized on occasion to help and advise a young widow (Gene

THE CANTERVILLE GHOST (1944). Charles Laughton as Sir Simon de Canterville does a jig step for Robert Young and Margaret O'Brien.

I MARRIED A WITCH (1942). Fredric March is startled to find lovely witch Veronica Lake in his armchair.

Tierney) and her children. The direction by Joseph L. Mankiewicz faltered at times but the movie was a charming whimsy.

One of the most adroit of these ghostly comedies was the 1942 fantasy, *I Married a Witch*. Thorne Smith supplied the original premise in his uncompleted novel, which was adapted into a delightful screenplay by Marc Connelly and Robert Pirosh. Under René Clair's direction (his second American film), Veronica Lake and Cecil Kellaway played the father-and-daughter ghosts of sorcerers burned at the stake in Puritan days who return to torment the descendant (Fredric March) of their persecutors. An odd romance ensues between the bewitching spirit and the love-struck gentleman, who happens to be a candidate for governor. Susan Hayward played March's edgy fiancée and Robert Benchley was on hand, as fuzzy-minded as ever. But the best performance was given by the always reliable Cecil Kellaway as the perennially tipsy, lighthearted ghost.

Ghosts may have been a source of movie merriment, but in the forties they were surpassed by another group of fantasy figures who enjoyed wide popularity for a time. Not usually associated with hilarity, heavenly angels as emissaries of good will, salvation, or otherworldly assistance began to appear regularly on movie screens.

The film that brought about an influx of angelic visitors was Columbia's 1941 comedy-fantasy, *Here Comes Mr. Jordan*. Adapted by Sidney Buchman and Seton I. Miller from a play by Harry Segall, this movie pleased audiences with its combination of whimsy, sentiment, and romance. It dealt with Joe Pendleton (Robert Montgomery), a genial prizefighter who enjoys flying planes and playing his saxophone. Following a plane crash, he is brought to heaven by fussy, petulant Messenger 7013 (Edward Everett Horton) and his body is cremated. But the Messenger has made a mistake, prematurely removing Joe's soul, when actually he would have been able to pull out of the seemingly fatal dive; now Joe's body has been destroyed and they must find another one for him to inhabit.

With the help of the dignified Mr. Jordan (Claude Rains), who is charged with transporting the souls of the deceased on their predestined journeys, Joe searches for the "perfect" body—after all, he was "in the pink." He first takes over the body of Bruce Farnsworth, a nasty playboy whose wife (Rita Johnson) and confidential secretary (John Emery) have drowned him in the bathtub. When he is obliged to leave this body, he selects the body of K.O. Murdock, once his foremost competitor for the heavyweight championship, who has been shot by gangsters for refusing to "throw" a fight. When, as

Murdock, Joe wins the fight and the championship, Mr. Jordan decrees that he will remain K.O. Murdock for the rest of his life. Along the way, as each transformation takes place, Joe confounds his crusty but good-hearted manager Max Corkle (James Gleason) and finds love with Bette Logan (Evelyn Keyes), a girl whose father had been wronged by Bruce Farnsworth in their business dealings.

For most of its length, *Here Comes Mr. Jordan* is a pleasing film, competently directed by Alexander Hall. Its vision of "heaven" may be Hollywood-traditional, with lots of clouds and mist, but the situation is original and skillfully handled. Occasionally, a faint echo of Frank Capra can be heard, especially when Joe, as Farnsworth, returns all the money he has stolen to the grateful "little people," and there are also a few uneasy "metaphysical" moments, as when Jordan tells Joe: "Eventually all things work out. There is design in everything. You were meant to be a champion. You *are*." But on the whole the script succeeds in avoiding many of the pitfalls of film fantasy. Only towards the end does the movie lose its way and become strained and silly.

The performances are all fine, with Robert Montgomery winning as Joe Pendleton and Claude Rains bringing his mellifluous voice and dignified bearing to the role of Mr. Jordan. But the best performance is given by James Gleason, who is splendid and even poignant as Max Corkle, reacting in amazement at each "return" of his beloved Joe, struggling to keep from addressing the empty air, and finally realizing that Joe now *is* K.O. Murdock. He repeated the role in Columbia's 1947 Rita Hayworth musical, *Down to Earth*, as did Edward Everett Horton as Messenger 7013. (Mr. Jordan also showed up in this film, played by Roland Culver.)

The success of *Here Comes Mr. Jordan* did not go unnoticed by film producers,* and the balance of the forties found the visitations from above (and below) turning up frequently. In Paramount's *The Remarkable Andrew* (1942), written by Dalton Trumbo, the spirit of Andrew Jackson (Brian Donlevy) returned to earth to help out a young small-town politician (William Holden) who uncovers skulduggery in the town's government. Stuart Heisler directed this comedy, which also brought in the shades of Washington, Jefferson, Franklin, and Marshall to save the day for the hero. Universal's *That's the Spirit* (1945)

---

*It won two Academy Awards—Best Original Story (Harry Segall) and Best Written Screenplay (Sidney Buchman and Seton I. Miller). The film itself was nominated for the Best Picture award, as was Robert Montgomery for Best Actor.

Left: HERE COMES MR. JORDAN (1941). Boxer Joe Pendleton (Robert Montgomery) meets Bette Logan (Evelyn Keyes), with heavenly emissary Mr. Jordan (Claude Rains) as an invisible onlooker.

Right: THE REMARKABLE ANDREW (1942). One Andrew—Andrew Jackson (Brian Donlevy)—helps another (William Holden).

HEAVEN CAN WAIT (1943). Henry Van Cleve (Don Ameche) is introduced to the lovely Martha (Gene Tierney) by his cousin Albert (Allyn Joslyn).

starred Jack Oakie as the ghost of a long-dead vaudevillian who returns to earth to get his daughter (Peggy Ryan) on the stage and out of the clutches of her cantankerous grandfather (Gene Lockhart). Charles Lamont directed the scenario by Michael Fessier and Ernest Pagano.

Emissaries from the Hollywood heavens materialized for every purpose. Warners' *The Horn Blows at Midnight* (1945), directed by Raoul Walsh, offered Jack Benny as the Angel Athanael, brought to earth to sound the trumpet of doom for mankind. *The Cockeyed Miracle* (MGM, 1946) presented Frank Morgan as a recently deceased codger whose long-dead father (Keenan Wynn) appeared to help the old man settle his family problems before passing into a void. S. Sylvan Simon directed the Karen De Wolf screenplay from a play by versatile producer-director-writer George Seaton. *Heaven Only Knows* (1947) starred Robert Cummings as the Archangel Michael, dispatched to a Western mining town to change the nasty and despotic ways of one Duke Byron (Brian Donlevy). Albert S. Rogell directed this tame fantasy. And in *The Bishop's Wife* (Goldwyn, 1947), an angel named Dudley (Cary Grant) answers a bishop's prayer for guidance and comfort. This film, at least, had solid virtues—a gently amusing screenplay by Robert Sherwood and Leonardo Bercovici (from Robert Nathan's novel), smooth direction by Henry Koster, and an exceptionally fine cast that included David Niven, Loretta Young, Monty Woolley, James Gleason, Elsa Lanchester, and Gladys Cooper.*

Occasionally, as a variation on all the heavenly messengers, a figure from the nether regions, unmistakably representing the devil, materialized on the screen. In Fox's *Heaven Can Wait* (1943), a Technicolor comedy stylishly directed by Ernst Lubitsch, Don Ameche played a recently deceased elderly rake who appears before Lucifer (Laird Cregar), here called His Excellency, and reviews his long, ill-spent life ("I have no illusions," he remarks. "I know where I belong.") The screenplay by Samson Raphaelson (from a play by Ladislaus Bus-Fekete) was highly engaging, filled with satirical moments as Henry Van Cleve relived his family life and his marriage to Martha (Gene Tierney). The funniest moments were contributed by Charles Coburn as Henry's salty grandfather, and by Marjorie Main and Eugene

---

*Angelic visitors have not disappeared entirely from the screen. As recently as 1970, Harry Belafonte starred in *The Angel Levine* as an angel who may or may not be authentic but who, at any rate, is visible to a poor tailor played by Zero Mostel.

Pallette as a squabbling Kansas couple. (Their noisy fight over the funnies is a classic encounter.) Allyn Joslyn was also splendid as a priggish cousin. The film was nominated for an Academy Award.

Lucifer also turned up in *Angel on My Shoulder* (1946) and oddly enough he was portrayed by Claude Rains, who had played the heavenly Mr. Jordan. Here, known simply as Nick, he makes a pact with a murdered gangster (Paul Muni), allowing him to return to earth to exact revenge on a double-crossing colleague in exchange for his taking over the body of an honest judge he (Nick) wishes to disgrace. Of course the gangster outwits the devil because of his love for the judge's fiancée (Anne Baxter) and sets things rights before returning to Lucifer. The screenplay was by Harry Segall (author of the original stage version of *Here Comes Mr. Jordan*) and Roland Kibbee, and the director was Archie Mayo. Despite the worn material, the film was enjoyable, largely due to the seasoned acting of Muni and Rains.*

*Perhaps the most unusual variation on the heavenly visitor theme was Universal's forgotten 1951 fantasy, *You Never Can Tell*, in which Dick Powell played a murdered *dog* who returns to earth in human form to find his killer.

CHAPTER EIGHT

BOSS-LADIES AND OTHER LIBERATED TYPES

"You're free, baby. Step out and be yourself."—Melvyn Douglas to Irene Dunne in *Theodora Goes Wild*

"You're a machine—not a woman."—Melvyn Douglas to Joan Crawford in *They All Kissed the Bride*

In the world of movies, where independent-minded heiresses could thumb their noses at high society, where ambitious working girls could set their traps for wealthy husbands, it was inevitable that the ladies would set out to invade the male-dominated bastions of Big Business, or make their mark in professions usually associated with men. Why, they asked, couldn't a woman run a company, or a staff of office workers, or a hung-over playboy with no head for business? Why couldn't they preside over a courtroom, write the Great American Novel, diagnose an illness, or edit a magazine?

The fact is, of course, that they *could,* and so a series of comedies appeared during the thirties and forties in which the broad-shouldered lady in a tailored suit played the "boss," snapping out orders to her intimidated staff, dismissing the competition with an airy wave of her well-manicured hand, and behaving like John D. Rockefeller on one of his bad days. Or she might turn up as a formidable, lionized author of a tome on the pitfalls of marriage and romance, or as a man-eating tigress ostensibly engaged in the practice of law or medicine.

Yet this was the lotus-land of Hollywood, where women must remain women, and so the "feminist" attitude was really a sham: the "liberated" lady had to discover romance before the final reel, was obliged to reveal the femininity behind her iron corset and truculent

HONEYMOON IN BALI (1939). Boss-lady Madeleine Carroll is clearly startled by what Fred MacMurray is telling her about women and marriage.

THIRD FINGER, LEFT HAND (1940). Melvyn Douglas examines the sculpture shown to him by Donald Meek, watched by a dubious Myrna Loy.

manner. As Helen Broderick explains to Madeleine Carroll, boss-lady extraordinary in *Honeymoon in Bali* (1939): "You're going to find out you're a human being."

Until Rosalind Russell appeared a few years later (after an assortment of roles) to virtually corner the market on boss-ladies, the formidable Gail Allen played by Madeleine Carroll in this Paramount comedy was a prime example of the businesswoman who has little time (or use) for men. As the head of Morrisey's Department Store, she reigned supreme in a masculine world, hiring and firing with dispatch and looking upon love and marriage with irritation and disdain.

As acted by the beauteous Miss Carroll under Edward H. Griffith's direction, Gail Allen is, of course, a sitting target for a comeuppance. This appears promptly in the guise of one Bill Burnett (Fred MacMurray), an easygoing, freewheeling sort who meets her in a boat shop. With a house in Bali and an adopted little girl named Rosie (Carolyn Lee), he is not averse to a romantic or even marital entanglement, and Gail seems a likely contender. In the manner of movie "male chauvinists" of the time, he is startled and amused to discover that she is a high-powered executive.

Though they spend much time together, Gail and Bill express opposing attitudes with conviction. "I'm not a feminist," Gail claims, "but the expression 'It's a man's world' irritates me." His rejoinder: "Men use their heads. Women use their emotions." "Why do I need a husband?" she asks him. "I don't intend to fall in love." (This, despite the evidence of a patient longtime boyfriend, an opera singer named Eric—played by Allan Jones.) Clearly, Bill and Gail are meant for each other in a movie world where opposites attract in a matter of minutes.

The softening of Gail's point of view comes by way of Rosie, a not too oppressively cute child who comes to stay with her for a while. (Rosie, it seems, prays every night to the Devil. "*Everybody* prays to God," she explains.) After a while, Gail's affection for Rosie begins to extend to her adoptive father, though she refuses to admit it even to herself. She takes Rosie to Nassau for a brief vacation, and when Bill shows up, the three have a charming scene together in which they sing a "pidgin English" song. But when Bill becomes amorous, she resists him. "You're afraid of becoming Miss Nobody," he tells her. She calls him "a liar, a cheat, and a coward," and flies back to New York and her job.

Brooding and unhappy despite Eric's attentions, Gail finally decides to go to Bill in Bali, and in abject surrender she tells him: "I kept crying for Rosie and you. A husband and children are necessary to make me complete." Inexplicably, Bill is cold to her, tells her he is marrying his old girlfriend Noel Van Ness (Osa Massen). Leaving in tears, Gail returns to accept Eric's proposal—but not for long. A friendly, philosophical window-washer (Akim Tamiroff) advises her to fight for Bill. "Your kind of woman," he tells her, "needs a guy —not a fine gentleman." And Eric, in a dubious display of generosity, also advises her that Bill is the man for her. "A woman's not supposed to be a boss," he says. "Your kind of boss-woman needs a boss-man." The fact that he is unquestionably serious speaks volumes for the screen's attitude toward women in those years. Of course the ending finds Gail, Bill, and Rosie on the beach at Bali, singing their "pidgin English" song.

If *Honeymoon in Bali* is calculated to offend every woman in the movie audience, it is still reasonably amusing, with an agreeable script by Virginia Van Upp (based on stories by Grace Sartwell Mason and Katharine Brush). Though the characters frequently behave in irrational ways, without the insane logic of the best screwball comedies, the pace is brisk and the leads are adept. (By 1939 Fred MacMurray already had a patent on the sort of role he plays here.) Their best support comes from Helen Broderick, bringing her inimitable wry delivery to the role of Gail's sensible novelist friend, Lorna Smith.

Lady executives hovering reluctantly on the brink of romance persisted into the forties. MGM's *Third Finger, Left Hand* (1940) starred Myrna Loy as high-ranking magazine editor Margot Sherwood, who avoids suitors by simply pretending to *be* married. Then she meets artist Jeff Thompson (Melvyn Douglas), who falls in love with her. Since she clearly feels the same way, there would be no reason for her to continue her ruse. Nevertheless, to sustain an hour and a half of film comedy, she continues to pretend having a husband, with inevitable complications. The Lionel Houser screenplay was flat, as was Robert Z. Leonard's direction, but the cast, including Raymond Walburn, Lee Bowman, and Donald Meek, tried to supply some of the missing sparkle.

In *They All Kissed the Bride* (Columbia, 1942), the studio's resident comedy director, Alexander Hall, led Joan Crawford through her paces in a role originally intended for Carole Lombard, who had been killed in an airplane crash. She played M. J. (Margaret) Drew, the strong-minded head of a trucking company, who is steering her

THEY ALL KISSED THE BRIDE (1942). Melvyn Douglas and Joan Crawford "mix it up" with the ordinary people.

TAKE A LETTER, DARLING (1942). Advertising executive Rosalind Russell goes shopping with Fred MacMurray.

younger sister Vivian (Helen Parrish) towards a rich but loveless marriage. ("Intelligent people don't marry for better or worse. They marry for better and better.") Then journalist Mike Holmes (Melvyn Douglas) shows up at Vivan's lavish wedding and proceeds to give the bride several long kisses. Margaret mistakes him for one of her sister's former boyfriends, but when they are alone and she learns his name, she finds herself alarmingly attracted to him.

The rest of the film involves her refusal to admit that she's fallen in love—instead she acquires a variety of physical symptoms—while Mike goes about organizing and haranguing her drivers and making nasty remarks about her lack of femininity. "You're a machine, not a woman!" he shouts. Even when he sends her flowers, he cannot resist remarking: "I debated before sending these. With these on, you might be mistaken for a girl!"

Goaded into proving she can be just like anyone else, Margaret attends the annual dance for the Drews' drivers where she does a jitterbug routine with Mike's friend Johnny Johnson (Allen Jenkins). Later, she gets decorously drunk with Mike and his friends. But when her misunderstood directive gets all the drivers fired from the company, her progress towards becoming a "human being" is halted abruptly and she and Mike have a falling out. By the time the film ends, however, M. J. Drew is a creature of the past, and Margaret Drew is on her way to becoming a radiant bride.

Never too happy in comedy roles, Joan Crawford plays M. J. Drew with a grim determination that sinks the enterprise almost as quickly as it gets under way, and not even Roland Young, Billie Burke, and Allen Jenkins, professionals all, can keep it afloat. For Melvyn Douglas, the film provided one of his last roles in the suave romantic vein he had perfected since the mid-thirties. He progressed to genial character roles in the forties and later to the colorful, cantankerous old men of the sixties.

Also in 1942, Rosalind Russell appeared in one of the films that contributed to her lasting reputation as the screen's most high-pressured boss-lady. In 1940, she had played Brian Aherne's demonically efficient executive secretary in Universal's *Hired Wife* (1940). In Paramount's *Take a Letter, Darling*, she was an advertising executive named A. C. MacGregor. (Apparently, as with Joan Crawford's M. K. Drew, two initials instead of a first name give instant status to a lady executive.) To calm the suspicious wives of her clients, she hires Tom Verney (Fred MacMurray) to act as her general flunkey and nighttime escort. But when an important client turns out to be young and pretty

Ethel Caldwell (Constance Moore), A. C. MacGregor loses her aplomb and begins to acquire unmistakable signs of jealousy.

Around this familiar situation, director Mitchell Leisen and scenarist Claude Binyon, both old hands at this sort of nonsense, spin a fair amount of verbal and physical comedy. Russell's desperate attempts to suppress her growing affection for her easygoing hireling; MacMurray's losing battle with an opera hat; Robert Benchley's insistence on playing ring-toss and ski-ball during business hours—these are among the highlights. As Russell and MacMurray move from an employer-employee relationship to something warmer and more lasting, the film begins to run out of steam and sputters to a conclusion. (The cast includes Macdonald Carey in his film debut.)

There was one standard variation in these films. Occasionally, the businesslike lady suspected all along that she craved a husband and family instead of a carpeted office, but her domestic yearnings went unrecognized by the male in question. In these cases, *he* was deaf to the blandishments of love and marriage.

Paramount's *She Married Her Boss* (1935), directed by Gregory La Cava, was an early example. Here, Claudette Colbert played Julia Scott, crisply efficient assistant to widower and department-store owner Richard Barclay (Melvyn Douglas), who turns down a high-paying job in Paris because she loves her boss. ("He's just forgotten about women," she tells a friend.) Even willing to be helpful outside the office, Julia takes charge of Barclay's obnoxious sister Gertrude (Katharine Alexander)—Julia calls her a "professional pall-bearer"— and his bratty daughter Annabelle (Edith Fellows). Asked by Barclay to set his household in working order, she promptly fires the slovenly cook and butler, spanks Annabelle, and intimidates Gertrude. When she opens the shades and turns on the radio, Barclay is ecstatic: "That's the first music I've heard around this house for months."

When Julia realizes that she has behaved like a "first-class fishwife," she decides to leave her job at last. Barclay counters this by making her general manager and giving her a vacation with pay. It is only when he is on the verge of losing her for good that he is prodded to the point Julia has wanted him to reach: a glancing, unromantic proposal of marriage. "I've passed that romantic nonsense of adolescence," he tells her. Julia decides to accept him anyway.

The balance of this predictable but moderately funny film is devoted to Julia's efforts to put their marriage on a more permanent, more romantic footing, despite the opposition of Richard's family. "Is our marriage just a bargain to you?" she asks her blankly insensitive husband. "You've changed," he tells her. "You're not the Julia Scott I know. I don't understand you any more." Glumly, she responds: "It was just my idea of being a woman."

For this boss-lady, "being a woman" is more important than running an office or earning a large salary. Her secretary admires her, wants to be just like her. "My career means everything to me," she tells Julia. But Julia, expressing the attitude of countless thirties heroines, reprimands her gently. "Sit in the moonlight and hold hands," she advises. "A career leaves you empty. Do something really important." And when her marriage is falling apart, she exclaims: "I hate business, stores, everything that turns people into pieces of machinery!"

The film's funniest sequence occurs when Richard finally realizes that he has lost Julia and proceeds to get riotously drunk with his butler Franklin (played by the unfailing Raymond Walburn). Singing "Home on the Range" in a noisy duet, they spirit Julia away from the wealthy businessman with whom she is running off, and go on a wild ride through the city streets. They gather bricks and heave them joyfully through the window of Barclay's Department Store. Love, femininity, and domesticity conquer all. Moral: a girl out for money in the heartless world of big business should settle for romance and marriage.

In Columbia's *More Than a Secretary* (1936), under Alfred E. Green's direction, Jean Arthur also played a businessgirl in love with her boss (George Brent), who finally snares him. The boss happens to be a dedicated "health-nut," the editor of *Body and Brain* magazine, who insists on "correct living." ("This office is a shrine—a shrine to health," he announces when he hires her as his secretary.) Carol Baldwin (Arthur) is actually the owner of a secretarial school but one look at Fred Gilbert (Brent) and she changes jobs.

Unfortunately, this comedy's best scene takes place at the beginning and is never topped. On her first morning, Carol is introduced to the regimen of staff exercises at *Body and Brain*. This regimen, called "Mr. Gilbert's 11 o'clock cobweb-chaser," has the workers crawling along the floor in grotesque fashion and features a lunch, served at the desks, of buttermilk and a bran muffin. At the end of the day, Carol comments "I felt fine before I got healthy." But she is still attracted to the man she calls "a slave driver, a calisthenic expert, and a guy who lives on mattress stuffing." "There's nothing human about him," she adds.

SHE MARRIED HER BOSS (1935). Tipsy butler Raymond Walburn and his equally tipsy employer, Melvyn Douglas, are admonished by Jean Dixon and Claudette Colbert.

MORE THAN A SECRETARY (1936). Jean Arthur shows the new cover of *Body and Brain* magazine to boss George Brent. At left: secretary Dorothea Kent.

Nevertheless, she is determined to find his "human" streak and, incidentally, to help him save the failing magazine by using decidedly "healthy" pin-up girls as a spur to circulation. She is scoring well in both these endeavors until a secretary named Maizie appears on the scene. Bequeathed to Fred by a friend whose wife is suddenly returning home, Maizie turns out to be a blonde with a roving eye and a unique point of view. Played with comic zest by Dorothea Kent in her first role, she is given to such remarks as: "I think education is terribly important. I came pretty near to getting a dose of it myself." (Her mother told her: "Take care of your body, Maizie, because it's all you've got.")

To Carol's dismay, Maizie promptly sinks her fangs into Fred and succeeds in luring him away from his health "regimen." (She complains to Fred about Maizie's error-studded letters. Fred: "Her mind must have been wandering." Carol: "It's been on a Cook's Tour.") Unable to compete with Maizie, she quits, and the magazine plummets in circulation without her sensible touch. But she refuses to return to her "stubborn, conceited, selfish, incompetent" boss and vanishes with her friend Helen (Ruth Donnelly). Following the reversal pattern of these comedies, Fred now realizes that he loves Carol and wants her back. After managing to foist Maizie on his unsuspecting publisher, Crosby (Charles Halton), he decides to locate Carol by running a full-page ad in the magazine and using her face on the cover. The ruse works, and after some confusion, they are back together again.

Frail but amusing, *More Than a Secretary* was hardly one of Jean Arthur's best comedies of the thirties—after *Mr. Deeds Goes to Town*, she merely coasted until *Easy Living* the following year—but she is capable, as usual, as are Ruth Donnelly, Charles Halton, and Lionel Stander as a pragmatic aide to Fred Gilbert. The film, however, really belongs to Dorothea Kent as the single-minded Maizie, cheerfully sprinting from man to man. (Her comment on Crosby, her latest project: "You'll never know how he leans on me.")

The executive suite may have been successfully invaded by the movie heroines of the thirties and forties, but they had other worlds to conquer (and then, of course, promptly surrender to men). One was the world of letters, and occasionally a lady author appeared who demonstrated that a sharp mind and outspoken point of view need not be confined to male writers. Theodora Lynn was a case in point, and as played by Irene Dunne in Columbia's entertaining 1936 comedy, *Theodora Goes Wild*, she was one of the most effective literary gadflies of the thirties.

A resident of Lynnfield, Connecticut, Theodora appears at first to be the epitome of the small-town girl, modest, demure, and sensible. In reality, Theodora has a secret: under the pseudonym of Caroline Adams, she is the author of the year's sexiest, most titillating novel, condemned by Lynnfield's moral guardians as "unmoral and not fit to print." Only the newspaper editor, Jed Waterbury (Thomas Mitchell), defends the novel, claiming that the town should learn "how people live and love in the wide awake world." "You can't keep civilization out of Lynnfield forever," he asserts.

Theodora's adventures begin on a trip to New York City to visit her publisher where she expresses her dismay at Caroline Adams' reputation and defends her own timidity: "Were you ever raised in a small town by two maiden aunts? Have you played the organ in church since you were fifteen? No, well, I have. And right now I ask myself: where did Caroline Adams come from? How did all this start?" Then Theodora meets Michael Grant (Melvyn Douglas), the lighthearted artist who designed the cover of her book, who begins to change her attitude. Surprised and intimidated by her small-town point of view, he gets mildly tipsy and then, in his apartment, deliberately duplicates the seduction scene in her book. Theodora's reaction doesn't match her fictional heroine's: "Don't you dare!" she cries, warding him off.

Attracted to Theodora and determined to "free" her, Michael comes to Lynnfield and gets a job as gardener to Theodora's aunts. (One of the aunts comments: "He's much too happy for Sunday, if you ask me.") Theodora, of course, is annoyed, but Michael tells her: "I'm going to break you out of this jail and give you the world." He insists: "You're a strange, sad case, girlie. Desires being strangled to death. Break loose. Be yourself." But she insists that Caroline Adams was an accident.

When they go on a fishing trip together on a Sunday, Theodora is whispered about by a shocked townspeople and her aunts demand that Michael leave town at once. Bitter and angry at their small-mindedness, Theodora finally rebels: "I'm sick of it. You've scolded and frightened me all I'll stand for . . . I invite the whole town to take a jump in the lake!" But Michael leaves abruptly, telling Theodora: "You're free, baby. Step out and be yourself. There are big things ahead and you'll travel faster alone."

When Theodora follows him to New York, the sort of reversal favored by thirties comedies occurs. Thoroughly liberated now, Theodora becomes the champion of rebellious womanhood, presiding at press conferences where she sounds her call to arms: "I say this

THEODORA GOES WILD (1936). A forlorn Theodora (Irene Dunne) reads Michael's farewell note.

to the modern young girl—be free—express yourself. Take your life in your own hands and mold it." She is even named by her publisher's wife in a divorce action, though of course she is entirely innocent. On the other hand, Michael turns out to be married to a hateful woman, Agnes (Leona Maricle). What is more, he is under the thumb of a father (Henry Kolker) prominent in state politics, who insists on Michael's remaining married in name only! Now *Theodora* is urging *Michael* to throw off his shackles, and when she kisses him just for "a memory," the reporters photograph the act. Result: another divorce action, this one by Agnes.

Surprisingly, Theodora's aunts defend her behavior and in a delightful scene expressing small-town attitudes, they march down the church aisle, proudly ignoring the hostile stares of the parishioners. "What's so scandalous about Theodora's behavior?" her Aunt Mary (Elizabeth Risdon) asks. When their wayward niece turns up at the railroad station, she causes more consternation than ever: she is holding a newborn baby! But the baby, it seems, belongs not to Theodora but to the secretly married daughter of a local townswoman. Michael, waiting to admit that he loves her, is startled by the baby until Theodora tells him: "It isn't mine, stupid." And though Theodora will probably never be Lynnfield's favorite citizen, she has come into her own at last.

Another "liberated" lady took a stand (for at least the length of the film) in Columbia's *The Doctor Takes a Wife* (1940). In this breezy comedy directed by Alexander Hall, Loretta Young played professional bachelor girl June Cameron, who has written a popular tome entitled *Spinsters Aren't Spinach*. ("Marriage is no longer the answer to a maiden's prayer.") Ray Milland was co-starred as Tim Sterling, a young surgeon with opposite ideas about women. (He scoffs at "the independent but frustrated female.") Under circumstances only desperate screenwriters could invent—in this case George Seaton and Ken Englund—the two are forced to pretend they are married. Sharing the same apartment, they exchange the sort of vitriolic insults which, in movie lore, can only lead to romance. And so it does, despite the opposition of Dr. Sterling's fiancée Marilyn (Gail Patrick) and other complications.

Though the plot is foolish, the movie has a surprising number of funny moments: the new "bride" bewildered at a gathering of her "husband's" colleagues, who seem to speak in nothing but medical terminology; Tim forced to scamper frantically between two apartments to keep Marilyn from discovering that he is "married" to June;

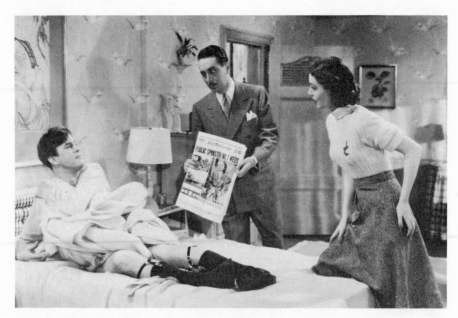

THE DOCTOR TAKES A WIFE (1940). A shocked Ray Milland learns from Reginald Gardiner and Loretta Young that he has "married" Public Spinster No. One.

WHEN LADIES MEET (1941). Novelist Mary Howard (Joan Crawford) meets journalist Jimmy Lee (Robert Taylor).

June arriving at a party where Marilyn is about to announce her engagement to Tim, and sweetly beginning to knit baby clothes. The support by Reginald Gardiner, Edmund Gwenn (as Tim's father), and Gail Patrick is adequate, though the elegant Miss Patrick, usually the essence of icy sophistication, is called upon to behave like a simpering nincompoop.

Other women writers with romantic problems continued to find their way into forties comedy, usually making their way from austerity to glowing ardor by the last reel. MGM's *When Ladies Meet* (1941), directed by Robert Z. Leonard, offered Joan Crawford as novelist Mary Howard, long enamored of her publisher Rogers Woodruff (Herbert Marshall) but pursued by a carefree young journalist named Jimmy Lee (Robert Taylor). The S. K. Lauren–Anita Loos screenplay (from Rachel Crothers' 1932 play) complicated the triangle by bringing in Woodruff's lovely wife Clare (Greer Garson), whose nobility of character and general all-around decency inspire Mary to forget her feelings for Woodruff and accept Jimmy Lee. A remake of MGM's 1933 film, which had Ann Harding, Myrna Loy, Robert Montgomery, and Frank Morgan in the Garson-Crawford-Taylor-Marshall roles, respectively, *When Ladies Meet* was a garrulous exercise in pointlessness.

Nobility of character was also expressed by Bette Davis as novelist Kit Foster in Warners' film version of John Van Druten's play, *Old Acquaintance* (1943). Van Druten collaborated with Lenore Coffee on the screenplay, which sacrificed much of the brittle amusement of the play to the typical *Sturm und Drang* of the studio's vehicles for Bette Davis. It dealt with Kit Foster's long and stormy friendship with Millie Drake (Miriam Hopkins), a vicious and hysterical woman whose jealousy of Kit compels her to write a series of pulpish but successful novels. Through the years the women clash over a number of emotional issues. Though Vincent Sherman's direction was competent, there was less pleasure in the dialogue than in watching two stars locked in contention for camera supremacy, and the moment in which Davis finally throttled Hopkins never failed to draw applause. In RKO's 1946 comedy, *Without Reservations,* Claudette Colbert also played a famous novelist, but one beset by less weighty problems as she traveled incognito across the country, finding comic adventures and romance with a Marine captain (John Wayne).

Another outlet for the screen's literary ladies was the magazine, usually chic, where a haughty attitude toward men could be handily combined with a glamorous wardrobe. In Paramount's *Lady in the*

OLD ACQUAINTANCE (1943). Kit Foster (Bette Davis) and Millie Drake (Miriam Hopkins) toast their long friendship.

WITHOUT RESERVATIONS (1946). John Wayne and Claudette Colbert discuss matters with Thurston Hall.

Dark (1944), Ginger Rogers, as coolly efficient, vitriolic fashion editor Liza Elliott, was actually addressed contemptuously as "boss-lady" by editorial associate Charley Johnson (Ray Milland). In this leaden Technicolor version of the Moss Hart–Kurt Weill–Ira Gershwin musical play, Liza is revealed as a lady burdened with a deep-seated neurosis caused by a wretchedly unhappy childhood. Her psychoanalysis takes the form of grandiose production numbers (including the celebrated "Saga of Jenny") and her cure comes in exorcising the past. Not unexpectedly, after toying with the affections of several men (Warner Baxter, Jon Hall), she discovers that the blunt Mr. Johnson is the one true love in her life. In *Christmas in Connecticut* (Warners, 1945), Barbara Stanwyck appeared as magazine columnist Elizabeth Lane, whose expertise on home matters is pure sham. She is put to the test when her publisher (Sydney Greenstreet) forces her to prepare a Christmas dinner for a war hero at her nonexistent Connecticut farm. The rather inane plot had her desperately trying to acquire a home and family in a matter of hours, at the same time that she finds herself falling in love with the hero (Dennis Morgan.) Peter Godfrey directed this intermittently clever farce, and Reginald Gardiner, S. Z. Sakall, and Una O'Connor contributed to the limited fun.

Warners' *June Bride* (1948) also attempted to mix magazine sophistication with rural simplicity, with happier results. Here, Bette Davis played Linda Gilman, chic editor of *Home Life* magazine, who ventures to Indiana in a wintry March to stage an article on a local June bride. She is accompanied by her star reporter and ex-lover Carey Jackson (Robert Montgomery), who persists in trying to win her back though he is well aware of her frosty attitude. ("Even when I was making love to you, I felt you were wondering what time it was.") The screenplay by Ranald MacDougall (from a play by Eileen Tighe and Graeme Lorimer) contained a number of sharply funny lines, which Davis delivered with surprising aplomb, bolstered by Montgomery's easy charm. Bretaigne Windust directed a good cast that included Fay Bainter (in another patented wise-friend-of-the-heroine role) and Tom Tully, Barbara Bates, Betty Lynn, and Marjorie Bennett as a small-town family.

For Bette Davis, playing an aggressive boss-lady in *June Bride* was clearly a lark, a welcome respite before returning to tear-drenched dramas. (The following year she appeared in *Beyond the Forest*, an overwrought soap-opera and her last Warners film for many years.) For an actress like Rosalind Russell, however, the boss-lady was a

CHRISTMAS IN CONNECTICUT (1945). Magazine editor Barbara Stanwyck finds herself mellowing with naval hero Dennis Morgan.

JUNE BRIDE (1948). Editor Linda Gilman (Bette Davis) and her star reporter and ex-lover Carey Jackson (Robert Montgomery).

definitive characterization, to be refined in film after film throughout
the forties. Elaborately gowned or smartly turned out in a business
suit, her voice ringing out notes of haughty amusement, condescen-
sion, or mild dismay, she perfected the image of the career woman,
too busy for romance, but too womanly to ignore it completely.

In *Take a Letter, Darling*, she had leaped from behind her executive
desk into the waiting arms of Fred MacMurray. In Columbia's *What
Woman* (1943), she took much longer to realize that she loved magazine writer Brian Aherne. In this foolish but pleasant comedy, she
played Carol Ainsley, the country's most successful literary agent,
who is assigned to locate a new actor for the lead in the film version
of the fabulously successful novel she sold to the movies. She settles
on the author himself, a ruggedly handsome but straitlaced college
teacher named Michael Cobb (Willard Parker), who wrote the book
under a pseudonym. She lures him into accepting the role but trouble
sets in when the sober professor misconstrues her interest in him and
turns into a raging Romeo. He pursues her relentlessly, even to the
point of deluding himself that they are engaged, but she succeeds in
extricating herself from the dilemma. Finally, she admits her love for
capricious writer Henry Pepper (Aherne).

As Henry Pepper, assigned by *Knickerbocker* magazine to write a
profile of Carol, Brian Aherne is given the obligatory lines for this
species of comedy. At first amused and mildly annoyed by her "blank
efficiency," he tells her that "only ten percent of you exists." But
later, when he begins to truly care for her, his criticism takes on a
more urgent edge, as he remarks: "You never felt anything in your
life." She resists his amorous advances but of course there are tears
in her eyes (also obligatory) after she sends him packing. It takes only
a few more scenes for Carol to settle for a happy, nonbusiness existence as Mrs. Henry Pepper.

Since neither Irving Cummings' direction nor the Therese Lewis–
Barry Trivers scenario (from a story by Erik Charell) is very helpful,
the burden for making *What a Woman* tolerably entertaining rests on
Rosalind Russell's broad shoulders, and she comes through with a
typically expert comedy performance. The gleam in her eyes at the
first sight of Michael Cobb, her desperation and exhaustion as he
drags her about the room in an abandoned rhumba, her looks of icy
disdain for Henry Pepper's theories about her childhood—these and
other moods ranging from glee to exasperation are conveyed with
finesse by this thoroughly professional comedienne. Brian Aherne
merely repeats his performance in Paramount's *Skylark* the year

WHAT A WOMAN (1943). Writer Brian Aherne lights a cigarette for authors'
agent Rosalind Russell.

DESIGN FOR SCANDAL (1942). Judge Cornelia Porter (Rosalind Russell) takes
a wary look at Jeff Sherman (Walter Pidgeon).

before—that of the whimsical spirit urging the heroine to throw aside discretion and "live"—and Willard Parker overplays Michael Cobb badly. But Russell remains elegantly right, blissfully unaware that she may be the only surviving passenger on a sinking ship.

As a figure of authority fully in command of her fate, Russell appeared in other comedies throughout the forties, all dominated by her forceful personality. In MGM's *Design for Scandal* (1942), she was directed by Norman Taurog as Judge Cornelia Porter, who decrees that tycoon Judson Blair (Edward Arnold) must pay $4,000 weekly to a girl whose "affections" he has slighted. Irate at the decision, Blair hires one Jeff Sherman (Walter Pidgeon) to discover the lady's weakness, only to learn that Jeff himself is her weakness. The Lionel Houser screenplay moved briskly through some predictable plot maneuvers. In Columbia's *She Wouldn't Say Yes* (1945), the title told the story. As prominent psychiatrist Susan Lane, she again found herself castigated by an amorous fellow for her inhibitions and lack of emotional response—and, of course, her disinclination to fall in love. This time he was a jaunty comic-strip artist (Lee Bowman), and he was encouraged by Dr. Lane's whimsical father, played by Charles Winninger. The tired scenario, courtesy of Virginia Van Upp, John Jacoby, and Sarett Tobias (from a story by Laslo Gorog and William Thiele), was limply directed by Alexander Hall.

Seven years after *Design for Scandal*, Rosalind Russell again had her eye on the judge's bench. In Columbia's *Tell It to the Judge* (1949), directed by Norman Foster, she played prominent lawyer Marsha Meredith, anxious to be appointed a federal judge, who divorces her lawyer husband Pete (Robert Cummings) when she catches him with dumb blonde Marie MacDonald. Most of Nat Perrin's screenplay (from a story by Devery Freeman) involved his frantic efforts to win her back. He pursues her from Florida to the Adirondacks, where Marsha is obliged to pretend being married to amorous playboy Gig Young (who else?). The comedy's funniest scene had Cummings and Young competing in a ski competition but there was enough pell-mell activity by the hard-working cast to guarantee at least a few laughs. Reliable old Harry Davenport was present as Russell's father.

Rosalind Russell may have dominated the movie market for lady executives, editors, and judges, but it remained for Irene Dunne to achieve elective office. In Columbia's *Together Again* (1944), she played Anne Crandall, mayor of the small town of Brookhaven, whose late husband had been mayor before her. Afflicted with what her father-in-law (Charles Coburn) calls "a swollen sense of duty,"

SHE WOULDN'T SAY YES (1945). A crucial moment with Percy Kilbride, Rosalind Russell, Charles Winninger, and Lee Bowman.

TELL IT TO THE JUDGE (1949). Lawyer Rosalind Russell is assisted by her disgruntled ex-husband, Robert Cummings.

TOGETHER AGAIN (1944). Small-town mayor Irene Dunne is courted by sculptor Charles Boyer.

ADAM'S RIB (1949). Amanda Bonner (Katharine Hepburn) breaks into tears at wrongful "abuse" of husband Adam (Spencer Tracy).

THEODORA GOES WILD (1936). A liberated Irene Dunne disconcerts Melvyn
Douglas while the ladies of Lynnfield look on.

LADY IN THE DARK (1944). A restaurant encounter with Ray Milland, Frances
Robinson, Jon Hall, and Ginger Rogers.

she has remained a widow. She claims, nevertheless, to be a "free soul," entirely happy and secure in her life. Then an electrical storm knocks the head off her late husband's statue and she goes to New York to interview sculptor George Corday for the job of creating a new statue. The sculptor turns out to be suave, romantic Charles Boyer, and thereby hangs the tale of *Together Again.*

Under Charles Vidor's direction, the F. Hugh Herbert–Virginia Van Upp screenplay (from a story by Stanley Russell and Herbert Biberman) moves agreeably through a number of unsurprising turns, as Corday finds Mayor Crandall enchanting, and she tries to resist his Gallic charm. For a while the film is pleasurable as the two players conduct their bemused, understated courtship, she trying delicately to keep her attraction under control, he discreetly biding his time, amused by her reticence. (In an amusing scene, he finally whispers a proposal of marriage to her while they attend her stepdaughter's piano recital.) Unfortunately, after he follows her home, the film plummets into silliness as the stepdaughter (Mona Freeman) gets the mistaken impression that George wants to marry *her,* while her callow boyfriend (Jerome Courtland) starts believing that *he* is engaged to Anne. Despite stalwart efforts by Dunne and Boyer, the film shows signs of strain at mid-point and eventually collapses into frantic farce.

By the late forties, the boss-lady and all her attendant professional women were becoming figures out of the movie past, although now and again they surfaced, ready to succumb to romance, or to be cut down to size by some persistent male. One conspicuous exception to this Hollywood-formed idea of the compliant female closed out the decade in high style and showed that *some* women were a formidable match for men. This was Amanda Bonner, lawyer and ardent defender of women's rights, as played by Katharine Hepburn in MGM's 1949 comedy, *Adam's Rib.*

In this scintillating Ruth Gordon–Garson Kanin screenplay, Amanda, the outspoken wife of Assistant District Attorney Adam Bonner (Spencer Tracy), decides to confront her husband as an adversary in the courtroom by defending a woman accused of shooting her unfaithful husband. For Amanda it is a matter of principle: women should (but seldom do) have equal rights before the law, and she is determined to take a stand. ("Lots of things a man can do and in society's eyes it's all honky-dory. A woman does the same things, and she's an outcast.") For Adam, a crime is a crime, regardless of sex, and he becomes increasingly furious with her "causy" attitude. ("You're shaking the tail of the law, Amanda, and I don't like it.")

ADAM'S RIB (1949). At the trial: prosecutor Adam Bonner (Spencer Tracy), defendant Doris Attinger (Judy Holliday), and defense attorney Amanda Bonner (Katharine Hepburn).

Loving each other and yet bitterly at odds in the courtroom, Adam and Amanda begin a duel of wits in the familiar but always dazzling and elegant style that perhaps only Tracy and Hepburn could carry off together. To prove her point, Amanda summons a series of women witnesses—a chemist, a factory foreman—each of whom demonstrates that women can excel in occupations usually reserved for men. The last is a circus weight-lifter named Olympia LaPere (Hope Emerson) who, in a hilarious moment, lifts a startled Adam into the air to display her prowess.

Irate at Amanda's courtroom antics, Adam reaches the breaking point and is even willing to dissolve their marriage. In a speech that would surely make a seventies advocate of Women's Liberation turn pale, he tells her: "All of a sudden I don't like being married to what's known as the *new* woman! I want a wife—not a competitor! *Competitor! Competitor!*" But Amanda will not compromise her principles, and they separate. His final, irrevocable ploy occurs when he walks in on Amanda as she is being embraced by her whimsical longtime admirer, Kip Lurie (David Wayne). In a jealous rage he pulls out a gun, threatening to shoot them both, but when Amanda shouts *"You have no right!"*, he proceeds to eat the barrel—the "gun" is merely licorice! Those are the exact words Adam has wanted to hear, and he feels vindicated. Their divorce seems inevitable but in their lawyer's office, brought together for a property settlement, Adam uses some fake "tears" to soften Amanda's stance, and they decide to stay together.

In *Adam's Rib*, all elements combine to create one of the screen's best comedies: the witty and observant scenario, George Cukor's expert direction, and the smooth teamwork of Hepburn and Tracy. Yet even their silken professionalism pales before the presence of Judy Holliday as Doris Attinger, the defendant in the case. In her first major role, she is memorable as a lady of basic needs and straightforward emotions saddled with a wandering husband who despises her. Questioning her at police headquarters, Amanda asks: "After you shot him, how did you feel then?" Doris replies: "Hungry." (She had trailed her husband throughout the fatal day, munching candy bars.) On the stand, she gives a precise and extremely funny description of her rocky marriage. ("I says: 'Don't you try to make some kind of part-timer out of me.' So he says: 'Bite your lip, Fatso.' ")

Equally good are Tom Ewell in his film debut as the wounded husband, turned into a "nervous wreck" by his "crazy" wife; Jean Hagen, also in a screen debut, as his simpleminded paramour Beryl Caign (On the witness stand, she is asked by Amanda if Attinger ever "touched" her before. ("We used to shake hands a lot," she replies), and David Wayne as Kip, Amanda's persistent and slightly obnoxious song-writing suitor whose tune in her honor, "Farewell, Amanda," was actually written for the movie by Cole Porter.

These, then, were the forceful ladies who made their mark and cut their professional niche in Hollywood's Never-Never Land, only to discover that in this land at least, love and marriage were the only real goals, and the men who brought them both were the only true necessities. A pernicious lie, no doubt, and the Women's Liberation movement would not approve. But in Never-Never Land, Women's Liberation is the stuff of farce.

CHAPTER NINE

THE AMAZING MR. STURGES

"This is the land of opportunity. Everybody lives by chiseling everybody else."—Akim Tamiroff to Brian Donlevy in *The Great McGinty*

"There's a lot to be said for making people laugh! It isn't much but it's better than nothing in this cockeyed caravan!"—Joel McCrea in *Sullivan's Travels*

A wealthy young man who prefers snakes to women meets the girl of his dreams and reacts by continually tripping and falling. A stammering, small-town boob who keeps breaking out in spots turns up at his 1944 wedding wearing a World War I uniform. An eccentric millionaire insists on recording minute expenditures in his little black book. A bus filled with scrounging Hollywood types careens down the road in mad pursuit of a hot-rod jalopy.

Lunatics all? No, merely the inhabitants of a special film world, irrational, irreverent, ferocious, and funny, created by writer-director Preston Sturges. Appearing in the early forties at a time when most films were striving to celebrate America's virtues either in patriotic spectacles or in nostalgic hymns to the past, Sturges' films used slapstick as a weapon to poke gentle (and sometimes not so gentle) fun at the country's most cherished ideals and most ill-advised pretensions. From *The Great McGinty* (1940) to *Hail the Conquering Hero* (1944), he thumbed his nose at politics, romance, heroism, motherhood, and the "serious" intentions of many of his colleagues in motion pictures. When he declined badly after *Hail the Conquering Hero*, the screen lost one of its genuine originals, a brilliant but untidy jester whose witticisms were occasionally tinged with bitterness and malice.

Some of the harshness beneath the custard-pie slapstick of Sturges' films may have been the result of a highly unorthodox life. He was born in Chicago in 1898, the son of Solomon Sturges, a stockbroker and socialite, and Mary Dempsey (later Mary Desti), who was a close friend of Isadora Duncan. Determined to make her son an "artist," she apparently forced him to accompany her from gallery to gallery, from opera to opera. (He is reputed to have said: "I was dragged into every goddamn museum in the world.") The result was young Sturges' aversion to "aesthetics" and "culture," coupled with a strong desire to succeed in the business world. At sixteen, he was the manager of one of the branches of his mother's cosmetics firm. After serving in the Air Corps during World War I, he returned to the firm, Maison Desti, where he invented the first nonsmear, kissproof lipstick. When he left the cosmetic business, he worked for years as a free-lance inventor, but nothing succeeded.

A dejected failure at thirty, Sturges was suddenly obliged to think about the direction of his life when he was rushed to a Chicago hospital with a ruptured appendix. He lay on his back for six weeks, solemnly vowing to achieve success—as a playwright. After working for a time as a stage manager, he reached his goal with his second play, *Strictly Dishonorable.* A lively comedy about a romance in a speakeasy between an Italian opera singer (Tullio Carminati) and a Southern belle (Muriel Kirkland), it opened in September, 1929 to excellent reviews and was the first success of the season. The play ran for sixty-nine weeks and was filmed twice, in 1931 and then in 1951 as a vehicle for MGM's short-lived "mature" star, Ezio Pinza.

His next three plays, however, were failures. *The Well of Romance,* an operetta, ran for eight performances in 1930, with Norma Terris, the star of the original *Show Boat,* in the leading role. Also in 1930, his drama *Recapture,* with a plot strikingly similar to Noël Coward's *Private Lives* (divorced couple meet and rekindle their love), fared badly. Melvyn Douglas starred with Ann Andrews and Glenda Farrell, but the play lasted only twenty-four performances. *Child of Manhattan,* a comedy about a dance hall hostess (Dorothy Hall) who has an affair with a wealthy New Yorker (Reginald Owen), opened in March, 1932 and ran for eighty-seven performances. The cast included Jessie Ralph, who played many a salty old lady in thirties films, and Douglas Dumbrille, one of the best-known stock villains in the thirties and forties. The play was filmed in 1933 with Nancy Carroll and John Boles.

Discouraged by his inability to repeat the success of *Strictly Dishon-*

orable, Sturges went to Hollywood to make his mark as a screenwriter. In the thirties, he wrote or collaborated on a number of scenarios, ranging from *The Power and the Glory* (1933), a striking and unusual forerunner of *Citizen Kane,* to *Remember the Night* (1940), a pleasant comedy-drama for Paramount. Not surprisingly, the comedy screenplays on which he worked alone proved to be the most successful. *The Good Fairy* (1935) was an airy confection from Ferenc Molnar's play. *Easy Living* (1937) was a bright Cinderella tale that gave Jean Arthur one of her best opportunities to shine in the thirties and featured the slapstick Automat scene that, more than any other, foreshadowed Sturges' penchant for knockabout farce in the forties. Other efforts included Universal's *Diamond Jim* (1935), a highly fictitious biography of the legendary "Diamond Jim" Brady; MGM's *Port of Seven Seas* (1938), a groping attempt to film an English version of Marcel Pagnol's *Fanny,* that well-known tale of life among Marseilles fishermen; and Paramount's *If I Were King* (1938), a colorful, nonmusical version of Justin Huntly McCarthy's fanciful play about poetrogue François Villon.

Though *Easy Living* was closest to the sort of comedy Sturges would create at Paramount in the forties, his screenplay for *Remember the Night,* his last before turning to direction, has several glowing virtues that make it a highly watchable movie. Its tale of an earnest young assistant district attorney (Fred MacMurray) who falls in love with the contrite jewel thief (Barbara Stanwyck) he is obliged to prosecute is hardly original, but Sturges' script and Mitchell Leisen's unforced direction make something warm and genial out of the familiar material. The long central section of the screenplay, in which attorney John Sargent brings Lee Leander home to his Indiana farm to spend the Christmas holiday with his family before her trial, is graced with a sentiment that is appealing rather than maudlin. As Lee settles in with John's mother (Beulah Bondi), aunt (Elizabeth Patterson), and handyman (Sterling Holloway), she is touched by their mutual concern and devotion.* (In an earlier scene, she had held a painful reunion with her slatternly mother after many years. "I'd forgotten how much that woman hates me," she tells John, "and how much I hate her!") Though she loves John, Lee recognizes that any permanent relationship is out of the question, since it would damage

---

*One oddly moving scene, somehow remembered by many filmgoers, occurs when the family is gathered together in the evening to rest and talk. Sterling Holloway breaks into a chorus of "The End of a Perfect Day," and this unparalleled moment of rural nostalgia stays in the mind.

REMEMBER THE NIGHT (1940). Fred MacMurray and Barbara Stanwyck share a happy moment in his Indiana home, watched by handyman Sterling Holloway.

THE GREAT MCGINTY (1940). Dan McGinty (Brian Donlevy) is sworn in as governor. Behind him: Allyn Joslyn, Muriel Angelus, and William Demarest.

his career and hurt his mother, who has learned of her past. In a burst of honesty and integrity, she pleads guilty at her trial, despite John's protests. ("I am guilty. When you make a mistake, you have to pay for it.")

In the middle of all this sacrificial emotion, Sturges takes only one opportunity to insert the sort of scene that would turn up regularly in his forties farces. On their way to Indiana, Lee and John fall asleep in a field and wake up to find themselves surrounded by cows. Arrested by a farmer for trespassing, they are arraigned before the local judge. Lee gives the wrong name, claims she is a "bubble dancer." And John insists he is a steam-fitter named Henry Wadsworth Longfellow. The irate judge is determined to send them to jail for mocking justice, until Lee starts a fire in a waste basket and flees with John.

Following *Remember the Night*, Sturges wrote *The Great McGinty*, which dealt, rowdily and pointedly, with political chicanery in the early years of the century. The studio balked, until Sturges offered to sell it to them for $10—if they allowed him to direct the film. William Le Baron, the Chief of Production, agreed, and Sturges made his debut as a director with a screenplay that revealed his original comic talent and won for him his only Academy Award (Best Original Screenplay).

The story of *The Great McGinty* is told by Dan McGinty (Brian Donlevy) himself, once a leading politician and now a bartender in a banana republic. He relates how, years back, he had changed from a hungry tramp to a nattily dressed "strong-arm" man for New York City's most powerful political boss, known appropriately as the "Boss" (Akim Tamiroff). Their meeting is a memorable encounter: McGinty asks to be paid $74 for voting thirty-seven times for the incumbent mayor, a willing tool of the Boss'. Intimidated and amused by McGinty's toughness, the Boss slaps him and is slapped in return. "Get your finger out of my face!" McGinty shouts. The Boss is astonished: "He thinks he's me!"

From this point, the film traces McGinty's inevitable rise up the political ladder. As a conscientious collector of protection money for the Boss, he is entirely reasonable (by his standards) with every "client." "You want to be at the mercy of every slug who wears a uniform?" he asks. "You need someone to protect you from human greed." The Boss, of course, is pleased by McGinty's firm methods. Eyeing McGinty's flamboyant jacket, he tells him: "The reason you're alive and walking around in that horse blanket isn't because I like you." But he adds expansively: "This is the land of opportunity.

Everybody lives by chiseling everybody else." Occasionally, the Boss and McGinty battle, and in one hilarious scene we hear them grappling ferociously in the back seat of a car, while the Boss' deadpan lackeys continue their trivial conversation in the front.

When a city-wide shakeup deposes forty-two members of the local government, the Boss decides that a new mayor is badly needed. The obvious candidate: Dan McGinty. McGinty, he decides, has all the necessary attributes but one: a wife. "Marriage," the Boss remarks in a rare moment of sentiment, "has always been the most beautiful set-up between the sexes." McGinty is indignant at first but is surprised to find a willing "partner" in his pretty secretary Catherine (Muriel Angelus), who has always loved him. With a new wife and the Boss' backing, McGinty wins an easy victory for mayor of the city. He even comes to feel genuine affection for Catherine, and his future looks bright.

At this point, under Catherine's righteous, ennobling (and slightly smug) influence—she sincerely believes he's "a fine, honest man of decent impulses"—McGinty begins to reform and the script loses some of its bite and pungency. He tries earnestly to resist; when she tells him to help the poor, he refuses: "They want to be left alone. They like to be dirty." But her blandishments are too strong, and he begins to oppose the Boss' corrupt schemes, especially after being elected governor. (The Boss wants to build a new state capitol building. The "old one ain't safe," he insists.) In a violent quarrel with the Boss, McGinty barely escapes being shot and has the Boss sent to prison as an attempted "assassin." On his own at last, he is supported by Catherine, who insists: "You're going to be the finest governor the state ever had." Ironically, McGinty is now arrested on a graft charge involving a bridge he built when he was mayor. Integrity has come too late, and he is sent to prison.

In an improbable climax, McGinty finds himself in a cell next to the Boss' and together they break out of prison. McGinty flees the country, but not before he has called Catherine to ask her to forget him, and to let her know about the safety deposit box in which his money is hidden. His story ended, McGinty begins a round of fisticuffs with the owner of the bar: the Boss.

As McGinty and the Boss, Brian Donlevy and Akim Tamiroff give surprisingly good performances, with Donlevy adding flavor and color to his usual forthright but dull characterizations, and Tamiroff making a virtue of his customary flamboyance. Best of all is William Demarest, soon to be a regular member of Sturges' "stock" com-

CHRISTMAS IN JULY (1940). The bubble of fame and fortune bursts for Dick Powell and fiancée Ellen Drew. Ernest Truex raises a point of order in the crowd.

THE LADY EVE (1941). Eric Blore, Melville Cooper, Barbara Stanwyck, and Charles Coburn discuss developments.

pany, playing the Boss' chief aide. Listed in the credits only as "the Politician," he offers a persuasive characterization of a man for whom the skulduggery of politics is a way of life. "If you didn't have graft," he tells McGinty, "you'd have a lower class of people in politics." At the end, he turns up in the same bar as McGinty and the Boss, another victim of "honest" politics.

With *The Great McGinty*, Preston Sturges immediately attracted the attention of every critic who thirsted for originality in films. Bosley Crowther's review in the *New York Times* praised the film's "racy wit," and its "superior acceleration of action and a flavor as pungent and infectious as the fumes of a red-fire torch." In the *New Yorker*, Russell Maloney remarked: "If somebody in Hollywood were smart, you could have pictures this good every week in the year, and Mickey Rooney could be sent to a good, strict military school." Otis Ferguson wrote in *Newsweek* that *The Great McGinty* "took delightful and wicked jabs at the various forms of the squeeze, the shakedown, and ballot-stuffing as practiced by a Tammany set-up."

The Great McGinty was lightly sprinkled with satire. Sturges' next film, *Christmas in July* (1940), went one small step further to take on a few easy targets: America's mania for contests of every kind, its fondness for creating "instant" celebrities and "instant" experts, and the mistaken belief that money can be equated with happiness. A minor but likeable Sturges film, it revolves about Jimmy (Dick Powell) and Betty (Ellen Drew), an average engaged couple low in funds, who suddenly find themselves in the middle of a whirlwind when Jimmy is deluded into thinking he has won $25,000 in the Maxford House Coffee Contest.

Sturges' scalpel gleams sharply, cutting through layers of greed and fatuousness, in his first introduction of the Maxford Company president and staff. Here we see many stalwart members of his repertory company assembled for the first time. Caught up in the frenzy of trying to select a winner for their contest are Dr. Maxford (Raymond Walburn), certain that doom is just around the corner—"$25,-000! All that sugar attracts a lot of flies!"; the Maxford radio announcer Don Hartman* (Franklin Pangborn), on the verge of nervous collapse; and a jury of Maxford staff members that cannot decide on a winner. Holding up the decision is the cantankerous Bildocker (William Demarest).

Jimmy, of course, has entered the contest—he apparently enters *every* contest—and he is certain that he has a winner in "If you can't

---

*An inside joke. Don Hartman was a staff writer at Paramount, later a producer and director.

sleep at night, it isn't the coffee, it's the bunk!" With Betty, he dreams of having all that first-prize money: "Everything that means happiness costs money," he tells her, wistfully expressing that fondest of delusions. Then his colleagues at his office decide to carry out a nasty prank. They send him a telegram ostensibly from the Maxford Company, telling him that he's won the contest. Naturally, he erupts into gleeful hysteria, telephoning his mother and sending the office into an uproar.

When he arrives at the Maxford office to collect his prize he causes total confusion, but Maxford, thinking that the jury has decided on a winner without informing him, gives Jimmy the check. Jimmy even achieves immediate status as an "expert" on slogans. When he suggests "Bred in the Bean" as another possibility, Maxford and company nod sagely and find it "functional." Armed with his newfound riches, Jimmy goes on a frantic shopping spree with Betty, buying her a ring ("It's a friendly little piece," the clerk tells him), a sleep sofa, and dozens of other items. He is fawned upon, flattered, and pampered, and his neighbors regard him with awe and delight. (Sturges intrudes one sentimental touch by having Jimmy give a doll to a crippled little girl.)

Of course pandemonium breaks loose at the Maxford Company when Maxford discovers that no winner has actually been chosen, and that he has given $25,000 to a perfect stranger. Furious in the dim-witted way that Raymond Walburn could manage so skillfully, he descends upon Jimmy in the midst of his neighborhood celebration, along with the store manager who had sold Jimmy his furniture. A near-riot ensues but the ending is all too clear: Jimmy has been treacherously deceived and he is just as poor as ever. Later, at the office, his cronies confess their prank, which does little to allay his depression. In a speech worthy of Frank Capra at his most sentimental, Betty defends Jimmy and pleads for "just a chance" for young people like themselves to be happy.

A final scene: the Maxford jury has broken its deadline. Triumphantly, Bildocker announces the winner: "If you can't sleep at night, it isn't the coffee, it's the bunk!"

Sturges followed *Christmas in July* with a sparkling romantic comedy called *The Lady Eve* (1941). Here, the combination of stinging satire and knockabout slapstick that marked his later Paramount films was not yet in evidence. But there were an ample number of Sturgesian turns of phrase and bits of characterization that bespoke an original and inventive sense of comedy.

The hero is a typical Sturges figure: a well-meaning but cotton-headed oaf who finds himself in dilemmas not of his own making. Charles Pike (Henry Fonda) is a wealthy young man whose sole interest is snakes. ("You know me. Nothing but reptiles.") Returning on a boat to New York from an expedition up the Amazon, he meets cardsharps Jean Harrington (Barbara Stanwyck) and her father, "Handsome" Harry (Charles Coburn), in search of a millionaire ripe for bilking. Harry's motto is aptly stated as "Let us be crooked but never common."

Pike, of course, is a first-rate prospect for their conniving, and Jean arranges to meet him by simply tripping him as he passes by and claiming that he has knocked off the heel of her shoe and must accompany her to her cabin. ("Funny our meeting like this," she remarks.) In the cabin, he is overcome by her perfume, though he persists in telling her that he cares only about snakes. He also has a special loathing for beer and ale, possibly because his family has made Pike's Ale, "the Ale that won for Yale," for many years. (He is known familiarly as "Hoppsy.") Jean ignores his protests and continues to use her feminine wiles to lure him into a card game. Her only opposition is Hoppsy's suspicious bodyguard Muggsy (William Demarest), who has had previous dealings with slick operators like Jean.

Jean introduces Hoppsy to her father ("He does card tricks"), who comments: "You look as honest as we do." At the same time she continues her efforts to seduce him in scenes that are well written and played. "You have a definite nose," he tells her shakily. Coyly, she asks: "Do you like any of the rest of me?" "You're certainly a funny girl for anyone to meet who's been up the Amazon," he comments. In the time-honored tradition of romantic comedy, she finds herself falling in love with the "poor fish" and reluctant to make him a victim. "I'm going to be exactly the way he thinks I am," she tells her father. Harry's reaction is glum: "Children don't respect their parents any more."

He is even more glum when the card game finally takes place and Jean deliberately outfoxes her father so that Hoppsy will lose very little. But when she leaves, Harry manages to trick Hoppsy into giving up a large sum. "This is very embarrassing," he tells Hoppsy, but quickly adds: "Just make it out to cash. $32,000—and no cents." Later, he pretends to tear up the check for Jean's benefit, and even pretends to be thunderstruck when Hoppsy announces that he wants to marry Jean.

Jean and Hoppsy are now genuinely in love, but then Hoppsy learns the truth about her and her father from the ship's purser and is bitterly disillusioned. Jean tries to explain that she did try to snare him, but now loves him, "which wasn't in the cards." To soothe his injured pride, he insists that he knew about her plan all along, and now Jean feels "cheap and hurt." She vows to get even with him at the earliest opportunity. Her chance comes at the races where she meets the dapper Sir Alfred McGlennan Keith (Eric Blore), a fellow cardsharp playing the contract bridge circuit in Connecticut. He is now a houseguest of the Pikes and has known Hoppsy since he was a boy ("a tall, backward boy always toying with toads"). He is even fond of Hoppsy's product: "I positively swill in his ale." Jean asks if she could visit him there as his "niece." "I've been British before," she tells him. "Glenny" agrees to the ruse.

From this point, the film brightens noticeably as Sturges assembles the principals at the Pike house for a merry round of deception and romantic raillery. At the house, the elder Mr. Pike (rotund Eugene Pallette at his most crotchety) is incensed at the confusion surrounding the party they are giving that evening. Finding no food for breakfast at his table, he clashes the dish covers together like cymbals. At the same time, the cook is in a fury, and the butler is walking about with one of Hoppsy's snakes draped about his leg.

At the party, Glenny arrives with Jean on his arm, now transformed into the ravishing Lady Eve Sidwich. She proceeds to captivate every man with her beauty, humor, and charm, but Hoppsy, startled by her resemblance to Jean, reacts with a series of hilarious and beautifully timed pratfalls, once getting himself enveloped in drapes. Muggsy is convinced that the Lady Eve *is* Jean Harrington, but Hoppsy insists, "They look too much alike to be the same." At dinner, Jean regales the guests with a description of how she came to America in a submarine, while Muggsy tries to get close to her. In his zeal to expose her, he only ends up quarreling with the servants and dumping a tray on Hoppsy. Meanwhile Glenny tells Hoppsy a wild story about Jean being the daughter of the coachman in her British household.

Jean's plot is now to "hook" Hoppsy and then drop him in six weeks. Completely enchanted by her, he finally proposes marriage, and she accepts. On a train, headed for their honeymoon, Jean gets her "revenge" in a scene that is the best-remembered in the film. As he tries to get amorous, she tells him all about her previous "marriages": first to Angus, a stableboy on her father's estate, followed by Herman, Vernon, Cecil, and others. Each time, as she begins to relate the lurid details, the train goes into a tunnel and the roar of the train cleverly punctuates her sordid confessions. Hoppsy flees into the

Left:

THE LADY EVE (1941). As "Lady Eve Sidwich" Barbara Stanwyck dazzles the junior and elder Pikes (Henry Fonda and Eugene Pallette).

SULLIVAN'S TRAVELS (1942). Sullivan (Joel McCrea) and the Girl (Veronica Lake) on the road.

SULLIVAN'S TRAVELS (1942). Sullivan (Joel McCrea) and the Girl (Veronica Lake) at his Hollywood home.

night, and shortly afterwards he is asking for an annulment. Harry sees this as a splendid opportunity to make a large sum of money, but Jean now regrets her actions and realizes that she still loves him. On a boat to the Amazon, as Jean Harrington, she is reunited with him. "I'm married," he tells her. "So am I," she retorts, and the film ends with the jaunty animated snake that had appeared on the front titles now draped, exhausted, across the end title.

Though the film is not without flaws (Jean's revenge, the crux of the film, seems far-fetched and excessive), it is still sleekly entertaining, with Stanwyck at her best as the hard-as-nails but basically womanly Jean-Eve and Coburn in good form as Handsome Harry. Once again, much of the pleasure comes from Sturges' astute casting of supporting roles, with Eugene Pallette, Eric Blore, and William Demarest giving the story an added measure of color and bite. (The film was poorly remade in 1956 as *The Birds and the Bees*, with George Gobel, Mitzi Gaynor, and David Niven in the Fonda-Stanwyck-Coburn roles.)

Early in 1942, Paramount released Sturges' next and most unusual film. Apparently, as war raged in Europe and threatened to engulf the United States, Sturges had felt that he needed to justify his preoccupation with frivolous and lighthearted matters in his comedies. At the same time, he was clearly irritated with film producers who insisted on investing their films with what they considered "significance" and stark "realism." At any rate, he dedicated *Sullivan's Travels* "to the memory of those who made us laugh," and this brilliant and curious film has as its theme the value—and even the importance—of comedy in a tragic world.

One of the few Sturges comedies to blend serious and even grim ingredients with the usual dosage of slapstick, *Sullivan's Travels* centers on film director John L. Sullivan (Joel McCrea), who is tired of working on movies with such titles as *Hey, Hey in the Hayloft* and *Ants in Your Plants of 1939* and now wants to "hold a mirror up to life," to create "a canvas of suffering humanity." "I want to direct a film," he states, "that will reveal the "sociological and artistic potentialities of the medium." (Its working title: *Brother, Where Art Thou?*) When he asserts that he wants to show "life's garbage cans," his lackeys ask: "What do you know about garbage cans?"

Sullivan decides to learn about life at first hand by hitting the road in shabby clothes, with ten cents in his pocket. His butler (Robert Grieg) is highly skeptical. "Isn't that overdoing it a bit?" he asks. "The poor know all about poverty. Only the morbid rich would find the subject interesting." He warns Sullivan about poverty: "Greed. Criminality. Filth. Despair. These are only a few of its symptoms."

But Sullivan is determined to set out on his personal odyssey. On the road, he is followed at a discreet distance by a bus carrying his nervous staff and other studio people anxious to guard their interests. When he hitches a ride with a teenaged hot-rodder, the bus tries frantically to catch up with him, resulting in an uproarious chase scene, one of the funniest in films. As the bus pursues Sullivan at breakneck speed, the police race after the bus, and the result is a comic symphony of sirens, screeching brakes, and near-collisions. Sullivan continues on his way alone, telling his staff that he'll meet them in Las Vegas in two weeks.

After an absurd adventure with two spinster sisters (Esther Howard and Almira Sessions), Sullivan finds himself back in Hollywood, where, in a diner, he meets a hungry, despondent girl (Veronica Lake) who is ready to return home after failing to find a job in films. He offers to let her stay in his house for two weeks while he's away, and they discuss Sullivan the director and his movies. In the film's first of many swipes at serious films, she tells him that she liked his film *Hey, Hey in the Hayloft* and that "there's nothing like a deep-dish picture to drive you into the open."

With the girl in tow, Sullivan goes on his way but soon they are thrown into jail for stealing his own car and he is obliged to reveal his true identity to her. Angry at first, she asks him to take her along on his experiment. In a marvelous scene, Sullivan's people arrange his schedule for his earnest voyage into poverty. On the telephone with the railroad, his butler asks: "Does that train carry tramps?" He is driven to a freight train in his limousine, accompanied by the girl, now disguised as an improbable boy. They join a tramp colony where one of the residents observes them and comments bluntly to another: "Amateurs." And in fact, with the girl whining and hungry, with Sullivan sneezing badly in the drafty train, it appears that the comment is apt.

Sullivan's first encounter with "reality" in the hobo colony seems to echo his butler's warning about the dire symptoms of poverty. The camera pans across the lost, ravaged, lonely faces of the tramps, dwelling on the depressing community shower rooms, the awful food, the cramped sleeping quarters. This sort of existence, Sturges appears to be telling us (and Sullivan), is too bleak, too harsh to be depicted in films, and Sullivan duly flees from the colony back to the studio. Yet Sturges' point is marred by having the tramp colony patently phony and self-consciously photographed from Hollywood's traditional point of view (as in *Man's Castle*, 1933, or *My Man Godfrey*, 1936).

Now Sullivan has a simpler plan that will ease his conscience but keep him away from hobo colonies. He will give away money, five dollars at a time, to the needy poor. The studio publicizes his "generosity" and a lackey admiringly asks: "Doesn't that give you a lump in your throat?" At the same time, Sullivan tells the girl about his wife. He is married to a "vulture"—he is unable to get a divorce without collusion, and he "won't collude."

At this point, the film takes a strange and unexpected turn and the slightly sour humor of the first part becomes rancid. Handing out his five-dollar bills, Sullivan is followed by a tramp who knocks him down and steals his wallet. In his flight, the tramp drops it on a railroad track and is killed by a speeding train (a vivid and harrowing sequence). When his body is found, it is assumed that he is Sullivan, and the director's death is announced in the newspapers.

Waking up in a freight car, bewildered and groggy, Sullivan is treated brutally by the guard who finds him and he strikes back. In an oddly expressionistic scene, he is brought to trial and sentenced to six years at hard labor in a vicious prison. Beaten furiously when he tries to reveal his identity, he ends up in the "sweatbox" designed to reduce a "troublesome" prisoner to abject surrender. Sullivan is virtually destroyed as a human being, until an evening when he is led with other convicts into a Negro church where they watch a Disney cartoon. As the hard-bitten convicts dissolve in hysterical laughter, Sullivan perceives that the laughter supplied by movies is a soothing balm for the wounds of the wretched and downtrodden of the earth.

He announces: "I haven't got the time to spend here" and confesses to the murder of "Sullivan." The public uproar uncovers the full story and he is restored to his former position. (His wife has conveniently divorced him.) Now he is certain that he doesn't want to make *Brother, Where Art Thou?*, but a comedy film. In a closing speech presumably expressing Sturges' own feelings, he proclaims: "There's a lot to be said for making people laugh! It isn't much but it's better than nothing in this cockeyed caravan!"

More than an abrupt change of mood in what is essentially a comedy, this long section involving Sullivan's plight as a chain-gang convict is an uncertain and unconvincing expression of Sturges' attitude toward the responsibilities of film-makers. Sturges seems to be saying that like himself, they should devote their time to making

THE PALM BEACH STORY (1942). Gerry (Claudette Colbert) and her husband Tom (Joel McCrea).

THE PALM BEACH STORY (1942). A meeting of the principals: Joel McCrea, Rudy Vallee, Mary Astor, and Claudette Colbert.

people (the Negroes and convicts in the church, for example) laugh and forget their troubles—that "real" life is too grim, too horrifying to be mirrored on the screen. Yet the scenes with which he chooses to demonstrate sordid reality are every bit as phony as the tinsel and glitter Sullivan wants to put behind him. The incidents in the brutal prison are as "stagey," as artfully calculated, as those in the hobo colony. Ironically, these scenes belong, not in *Sullivan's Travels*, but in *Brother, Where Art Thou?*, the pretentious movie Sullivan would have made before his "travels."

Despite its cloudy viewpoint, *Sullivan's Travels* is a fascinating film, ably performed by the Sturges company of players. As Sullivan, Joel McCrea even drops his usual flat, gray manner and invests the role with a reasonable amount of flesh and blood. As the girl who accompanies him on his journey, Veronica Lake gives her familiar toneless readings of the lines, but she is still recognizable as a person instead of a manufactured Hollywood product. William Demarest, Franklin Pangborn, Porter Hall, and Robert Warwick make a fine group of studio lackeys and except for the sodden drama in the second half, the film has solid virtues as another original contribution from Preston Sturges.

Most of the critics of the day found the film impressive. Bosley Crowther wrote in the *New York Times* that it was "a beautifully trenchant satire, one of the screen's more 'significant' films, and the best social comment made upon Hollywood since *A Star is Born.*" Otis Ferguson's review in the *New Republic* (January 26, 1942) said that the film had "suspense, odd situations, and a lot of crackle in the lines." But he added that the slapstick was "the size of a whaleboat oar." Ferguson wrote: "When [Sturges] wants anything at all in visual effect he does himself the rather serious disservice of talking down to the public as a bunch of mugs, making too much noise and too little connection with the sustained mood of true-to-life."

The Palm Beach Story (1942), Sturges' next film, represented a marked falling-off, though it too had hilarious moments. A madcap marital comedy, it centered on Gerry (Claudette Colbert) and Tom (Joel McCrea), broke and down on their luck. He is an inventor who is currently trying to sell his plan for a new kind of airport. But nobody cares to listen and they are forced to rent their apartment to a rich and eccentric Texan (Robert Dudley), the "Wienie King." ("Lay off 'em," he advises Gerry. "You'll live longer.") When the Texan gives Gerry $700 to pay their debts, Tom is furiously suspicious of the motive—"Sex didn't enter into it, did it?" Gerry loses her temper in turn, claiming he is jealous of any man who tries to help him. Convinced that she is simply no good for him, she leaves to get a divorce.

Over Tom's strenuous objections, Gerry manages to break away and board a train bound for Palm Beach. On the train she meets a group of rowdy millionaires who call themselves the Ale and Quail Club. They adopt her as their "mascot" and in a self-contained section of riotous slapstick, involve her in one noisy fracas after another, shooting up the train and rushing pell-mell through the cars with their hounds. Happily, the members of the club are played by proficient Sturges regulars William Demarest, Jack Norton, Roscoe Ates, Robert Grieg, and Dewey Robinson. Gerry also meets a dim-witted millionaire named John D. Hackensacker III in the ludicrous person of Rudy Vallee.

In Palm Beach Gerry is completely taken over by John who buys her elaborate clothing and jewelry, but also keeps a detailed record of expenses, however small, and carefully evaluates the various prices of breakfast. Gerry also meets John's sister (Mary Astor), a giddy, much-married lady, currently a princess, who has a devoted admirer (Sig Arno) incapable of saying anything but "Neetz!" Noting their vast wealth, Gerry decides to get the money for Tom to build a model of his new-style airport. Meanwhile, Tom has pursued her to Palm Beach and John's yacht.

Disconcerted by Tom's presence, Gerry introduces him as her brother "Captain McGloo" and the princess is immediately taken with him. ("I grow on people—like moss," she tells him after a few days of active pursuit.) Tom is annoyed by Gerry's new wardrobe and also by having to pretend that she is his sister. He is also not pleased by Gerry's efforts to get the money for his airport model from John and tells John that the money Gerry wants is actually for her nasty husband. John, however, is undaunted and continues to court Gerry in his own odd fashion. In a funny climactic scene, he serenades her with "Goodnight, Sweetheart," while Gerry in her room above is resisting and then responding to Tom's amorous attentions. The following morning, Gerry reveals Tom's true identity to John, who is disconsolate. But he perks up considerably when he learns that Gerry has a twin sister. Tom, it turns out, has a twin brother and in a "trick" ending, there is a group marriage with everyone paired off satisfactorily.

Sturges is not able to make much of this thin material, and the humor throughout is only fitful. Serviceable comic ideas are set up,

THE MIRACLE OF MORGAN'S CREEK (1944). The Kockenlocker girls: Emmy
(Diana Lynn) and Trudy (Betty Hutton), and a frightened Norval Jones
(Eddie Bracken).

THE MIRACLE OF MORGAN'S CREEK (1944). Trudy (Betty Hutton) discusses her
plight with lawyer Johnson (Alan Bridge) and sister Emmy (Diana Lynn).

then dropped, and the dialogue is not especially bright. However, *The Palm Beach Story* offers Mary Astor in a delightful performance as the irrepressible and predatory princess and Rudy Vallee in one of the first of his many roles as an addled playboy.

The beginning of 1944 brought Sturges' return to full-bodied satire after the apologia of *Sullivan's Travels,* the romance of *The Lady Eve,* and the marital frivolity of *The Palm Beach Story.* In *The Miracle of Morgan's Creek,* he sought to puncture holes in several of America's most revered institutions: motherhood, marriage, and, as in *Christmas in July,* the fondness for "instant" or "overnight" celebrities.

The movie begins over the credits with excitement rampant in the small town of Morgan's Creek. The town doctor is on the phone with the governor (Brian Donlevy, repeating briefly as McGinty), discussing feverishly how the event will be handled, why it is a matter of national policy, etc. In a flashback, we learn the cause of all this hysteria.

The town constable, named Kockenlocker (William Demarest), is a perennially irate and suspicious man with two daughters, Trudy (Betty Hutton) and Emily (Diana Lynn). For years Trudy has been loved by a meek, stammering idiot named Norval Jones (Eddie Bracken), whom she virtually ignores. She prefers instead to socialize with the soldiers who fill the town. One fatal night, despite the violent objections of her father, Trudy arranges to attend a "farewell" dance for the troops by pretending that Norval is taking her to the movies. She even persuades Norval to let her borrow his car. The party is a wild affair, replete with noisy laughter, group singing—and lots of liquor. (Jack Norton is conspicuously present as an enthusiastic drunk.) At 8:00 A.M., Trudy turns up with Norval's car, tipsy, bedraggled, and with a "Just Married" sign on the car!

In deep trouble, Trudy realizes that she did indeed marry a soldier at the peak of the night's festivities. Unfortunately, she can only remember him as "Private Ratski-Watski" and never gave her own right name to the judge. What is worse, she is pregnant! Practical-minded Emmy suggests an emergency solution: Trudy must find a husband—quickly. The obvious nomination for this honor is Norval Jones. After all, Emmy points out, their father will probably blame him anyway. (Mr. Kockenlocker's opinion of daughters is that they are either pretty and "trouble" or "so homely they hang around the house like Spanish moss.")

Trudy gets Norval to propose easily, but he is so overwhelmed with gratitude, so astonished that she could accept his hopelessness, his ugliness, that she bursts into tears and tells him the true story. Norval becomes a hysterical, stammering mess, covered with spots. "I knew the idea might not appeal to you entirely," Trudy says. With Emmy, Trudy is morose about treating Norval so shabbily: "He went to sewing and cooking classes just to be near me." "How perfect," Emmy comments. "He could take care of the house."

Norval persists in wanting to marry Trudy, despite the circumstances, especially when he hears she is contemplating drowning herself in the creek. "But I'm too good a swimmer," she notes, glumly. Mr. Kockenlocker approves of Norval as a son-in-law and finally Trudy is convinced that marrying Norval is the only solution to her dilemma, even if she runs the risk of committing bigamy. In a very funny scene, Trudy and Norval, accompanied by Emmy, go off to be married, while Mr. Kockenlocker thinks they are off to the movies. Their tearful, emotional farewell completely confounds and bewilders him.

The film's most hilarious scene is the "wedding" of Trudy and Norval. To pretend that he is Private Ratski-Watski, Norval puts on an Army uniform, only it turns out to be a World War I uniform. The ceremony is a comic shambles in which the justice of the peace (Porter Hall) tries to make out their names without success and then causes an uproar when Norval signs his true name by mistake. "Lock the doors!" the justice shouts. "This man is an abductor!" In the resulting chaos, Norval is accused of various crimes, set upon by Trudy's blazingly angry father, and finally tossed into jail. When Mr. Kockenlocker learns about the baby, he goes into shock. "What do you want me to do," he asks, "learn to knit?"

Determined to get Norval to marry Trudy, Constable Kockenlocker desperately tries to get him to escape from his cell, practically handing him a blackjack and opening the rear window, but stupid, honest Norval fails to get the idea. When he does "break out," it is only to step into further trouble as he breaks into the bank at night to steal the bonds he needs to get away, accompanied by the Kockenlockers. Of course he accidentally sets off the alarm, and they flee.

Six months later, Norval returns to find that the Kockenlockers have left town after the constable was fired. He is discovered and arrested again, but now Trudy learns of his plight and loving him after all, is determined to tell the truth and get him freed. Instead she is rushed to the hospital to give birth. With nurses and doctors in disbelieving shock and surprise, her babies are born—*six* of them and all boys!

In the ensuing bedlam, Norval becomes a national hero and the governor not only frees him but puts him in the National Guard with a commission. The headlines read: "MUSSOLINI RESIGNS!" "HITLER DEMANDS RECOUNT!" Trudy's "Ratski-Watski" marriage is annulled and she and Norval are ecstatically happy. The closing legend reads: "Some are born great, some achieve greatness, and some have greatness thrust upon them."

Although it now seems more frantic than funny, *The Miracle of Morgan's Creek* appeared as a refreshing new note on the movie scene. The idea of a pregnant small-town girl trapping an innocent boob into marriage to make her baby legitimate seemed the height of bad taste to many filmgoers, but most critics were delighted by Sturges' thumbing his nose at the sanctity of motherhood, or his demonstrating that moral rightness did not always win over desperate expediency. They enjoyed Sturges' skill with wild farce, or his uncanny ability to cast even the smallest roles with interesting or outlandish types: at the "farewell" party for the soldiers, the trombonist with the band is a formidable matron; a local merchant named Mr. Rafferty turns out to have (with no explanation from the script) a heavy Yiddish accent; a nurse delivering the sextuplets suddenly breaks out with a shout of "Whoopee!"

Writing in the *Nation*, James Agee summed up the general reaction to the film: *"The Miracle of Morgan's* Creek seems to me funnier, more adventurous, more abundant, more intelligent, and more encouraging than anything that has been made in Hollywood for years." Bosley Crowther in the *New York Times* was equally enthusiastic: "A more audacious picture—a more delightfully irreverent one—than this new lot of nonsense has never come slithering madly down the path." Manny Farber, writing in the *New Republic* (February 7, 1944), called it Sturges' "most entertaining film, carried out with speed, positiveness, and pleasure," but he had some perceptive reservations:

> There is always in a Sturges film the feeling that he is above most of his comedy effects and that he is stooping quite far to make use of a comedy of which he realizes the entertainment value, as well as the fact that he realizes that a more profound, devastating picture (which he is more capable of in movies than anyone I know) is impossible in Hollywood and slapstick is a formula to rest comfortably with.

Viewing the film thirty years later, one is inclined to modify the general praise with a few churlish reservations: Betty Hutton is fren-

HAIL THE CONQUERING HERO (1944). "Hero" Woodrow Truesmith (Eddie Bracken) and his girlfriend Libby (Ella Raines).

HAIL THE CONQUERING HERO (1944). Woodrow (Eddie Bracken) surrounded by proud friends and family: (left to right) Freddie Steele, Georgia Caine, Ella Raines, and Elizabeth Patterson.

etic and not very appealing as Trudy, and yet she is a model of charm compared with Eddie Bracken's grating, nerve-wracking performance as Norval. (The *New Yorker* review remarked that they had "apparently been instructed to act as much like incipient breakdown cases as possible.") The best performances are given by William Demarest, combining rage, concern, and muddle-headedness in one perfect characterization; Alan Bridge as the practical and unflappable lawyer Johnson; and Diana Lynn, who gives a nice edge of astringency to the role of Emmy. When her father, whom she clearly loathes, expresses his suspicions of every soldier's intentions, Emmy tells him bluntly: "You have a mind like a swamp."

Later in 1944, Eddie Bracken appeared in the leading role of Sturges' *Hail the Conquering Hero* and though he was no more endearing than in *The Miracle of Morgan's Creek*, the movie was much funnier and in many ways the director's best film. This time his target was even more sacrosanct than motherhood, although he took a few healthy swipes at mother-worship along the way. Here he was aiming at America's devotion to mindless hero-worship, to the wartime penchant for raising a banner to every serviceman who managed to kill more than his quota of the enemy. It was a dangerous subject to be satirizing in 1944, but Sturges' wit and his ability to keep the bitterness within reasonable bounds kept the film from being condemned by patriots.

The "hero" is Woodrow Lafayette Pershing Truesmith (Bracken), glum, lonesome, and decidedly 4–F, who meets six Marines in a bar and tells them his pathetic story: the son of a famous World War I hero, "Hinky Dinky" Truesmith, he has been rejected by the Marines and cannot muster the courage to return home. One of the Marines, a shell-shocked fellow named Bugsy* (Freddie Steele), suffers from a highly advanced mother complex and impulsively calls Woodrow's mother, telling her that Woodrow is a great hero who has distinguished himself in battle.

Much against his will, the terrified Woodrow is forced into putting on a uniform with many decorations and returning to his hometown for a hero's welcome. The townspeople are in an uproar only Sturges (or possibly Capra) could devise: the mayor (Raymond Walburn), a

---

*Calling a shell-shocked Marine "Bugsy" is only one example of Sturges' cruel streak, which sometimes surfaces in his films. Others include his characterization of the spinster sisters in *Sullivan's Travels*, one hatchet-faced and grim, the other foolishly flirtatious; and virtually every scene in *The Miracle of Morgan's Creek*, where the basic situation teeters on the edge of a true, deep-seated nastiness.

blowhard and idiot, is trying to remember his speech, without success; the chairman of the Reception Committee (Franklin Pangborn in a deliriously funny performance) is totally distraught, shouting "Oh, death, where is thy sting?" when the band members begin feuding. Only Woodrow's girlfriend Libby (Ella Raines) is less than ecstatic—while Woodrow was away, she has become engaged to the mayor's son.

Woodrow's reception is glorious—and hilarious. With Pangborn in hysterics, the mayor tries to deliver his speech ("deep humility" . . ."home to the arms of his mother") but is constantly being interrupted by the band. Woodrow's mother is all atwitter at her "hero" and later, in the church, the minister delivers an emotional speech praising Woodrow. Woodrow watches in horror as the minister burns the mortgage on his mother's house, and he is mortified to learn that the town is raising money for a monument reading: "Like Father, Like Son." But the Marine sergeant (William Demarest) is pleased: "Everything is perfect, except for a couple of details." "You can be hanged for a couple of details!" Woodrow wails.

Libby tries to tell him about her engagement, but she is interrupted by a delegation that comes to tell Woodrow he is their candidate for mayor! Desperately, he tries to confess to the assembled townspeople that he is no hero, but they are agog with admiration at his every word. Judge Dennis (Jimmy Conlin) remarks: "He has a natural flair for politics," and his comment on Woodrow's stammering apology is: "That's as fine a political speech as I've heard since Bryant's Crown of Thorns!" To make a bad situation worse, the sergeant regales everyone with melodramatic stories about Woodrow's heroism in saving his life. Hearing that Woodrow will oppose him in the coming election, the mayor is confounded and dismayed.

Woodrow's political steamroller gains momentum. At a rally the sergeant churns up enthusiasm by having the other Marines join in telling fabricated tales about Woodrow: "Every one of these boys is telling the truth, except that they're changing the names a little." Pangborn leads the crowd in a campaign song, beamingly pleased to be in control of the situation for once. When Libby finally manages to tell Woodrow that she is engaged, he reacts with surprising pleasure which causes her to burst into tears. Woodrow tries to tell her the truth about himself but she refuses to believe him and confesses that she still loves him.

Violently upset at the turn of events, the mayor prepares a speech against Woodrow: "Every man must do what he does best—and what

THE GREAT MOMENT (1944). Dr. William Morton (Joel McCrea) continues his experiments with ether, supported by his loyal wife (Betty Field).

UNFAITHFULLY YOURS (1948). A clearly unhappy moment with Sir Alfred de Carter and wife (Rex Harrison and Linda Darnell).

he does best can be done best in Guadalcanal." Only his constantly
hungry aide (Alan Bridge) keeps his wits about him and decides to
check on Woodrow's story. After one frantic but unsuccessful attempt by Woodrow to get out of his dilemma—he fakes a call to his
house saying that Sergeant Truesmith must return to the Marine base
for "limited service"—the mayor receives a telegram stating that no
Woodrow Truesmith ever served in the Marine Corps. Elated, he
plans to expose the hoax, but Woodrow bravely decides to reveal
the truth himself. In a moving speech, he tells the townspeople that
this is "the bitterest day" of his life. "My cup runneth over—with
gall," he says. "The coward is at last cured of his fear. If I could
reach as high as my father's shoestrings, my whole life would be
justified."

To Woodrow's astonishment, his painful candor only serves to
endear him to the town, and a mob assembles outside his house to
urge him to stay and run as an "honest, courageous, veracious"
mayor. Even Libby is breaking her engagement to return to him. It
is the sort of reversal common in American films—hero embraced for
his sins and his failings—but Sturges manages to invest it with an
edge of cynicism and malice, making the townspeople seem more
fatuous and hypocritical than kind and tolerant. As the Marines leave
town, Woodrow, smiling and happy, mouths: "Semper Fidelis."

Hail the Conquering Hero was warmly received by the critics, with the
New York Times calling it "riotously funny" and "one of the wisest ever
to burst from a big-time studio." *Newsweek* wrote: "His latest human
comedy is all of a piece in the blending of satire and broad slapstick,
the deft dialogue, and vivid characterizations." In the *New Yorker*,
John Lardner called it "a fine comic performance," adding: "Mr.
Sturges is . . . a master of an abundant vein of entertainment, and he
is nicely at home in his medium, filling the screen with movement,
people, and droll asides." Only James Agee, writing in the *Nation*,
modified his praise by criticizing the film's failure to follow through
on any one of many themes:

> This film has enough themes for half a dozen first-rate American
> satires—the crippling myth of the dead heroic father, the gentle
> tyranny of the widowed mother, the predicament of the only child,
> the questionable nature of most heroes, the political function of
> returning soldiers, these are just a few . . . But not one of these
> themes is honored by more attention than you get from an incon-
> tinent barber in a railway terminal, and the main theme, which I

take to be a study of honor, is dishonored by every nightingale in Sturges' belfry.*

Yet he called the movie "remarkable" and praised Sturges' "fine and comic gifts." In his anonymous *Time* review, he hailed it as "one of the year's most ingratiating pictures."

None of the five films Sturges wrote and directed after *Hail the Conquering Hero* could match the corrosive wit and ebullience of his early work. *The Great Moment* (1944), originally called *Great Without Glory*, was a very curious film, the mostly serious story of Dr. William Morton, the Boston dentist who successfully demonstrated the use of ether as an anesthetic. Joel McCrea starred as Dr. Morton, earnest and sober-sided, but the supporting cast included William Demarest, Franklin Pangborn, Porter Hall, and other comedians of the Sturges repertory company, who contributed several slapstick sequences in their familiar style. As film biography it was decidedly unconventional, but the mixture of drama and farce bewildered and irritated most audiences, and the film was largely dismissed.

After a four-year hiatus, Sturges returned to films with *Unfaithfully Yours*** (Fox, 1948), an uneven but disarming and often amusing comedy with a clever idea: a volatile symphony conductor (Rex Harrison) suspects his lovely wife (Linda Darnell) of infidelity and while leading his orchestra in several musical selections, he envisions various forms of revenge, all of them broadly acted out. He tries to carry out his first plan—murdering his wife and placing the blame on her lover—but his effort fails comically. The *New York Times* called the film "cheerful entertainment, the work of an adult, agile mind" and praised the "fully and richly presented" symphonic music. But the movie did not attract wide attention.

Sturges' remaining films were minor: *The Beautiful Blonde From Bashful Bend* (Fox, 1949), a generally flat-footed Technicolor farce about a straight-shooting frontier girl (Betty Grable), which brought on a few familiar Sturges people—Rudy Vallee, Porter Hall, Alan Bridge, and Sterling Holloway—for brief but not very funny turns; *Mad Wednesday (The Sin of Harold Diddlebock)* (RKO, 1951), concerning a mild bookkeeper (Harold Lloyd) who goes on a wild spree after being fired—here the cast included a large contingent of Sturges regulars:

*James Agee, *Agee on Film* (New York: McDowell, Obolensky, 1958), p. 16.
**Sturges' film with Harold Lloyd, *The Sin of Harold Diddlebock*, had been produced earlier but it was not released until early in 1951 under a new title, *Mad Wednesday.*

THE FRONT PAGE (1931). Reporter Frank McHugh tangles with prostitute Mae Clarke, while Matt Moore looks on.

Jimmy Conlin, Raymond Walburn, Franklin Pangborn, Alan Bridge, Jack Norton, and Georgia Caine; and *The French They Are a Funny Race* (1957), which Sturges adapted from Pierre Daninos' *The Notebooks of Major Thompson*. This was a tired film about a pompous English major (Jack Buchanan), his French wife (Martine Carol), and his friends. The *New York Times* called it "a generally listless picture, without wit, electricity, or even plot." It was a sad ending to a notable career. Sturges died in 1959.

Over the years, Preston Sturges has been one of the few comedy directors of the sound era to be discussed, explicated, and puzzled over. Even at the height of his career, reputable critics and colleagues wrote about him ambiguously, praising his artistic gifts and condemning his failure to use them fully. In his *Time* review of *The Miracle of Morgan's Creek*, James Agee wrote that Sturges "has given the slick, growing genteelism of U.S. cinema the roughest and the healthiest shaking up it has had since the disease became serious." But a year later, in his review of *Hail the Conquering Hero*, he called Sturges "a never-quite-artist of not-quite-genius." French director René Clair said: "If he could slow down, he would be great; he has an enormous gift, and should be one of our leading creators. I wish he would be a little more selfish and worry about his reputation."

A brilliant, if somewhat overappreciative estimate of Sturges was written by critic Manny Farber in a 1954 essay.* Calling Sturges "the most spectacular manipulator of sheer humor since Mark Twain," and "the most original movie talent produced in recent years," Farber astutely maintained that he was actually the inheritor of silent comedy, who combined its methods, added new perspectives, and developed the whole in a form suitable to the sound film. Sturges' freewheeling dialogue—"his most original contribution to films"— was "a special, jerky, spluttering form of talk that is the analogue of the old, silent-picture firecracker tempo."

From the silent film, Sturges also learned that the only American characteristics that could possibly be satirized were the mania for speed and the equally manic pursuit of success. "The image of success," Farber writes, "stalks every Sturges movie like an unlaid ghost, coloring the plots and supplying the fillip of his funniest scenes." Ironically, the silent comedian who embodied the success-obsessed but disaster-prone purveyor of speed was Harold Lloyd, who starred in Sturges' last American-made film, *Mad Wednesday*.

*Reprinted in Manny Farber, *Negative Space* (New York: Frederick Praeger, 1972), pp. 89–104.

Sturges has often been criticized for his misplaced slapstick, but Farber finds it a defensible virtue: "The nervous tantrums of slapstick in a Sturges movie, the thoughtless, attention-getting antics combined with their genuine cleverness give them an improvised, blatant immediacy that is preferable to excesses of calculation and is, in the long run, healthier for the artists themselves." Farber also defends Sturges' sudden shifts of mood, claiming that the sentimental forgiveness at the end of *Hail the Conquering Hero* is intended ironically and dismissing other mixings of moods, such as the abrupt veering into grim drama of *Sullivan's Travels*, as a "dislike of fixed purposes," a case of "resourcefulness, intelligence, and Barnum-and-Bailey showmanship" misinterpreted as clumsy writing.

Whatever his faults—his muddled points of view, his resorting to easy slapstick, his childish fondness for "comic" names (Hackensacker, Kockenlocker, Diddlebock)—Preston Sturges was unquestionably unique, a gifted if erratic writer-director who created a small but valuable group of film comedies in the early forties. His reputation may have faded slightly, but the gallery of mountebanks, charlatans, blowhards, and stammering victims he brought to life are durable indeed.

CHAPTER TEN

STAGE TO SCREEN

"When I love a woman, I'm an Oriental. It never goes. It never dies."
—John Barrymore in *20th Century*

"For a place with a bad location and no neon sign, we're doing a heck of a business!"—Rosalind Russell in *My Sister Eileen*

The advent of sound brought panic to the movies, evidenced not only by the sudden influx of "elocution" teachers for silent film stars (a phenomenon satirized in *Once in a Lifetime*) but by the studios' desperate search for writers who could replace printed titles with believable, audible dialogue. Words and more words became necessary for even the grating screech of the earliest soundtracks. Inevitably, the movies turned to their arch-enemy, the stage, to recruit playwrights who could turn out badly needed screenplays for sound, or they burrowed deeply into the literature of the stage to find vehicles for their contract players. Some of the silent stars survived; many did not. And a new breed of actors, whose voices and personalities were appropriate for sound, came on the scene.

In the profusion of stage comedies adapted to the screen in the early thirties, not many had a contemporary American ambience. A number of them were adapted from British drawing-room comedies, which offered readily available dialogue that the current crop of players could handle with relative ease. (They were also suited to the still-inflexible cameras, which permitted little venturing outside of single, stationary sets.) John Van Druten's play *After All*, concerning the perennial gap between parents and children, was adapted by MGM into *New Morals for Old* (1932), with Robert Young, Myrna Loy, and Lewis Stone. Three of Noël Coward's comedies—*Private lives*

(1931), *Tonight is Ours* (1933, from *The Queen Was in the Parlor*), and *Design for Living* (1933)—offered good opportunities for rising young players, including Claudette Colbert, Fredric March, Norma Shearer, Gary Cooper, and Miriam Hopkins, to gain needed experience. Somerset Maugham's play *Our Betters* became a 1933 RKO film with Constance Bennett and Gilbert Roland. Even James Barrie's old warhorse of a play, *What Every Woman Knows*, was adapted by MGM in 1934 to permit Helen Hayes to repeat her famous stage role as Maggie Wylie opposite Brian Aherne.

Many of the American plays brought to the screen in the early thirties emulated the British style in their witty, elegant, and sometimes tiresome palaver, their emphasis on discreetly handled love affairs or extramarital dalliances in lavishly appointed sets. *The Animal Kingdom* (RKO, 1932, later remade by Warners as *One More Tomorrow*) dealt with Leslie Howard, married to Myrna Loy, but still in love with old flame Ann Harding. MGM's *Forsaking All Others* (1934), from the play by Edward Barry Roberts and Frank Morgan Cavett, had Joan Crawford in Tallulah Bankhead's stage role as the apex of a triangle, with Clark Gable and Robert Montgomery courting her dutifully at either side. MGM also adapted S. N. Behrman's *Biography* to the screen, adding an unwarranted note of titillation by calling it *Biography of a Bachelor Girl* (1935). Ann Harding was unconvincing as an artist who falls in love with radical editor Robert Montgomery. Other plays-into-films were contributed by genteel women playwrights of the day, including Rose Franken (*Another Language*, MGM, 1933) and Rachel Crothers (*When Ladies Meet*, MGM, 1933; *As Husbands Go*, Fox, 1934).

Comedies based on stage plays with distinctly American characters and attitudes were not as frequent but when they appeared, their brisk pace, slangy dialogue, and brash, unaffected actors made them a welcome relief from the "highfalutin' " milieu of the society films. Lewis Milestone directed Pat O'Brien (in his film debut) and Adolphe Menjou in the first screen version of Ben Hecht and Charles MacArthur's raucous comedy, *The Front Page* (United Artists, 1931).* Edna May Oliver appeared in Minnie Maddern Fiske's stage role as a

---

*About nine years later, Columbia remade this comedy as *His Girl Friday*, turning Pat O'Brien's reporter into a woman (Rosalind Russell) named Hildy Johnson. In her running battle with editor Cary Grant, the pungent Hecht-MacArthur dialogue was delivered at a speed that has possibly never been matched by another film. Howard Hawks directed at a breakneck pace, and Ralph Bellamy, Gene Lockhart, and Porter Hall joined in the antic spirit of what the *New York Times* called "the maddest newspaper comedy of our times."

BIOGRAPHY OF A BACHELOR GIRL (1935). A meeting of editor Richard Kurt (Robert Montgomery), artist Marion Froude (Ann Harding), and composer Melchior Feydak (Edward Arnold).

HIS GIRL FRIDAY (1940). Reporter Hildy Johnson (Rosalind Russell) aims her handbag at editor Walter Burns (Cary Grant).

wealthy and imperious juror in *Ladies of the Jury* (RKO, 1932), adapted from Frederick Ballard's 1929 play. Warners' *Blessed Event* (1932) was an adaptation of the comedy by Manuel Seff and Forrest Wilson about an unscrupulous Winchell-like gossip columnist (Lee Tracy) who tangles with gangsters and a radio crooner (Dick Powell).

Similar stage comedies, all wisecracks and fast action, turned up intermittently as films in the early thirties. Bella and Samuel Spewack adapted their own 1932 play, *Clear All Wires*, for MGM in 1933, offering Lee Tracy as Buckley Joyce Thomas, head of the Chicago Globe's foreign service, whose globe-trotting stunts and outrageous activities make him "the ace of correspondents." Joe E. Brown appeared as a baseball homerun king in Warners' version of Ring Lardener and George M. Cohan's 1928 comedy, *Elmer the Great* (1933). (His role was played on the stage by Walter Huston.) Gertrude Tonkonogy's *Three-Cornered Moon*, about a family of scatterbrains that included Mary Boland and Claudette Colbert, was filmed by Paramount in 1933. In 1934 George Bancroft and Frances Fuller co-starred in *Elmer and Elsie*, Paramount's adaptation of *To the Ladies*, a 1922 comedy by George S. Kaufman and Marc Connolly.

Several comedies were especially noteworthy. In 1932, Universal produced an adaptation of George S. Kaufman and Moss Hart's first major success, *Once in a Lifetime*, a broad and hilarious satire of the coming of sound to Hollywood. Directed by Russell Mack, the Seton I. Miller screenplay wisely preserved much of the lunatic atmosphere of the play as it related the improbable adventures of a trio of Broadway types in the wilds of Beverly Hills. Aline MacMahon gave one of her expert performances as wise, cynical May Daniels, who forms a bogus "elocution" school with cohorts Russell Hopton and Jack Oakie, the latter as a nut-cracking simpleton named George Lewis. Through sheer, dauntless stupidity, George becomes an important fixture at the studio and wins the hand of an aspiring actress (Sidney Fox). Most of the fun came from the authors' barbs at Hollywood's idiotic denizens: the apoplectic head of the studio (Gregory Ratoff in a marvelous performance), the bird-brained actresses (Mona Maris and Carol Tevis), the shrill gossip columnist (Louise Fazenda), and an unflappable receptionist with a short memory (ZaSu Pitts). Onslow Stevens appeared in the role George S. Kaufman himself had played on the stage: the increasingly irritated writer who waits for months to see the studio head.

An even funnier Hollywood spoof was released in 1933. MGM's *Bombshell*, based on a play by Caroline Francke and Mack Crane, gave

BOMBSHELL (1933). Agent Space Hanlon (Lee Tracy) and his temperamental client, Lola Burns (Jean Harlow).

DINNER AT EIGHT (1933). Wallace Beery tangles with wife Jean Harlow.

20TH CENTURY (1934). Mad stage producer Oscar Jaffe (John Barrymore) and his star actress, Lily Garland (Carole Lombard).

THE PURSUIT OF HAPPINESS (1934). In their New England household, Prudence Kirkland (Joan Bennett) discusses matters with her mother (Mary Boland).

Jean Harlow one of her best roles as Lola Burns, a volatile movie star forever caught up in headlined scandals engineered by her publicity agent, Space Hanlon (Lee Tracy). The dialogue by John Lee Mahin and Jules Furthman crackles throughout the film as Space spoils Lola's plans to adopt a baby and even hires an actor (Franchot Tone) to impersonate a wealthy Boston scion in amorous pursuit of Lola. (At one point, overwhelmed by Tone's love-making, she murmurs: "Not even Norma Shearer or Helen Hayes in their nicest pictures were ever spoken to like this!") Harlow's best moment comes in an interview with a gossip columnist in which she prattles on in a mock-elegant style while the columnist makes terse, realistic notes. Harlow concludes with a comment on her scandalous publicity: "I ask you as one lady to another—isn't that a load of clams?"

MGM's impressive roster of leading players helped to make its film version of the George S. Kaufman–Edna Ferber play, *Dinner at Eight,* into one of the most popular movies of 1933. Adapted by Frances Marion and Herman J. Mankiewicz (with additional dialogue by Donald Ogden Stewart) and directed with his usual expertise by George Cukor, *Dinner at Eight* was a comedy-drama that succeeded not because of its screenplay, which had some tragic and soap-operatic elements along with its cutting satirical wit, but because of its fascinating interplay of "star" personalities.

The dinner guests invited to the home of Millicent and Oliver Jordan (Billie Burke and Lionel Barrymore) include: Larry Renault (John Barrymore), a vain but washed-up actor who is having an affair with the Jordans' daughter Paula (Madge Evans); Carlotta Vance (Marie Dressler), a once-glamorous stage star down on her luck; Dr. Wayne Talbot (Edmund Lowe), a society doctor; and Dan and Kitty Packard (Wallace Beery and Jean Harlow), a vulgar, newly rich couple given to violent shouting matches. The situation is complicated by several factors: Oliver Jordan's serious heart condition, Dan Packard's desire to take over Jordan's business, and Dr. Talbot's secret romance with Kitty Packard. By the time the dinner begins, several lives have been changed drastically—and one has ended: Larry Renault has killed himself in a scene superbly played by John Barrymore. (He turns on the gas in his hotel room, then arranges the lighting so that, even in death, his famous profile will be shown to advantage.)

Many of the scenes in *Dinner at Eight* have become legendary: Marie Dressler's reunion with Lionel Barrymore at which she gallantly and bemusedly admits to being in dire need of money after years of riches; John Barrymore's increasing despair as he suffers defeat and humiliation by his agent, the hotel manager, and even the hotel bellboy; and especially Beery and Harlow in their raucous brawl, she propped up in bed all in white and veering from baby talk to brassy invective. As the Jordans' dinner begins, Harlow tells Dressler: "I was reading a book the other day. It's all about civilization or something. Do you know the guy said machinery is going to take the place of every profession?" Dressler responds with a famous line as she ogles Harlow: "Oh, my dear, that's something you'll never have to worry about."

Best of all the early stage-to-screen translations was Columbia's version of Ben Hecht and Charles MacArthur's rowdy farce, *20th Century* (1934). Wilder and, at the same time, more sophisticated than most of the film comedies of the day, it brought together several rare talents for one memorable encounter. Hecht and MacArthur adapted their play to the screen, dropping or changing very little of the original; director Howard Hawks had already proven his ability to rivet an audience's attention with a group of hard-bitten melodramas (*Scarface*, *The Crowd Roars*, etc.); and the stars, John Barrymore and Carole Lombard, were two of the screen's most gifted performers. Lombard, in particular, was ready for a role that would reveal her ability to play slapstick comedy.

All forces converged on *20th Century* and the result was a very funny film. The movie revolves about Oscar Jaffe (Barrymore), a flamboyant and conniving theatrical producer, and his roller-coaster relationship with Lily Garland (Lombard), the girl he develops from a frightened, budding actress named Mildred Plotker into a stage star. His training techniques involve long hours of hard work and screaming ("You're not demonstrating underwear, do you hear?") and even physical violence. (He sticks Lily with a pin to get her to scream realistically.) But his drastic measures work, and on her opening night, Jaffe greets her humbly as a "great actress."

Three years later, however, Lily is rebelling against Oscar's control of her life ("I'm no Trilby!"), and she is determined to leave him for Hollywood and movie stardom. Oscar falls into a violent tantrum, shouting "Oblivion! Oblivion!", and he even threatens suicide, but his agent, Owen O'Malley (Roscoe Karns), knows better: "He won't shoot himself. It would please too many people." Apparently nothing can convince Lily to return to Oscar and spend days listening to him discuss his "genius."

Fate, helped by the writers' machinations, brings them together on

HAVING WONDERFUL TIME (1938). Ginger Rogers and Douglas Fairbanks, Jr. discover each other at a resort camp.

MY SISTER EILEEN (1942). Appopolous (George Tobias) shows his "apartment" to the Sherwood sisters (Janet Blair and Rosalind Russell).

the "20th Century Limited," where most of the film's action takes place. Oscar comes aboard in disguise, hiding from the police for nonpayment of debts and very much down on his luck. His manager, Oliver Webb (Walter Connolly), who has tried to get in touch with Oscar's arch-rival Max Jacobs (born Mandelbaum) and been fired for the umpteenth time for his efforts, learns that Lily is on the train. Oliver pleads with Lily to come back to Oscar—"You're his only chance"—but she is adamant and also perfectly content with her new fiancé, George Smith (Ralph Forbes). When Oscar hears about Lily, he pretends to be just as stubborn: "I wouldn't take that woman back if we were the last two people on earth and the future of the human race depended on us!" His reaction to her new companion: "She's mousing around with boys!"

But of course they meet again, and in an uproarious scene, he begins to court her recklessly. "When I love a woman," he remarks, "I'm an Oriental. It never goes. It never dies." But she is glum: "We're not people. We're lithographs." He tries to tell her about the play he has in mind for her, in which she would play Mary Magdalene ("running the gamut from the gutter to the glory!"), but Lily is unconvinced and hostile. Exasperated, Oscar leaves her with a final volley: "If there's any justice in the world, Mildred Plotker, you'll end up where you belong—in a burlesque house!"

Oscar and Lily are not the only screwballs aboard the train. There are two bearded Russians who want to appear in Oscar's *Passion Play*, and Mr. Clark (Etienne Girardot), a mousy little man with a penchant for placing stickers throughout the train reading, "Repent, for your time is at hand!" Obviously a candidate for a padded cell, Mr. Clark is under the delusion that he is wealthy and gives Oliver a worthless check for backing Oscar's return to the stage. Elated, Oscar begins to order elaborate scenery. But then his troubles mount: he learns to his dismay that the check has no value, he is attacked by the police, who think he is Clark, and then Lily discovers the truth about his generous "backer." "Lily, I've been bamboozled!" he tells her plaintively. But she has also been "bamboozled" once too often.

As Oliver and Owen both get noisily drunk, Oscar decides on one final ruse to win Lily: he pretends to be dying. Tearfully, she fills his "dying" request by signing a contract with him for her next play. When Max Jacobs suddenly appears on the scene, Oscar rises from his "deathbed" like a demented wraith and cackles: "You're too late, Max Mandelbaum!" We last see Oscar and Lily at a rehearsal, still fighting ferociously but together again.

Never slackening in its pace, *20th Century* has the same sort of inspired insanity that Howard Hawks would sustain four years later in *Bringing Up Baby*. Ranging from honeyed tones to ear-piercing bellows, John Barrymore pulls out all stops characteristically, making Oscar Jaffe a kind of outrageous but likeable monster. Lombard here shows the ability to combine both high and low comedy in a single performance, an ability she was to develop more fully in the late thirties. The stars are given exceptionally solid support by Walter Connolly, Roscoe Karns, Etienne Girardot, and Charles Levison as Max Jacobs-Mandelbaum.

In its nervous, broadly mocking style, *20th Century* represented a kind of comedy that was natively American. A number of other stage adaptations of the early and mid-thirties, though often gentler and certainly quieter than the Hecht-MacArthur farce, had a similar feeling for American types and their quirky, teasing, self-disparaging humor.

Several of these comedies were intended as nostalgic evocations of the country's past, colored with mildly spoofing reminders of our naïveté and innocence. Paramount's *The Pursuit of Happiness* (1934), adapted from the Lawrence Langner–Armina Marshall play and directed by Alexander Hall, took up the old colonial custom of "bundling," which permitted an unmarried couple to share a bed on a cold winter's night—provided they were separated by a center-board. The plot hinged on a cheerful, smooth-talking Hessian soldier (Francis Lederer), who disrupts a colonial community by wooing—and attempting to "bundle" with—a virginal local girl named Prudence (Joan Bennett). Mary Boland and Charlie Ruggles played the girl's bewildered parents, and Walter Kingsford, repeating his stage performance, played the zealous, fire-breathing minister who is shocked by Prudence's bundling partner.

Other stage-originated comedies set in the "good old days" appeared about the same time, painting a rose-colored portrait for filmgoers who found the present barely tolerable. The films included: Paramount's *One Sunday Afternoon* (1933), the first screen version of James Hagan's play about the vicissitudes of a dentist (Gary Cooper in Lloyd Nolan's stage role) at the turn of the century;* *The Farmer Takes a Wife* (Fox, 1935), adapted from the Frank B. Elser–Marc

*Warner Brothers filmed the story again, once in 1941 as *The Strawberry Blonde*, with James Cagney, Olivia De Havilland, and Rita Hayworth, and then again in 1948 under its original title, but this time as a Technicolor musical with Dennis Morgan, Janis Paige, and Dorothy Malone.

Connolly play about life on the Erie "Canawl" in the 1850s, with Henry Fonda repeating his stage performance in his screen debut; and *Ah, Wilderness!* (1935), MGM's pleasing adaptation of Eugene O'Neill's comedy of adolescence in the Connecticut of 1906.

As the thirties waned and the forties approached, film versions of stage plays showed contemporary Americans in their native habitats, either puffed up with self-importance or steeped in dreams of romance, wealth, or success. Sometimes the delusion was treated gently, as in RKO's *Having Wonderful Time* (1938), which took the Jewish flavor out of Arthur Kober's play about a summer resort colony and turned it into a conventional story about two romantically inclined young people (Ginger Rogers and Douglas Fairbanks, Jr.) who discover each other at a summer camp. Surprisingly, the screenplay was written by Kober himself, who apparently thought he could make his play more palatable to a general audience by extracting its ethnic bite and color. Fortunately, the cast included such stalwart performers as Lucille Ball, Eve Arden, Jack Carson, and Red (here called Richard) Skelton, who, under Alfred Santell's direction, managed to restore some of the fun to the bland proceedings. Warners' *Saturday's Children* (1940), adapted—for the third time—from Maxwell Anderson's 1927 play, was another softly focused comedy about a young married couple (John Garfield and Anne Shirley) trying to survive on a meager income. Vincent Sherman supplied the placid direction, and Claude Rains took the acting honors as the girl's troubled father.

One of the funniest comedies to deal with unquenchable hopes and aspirations, despite mounting odds, was Columbia's 1942 version of the Joseph Fields–Jerome Chodorov play *My Sister Eileen*, which had been produced on the stage in 1940. In this case, the authors adapted their play without diluting the flavor or reducing the hilarity of the antic farce about two naïve Ohio sisters seeking fame and fortune in Manhattan. With Alexander Hall handling the direction, and Rosalind Russell bringing her special flair for comedy to the Shirley Booth role, *My Sister Eileen* was a merry, madly spinning, and entertaining film.

From the moment the Sherwood sisters, Ruth (Rosalind Russell) and Eileen (Janet Blair), arrive in New York, they are the easy prey of everyone they meet. (At the station, a flashy type remarks "Hot, isn't it?" and Ruth responds in her most acid tone, "Yes, but you'll cool off.") Weary and confused, they are badgered into taking a ramshackle basement apartment in Greenwich Village by Appopolous (George Tobias), an effusive but shifty Greek landlord. (He points out the "exquisite imitation fireplace.") Only after they have moved in do they learn, by way of an ear-splitting blast, that their apartment is perilously close to where a new subway is under construction. "What'll we do?,'" Eileen cries. Ruth's answer is flatly realistic: "We'll do thirty days."

Ruth has aspirations as a writer, Eileen as an actress—but both find the going rough, though Eileen's dewy-eyed and innocent look attracts many men, especially reporter-on-the-make Chick Clark (Allyn Joslyn) and soda-jerk Frank Lippincott (Richard Quine). Ruth gets to meet Bob Baker (Brian Aherne), editor of *Manhatter* magazine, only to attack the magazine as "unreal" and leave in a huff. At home in the Village, the girls confront all sorts of odd neighbors and visitors: the "Wreck" (Gordon Jones), an amiable but dense ex-football player and his wife Helen (Jeff Donnell); Effie, (June Havoc) a former tenant and her "customers"; Eileen's baffled suitors; and even a dog. The Wreck does all the ironing for the girls—"Which way do you want the pleats turned?" he asks Ruth. "Towards Mecca," she replies —and he even comes to sleep in their kitchen when he and Helen want to keep their marriage a secret from his mother. Ruth remarks ruefully: "For a place with a bad location and no neon sign, we're doing a heck of a business!"

Bob Baker comes to the apartment in search of Ruth, telling her that he likes her writing style but urging her to write about her own experiences. Attracted to Bob, she turns out a fresh batch of stories, which Bob admires. But he is fired when he quarrels with the publisher about printing them. Deeply dejected, Ruth gets a telephone call ostensibly from Chick's newspaper, giving her an assignment to cover the arrival of the Portuguese merchant marine in Brooklyn. In a riotously funny scene, she is pursued back to the Village by an enthusiastic group of Portuguese mariners who speak no English. "The fleet's in!" she bellows, as the men romp through the neighborhood and into their apartment, where they find delectable Eileen. "What are they tossing for?" Eileen asks. "I have a hunch it's not me!" Ruth shouts as Eileen leads an uninhibited conga into the street. Soon the area is in total turmoil, and Eileen ends up in jail, the pampered darling of the police force.

When the girls' father and grandmother (Grant Mitchell and Elizabeth Patterson) arrive in New York, their shock at discovering how the two have been living is compounded when the Wreck announces that he doesn't have to live in the apartment any more—his marriage is no longer a secret—and the Portuguese mariners show up in full regalia to apologize for their behavior the night before. The girls are ready to return home, until Bob appears to tell Ruth that she has sold the stories to *Manhatter* after all. What is more, he and Ruth are going to be married.

All is well, and for a happy moment, even the subway blasting stops. But then the drilling begins and the film closes with the Three Stooges drilling their way into the apartment. Their remark: "We must have made a wrong turn."

My Sister Eileen is certainly one of the most durable of theatrical properties—it was turned into a 1953 stage musical, *Wonderful Town*, with Rosalind Russell repeating her role, then remade as a Technicolor musical in 1955 under its original title, with Betty Garrett and an entirely new score. It was even a television series in the 1950s, with Elaine Stritch. In this original version, the pace never falters and the cast moves through its paces with obvious pleasure. The film is sparked by Rosalind Russell's marvelously blunt and endearing performance as Ruth, her no-nonsense voice expressing unvarnished truth as she informs Eileen: "Something tells me you weren't ready to leave Columbus." Commenting on their eating lots of roughage on their skimpy diet, she says: "I'd like to mix it with a little smoothage."

Other screen adaptations at the beginning of the forties dealt facetiously with human foibles and weaknesses, and several seemed to take a special delight in poking fun at the kind of scatterbrained woman who precipitates trouble. In *Susan and God* (MGM, 1940), Joan Crawford took on Gertrude Lawrence's stage role as a foolish wife who becomes enthusiastic about a religious "movement" and tries to convert her society friends, all the while damaging her none-too-strong marriage to a hard-drinking weakling (Fredric March). The humorous possibilities of the story were lost as Anita Loos' scenario from the Rachel Crothers play became heavily dramatic (a frequent occurrence when Joan Crawford was the star). George Cukor was unable to instill any life into the proceedings, despite a supporting cast that included Ruth Hussey, Nigel Bruce, Marjorie Main, John Carroll, Constance Collier, and Rita Hayworth in her only MGM film in the forties.

Another flighty female appeared on the scene in MGM's *Dulcy* (1940), adapted by Albert Mannheimer, Jerome Chodorov, and Joseph A. Fields from the George S. Kaufman–Marc Connelly play produced in 1921. (A silent film version appeared in 1923.) Ann

SUSAN AND GOD (1940). A moment of contention shared by Joan Crawford, John Carroll, Nigel Bruce, and Rita Hayworth.

DULCY (1940). Ian Hunter discusses his invention with Ann Sothern and Reginald Gardiner.

Sothern starred in Lynn Fontanne's stage role as the bird-brained Dulcy Ward, who tries to help her fiancé (Ian Hunter) sell his invention by inviting the prospective buyer and his wife and daughter to spend a weekend with them in the country. Inevitably all sorts of disasters ensue but Dulcy perseveres in her nitwit way and all ends happily. The funniest moments were contributed by Reginald Gardiner as a crackpot who finally buys the invention, and others on the scene were Roland Young, Billie Burke, and Dan Dailey, the latter in his second film. S. Sylvan Simon directed. An equally light-headed heroine was *Claudia* (Fox, 1943), adapted by Morrie Ryskind from Rose Franken's popular stories and play. In her screen debut, Dorothy McGuire repeated her stage role as the immature but engaging young wife who finally approaches adulthood after several comic and poignant confrontations with life. Robert Young played her sensible husband, and Ina Claire gave a lovely performance—her last in films —as Claudia's mother, whose imminent death helps Claudia finally recognize her responsibilities.

These views of women, courtesy of the theatre, were all gently satirical, but one was withering and scornful. This was MGM's version of Clare Boothe's play *The Women* (1939), which was produced on the New York stage in 1936. Adapted by Anita Loos and Jane Murfin and directed by George Cukor, it presented a jaundiced composite portrait of a group of ladies whose unrelenting viciousness is the prime cause of wrecked marriages and friendships. The studio gave the film one of its glossiest productions, with lavish settings and costumes by art director Cedric Gibbons (including a fashion show in Technicolor) and a star-heavy cast headed by Norma Shearer, Joan Crawford, and Rosalind Russell.

Like the play, the film of *The Women* leans more heavily on insult and invective than on wit to satirize the petty, selfish, nasty, and often stupid behavior of its all-female characters. The film, however, tempers some of the harshness by casting Norma Shearer, one of MGM's favorite Weeping Heroines, in the central role of Mary Haines, the noble, wronged young wife who learns to swallow her pride and fight for her husband. Whether bearing up stoically with her small daughter or sobbing her heart out to her mother, Miss Shearer waters the film's vitriol with her tears.

Sweeping from beauty salon to exercise parlor, and from lavish apartments to a dude ranch in Reno, *The Women* revolves about Mary Haines' discovery, by way of her maliciously gleeful friends, that her husband is cheating on her with a greedy salesgirl named Crystal

CLAUDIA (1943). Young bride Claudia (Dorothy McGuire) and her David (Robert Young).

THE WOMEN (1939). A gathering of the ladies at a Reno ranch: (left to right) Joan Fontaine, Norma Shearer, Rosalind Russell, Mary Boland, and Paulette Goddard.

Allen (Joan Crawford). Her friends include Sylvia Fowler (Rosalind Russell), fairly oozing with malice and spite; Edith Potter (Phyllis Povah), continually pregnant; Peggy Day (Joan Fontaine), gentle but lame-brained; and Nancy Blake (Florence Nash), a novelist and the only sensible member of the group. The film begins with a well-remembered scene in a beauty salon, as the camera passes from foolish matrons to overly polite employees, finally settling on Sylvia as she learns about Stephen Haines' indiscretion with Crystal from a talkative manicurist.

Sylvia's pleasure in the news is apparent and she hurries to tell Edith, who is titillated by the prospect of serenely happy Mary Haines' learning the truth about her husband. ("Suppose Mary should hear about it? Wouldn't it be *awful?*") Sylvia, of course, manages to mention the manicurist's name to Mary, who asks for the girl at the salon and is rewarded with the full, shocking story about Stephen. Bitter and anguished, Mary confides in her mother (Lucile Watson), whose "sage" advice is heavy with philosophical platitudes. ("A man has only one escape from his old self, to see a different self —in the mirror of some woman's eyes.") Though she still loves Stephen, Mary is unable to tolerate his indiscretion, especially after she meets Crystal at a fashionable dress shop. Their confrontation in a fitting room provides one of the film's highlights as lofty society woman meets girl-on-the-make. (Mary: "He couldn't love a girl like you." Crystal: "If he couldn't, he's an awfully good actor!")

Despite her best instincts, Mary finds that she cannot forgive her husband, and she sues for divorce.* She goes off to Reno, where, on the Double Bar T Ranch, she meets a colorful group of divorcees, including cowgirl Miriam Aarons (Paulette Goddard), a realistic-minded girl whose next husband happens to be Sylvia Fowler's ex-husband; and the Countess de Lave (Mary Boland, giving the film's funniest performance), a much-married lady who enjoys drinking toasts to "L'amour! Toujours! L'amour!" She also has an absurd but endearing way of speaking: "My dear, you've got the Reno jumpie-wumpies!" The ranch housekeeper is Lucy (Marjorie Main, repeating her stage role), a cheerful slattern who knows the divorce route all too well. While Mary waits fretfully for a call from Stephen, the

---

*Despite all the sharp edges in the screenplay, the satire does not cut very deeply. Only one curious little scene has moments of genuine bitterness. Stephen's frustrated secretary (Ruth Hussey), while arranging for his divorce settlement, confesses to a co-worker that she not only loves him but that she has contempt for his women. ("He could get along better without Mrs. Haines or Allen than he could without me.")

"girls" carry on at the ranch, especially when Sylvia arrives and engages in a noisy and hilarious kicking-and-screaming match with Miriam Aarons.

Mary's hopes are shattered when the divorce becomes final and Stephen marries Crystal. But Crystal is quickly bored with conventionality and begins to cheat on Stephen with "Buck" Winston, a singing cowboy who is the Countess de Lave's latest acquisition. When Mary learns in a conversation with her daughter (Virginia Weidler) that Crystal is faithless and that Stephen is lonely and unhappy, she finally springs into action. In a final scene in the ladies' dressing room of the posh Casino Roof, she uses some of the "female" tactics learned from Sylvia and Crystal to generate trouble and win her husband back. Crystal is glad to bequeath her "leavings" to Mary and go off with Buck Winston, only to learn that he has no money after all—he was "subsidized" by the countess. Happy again, Mary rushes to Stephen's arms.

Despite its uneasy combination of relentless bitchiness and Shearer-soaked sentiment (her scenes with her daughter are particularly saccharine), *The Women* is an entertaining film that provides a number of "star" turns for its principals. Joan Crawford is given a scene that was widely publicized at the movie's release: while soaking luxuriously in a bathtub, Crystal dispenses nastiness in all directions. Rosalind Russell is taken through a series of strenuous exercises in a figure salon, but nothing can turn off her steady flow of vicious gossip. (The instructor asks her to "crawl slowly up the wall" with her legs. Sylvia: "The way you say that makes me feel like vermin." Instructor: "That shouldn't be much effort." [Pause] "I mean, crawling up the wall.") Paulette Goddard (in her fourth film) is fine as Miriam Aarons, though she is also called on to deliver a few of the movie's fatuous homilies. She tells Mary: "Don't you know that we dames have got to be something more to the guy we marry than a schoolgirl sweetheart? We've got to be a wife—a *real* wife. A mother, too, and a pal. *And* a *nursemaid!*" Mary Boland makes a delightful countess, very fond of her "drinkie-winkies." At one point she says: "It's so wonderful to see all our lives so settled—temporarily."

In the late thirties and early forties, virtually every studio turned to the stage for material, but none so frequently as Warner Brothers. No sooner had a play demonstrated its popularity with theatregoers than the studio acquired it and moved it quickly into production, assigning the screenplay to the busy Epstein brothers, Julius and

Philip, or other staff writers. The trend to stage adaptations began as early as 1936, when the studio released Howard Hawks' *Ceiling Zero*, a lively version of Frank Wead's 1935 play about intrepid fliers, with James Cagney as the brashest of them all and Pat O'Brien as his boss and rival in romance. The same year, the studio presented a lavish production of Marc Connelly's Pulitzer Prize play, *The Green Pastures*, a "fable" recreating Bible stories as imagined by black children in a poor Southern Sunday school.

Most of the Warners' stage-to-screen adaptations were comedies in the middle range: inoffensive, often veering towards farce, and studded with juicy roles for their "stock-company" players. *Three Men on a Horse* (1936), became a vehicle for Warners' ubiquitous featured player Frank McHugh, who appeared as Erwin Trowbridge in Laird Doyle's version of the John Cecil Holm–George Abbott stage farce. McHugh was the mild-mannered writer of greeting card verse whose surefire system for picking the winner in a horse race (but never betting) attracts the attention of a group of raffish gamblers. Sam Levene repeated his stage role as head gambler Patsy, delighted with his treasure named "Oiwin," and Joan Blondell, forcing a Brooklyn accent, appeared as Patsy's girlfriend Mabel. Directed by Mervyn LeRoy, the movie was fairly ramshackle, but there were some laughs, contributed particularly by Teddy Hart (also from the original cast) as Frankie, one of Patsy's faithful lackeys. Both simpleminded and literal-minded, Frankie is involved in the film's funniest sequence: a visit to a hospital where he asks to see a man named Leibowitz and is shown Leibowitz' newborn grandson instead. He emits an outraged roar: "This guy is a *baby!*"

Occasionally, there were light touches of "sophistication" in the adaptations. In 1937, Kay Francis tried, without success, to emulate Jane Cowl in the leading role of the Katharine Dayton–George S. Kaufman 1935 play, *First Lady*, concerning open "warfare" between two prominent Washington ladies. As Lucy Chase Wayne, wife of the Secretary of State, the regal but unanimated Miss Francis was outacted by Verree Teasdale, biting and venomous as the wife of a Supreme Court Justice (Walter Connolly). Rowland Leigh's screenplay preserved some of the play's brittle humor, and a host of reliable supporting actors, including Marjorie Rambeau, Louise Fazenda, Harry Davenport, and Victor Jory were present and accounted for as Washington residents. Also in 1937, Charles Boyer and Claudette Colbert co-starred in *Tovarich*, Casey Robinson's version of the Jacques Deval play, which Robert E. Sherwood had adapted for the

THREE MEN ON A HORSE (1936). Erwin Trowbridge (Frank McHugh) and his new friends, Mabel (Joan Blondell) and Patsy (Sam Levene).

FIRST LADY (1937). A Washington tea party with Kay Francis, Verree Teasdale, and Victor Jory.

Broadway stage in 1936. Under Anatole Litvak's direction, they played a Russian emigré couple in Paris, obliged to take jobs as butler and maid in a banker's home.

Much more typical were Warners' versions of two long-running stage comedies, *Brother Rat* (1938) and *Boy Meets Girl* (1938). *Brother Rat*, with a plot line that might have served for a Dick Powell–Ruby Keeler musical a few years earlier, dealt with hectic activities at a Hollywood version of Virginia Military Institute. Derived from the 1936 play by John Monks, Jr. and Fred F. Finklehoffe, in which Eddie Albert, Jose Ferrer, and Frank Albertson had appeared, it focused on three cadets (Ronald Reagan, Wayne Morris, and Eddie Albert in his original role) who experience all sorts of comic difficulties, ranging from Reagan's secretly courting the commandant's daughter to Albert's dazed hysteria over his wife's pregnancy. (They also have trouble with their studies, which are apparently only incidental.) Priscilla Lane, Jane Wyman, and Jane Bryan provided the feminine interest, and William Tracy, in the role Ezra Stone had played on the stage, was funny as a gawky cadet with the improbable name of Misto Bottome. William Keighley directed briskly.

Boy Meets Girl was adapted by Bella and Samuel Spewack from their own stage play, which had been one of the successes of the 1935 theatre season. (The stars were Allyn Joslyn and Jerome Cowan, with Garson Kanin in a featured role.) For this broad spoof of Hollywood's manic ways, the studio cast James Cagney and Pat O'Brien as Benson and Law, playful writers who take Susie (Marie Wilson), a pregnant waitress, under their protective wing. (Unlike the stage play, Susie's baby "Happy," who becomes a movie star, is legitimate, Susie being given the benefit of a British husband.) Some of the teeth in the original play were extracted by the authors themselves to accommodate the "star" turns by Cagney and O'Brien and possibly to soothe Hollywood's sensitive feelings about criticism, but there was still some humor in the satirical portraits of Hollywood types: the numbskull producer (Ralph Bellamy), the aggressive agent (Frank McHugh), the idiot Western star (Dick Foran), etc. Ronald Reagan appeared briefly as a radio announcer at Happy's premiere. Director William Keighley kept things moving, but the film was not favorably reviewed.

A few of the stage properties became vehicles for Edward G. Robinson, one of Warners' most popular stars since his early *Little Caesar* days. In 1938, he appeared in two: *The Amazing Dr. Clitterhouse* and *A Slight Case of Murder*. Derived by John Wexley and John Huston

TOVARICH (1937). Down on their luck in Paris, Russian emigrés Mikail (Charles Boyer) and Tatiana (Claudette Colbert) must find work.

BROTHER RAT (1938) Happy cadets at Virginia Military Institute: (left to right) Wayne Morris, Johnnie Davis, Eddie Albert, and Ronald Reagan.

BOY MEETS GIRL (1938). Hollywood writers Benson and Law (Pat O'Brien and James Cagney) comfort pregnant waitress Susie (Marie Wilson).

THE AMAZING DR. CLITTERHOUSE (1938). Claire Trevor in a tense moment with nasty boyfriend Humphrey Bogart.

from Barré Lyndon's play starring Cedric Hardwicke, *The Amazing Dr. Clitterhouse* was a rather bizarre comedy-melodrama concerning a doctor (Robinson) who turns to crime merely as an exercise in research. (He is interested in the psychological makeup of the criminal.) Inevitably he becomes involved with a gang headed by "Rocks" Valentine (Humphrey Bogart) and is forced to extricate himself by desperate measures. In a disturbing sequence, he poisons Valentine and calmly studies the gangster's reaction as he dies. Claire Trevor appeared as a lady with a "questionable" occupation.

A Slight Case of Murder, adapted from a Damon Runyon–Howard Lindsay play by Earl Baldwin and Joseph Schrank, was a boisterous farce about Remy Marko (Robinson), a retired bootlegger who has to get rid of the four dead bodies left unceremoniously in his Saratoga home by his enemies in the rackets. (His solution: he simply has his men deposit the bodies on selected doorsteps.) Marko has other problems as well: a social-climbing wife (Ruth Donnelly); a daughter (Jane Bryan) who embarrasses him by becoming engaged to a state trooper (Willard Parker); an enormous debt on his brewery; and the presence of an obnoxious orphan named Douglas Fairbanks Rosenbloom (Bobby Jordan). Helped by the screenplay's flavorful dialogue, director Lloyd Bacon kept the movie spinning from one outlandish situation to another, climaxed by a hilarious "shoot-out" involving the entire cast. In the confusion, the flying bullets not only strike the corpses in Marko's closet but wound a hood about to escape from the balcony! With a few nondescript songs added, the movie was poorly remade by Warners in 1952 as *Stop! You're Killing Me!,* with Broderick Crawford and Claire Trevor in the Robinson-Donnelly roles.

Adaptations of stage comedies picked up momentum at Warners at the start of the forties. S. N. Behrman's play *No Time for Comedy,* which had served as a successful vehicle for Katharine Cornell and Laurence Olivier in 1939, became a 1940 film starring Rosalind Russell and James Stewart. Rosalind Russell played Linda Esterbrook, a prominent stage actress whose playwright husband Gaylord (James Stewart) suddenly decides to stop turning out frivolous comedies for his wife and to create more serious and socially conscious works. ("I'm blue. I'm sunk. I'm low. I'm bored with myself.") He is taken under the wing of Amanda Swift (Genevieve Tobin), a giddy, self-proclaimed "patroness of the arts" whose husband Philo (Charlie Ruggles) has seen her "protégés" come and go. Written by the Epstein brothers, the film was blithe entertainment that reached its peak

A SLIGHT CASE OF MURDER (1938) Orphanage head Margaret Hamilton expresses disapproval as Remy Marko (Edward G. Robinson) takes on his latest charge, Douglas Fairbanks Rosenbloom (Bobby Jordan).

THE MAN WHO CAME TO DINNER (1942). Sheridan Whiteside (Monty Woolley) and friend Banjo (Jimmy Durante) conspire to get actress Lorraine Sheldon (Ann Sheridan) into a mummy case.

in the confrontation of Linda and Amanda. "Love Gay if you must," Linda tells her, "but please don't ruin his style." "You can't give him anything but foolish, empty laughter," Amanda insists. Linda is dejected: "If he believes that, I'm sunk." But of course Gay returns to Linda, after a humiliating disaster with his "serious" play.

Russell and Stewart were competent in the leading roles but the film's best performance was given by Charlie Ruggles as Philo Swift. His amused tolerance of Amanda's inane behavior, his quizzical reaction to Linda's calm, unruffled demeanor, are played with skill and enormous charm by this sterling actor. Allyn Joslyn was also excellent as sardonic director Morgan Carrel.

Warners released three versions of stage comedies in 1942. Appearing earliest in the year was the Epstein brothers' adaptation of George S. Kaufman and Moss Hart's play, *The Man Who Came to Dinner*, first produced in 1939. Wisely, to screen this broad and hilarious lampoon of the irascible, gushily sentimental "Town Crier," Alexander Woollcott, the studio cast the stage's original Sheridan Whiteside, Monty Woolley. As the world-renowned writer and raconteur spewing forth invective as he took charge of an Ohio household, Woolley was perfect. (He had appeared in small movie roles since 1937, most notably as the judge in *Midnight*.) By and large, the film followed the outlines of the play: Whiteside, confined to a wheelchair with a broken hip, bedevils his hosts, the Stanleys (Grant Mitchell and Billie Burke), and works to wreck the romance of his loyal secretary, Maggie Cutler (Bette Davis), while cavorting with the famous friends who come to call. Just when he is about to be evicted by an irate Mr. Stanley, he recalls that Stanley's very odd sister, Harriet (Ruth Vivian), is a celebrated ax-murderess (shades of Lizzie Borden). He also redeems himself by restoring Maggie to her boyfriend, local newspaper editor Bert Jefferson (Richard Travis).

Most of the film's humor stems from Whiteside's poisonous wit, and from the irrepressible antics of his friends. He dismisses airily the befuddled doctor (George Barbier) who has written his autobiography. He interferes maliciously with the lives of the Stanley children. And he reserves his most scurrilous remarks for his hapless nurse, Miss Preen (memorably played by Mary Wickes). Calling her "Miss Bedpan," he casts aspersions on her love life ("What have you got in there, a sailor?"), her professional ability, and her appearance. When she tries to keep him from eating candy, he remarks: "My great-aunt Jennifer ate a whole box of candy every day of her life. She lived to be a hundred and two, and when she had been dead *three days*, she looked better than you do now!"

Whiteside's friends are clearly modeled after prominent theatrical figures: Lorraine Sheldon (Ann Sheridan), a predatory, self-dramatizing actress, reputedly resembling Gertrude Lawrence, who is summoned by Whiteside to break up Maggie's romance; Beverly Carlton (Reginald Gardiner), very British and sophisticated in the manner of Noël Coward; and Banjo (Jimmy Durante), obviously patterned after Harpo Marx and, except for Whiteside, the film's funniest character. In an uproarious sequence, it is Banjo who works with the contrite Whiteside to remove Lorraine Sheldon from the premises—she is carried off in a mummy case—and restore Bert Jefferson to Maggie. As directed by William Keighley, the film is played in the familiar Warners' style of overstating every situation, and racing through the lines as if the police are in hot pursuit of the actors, but it still draws many laughs. Reviewing the film at the start of the year, Bosley Crowther in the *New York Times* called it "unquestionably the most vicious but hilarious cat-clawing exhibition ever put on the screen, a deliciously wicked character portrait and a helter-skelter satire, withal."

The same unsubtle approach was used by Warners for *The Male Animal* (1942), derived from the James Thurber–Elliott Nugent play in which Nugent had starred in 1940. Henry Fonda played Tommy Turner, a teacher at a Midwestern university who starts a furor by wanting to read a letter by "radical" Bartolomeo Vanzetti to his students. Olivia de Havilland played his wife Ellen, who gives her husband an added problem by warming to the attentions of an old beau, ex-football hero Joe Ferguson (Jack Carson). The screenplay by the Epstein brothers and Stephen Morehouse Avery was briskly amusing and even pertinent for its time, especially in its satirical jabs at the mindless frenzy of college football and at the fatuousness of suspicious trustee Ed Keller (Eugene Pallette). Henry Fonda gave a commendable performance, particularly in a key scene in which, roaring drunk, he rages about being "the male animal" defending his lair and, in the film's climax, where he quietly reads the Vanzetti letter to a hushed crowd in the auditorium. The film was directed by Elliott Nugent, who presumably adapted himself to the Warners' way with comedy by having the cast perform at fever pitch.

In the fall of 1942, Warners released *George Washington Slept Here*, a film version of another (and not too successful) George S. Kaufman–Moss Hart stage comedy. Here, the authors were poking mild fun at city folk who longed to own "country" property and found themselves engaged in battle with Mother Nature. Reversing the play, which had Newton Fuller (Ernest Truex) buying an abandoned

THE MALE ANIMAL (1942). Pandemonium in the Turner household. Around the unconscious Henry Fonda: Jack Carson, Olivia de Havilland, and Don DeFore. On the telephone: Hattie McDaniel.

GEORGE WASHINGTON SLEPT HERE (1942). Ann Sheridan and Jack Benny inspect their ramshackle new Connecticut home.

farmhouse in Bucks County, Pennsylvania, to the dismay of his sharp-tongued wife Annabelle (Jean Dixon), the Everett Freeman screenplay made the wife (here called Connie and played by Ann Sheridan) the culprit who buys the house. Jack Benny played her husband (now named Bill), who expresses discomfort and outrage at becoming a country squire.

Under William Keighley's undisciplined direction, the film consisted of a series of farcical disasters to which Benny could react with his trademarked air of deep annoyance. He suffers the indignities of a collapsed floor and leaking roof, is forced to cope with an obnoxious nephew (Douglas Croft) and phony "rich uncle" (Charles Coburn), and nearly has his mortgage foreclosed by a hostile neighbor (Charles Dingle). (George Washington comes to his rescue with a valuable letter that permits Fuller to raise the necessary money.) The film's best performance was given by Percy Kilbride, repeating his stage role as the hilariously laconic caretaker, Mr. Kimber, who informs Benny of the house's many deficiencies with a unique nasal drone that turns each deficiency into a simple fact of life.

In the next few years, Warners' stage adaptations were meager. *Janie* (1944), a frail play by Josephine Bentham and Herschel V. Williams, Jr. that had eked out a modest run on Broadway, was turned into an equally frail movie by Warners, with Joyce Reynolds as the bird-brained teenage heroine, Edward Arnold and Ann Harding as her exasperated parents, and Robert Hutton as the soldier beau she married in the sequel, appropriately called *Janie Gets Married* (1946). Unaccountably, Michael Curtiz was saddled with the direction. *The Doughgirls* (1944), derived from the Joseph Fields play by James V. Kern (who directed) and Sam Hellman, was a hard-breathing farce set in a Washington hotel suite overrun with frantic characters. Among them were Ann Sheridan, Jane Wyman, Eve Arden, Jack Carson, and Charlie Ruggles. Many of the laughs came from Eve Arden (in Arlene Francis' stage role) as a formidable Russian sniper who takes walks to Baltimore between viewing double features and shooting pigeons from the hotel terrace.

Arsenic and Old Lace was also released in 1944, though it had been produced three years earlier. Adapted by the Epstein brothers from the long-running play by Joseph Kesselring, this was a macabre farce concerning two sweet old ladies in Brooklyn whose nephew discovers to his great shock that they are quietly poisoning the old men who come to rent a room and then burying their bodies in the cellar. To add to the mayhem, another nephew turns up from the past: a homi-

THE DOUGHGIRLS (1944). A climactic moment involving (among others) Jane Wyman, Jack Carson, Ann Sheridan, Alexis Smith, Barbara Brown, and John Ridgely.

ARSENIC AND OLD LACE (1944). A terrified Cary Grant tries to warn Edward McWade away from the elderberry wine. His startled aunts are Jean Adair and Josephine Hull.

cidally inclined gargoyle with a corpse of his own to bury in the cellar.

Though the plot is hardly the stuff of comedy, all these deadly doings are played for laughs from the moment the opening legend appears on the screen: "This is a Halloween tale of Brooklyn where anything can happen and usually does." The role of the distraught nephew Mortimer Brewster, a drama critic about to be married to the local minister's daughter, was assigned to Cary Grant, who pulled out all stops under Frank Capra's indulgent direction. Shouting, whinnying, and dashing about in continual frenzy as he uncovers his aunts' fondness for serving poisoned elderberry wine, Grant gives a forced, undisciplined performance. "Insanity runs in my family. It practically gallops!" he cries, and the viewer is inclined to believe him as nasty nephew Jonathan Brewster (Raymond Massey) stalks about the house like the Frankenstein monster transplanted to Brooklyn. (The stage role was played appropriately by Boris Karloff.)

Though the film broadens an already broad play, two performances remain serenely right and totally enchanting: Josephine Hull and Jean Adair, repeating their original roles as the darling but murderous aunts. As Aunt Abby, Josephine Hull is the very soul of old-fashioned innocence as she waddles about dispensing cheer with every fatal sip of wine. When Mortimer discovers a body in the window seat, she remarks petulantly, "We never dreamed you'd peek!" and she is properly indignant when Jonathan tries to bury a "stranger" in one of their cellar graves: "If he came here to be buried in our cellar, he's mistaken." The best line falls to Jean Adair as Aunt Martha, commenting on their private stock of wine: "One of our gentlemen found time to say 'How delicious!' "

Apparently unable to handle farce unsoftened by his usual sentimentality, Capra gives free rein to a good cast and they work strenuously to draw laughs: Peter Lorre as Jonathan's jittery companion, "Dr." Einstein, who maintains a comparative body count ("They've got twelve. You've got twelve."); John Alexander as the aunts' demented brother, who believes he is Teddy Roosevelt and charges up the staircase at every opportunity, thinking it is San Juan Hill; Jack Carson as a playwriting policeman; Priscilla Lane as Mortimer's baffled fiancée; and Edward Everett Horton as the owner of the "rest home" to which Aunts Abby and Martha are ultimately dispatched.

For the rest of the forties, movie versions of theatre comedies appeared sporadically. The trend towards mild adolescent farce begun by *Janie* in 1944 continued with *Junior Miss* (Fox, 1945), *Kiss and Tell* (Columbia, 1945), and *Dear Ruth* (Paramount, 1947), all stage successes. Other plays brought to the screen were such gentle period comedies as *Life with Father* (Warners, 1947) and *I Remember Mama* (RKO, 1948). The emphasis was on "niceness": even the film version of *The Late George Apley* (Fox, 1947) softened most of the satire, transforming J. P. Marquand's stuffy Boston Brahmin, played beautifully on the stage by Leo G. Carroll, into Ronald Colman's soft-focus charmer. Occasionally, a small amount of seasoned wit was introduced into te general blandness, as in MGM's adaptation of Philip Barry's *Without Love* (1945) and Howard Lindsay and Russel Crouse's *State of the Union* (1948), both starring Katharine Hepburn and Spencer Tracy.

What was lacking in these films was the zest and the freewheeling fun of earlier adaptations. It was as if the studios had decided that the moviegoing public had imbibed one too many cocktails, and were converting to a diet of skimmed milk. The thumb-to-nose gesture that had characterized *20th Century* and *My Sister Eileen* and even *Boy Meets Girl* gave way to the playful chucking-under-the-chin of *Junior Miss* and *John Loves Mary* (Warners, 1949).

But there was much for moviegoers to remember in all these stage-to-screen conversions: The legendary man-and-woman battles of John Barrymore vs. Carole Lombard, of Wallace Beery vs. Jean Harlow. The blunt and slightly rueful wit of Rosalind Russell as Ruth Sherwood. Mary Boland as the Countess de Lave, helplessly tangled in "l'amour." The scathing insults of Monty Woolley as Sheridan Whiteside. In their finest moments, these performers generated sparks, and even now, so many years later, the sparks can light the screen.

POSTSCRIPT

They have faded now: the aspiring Cinderellas, the spoiled heiresses, the battling couples, the "boss-ladies," the lambs who foiled the wolves. Many of the stars, directors, and writers whose wit and dexterity created a body of sparkling comedies are either gone or have become screen "institutions," shadows of the impudent, uninhibited people who worked in—or on—these films.

Yet occasionally, in "retrospective" showings, or on television screens, their work reappears to bring us pleasure. Susan Vance and David Huxley again chase a leopard across the Connecticut countryside. Nick and Nora Charles again exchange quips while solving a murder. The sentimental "little people" of Frank Capra and the addled clowns of Preston Sturges continue to pursue their dreams or follow their inclinations with little regard for convention or the laws of probability.

Once more we can enjoy this daft and dizzy world and the extravagantly foolish people who inhabit it. Once more we can be grateful for their legacy of laughter.

THE PLAYERS

Following is an annotated listing of the actors and actresses who appear most regularly in the pages of this book. These are the professional performers whose expertise and vivid personalities helped to create a matchless group of joyful, impudent screen comedies in the thirties and forties.

BRIAN AHERNE (1902–   )
This debonair Englishman made his American film debut in *The Song of Songs* (1933) as Marlene Dietrich's sculptor-lover, then went on to play both comedy and drama throughout the thirties and forties. As Maximilian von Habsburg he faced a firing squad stoically in *Juarez* (Warners, 1939), but he won Rosalind Russell in three comedies: *Hired Wife* (Universal, 1940), *My Sister Eileen* (Columbia, 1942), and *What a Woman!* (Columbia, 1943). But as a whimsical playboy in Paramount's *Skylark* (1941), he lost Claudette Colbert to Ray Milland.

LUIS ALBERNI (1887–1962)
Luis Alberni played volatile, eccentric Latin types in scores of films in the thirties and forties. He appeared in several of Grace Moore's musicals for Columbia and in such comedies as *The Gilded Lily* (1935) and *The Lady Eve* (1941). In *The Gay Deception* (1935), he had a riotous scene as a furious waiter, and in *Easy Living* (1937), he was the hotel owner who arranges to give Jean Arthur a lavish suite in the mistaken belief that she is Edward Arnold's mistress.

EVE ARDEN (1912–   )
After a brief career on the musical stage, Eve Arden wisecracked her way through innumerable movies, not all of them comedies. She varied very little in her delivery, but her acid, no-nonsense tones often helped to bring a

mediocre film to life. Her hilarious performance as a formidable Russian sniper at loose in Washington brightened *The Doughgirls* (Warners, 1944), and she played Olive Lashbrooke in the film version of *The Voice of the Turtle* (Warners, 1947). Prior to these she was featured in such comedies as *That Uncertain Feeling* (UA, 1941), *She Knew All the Answers* (Columbia, 1941), and *Bedtime Story* (Columbia, 1942).

JEAN ARTHUR (1905–   )
This delightful actress made her 1923 film debut in *Cameo Kirby*, a remake of a Booth Tarkington riverboat melodrama, with John Gilbert. After many silent one- and two-reelers, and a brief stretch as one of 1929's Baby Wampus Stars, plus several years on the stage, she played her first notable role opposite Edward G. Robinson in John Ford's *The Whole Town's Talking* (Columbia, 1935). From then on and especially after *Mr. Deeds Goes to Town* (Columbia, 1936), her piquant personality, distinctive voice, and comedy expertise were much in demand, and she was a major comedy star into the forties. Her best-known films include *Easy Living* (Paramount, 1937), *You Can't Take It With You* (Columbia, 1938), *Mr. Smith Goes to Washington* (Columbia, 1939), and *The More the Merrier* (Columbia, 1943).

MARY ASTOR (1906–   )
A fine and versatile actress in comedy and drama, Mary Astor has played both giddy and warmly sensible characters in films for many years. In *Midnight* (1939), she was John Barrymore's faithless wife who must cope with Claudette Colbert, hired by Barrymore to distract her latest lover. In Preston Sturges' *The Palm Beach Story* (1942), she was delightful as Rudy Vallee's sister, a predatory, much-married princess who sets her sights on Joel McCrea.

MISCHA AUER (1905–1967)
Mischa Auer played many roles, but he will always be remembered as Carlo, Alice Brady's gorilla-imitating "pet" houseguest, in *My Man Godfrey* (Universal, 1936). He played many mournful and manic Russians—in *You Can't Take It With You* (Columbia, 1938), *Twin Beds* (UA, 1942), *Up in Mabel's Room* (UA, 1944)—but the vision of him leaping onto a sofa and making monkey noises for Alice Brady's amusement is the one that endures. (At one point this absurd gigolo cries: "Money, money, money! The Frankenstein monster that destroys souls!")

LEW AYRES (1908–   )
Lew Ayres enjoyed a comfortable career at MGM as Dr. Jimmy Kildare (1938–1941), after scoring a notable success earlier in his first sound film, *All Quiet on the Western Front* (Universal, 1930). He was competent in several comedies of the late thirties, most notably as Katharine Hepburn's tipsy

brother in *Holiday* (Columbia, 1938). He also appeared that same year in *Rich Man, Poor Girl* (MGM) as a wild-haired "radical," and in *Spring Madness* (also MGM) as the object of Maureen O'Sullivan's affections. (The *New York Times* review of this film called him "the cinema's best unappreciated actor.")

BINNIE BARNES (1906–   )

Binnie Barnes played her first important role as Catherine Howard in *The Private Life of Henry VIII* (UA, 1933), then went on to make scores of films in which she was often brittle, scheming, and eloquently bitchy. Typically, she worked to snare wealthy Charles Winninger in *Three Smart Girls* (Universal, 1937), only to be thwarted by his daughters; tried to flatter Warner Baxter away from his wife Loretta Young in *Wife, Husband and Friend* (Fox, 1939); and locked swords with Claudette Colbert in *Skylark* (Paramount, 1941). She seldom had the opportunity to display her flair for lusty comedy, but in Fox's *Three Blind Mice* (1938), she was delightful as a lady with a penchant for beer, non sequiturs, and Joel McCrea.

RALPH BELLAMY (1904–   )

Until he went on to nobler pursuits, particularly as Franklin D. Roosevelt, Ralph Bellamy spent part of his film career chasing—and losing—his leading ladies. He played many kinds of roles, but most filmgoers remember him as Daniel Leeson, the Oklahoma oil millionaire who wants to marry Irene Dunne in *The Awful Truth* (Columbia, 1937), and as Bruce Baldwin (a very similar role), engaged to reporter Rosalind Russell in *His Girl Friday* (Columbia, 1940). Both characters were saddled with ogre-like mothers, and both were idiots.

ROBERT BENCHLEY (1889–1945)

The popular author of humorous essays enjoyed a second career as an actor and appeared in many comedies throughout the thirties and forties, mostly as an amiable bumbler. His short films—*How to Sleep,* etc.—were well-received, and his feature films included *Foreign Correspondent* (UA, 1940), *Bedtime Story* (Columbia, 1942), *The Major and the Minor* (Paramount, 1942), and *I Married a Witch* (UA, 1942).

CONSTANCE BENNETT (1905–1965)

A more assured actress but a less popular star than her sister Joan, Constance Bennett at her best had a brittle, acerbic style that was very agreeable. Her most famous role was as Marion Kerby, George's flippant and ghostly wife in two of the *Topper* films, *Topper* (MGM, 1937), and *Topper Takes a Trip* (UA, 1939). In MGM's *After Office Hours* (1935), opposite Clark Gable, she was a society girl turned newspaper reporter, and in *Merrily We Live* (MGM, 1938), she was the madcap daughter of an eccentric family. In *Two-Faced*

Woman (MGM, 1941), as Melvyn Douglas' discarded girlfriend, she stole the film from under Greta Garbo's classical nose.

JOAN BLONDELL (1909–   )

One of the busiest and most talented members of Warners' "stock company" of players in the thirties, Joan Blondell was an effervescent comedienne adept with a wisecrack. She appeared in the studio's outsize musical films *(Footlight Parade, Gold Diggers of 1933, Dames)* and in many of its entertaining low-budget programmers such as *Havana Widows* (1933), *I've Got Your Number* (1934), and *Kansas City Princess* (1934). She played Mabel, girlfriend to Sam Levene's Patsy, in *Three Men on a Horse* (1936). In the late thirties, she appeared in several amusing Columbia films opposite Melvyn Douglas: *There's Always a Woman* (1938), *The Amazing Mr. Williams* (1939), and *Good Girls Go to Paris* (1939). She has continued to give bright performances in leading and featured roles to the present.

ERIC BLORE (1887–1959)

Eyebrows raised, his voice a supercilious whine, his highly proper and subservient manner only faintly concealing his contempt, Eric Blore was the model of British smugness and obtuseness in scores of films. He was a memorable fixture in the Ginger Rogers-Fred Astaire musicals: as Everett Edward Horton's fussy manservant in *Top Hat* (RKO, 1935), as an inquisitive waiter in *The Gay Divorcee* (RKO, 1934), as the owner of a dance school in *Swing Time* (RKO, 1936), and as a hotel manager in *Shall We Dance?* (RKO, 1937). He was also pleasing as Leslie Howard's butler in *It's Love I'm After* (Warners, 1937), and in *The Lady Eve* (Paramount, 1941), as the bogus Sir Alfred McGlennan Keith.

MARY BOLAND (1882–1965)

This popular stage beauty and tragedienne became one of the screen's most skillful portrayers of shrill, domineering, and dim-witted matrons. In the thirties she made a series of comedies opposite that deftest of comedians, Charles Ruggles, but most filmgoers remember her as the much-married Countess de Lave in MGM's *The Women* (1939). "L'amour—l'amour—where love leads, I always follow," she cries as she lassoes cowboy star Buck Winston, only to have him stolen by Crystal Allen (Joan Crawford). She was also splendid as Mrs. Bennet in MGM's 1940 version of *Pride and Prejudice.*

ALICE BRADY (1893–1939)

A prominent stage actress in the twenties—she starred opposite Nazimova in the original production of *Mourning Becomes Electra*—Alice Brady made twenty-six films from 1933 until her untimely death in 1939. She won an Academy Award as Mrs. O'Leary (the lady with the cow) in Fox's *In Old Chicago* (1939), but she is most identified with her roles as giddy, addled matrons. She was unforgettable as Mrs. Bullock in *My Man Godfrey* (Universal, 1936), blithely overseeing an assortment of lunatics, including her two daughters.

HELEN BRODERICK (1890–1959)
One of the best of the wry, cynical, sharp-edged ladies of the thirties, Helen Broderick, mother of Broderick Crawford, was a bright feature in many comedies. She lent a refreshing note to two of the Astaire-Rogers musicals, *Top Hat* (RKO, 1935) and *Swing Time* (RKO, 1936)—in the latter film she even danced with Victor Moore—and she contributed a welcome astringency to *The Rage of Paris* (Universal, 1938), *Honeymoon in Bali* (Paramount, 1939, and *Nice Girl?* (Universal, 1941).

VIRGINIA BRUCE (1910–   )
Described in one 1935 review as "winsome and velvet-eyed," blondely beautiful Virginia Bruce appeared as one of Jeanette MacDonald's ladies-in-waiting in Paramount's *The Love Parade* (1929), then went on to play leading or secondary roles throughout the thirties, mostly for MGM. She was a nurse in the studio's *Society Doctor*, 1935, and a nightclub singer in *Society Lawyer*, 1939, also from MGM. Perhaps her best-known roles were as tipsy showgirl Audrey Vane in *The Great Ziegfeld* (MGM, 1936), and as a dedicated nurse in *Yellow Jack* (MGM, 1938), but she was also serviceable in many comedies: as a career-bent wife in *The First 100 Years* (MGM, 1938); as a meddlesome detective's wife in *There's That Woman Again* (Columbia, 1939), and as assorted "other women" (*Wife, Doctor and Nurse*, Fox, 1937; *Hired Wife*, Universal, 1940).

BILLIE BURKE (1885–1970)
Billie Burke had a long and illustrious career: as a popular stage beauty who married Florenz Ziegfeld; as a silent film actress; and throughout her later years, as a delightful portrayer of scatterbrained matrons. She began her sound career on a dramatic note as John Barrymore's troubled wife in *A Bill of Divorcement* (RKO, 1932), but most of her films were comic. She was Mrs. Topper in *Topper* (MGM, 1937) and its two sequels and at one time or another she was mother to most leading ladies of the time—to Constance Bennett in *Merrily We Live* (MGM, 1938), to Greer Garson in *Remember?* (MGM, 1939), and to Joan Crawford in *They All Kissed the Bride* (Columbia, 1942). To several generations of children, she will always be Glinda the Good Witch in *The Wizard of Oz* (MGM, 1939).

CHARLES BUTTERWORTH (1897–1946)
Slight, shy, diffident Charles Butterworth had his largest role as the Count de Savignac in Rouben Mamoulian's *Love Me Tonight* (Paramount, 1932), but played featured parts in a number of thirties comedies: *Baby Face Harrington*

(MGM 1935), *The Moon's Our Home* (Universal, 1936), *Thanks for the Memory* (Paramount, 1938), etc. He was invariably harried, unsmiling, and amusing.

SPRING BYINGTON (1893–1971)

Winsome, lovable Spring Byington was a popular stage actress whose first film, *Little Women* (RKO, 1933), established her gentle, motherly image for the rest of her film career. She made nearly 100 films, mostly as sweetly addled, well-meaning, pleasant ladies. She was mother of the Jones family in a series of low-budget Fox comedies in the thirties. Probably her best-known role is Penny Sycamore, the playwriting mother of *You Can't Take It With You* (Columbia, 1938), who uses a kitten as a paperweight.

MADELEINE CARROLL (1906–   )

One of the great film beauties of the thirties, blonde Madeleine Carroll was a charming comedienne even when her material was mediocre. In *It's All Yours* (Columbia, 1938), she was a secretary who inherits her boss' fortune, and in *Cafe Society* (Paramount, 1939), she was an heiress who marries Fred MacMurray to win a bet. MacMurray also taught "boss-lady" Carroll about love in *Honeymoon in Bali* (Paramount, 1939).

CHARLES COBURN (1877–1961)

At age sixty-six, Charles Coburn endeared himself to film audiences and won an Academy Award as Mr. Dingle, the portly, genial Cupid of Columbia's *The More the Merrier* (1943). In his long, distinguished film career, which began in 1935 (after many years on the stage), he played many gruff but kindly fathers, tycoons, and advisors. In two films he played the head of a department store—in *Bachelor Mother* (RKO, 1939), he was convinced that Ginger Rogers' foundling was his grandson, and in *The Devil and Miss Jones* (RKO, 1941), he joined the ranks of his workers to find out why he was hated. He was marvelous as Don Ameche's plain-speaking grandfather in Ernst Lubitsch's *Heaven Can Wait* (Fox, 1943).

CLAUDETTE COLBERT (1905–   )

One of the screen's most expert comediennes, French-born Claudette Colbert made only a modest impression in the early thirties, even when she bathed in asses' milk as the Empress Poppaea in Cecil B. DeMille's *The Sign of the Cross* (Paramount, 1932). Then she took to the road with Clark Gable, lifting her skirt to hitch a ride, and *It Happened One Night* (Columbia, 1934) won her an Academy Award and film fame. Her comedies in the thirties— *The Gilded Lily* (Paramount, 1935), *I Met Him in Paris* (Paramount, 1937), *Bluebeard's Eighth Wife* (Paramount, 1938), etc.—never equalled that classic film, but *Midnight* (Paramount, 1939) came reasonably close. She continued to play both comic and dramatic roles into the forties and early fifties, always with the ingratiating, womanly finesse that kept her a favorite of audiences.

WALTER CONNOLLY (1887–1940)

After a stage career, Walter Connolly started in films as Carole Lombard's self-sacrificing father in *No More Orchids* (1932) and as a gullible senator in *Washington Merry-Go-Round* (Columbia, 1932). But with his role as Claudette Colbert's irate father in *It Happened One Night* (Columbia, 1934), he became the screen's leading exponent of comic bluster and rage. He was Myrna Loy's angry millionaire-father in MGM's *Libeled Lady* (1936) and Fredric March's furious editor in *Nothing Sacred* (Selznick International, 1937), who threatened to take out March's heart and "stuff it—like an olive!" In Warners' *Four's a Crowd* (1938), as Olivia de Havilland's grandfather, he was proud to be known as America's most-hated capitalist. In *Fifth Avenue Girl* (RKO, 1939), he turned benign to help down-on-her-luck Ginger Rogers.

GARY COOPER (1901–1961)

Gary Cooper was not one of the screen's great (or even good) comedy actors, but he did his earnest, gangling best in a number of comedy films in the thirties. As Longfellow Deeds in Columbia's *Mr. Deeds Goes to Town* (1936), he was the perfect Capra hero, honest, eccentric, and likeable, and his playing of the courtroom scene, in which two elderly ladies accuse him of being "pixilated," is one of his finest moments. He was ill-at-ease as a much-married Parisian millionaire in Ernst Lubitsch's *Bluebeard's Eighth Wife* (Paramount, 1938), and in other comedies extending into the forties—*Ball of Fire* (RKO, 1941), *Casanova Brown* (RKO, 1944), etc.—he seemed to be wishing that he were back on the range, wearing spurs and a ten-gallon hat.

JOAN CRAWFORD (1904–   )

Joan Crawford was hardly known for her skill at comedy, yet MGM starred her in several romantic comedies during her peak years in the thirties. In *Forsaking all Others* (1934), she was the center of a triangle involving Clark Gable and Robert Montgomery, and in *Love on the Run* (1936), she was an heiress scampering across Europe with foreign correspondent Clark Gable. As Crystal Allen in *The Women* (1939), she was splendidly cold, ambitious, and vicious. One of her last comedy roles was in Columbia's *They all Kissed the Bride* (1942), as a broad-shouldered "boss-lady" tamed by Melvyn Douglas.

WILLIAM DEMAREST (1892–   )

William Demarest was a likeable fixture in comedies of the thirties and forties, often appearing in roles that called on him to be tough and apoplectic, but basically sentimental. He was a prominent member of Preston Sturges' stock company, and his best-remembered performance is probably as Officer Kockenlocker, irate father to the illegitimately pregnant Betty Hutton in Sturges' *The Miracle of Morgan's Creek* (1944). But he was equally good in *The Great McGinty* (Paramount, 1940), *Sullivan's Travels* (Paramount, 1942), and *Hail the Conquering Hero* (Paramount, 1944).

RUTH DONNELLY (1896–   )
One of the actresses most skillful at delivering the tart, slangy dialogue of thirties comedy was Ruth Donnelly. At Warners for many years, she appeared often as the confidante or mother of the heroine, or as the blunt wife or secretary who would tolerate no nonsense from husband or boss. She continued acting into the fifties. Among her many films are *Footlight Parade* (Warners, 1933), *Hands Across the Table* (Paramount, 1935), *A Slight Case of Murder* (Warners, 1938), in which she was hilarious as Edward G. Robinson's social-climbing wife, *Mr. Smith Goes to Washington* (Columbia, 1939), and *You Belong to Me* (Columbia, 1941).

MELVYN DOUGLAS (1901–   )
It is sometimes difficult to remember that the aged, cantankerous man of *Hud* (Paramount, 1963) and *I Never Sang for My Father* (Columbia, 1970) was once one of the screen's most debonair and expert comedians. Throughout the thirties, climaxed with *Ninotchka* in 1939, and into the forties, Melvyn Douglas was the impeccable, dry-voiced husband or lover to many leading ladies. He was pursued and won by Claudette Colbert in *She Married her Boss* (Columbia, 1935) and pursued and won her in *I Met Him in Paris* (Paramount, 1937). He captured Irene Dunne in *Theodora Goes Wild* (Columbia, 1936), but lost Jean Arthur to Fred MacMurray in *Too Many Husbands* (Columbia, 1940). On three occasions he played opposite Joan Blondell: *There's Always a Woman*, 1938; *Good Girls Go to Paris*, 1939; *The Amazing Mr. Williams*, 1940—all Columbia).

IRENE DUNNE (1904–   )
Irene Dunne's charm and grace adorned many films of the thirties and forties, and as a portrayer of sensible, cheerful, witty ladies, she was peerless. Her early roles were mostly dramatic and occasionally musical, but then *Theodora Goes Wild* (Columbia, 1936) revealed a flair for tongue-in-cheek comedy, and she went on to such lighthearted diversions as *The Awful Truth* (Columbia, 1937) and *My Favorite Wife* (RKO, 1940), both with Cary Grant and both first-rate screwball comedies. Her comedies in the forties were mostly feeble, and she turned to costumed sentiment with *Anna and the King of Siam* (Fox, 1946), *Life with Father* (Warners, 1947), and *I Remember Mama* (RKO, 1948). She was gracious in all these roles, but most filmgoers prefer to remember her in *The Awful Truth*, impersonating ex-husband Cary Grant's devastating, indiscreet Southern sister.

STUART ERWIN (1903–1967)
Bumbling hayseed or amiable sidekick, Stuart Erwin turned up in innumerable films of the thirties and forties, following his sound debut with Gloria Swanson in *The Trespasser* (1929). He was friend to Clark Gable in *After Office Hours* (MGM, 1935), to Joel McCrea in *Three Blind Mice* (Fox, 1938), and to

James Cagney in *The Bride Came C.O.D.* (Warners, 1941). He also played Judy Garland's brother in *Pigskin Parade* (Fox, 1936).

DOUGLAS FAIRBANKS, JR. (1909–   )

After four years at Warner Brothers in the early thirties, appearing mainly in breezy comedies and melodramas, Douglas Fairbanks, Jr. left the studio to play varied roles at other studios. He was the villainous Rupert of Hentzau in *The Prisoner of Zenda* (UA, 1937) and one of the lusty British soldiers in *Gunga Din* (RKO, 1939). His comedy films were spotty: he was an unlikely summer-camp waiter in RKO's tame version of *Having Wonderful Time* (1938); he tried to teach Irene Dunne about the *Joy of Living* (RKO, 1938); and he was a member of the larcenous Carleton family in *The Young in Heart* (Selznick International, 1938). In the forties, he emulated his father's dashing heroics in a series of swashbuckling adventure films.

HENRY FONDA (1905–   )

Henry Fonda's earnest, studied, slow-thinking manner was not exactly suitable for comedy, but he made an agreeable foil for the aggressive onslaughts of Barbara Stanwyck in three films: *The Mad Miss Manton* (RKO, 1938), *The Lady Eve* (Paramount, 1941), and *You Belong to Me* (Columbia, 1941). He also gave a genial performance opposite Olivia De Havilland as the beleaguered young professor in *The Male Animal*, Warners' 1942 version of the Elliott Nugent–James Thurber stage comedy. He was much happier, however, in a serious vein, giving his most eloquent performance as Tom Joad in *The Grapes of Wrath* (Fox, 1940).

CLARK GABLE (1901–1960)

Clark Gable's rank among the screen's comic actors is not especially high, but his rough-hewn, virile manner and easy, straightforward way with dialogue made his comedy films easy-to-take. Most famous, of course, is his performance as Peter Warne, the reporter on a cross-country bus tour with incognito heiress Ellie Andrews in *It Happened One Night* (Columbia, 1934), but he was also agreeable opposite Constance Bennett (*After Office Hours*, 1935), Joan Crawford (*Love on the Run*, 1936), Hedy Lamarr (*Comrade X*, 1940), and Rosalind Russell (*They Met in Bombay*, 1941), all MGM. His best co-star was undoubtedly Jean Harlow, whose earthy blonde beauty and raucous manner was the ideal complement for Gable's blunt way with women. They were perfect together in such MGM films as *Red Dust* (1932) and *China Seas* (1935).

REGINALD GARDINER (1903–   )

Reginald Gardiner played a variety of dapper and/or eccentric characters in scores of films in the thirties and forties. He was the maniacal Schultz in Charlie Chaplin's *The Great Dictator* (UA, 1940), supported Ray Milland and Loretta Young in *The Doctor Takes a Wife* (Columbia, 1940), and played the

Noël Coward-like Beverly Carlton in *The Man Who Came to Dinner* (Warners, 1942). Earlier he contributed a hilarious highlight to MGM's *Born to Dance* (1936), as a park policeman who, in a sudden fit of lunacy, decides to lead an imaginary symphony orchestra in a musical selection.

CARY GRANT (1904–   )

Many filmgoers would agree that Cary Grant is the screen's finest comic actor, a performer whose good looks, much-imitated aplomb, and comic flair have pleased audiences for nearly four decades. In the early thirties, he served as foil to some of the colorful and popular actresses of the period, notably Mae West. He first hit his stride as the dapper ghost George Kerby in *Topper* (MGM, 1937), then appeared in a series of comedies matchless for their bright, vigorous style: *The Awful Truth* (Columbia, 1937), *Holiday* (Columbia, 1938), *Bringing Up Baby* (RKO, 1938), *His Girl Friday* (Columbia, 1940), *My Favorite Wife* (RKO, 1940), etc. He continued making films until the mid-sixties, seldom faltering and lending his seemingly effortless skill even to frayed material.

JEAN HARLOW (1911–1937)

The brassy, heartily vulgar "platinum blonde" Jean Harlow was at her best in raucous comedy where her limited acting ability was no handicap. She was ideally cast as hot-tempered movie star Lola Burns in *Bombshell* (MGM, 1933), and even better as Gladys, Spencer Tracy's perennial girlfriend, in *Libeled Lady* (MGM, 1936). Flouncing into Tracy's newspaper office, dressed in her wedding gown and furious at being left at the altar (again), she was a sight to behold. As Wallace Beery's leather-lunged wife in *Dinner at Eight* (MGM, 1933), she was unforgettable, and her films with Clark Gable (*Red Dust*, 1932; *Hold Your Man*, 1933, etc.) were among the simple filmgoing pleasures of the thirties.

KATHARINE HEPBURN (1909–   )

After an auspicious start in *A Bill of Divorcement* (RKO, 1932), Katharine Hepburn starred in a number of films that either advanced her career (*Little Women*, RKO, 1933) or sent it plummeting (*Sylvia Scarlett*, RKO, 1936). But in all of them, she was the free and independent spirit, thwarted by or finding solace in romance. Then, just when her reputation as "box-office poison" threatened to ruin her career, Hollywood finally recognized that her perennial role of the independent lady had its comic aspects, and one of the screen's best and most enchanting comediennes emerged. In succession she appeared in three splendid comedies that have dimmed little with age: *Holiday* (Columbia, 1938), *Bringing Up Baby* (RKO, 1938), and *The Philadelphia Story* (MGM, 1940). Her unique beauty, her odd, Bryn Mawr voice, her refreshing, forthright approach to comedy captured the public's fancy and held it to the present day. The peak of her achievement in comedy came with a series of films opposite her close friend, Spencer Tracy. *Woman of the Year* (MGM, 1942), in particular, displayed a warm rapport between the two players that made a bright script glow even brighter. In recent years she has returned to solemn, overteary performances, but filmgoers remember and cherish the beautiful young actress who tamed men and leopards.

MIRIAM HOPKINS (1902–1972)
At the peak of her career in the thirties, Miriam Hopkins played both comic and dramatic roles with equal proficiency. In the same year—1932—she was Fredric March's pathetic victim in *Dr. Jekyll and Mr. Hyde* (Paramount) and Herbert Marshall's delightful partner in crime, his "sweet little pickpocket," in Ernst Lubitsch's *Trouble in Paradise* (Paramount). Her comedies in the thirties included *Design for Living* (Paramount, 1933), a diluted but amusing version of Noël Coward's play about a *ménage à trois; Woman Chases Man* (UA, 1937), about a girl architect in pursuit of a man; and *Wise Girl* (RKO, 1937), in which she played yet another of those incognito heiresses fleeing from all that cumbersome wealth.

EDWARD EVERETT HORTON (1888–1970)
Eternally fuming and fussing, prissily trying to maintain his decorum in the face of disaster, Edward Everett Horton was an enduring—and endearing—comic actor for four decades. He seldom varied in the scores of films he made, whether he was fleeing from Alice Brady in *The Gay Divorcee* (RKO, 1934), fretting over his plight as a downed airplane passenger in *Lost Horizon* (Columbia, 1937), or apologizing for his errors as Heavenly Messenger 7013 in *Here Comes Mr. Jordan* (Columbia, 1941). He was engaging as Cary Grant's friend Nick Potter in Columbia's *Holiday* (1938), but just as engaging, though considerably more wrinkled, nearly a quarter of a century later, as a very correct butler in Frank Capra's *Pocketful of Miracles* (UA, 1961).

RUTH HUSSEY (1914–   )
Ruth Hussey was never a major star but she was an able actress with an erratic career. She had featured or starring roles at MGM from 1937 to 1942, most notably as James Stewart's magazine colleague and girlfriend in *The Philadelphia Story* (1940). She was adept at comedy but the studio gave her little chance to shine. Other of her films included *The Women* (MGM, 1939), *Susan and God* (MGM, 1940), and *Our Wife* (Columbia, 1941), in which she played a lady scientist out to win Melvyn Douglas away from his scheming estranged wife, Ellen Drew.

RITA JOHNSON (1912–1965)
One of Hollywood's most attractive "other women," Rita Johnson appeared at her nasty best in *Here Comes Mr. Jordan* (Columbia, 1941), as a wife with homicide on her mind. But she was also causing trouble for the heroine in such films as *Rich Man, Poor Girl* (MGM, 1938), *The Girl Downstairs* (MGM, 1939), and *Appointment for Love* (Universal, 1941). She enjoyed a brief respite from her wicked ways as Mrs. Thomas Edison in MGM's *Edison the Man* (1940).

ALLYN JOSLYN (1905–)
Allyn Joslyn could aways be relied on for effective portrayals of an assortment of amiable or unpleasant crooks, cheaters, or otherwise dubious types. He was Melvyn Douglas' lawyer in *This Thing Called Love* (Columbia, 1941), a reporter out to make time with *My Sister Eileen* (Columbia, 1942), and Don Ameche's obnoxious cousin in Ernst Lubitsch's *Heaven Can Wait* (Fox, 1943).

FRANCIS LEDERER (1906–)
When he was not playing overwrought types in such films as *Confessions of a Nazi Spy* (Warners, 1939) and *The Man I Married* (Fox, 1940), this Czech-born actor was enjoying himself in comedy roles. In *The Pursuit of Happiness* (Paramount, 1934), he was a Hessian soldier who learns the colonial art of bundling from Joan Bennett. He was a playboy pursued by Madeleine Carroll in *It's All Yours* (Columbia, 1938), and yet another playboy with his eye on Claudette Colbert in *Midnight* (Paramount, 1939).

CAROLE LOMBARD (1908–1942)
Carole Lombard made twenty-six sound films as well as a number of silent films before she appeared in Columbia's *Twentieth Century* (1934) and established herself as a gifted comedienne. Her performance as tempestuous actress Lily Garland displayed a talent for zany comedy that carried her through a number of good films, including *Hands Across the Table* (Paramount, 1935), *True Confession* (Paramount, 1937), *My Man Godfrey* (Universal, 1936), and *Nothing Sacred* (UA, 1937). She was also a sensitive dramatic actress, as evidenced by *Made for Each Other* (UA, 1939), *Vigil in the Night* (RKO, 1940), and *They Knew What They Wanted* (RKO, 1940). Her last performance before her death in an airplane crash was opposite Jack Benny in Ernst Lubitsch's *To Be or Not To Be* (UA, 1942). Until Kay Kendall appeared in the fifties, no actress combined beauty and comic finesse to such a high degree as Carole Lombard.

MYRNA LOY (1905–)
After years of playing seductive Oriental wenches in silent films, Myrna Loy made her sound debut as a seductive native wench in *The Desert Song* (Warners, 1929)—she had a silent bit role in *The Jazz Singer*—then went on to make

twenty-six more films, mostly for Warners, in only two years. In 1932, she joined MGM to play the ingenue in *Emma* and remained until 1944. She was a popular actress but her fame was assured when she traded quips and shared adventures with William Powell in *The Thin Man* (MGM, 1934). As Nora, charming and sophisticated wife to detective Nick Charles, she indicated clearly that she loved her husband—a startling novelty for American films. Miss Loy and Powell played beautifully together in an enjoyable group of films, including the *Thin Man* series and such antic farces as *Libeled Lady* (1936), *I Love You Again* (1940), and *Love Crazy* (1941), all for MGM. She played many sensible, level-headed mothers through the forties and into the fifties, returning to MGM in 1947 to play Nora Charles once more in *Song of the Thin Man.*

JOEL McCREA (1905–   )

Until he turned to Westerns in the forties and fifties, Joel McCrea was the amiable if rather sober-sided hero of many films. He was solemn in *These Three* (UA, 1936) and *Dead End* (UA, 1937), but he managed to break loose into comedy a number of times, usually as a put-upon husband or fiancé. His comedy films include *Woman Chases Man* (Goldwyn, 1937), *Three Blind Mice* (Fox, 1938), *He Married His Wife* (Fox, 1940), and *The Palm Beach Story* (Paramount, 1942). His best comedy films were *Sullivan's Travels* (Paramount, 1942), Preston Sturges' Hollywood satire, and *The More the Merrier* (Columbia, 1943), in which he shared a Washington apartment with Jean Arthur and Charles Coburn.

FRED MacMURRAY (1908–   )

In his first major role in *The Gilded Lily* (Paramount, 1935), Fred MacMurray was already cast as the ingratiating, unprepossessing young man he played for many years afterwards. Although he seldom varied—one memorable exception was his murder-plotting insurance agent in Paramount's *Double Indemnity* (1944)—he was always likeable. He played well and often opposite Claudette Colbert: in *The Gilded Lily* (Paramount, 1935), *The Bride Comes Home* (Paramount, 1935), *No Time for Love* (Paramount, 1943), *Practically Yours* (Paramount, 1945), and other comedies. But he played equally well opposite other leading ladies of the thirties and forties, including Madeleine Carroll, Barbara Stanwyck, Rosalind Russell, and Jean Arthur. In his straightforward, artless way, he has managed to endure for nearly four decades.

HERBERT MARSHALL (1890–1966)

Reserved to the point of austerity and refined to the point of dullness, Herbert Marshall gave competent support to flamboyant actresses, notably to Bette Davis in *The Letter* (Warners, 1940) and *The Little Foxes* (Goldwyn, 1941). Occasionally he played in a comedy, where he was agreeable and polished but hardly animated, his best being *If You Could Only Cook* (Columbia, 1935). In that pleasant film, he played a millionaire who pretends to be poor and takes a job as a butler in the home of retired gangster Leo Carrillo.

DONALD MEEK (1880–1946)

For years the unique Mr. Meek virtually held a monopoly on the role of the timid, obsequious, befuddled little man who is usually the victim of fate, fortune, or adversity. Tiny, bald, and usually bleating, he made over 100 films from 1929 until his death. Everyone has his own favorite memory of Donald Meek: as the excitable little man who mistakes Edward G. Robinson for a hunted killer in *The Whole Town's Talking* (Columbia, 1935), as Mr. Poppins in *You Can't Take It With You* (Columbia, 1938), and—perhaps most memorably—as the judge in *State Fair* (Fox, 1945), who gets delicately drunk on Mrs. Frake's spiked mincemeat.

ADOLPHE MENJOU (1890–1963)

Perennially suave and dapper, Adolphe Menjou had a long career in films, extending from early silent days to the fifties. He played a variety of roles, both dramatic and comic, from the cynical Major Rinaldi in the 1932 version of *A Farewell to Arms* (Paramount) to a maniacal Russian impresario in *Gold Diggers of 1935* (Warners, 1935). He was often cast as a stage or film producer (*A Star is Born*, Selznick International, 1937; *Goldwyn Follies*, Goldwyn, 1938; *Stage Door*, RKO, 1937; etc.). Among his comedy films were *Convention City* (Warners, 1933), *The Housekeeper's Daughter* (Hal Roach, 1939), *Turnabout* (Hal Roach, 1940), and *Roxie Hart* (Fox, 1942).

UNA MERKEL (1903–   )

One of the steady delights of filmgoing in the thirties was watching blonde Una Merkel dispensing her caustic or sensible advice to the heroine, or conveying her sharp, no-nonsense opinion to a variety of suitors. She made her sound debut as Ann Rutledge to Walter Huston's Lincoln in 1930 but went on to much less ethereal roles. She gave countless good comic performances: as one of the discarded mates in *Private Lives* (MGM, 1931); as a tough chorine in *42nd Street* (Warners, 1933); as Eleanor Powell's sidekick in several MGM musicals; and as W. C. Fields' daughter in *The Bank Dick* (Universal, 1940). She continued to act in featured roles throughout the fifties and sixties, always a professional, always a pleasure.

RAY MILLAND (1907–   )

For the first six years of his film career, Ray Milland (usually billed as Raymond Milland) made only a mild impression as a serviceable leading man or supporting player. His first really good role came in Paramount's *Easy Living* (1937), in which he played opposite Jean Arthur as Edward

Arnold's independent-minded son. By the end of the thirties, he was a major
star, appearing in comedies, dramas, and adventure films with equal facility.
In the early forties, he appeared in a number of comedies, playing with
cheerful aplomb. The best of them was *The Major and the Minor* (Paramount,
1942), in which he was required to believe that Ginger Rogers was only
twelve years old. The fact that he was almost convincing was a testament to
his skillful acting. In 1945, he won an Academy Award playing a desperate
alcoholic in Paramount's *The Lost Weekend.*

ROBERT MONTGOMERY (1904–   )

One of the screen's most polished comedians for many years, Robert Montgomery made about sixty films before he retired from acting in 1950. Most
of them were made for MGM, where his bright insouciance and engaging
style made him a favorite leading man. He was not always playing comedy
—in *Night Must Fall* (1937) he was a deceptively charming murderer—but
most of the time he was pursuing Joan Crawford, Madge Evans, Rosalind
Russell, Norma Shearer, and other leading ladies in lightweight entertainments, including *When Ladies Meet* (1933), *Fugitive Lovers* (1934), *Forsaking
All Others* (1934), and *Live, Love, and Learn* (1937). One of his best roles was
as Joe Pendleton, the prizefighter in *Here Comes Mr. Jordan* (Columbia, 1941),
who is prematurely spirited to heaven and is forced to make serious adjust-
ments.

FRANK MORGAN (1890–1949)

Frank Morgan blustered his endearing way through dozens of films in the
thirties and forties, mostly at MGM. Some of his roles, as in *Tortilla Flat*
(1942) and *The Human Comedy* (1943), veered heavily into pathos and sentiment, but more often he was the hearty, fumbling con man in comedies and
musicals. In *The Shop Around the Corner* (1940), he combined comedy and
pathos in a fine performance as the cuckolded shop-owner. He was superb
in *The Great Ziegfeld* (1936), *Piccadilly Jim* (1936), *Saratoga* (1937), *Boom Town*
(1940), and scores of other films. He will always be remembered by millions
of children for one role: *The Wizard of Oz* (1939).

ALAN MOWBRAY (1896–1969)

Pompous, fatuous, elegant, or all three, British-born Alan Mowbray graced
hundreds of films playing an assortment of characters from butlers to kings.
He was the villainous de Sarnac in *Voltaire* (Warners, 1933) and Lady Hamilton's weak husband in *That Hamilton Woman* (UA, 1941), but more often he
appeared in comedy: as man-about-town Tommy Gray in *My Man Godfrey*
(Universal, 1936), as Topper's butler in *Topper* (MGM, 1937), as an idiotic
psychiatrist in *That Uncertain Feeling* (UA, 1941), and many others.

DAVID NIVEN (1911–   )
Impeccable and debonair, David Niven could usually be counted on to give graceful, relaxed performances in scores of films over three decades. In the middle and late thirties, he often appeared as the second male lead (*The Charge of the Light Brigade*, 1936; *The Dawn Patrol*, 1938; *Bluebeard's Eight Wife*, 1938; *Three Blind Mice*, 1938), then graduated to the leading role opposite Ginger Rogers in *Bachelor Mother* (RKO, 1939). He has starred in films of all kinds until the present, winning an Academy Award in 1958 for his portrayal of the pathetic British major in *Separate Tables* (UA). The year before he played William Powell's original role in an unsuccessful remake of *My Man Godfrey* (Universal).

LYNNE OVERMAN (1887–1943)
At Paramount in the late thirties, Lynne Overman was a reliable supporting actor whose querulous, often cynical manner and distinctive voice lent a cheerful note to many films. He was featured in *True Confession* (1937), *New York Town* (1941), and *Caught in the Draft* (1941) and shared a desert island no less than three times with Dorothy Lamour (*The Jungle Princess*, 1936; *Typhoon*, 1940; *Aloma of the South Seas*, 1941).

EUGENE PALLETTE (1889–1954)
Eugene Pallette played in many silent films, then made over 100 sound films before his retirement in 1946. He was invariably cast as the gruff, rotund, bass-voiced father, detective, business executive, or all-around boor, and he was invariably fun to watch. He was the long-suffering father of the Bullock family in *My Man Godfrey* (Universal, 1936), political hack Chuck McGann in *Mr. Smith Goes to Washington* (Columbia, 1939), Henry Fonda's put-upon father in *The Lady Eve* (Paramount, 1941), and bigoted college trustee Ed Keller in *The Male Animal* (Warners, 1942).

FRANKLIN PANGBORN (1893–1958)
The screen's No. 1 portrayer of fussy, hysterical, effeminate men, Franklin Pangborn was W. C. Fields' principal victim in *The Bank Dick* (Universal, 1940), and scores of harried hotel managers, shopkeepers, clerks, and officials throughout the thirties and forties. He was Longfellow Deeds' tailor in *Mr. Deeds Goes to Town* (Columbia, 1936) and a favorite member of Preston Sturges' company of players, appearing in *Sullivan's Travels* (1942), *The Palm Beach Story* (1942), and *Hail the Conquering Hero* (1944), all for Paramount. He almost walked off with the latter film, playing the desperately thwarted director of the ceremonies to welcome home "hero" Eddie Bracken.

GAIL PATRICK (1916–   )
Willowy brunette Gail Patrick played a variety of roles in many films in the thirties and forties but she is best remembered as one of the screen's iciest and most formidable "other women." In *My Favorite Wife* (RKO, 1940), she was Cary Grant's new second wife, unaware that his first wife, Irene Dunne, had inopportunely returned from the dead. She was also clearly destined to lose the heroes of *The Doctor Takes a Wife* (Columbia, 1940) and *Love Crazy* (MGM, 1941). In *My Man Godfrey* (Universal, 1936), she was Carole Lombard's unpleasant sister.

WILLIAM POWELL (1892–   )
William Powell would have to be considered one of the strongest candidates for the title of the screen's finest comic actor. In film after film from his sound debut in 1928, he was the epitome of sophistication and elegance, and his wry, ironic approach to a role was unique. After playing mostly villains in silent pictures, he appeared in many films for Paramount and Warner Brothers in the early thirties, then joined MGM in 1934. His second film for MGM was *The Thin Man* (1934) and it brought him fame as suave detective Nick Charles. He appeared opposite Myrna Loy in the *Thin Man* sequels and in a number of bright farces, including *Libeled Lady* (1936) and *I Love You Again* (1940). One of his most famous roles was Godfrey, the millionaire-turned-butler, in Universal's *My Man Godfrey* (1936).

GINGER ROGERS (1911–   )
After years as Fred Astaire's famous dancing partner, Ginger Rogers turned to straight acting roles, in which she proved to be an engaging if occasionally arch comedienne. She appeared as an ambitious actress in *Stage Door* (RKO, 1937), as a romantically inclined camper in *Having Wonderful Time* (RKO, 1938), as James Stewart's nightclub singer wife in *Vivacious Lady* (RKO, 1938), and as a salesgirl saddled with an abandoned baby in *Bachelor Mother* (RKO, 1939). After winning an Academy Award for *Kitty Foyle* (RKO, 1940), she appeared in two of her best comedies: *Tom, Dick and Harry* (RKO, 1941), as a dream-ridden girl with three suitors; and *The Major and the Minor* (Paramount, 1942), as a girl forced to impersonate a twelve-year-old. Later in her career, her performances became strained and heavy-handed, but her position as a favorite star remained secure.

CHARLES RUGGLES (1892–1970)
A comic actor of consummate charm and skill, Charlie Ruggles was unfailingly right as the genial, bumbling, and quizzical gentleman in many films of the thirties and forties. He was marvelous as the newly rich Egbert Floud in *Ruggles of Red Gap* (Paramount, 1935) and as the bewildered Major Applegate in *Bringing Up Baby* (RKO, 1938). But he was good in all his films, even in the series of low-budget programmers he made with Mary Boland in the

thirties. One of his last and best roles was as Lilli Palmer's witty father in Paramount's *The Pleasure of His Company* (1961).

ROSALIND RUSSELL (1908–   )
Rosalind Russell has ranged from stark drama to antic farce ovr her long career, but she is at her best in comedy, where her zest and her brilliant way with a brittle, acerbic line come to the fore. Until 1939, she usually played glum "other women," then MGM cast her as vicious gossip Sylvia Fowler in *The Women* (1939), and she was wonderful. In her next film, Columbia's *His Girl Friday* (1940), she was dazzling as fast-talking reporter Hildy Johnson. From then on, her comedy films were frequent and while many of them were not very good, she was always working hard to invest them with her own good humor and stylish presence. Among them: *This Thing Called Love* (Columbia, 1941), *Take A Letter, Darling* (Paramount, 1942), and *What a Woman!* (Columbia, 1943). She was at her best as wry, disenchanted Ruth McKenney in Columbia's *My Sister Eileen* (1942).

LIONEL STANDER (1908–   )
During the thirties, Lionel Stander's bushy eyebrows, disapproving grimace, and gravel voice were familiar fixtures in comedy films. He was notable as "Corny" Cobb in *Mr. Deeds Goes to Town* (Columbia, 1936), and as Flash, Leo Carrillo's suspicious henchman, in *If You Could Only Cook* (Columbia, 1935). He also appeared in *More than a Secretary* (Columbia, 1936) and *A Star Is Born* (Selznick International, 1937).

BARBARA STANWYCK (1907–   )
In the thirties and forties, Barbara Stanwyck epitomized the hard-as-nails, clear-thinking dame who knew—and usually got—what she wanted. Occasionally, she softened her image to play a self-sacrificing mother, notably *Stella Dallas* (Goldwyn, 1937), or to appear in several comedies, including *The Bride Walks Out* (RKO, 1936), *Breakfast for Two* (RKO, 1937), *The Mad Miss Manton* (RKO, 1938), and *You Belong to Me* (Columbia, 1941). Her best comedy by far was Preston Sturges' *The Lady Eve* (Paramount, 1941), where she was glamorous and beguiling in the title role. For the rest of her career, her appearances in comedy were infrequent and unsuccessful. She was at her best in Paramount's *Double Indemnity* (1944) as the icy murderess.

JAMES STEWART (1908–   )
James Stewart made his debut in MGM's *Murder Man* in 1935 and has enjoyed over thirty years of popularity playing the sincere, straightforward man of principles and ideals. His early MGM career was inauspicious—he was Jean Harlow's suitor in *Wife vs. Secretary* (1936) and an unlikely murderer in *After the Thin Man* (1936)—and he made his first major impression playing

the leading role in Columbia's *Mr. Smith Goes to Washington* (1939). From then on he was a major star, appearing regularly in comedies, Westerns, dramas, and adventure films until the present. His comic style was unvarying but ingratiating, and he was fine in *The Shop Around the Corner* (MGM, 1940), *The Philadelphia Story* (MGM, 1940)—he won an Academy Award for his performance as the reporter enchanted by Katharine Hepburn—and *Harvey* (Universal, 1950).

VERREE TEASDALE (c. 1897–   )
In the thirties, Verree Teasdale was haughty or frivolous in a number of comedies, including *The Milky Way* (1936), *First Lady* (1937), and *Topper Takes a Trip* (1938). In *Fifth Avenue Girl* (1939), she went from cheating to penitent as the wife of Walter Connolly.

GENEVIEVE TOBIN (1904–   )
This wide-eyed blond comedienne was skilled at playing frivolous or scheming ladies, which she did throughout the thirties, mostly at Warner Brothers. She was diverting as Charlie Ruggles' wife on two occasions: in *One Hour With You* (Paramount, 1932) and *No Time for Comedy* (Warners, 1940). Her best performance was not comic: she was Mrs. Chisholm, the bitter, frustrated wife in Warners' *The Petrified Forest* (1936).

FRANCHOT TONE (1905–1968)
Franchot Tone worked mainly at MGM from 1932 to 1939, often appearing as the debonair young man-about-town. In *The Girl from Missouri* (1934), he was a bachelor playboy who was pursued by Jean Harlow; in *The Bride Wore Red* (1937), he won Joan Crawford from Robert Young; and in *Three Loves Has Nancy* (1938), he lost Janet Gaynor to Robert Montgomery. He was not always the ardent swain—occasionally he appeared in large-scale adventure films such as *Mutiny on the Bounty* (1935), and in his later years, he tended to play tortured, neurotic roles. But in the thirties, few actors wore their dinner clothes with as much flair as Franchot Tone.

SPENCER TRACY (1900–1967)
One of the best-liked of film stars, Spencer Tracy was equally adroit at comedy or drama. His rugged Irish features, palpable warmth, and sincerity made his portrayals of Father Flanagan, Thomas Edison, and many other lesser men entirely memorable. He was winning as the brash editor in MGM's *Libeled Lady* (1936) and in a series of stylish, witty comedies with Katharine Hepburn, including *Woman of the Year* (1942) and *Adam's Rib* (1949).

RAYMOND WALBURN (1887–1970)
Whether he was playing the bumbling idiot or the crafty con man, Raymond Walburn was an inimitable comedian. He was delightful as the butler in *Mr. Deeds Goes to Town* (Columbia, 1936), practicing yodeling in the cavernous hallways of Deeds' house; and in *She Married Her Boss* (Columbia, 1935), he brightened a mediocre comedy as a tipsy butler. But he was equally good as the fatuous mayor in *Hail the Conquering Hero* (Paramount, 1944), trying to perserve his shaky status in a community gone beserk for its "hero."

CHARLES WINNINGER (1884–1969)
As an assortment of lovable and sometimes disreputable codgers, Charles Winninger had a long career in films. He came to movies from vaudeville and quickly established himself as a reliable character actor. He was best known for his performance as "Cap'n" Andy in Universal's 1936 version of *Show Boat* but also appeared to good advantage in *Destry Rides Again* (Universal, 1939), *Woman Chases Man* (Goldwyn, 1937), and *Nothing Sacred* (Selznick International, 1937).

LORETTA YOUNG (1913–   )
A beautiful woman and a competent actress, Loretta Young enjoyed a long career, beginning as Lon Chaney's co-star in *Laugh, Clown, Laugh* (1928) and progressing to demure heroine roles at Warners and Fox. At Fox, she starred in a series of light, unmemorable, but enjoyable comedies including *Love Is News* (1937), *Wife, Doctor, and Nurse* (1937), and *Wife, Husband, and Friend* (1937). At Columbia she was a decorative, harrassed wife in *The Doctor Takes a Wife* (1940), *Bedtime Story* (1942), and *A Night to Remember* (1942). In 1947, she won an Academy Award for her performance in *The Farmer's Daughter*.

ROBERT YOUNG (1907–   )
Long before he was playing wise fathers and physicians on television, Robert Young was a solid, dependable leading man in scores of films. Many of them were comedies in which he sometimes won, sometimes lost the leading lady, but whatever the outcome, his spirits remained high. His films included: *The Bride Comes Home* (Paramount, 1935)—he lost Claudette Colbert; *I Met Him in Paris* (Paramount, 1937)—he lost Claudette Colbert again; *Bridal Suite* (MGM, 1939)—he won Annabella; and *Married Bachelor* (MGM, 1941)—he won Ruth Hussey.

ROLAND YOUNG (1887–1953)
One of the screen's most delightful actors, Roland Young was best known for two contrasting characterizations: as the obsequious but sinister Uriah Heep in MGM's *David Copperfield* (1935) and as timid Cosmo Topper in

Topper (MGM, 1937). But he was equally marvelous as Colonel "Sahib" Carleton in *The Young in Heart* (Selznick International, 1938), as lecherous Uncle Willie in *The Philadelphia Story* (MGM, 1940) and in scores of other movies.

THE DIRECTORS

Following is an annotated listing of the directors who appear regularly in this book. Although they worked in many genres, they brought a zest and a skill to their work in comedy that made even their lesser efforts watchable and entertaining.

EDWARD BUZZELL (1897–   )
From starring on the stage in musical comedies (*The Gingham Girl*, 1922, etc.), Edward (then Eddie) Buzzell went to Hollywood where he appeared briefly as an actor (*Little Johnnie Jones*, 1930) and then turned to directing. At MGM from 1938 to 1949, he directed two Marx Brothers films (*At the Circus*, 1939; *Go West*, 1941), *Song of the Thin Man* (1947), and a cluster of musicals (*Ship Ahoy*, 1942; *Best Foot Forward*, 1943; *Neptune's Daughter*, 1949, etc.). His comedies include *Fast Company* (1938), *Married Bachelor* (1941), and—for Columbia—*A Woman of Distinction* (1950).

FRANK CAPRA (1897–   )
Frank Capra appears frequently in these pages as an innovative and important director who brought a refreshingly human note to film comedy with *It Happened One Night* (1934), *Mr. Deeds Goes to Town* (1936), *Mr. Smith Goes to Washington* (1939), and other films. He has described his long career in his autobiography, revealing the love for common humanity and the deep patriotic feelings that sometimes led him into excessive sentimentality and a simplistic attitude toward complex issues. (The humor of *You Can't Take It With You* (1938) is nearly smothered in buttered Capra-corn, and the effectiveness of *Mr. Smith Goes to Washington* is weakened by a view of government that third-graders might reject.) Yet his best films, including *Lost Horizon* (1937), still retain a glowing warmth and a charm that make them irresistible even today.

JACK CONWAY (1887–1952)

Starting under the aegis of D. W. Griffith, Jack Conway handled a great many silent films for MGM, including *Brown of Harvard* (1926) and the first film version of George McManus' famous comic strip, *Bringing Up Father* (1928). His sound films for the studio included many professional and entertaining efforts, such as *Viva Villa!* (1934), *The Girl From Missouri* (1934), *Boom Town* (1940), *Love Crazy* (1941), and especially the effervescent *Libeled Lady* (1936). He also had his share of disasters: *Saratoga* (1937), *Lady of the Tropics* (1939), *The Hucksters* (1947). His 1935 version of *A Tale of Two Cities* is considered a classic film, although critic Otis Ferguson called it "a bore . . . a public waste, and a stultifying influence on the industry" (*New Republic*, January 8, 1936).

GEORGE CUKOR (1899–   )

One of the screen's most durable and most distinguished directors, George Cukor can boast of an extraordinary list of credits, from the early thirties to the present day. He is perhaps best known for his handling of women stars, such as Greta Garbo (*Camille*, 1937; *Two-Faced Woman*, 1942), Katharine Hepburn (*A Bill of Divorcement*, 1932; *Little Women*, 1933; *The Philadelphia Story*, 1940; etc.), Ingrid Bergman (*Gaslight*, 1944), Judy Holliday (*Adam's Rib*, 1949; *Born Yesterday*, 1950; etc.), Judy Garland (*A Star is Born*, 1954), and Audrey Hepburn (*My Fair Lady*, 1964). Other of his best-known films are *Dinner At Eight* (1933), *David Copperfield* (1935), *The Women* (1939), and *A Double Life* (1947). In his last film to date, *Travels With My Aunt* (1973), he guided Maggie Smith through a bravura performance. Even when his films are far from excellent, Cukor brings an innate professionalism to them which makes them enjoyable to watch, and at his very best, he is incomparable.

TAY GARNETT (1898–   )

Tay Garnett's varied credits as a director include virtually every type of film: tear-jerker (*One Way Passage*, 1932; *Cheers for Miss Bishop*, 1941), war story (*Bataan*, 1943; *The Cross of Lorraine*, 1943), "prestige" drama (*Mrs. Parkington*, 1944; *The Valley of Decision*, 1945), and romantic comedy (*Love Is News*, 1937; *Eternally Yours*, 1939). Jean Harlow took the measure of Clark Gable in Garnett's *China Seas* (1935) and, clad entirely in white, Lana Turner sized up John Garfield in the director's steamy 1946 melodrama, *The Postman Always Rings Twice*. One of Tay Garnett's most raucous and colorful films was *Seven Sinners* (1940), which starred Marlene Dietrich as the alluring Bijou. Since the fifties, he has directed many television programs.

EDWARD H. GRIFFITH (1894–   )
Starting in the twenties with such "naughty" titles as *Scrambled Wives* (1921) and *Afraid to Love* (1927), Edward H. Griffith went on to direct film versions of stage plays (*The Animal Kingdom*, 1932; *Biography of a Bachelor Girl*, 1935), florid romances (*Ladies in Love*, 1936; *Cafe Metropole*, 1937), and musicals for Grace Moore (*I'll Take Romance*, 1937) and Fred Astaire (*The Sky's the Limit*, 1943). He also directed a number of Paramount films with beautiful Madeleine Carroll, including the "boss-lady" comedy, *Honeymoon in Bali* (1939), and the "flippant-heiress" farce, *Cafe Society* (1939). Griffith's *Bahama Passage* (1942), a film with Miss Carroll and Sterling Hayden (in his second role) was almost unforgettable in its awfulness.

ALEXANDER HALL (1897–1968)
At Columbia Pictures in the late thirties and early forties, Alexander Hall apparently had the market cornered on the studio's comedy films. He directed fourteen of them between 1938 and 1945. With the exception of the inane *Good Girls Go to Paris* (1939), they were all competent or better, the best being *Here Comes Mr. Jordan* (1941) and *My Sister Eileen* (1942). Even such routine entries as *There's Always a Woman* (1938) and *The Doctor Takes a Wife* (1940) had their moments. In his pre-Columbia years, he directed Shirley Temple in *Little Miss Marker* (1934), Joan Bennett in *The Pursuit of Happiness* (1934), and Mae West in *Goin' to Town* (1935). In the fifties, he directed a Mario Lanza musical, *Because You're Mine* (1952), for MGM and a musical remake of *The Awful Truth* called *Let's Do It Again* (1953). Unfortunately, they didn't.

LEIGH JASON (1904–   )
Leigh Jason directed some pleasant but forgettable comedies in the thirties and forties, including *The Mad Miss Manton* (1938), *Wise Girl* (1938), and *Model Wife* (1941). He also directed opera star Lily Pons in her second film, *That Girl From Paris* (1936). In later years, he directed for television.

GARSON KANIN (1912–   )
A distinctive writer and director since the late thirties, Garson Kanin attracted attention with his first film, a moving little "sleeper" called *A Man to Remember* (1938). In the next few years, he guided John Barrymore through *The Great Man Votes* (1939), a well-regarded film about a drunkard who turns sober for the sake of his children, and *They Knew What They Wanted* (1940), an adaptation of Sidney Howard's play. His best-remembered comedies are two with Ginger Rogers, *Bachelor Mother* (1939) and *Tom, Dick and Harry* (1941), and *My Favorite Wife* (1940), with Irene Dunne and Cary Grant. His writing credits (with his wife Ruth Gordon) include *A Double Life* (1947), *Adam's Rib* (1949), *The Marrying Kind* (1952), and *Pat and Mike* (1952). Singly he wrote *It Should Happen to You* (1954), one of Judy Hol-

liday's best films. Inexplicably, in 1950 his successful play *Born Yesterday* was adapted to the screen by Albert Mannheimer, rather than by himself.

WILLIAM KEIGHLEY (1893–   )

Prolific and proficient, William Keighley directed most of his films for Warner Brothers, including some of the most popular ever made by the studio—*G Men* (1935), *The Adventures of Robin Hood* (1938, with Michael Curtiz), *The Fighting 69th* (1940), etc. His comedy films for Warners were largely adapted from stage plays: *Brother Rat* (1938), *Yes, My Darling Daughter* (1939), *No Time for Comedy* (1940), *The Man Who Came to Dinner* (1942), and *George Washington Slept Here* (1942).

GREGORY LA CAVA (1892–1952)

The highlight of Gregory La Cava's career was his direction of the delightful *My Man Godfrey* (1936), but other of his notable films include *Private Worlds* (1935), one of the first films to deal with mental illness, and *Stage Door* (1937), which was generally conceded to be an improvement over the stage play. Early in the sound years, he directed the first version of Maxwell Anderson's *Saturday's Children* (1929), as well as *Gabriel Over the White House* (1933), a strange and controversial drama about a President of the United States (Walter Huston) who is inspired by a vision of the Archangel Gabriel to change his handling of the government. La Cava's comedies include *She Married Her Boss* (1935), *Fifth Avenue Girl* (1939), and *Primrose Path* (1940).

MITCHELL LEISEN (1898–1972)

Mitchell Leisen's long career as a leading director is worthy of careful and serious study. From his debut in 1933 with *Cradle Song* until the early fifties, he worked at Paramount, directing many popular films of those years with ease and efficiency. His second film, *Death Takes a Holiday* (1934), was a striking drama with Fredric March as the monocled Prince Sirki, personification of the grim reaper, and in a lighter vein Leisen directed three of the best romantic comedies of the thirties: *Hands Across the Table* (1935), *Easy Living* (1937), and *Midnight* (1939). In the forties, his films included *Remember the Night* (1940), with an engaging Preston Sturges script; *Hold Back the Dawn* (1941), a poignant drama with Charles Boyer and Olivia de Havilland, and *To Each His Own* (1946), for which Olivia de Havilland won an Academy Award. *Take a Letter, Darling* (1942) was a lighthearted comedy of the "boss-lady" school. Leisen had his share of failures—*Lady in the Dark* (1944), *Dream Girl* (1948)—but his record over the years was exceptionally good. His fifties films were not memorable, but in *The Mating Season* (1951), he directed Thelma Ritter in her best performance as John Lund's diamond-in-the-rough mother.

ROBERT Z. LEONARD (1889–   )
In the silent years, Robert Z. Leonard directed a number of films with those "titillating" titles so favored at the time: *The Restless Sex* (1920), *Jazzmania* (1923), *Dance Madness* (1926), and *The Waning Sex* (1926). At MGM from the mid-twenties until his retirement in the late fifties, Leonard was assigned to many of the studio's most prestigious films, including *The Great Ziegfeld* (1936), *Pride and Prejudice* (1940), and three of the Jeanette MacDonald–Nelson Eddy operettas: *Maytime* (1937), *The Girl of the Golden West* (1938), and *New Moon* (1940). Most of MGM's famous ladies were directed by Leonard in at least one movie: Greta Garbo *(Susan Lenox—Her Fall and Rise*, 1931), Joan Crawford *(Dancing Lady*, 1933; *When Ladies Meet*, 1941), Norma Shearer *(Strange Interlude*, 1932; *We Were Dancing*, 1942), and Lana Turner *(Ziegfeld Girl*, 1941; *Marriage is a Private Affair*, 1944; *Weekend at the Waldorf*, 1945). His comedies include *After Office Hours* (1935), *Third Finger, Left Hand* (1940), and *Grounds for Marriage* (1950).

LEO McCAREY (1898–1969)
Starting as a gag writer in the silent era, Leo McCarey went on to become a capable director of many outstanding films, as well as a writer and producer. In the early thirties, he went from Eddie Cantor *(The Kid From Spain*, 1932) to the Marx Brothers *(Duck Soup*, 1933) to Mae West *(Belle of the Nineties*, 1934) without missing a step. Also in the thirties, he directed four films that demonstrate his versatility: *Ruggles of Red Gap* (1935), a genial, low-key story about a British butler in the American West; *Make Way for Tomorrow* (1937), a touching drama of old age; *The Awful Truth* (1937), a riotous marital farce, and *Love Affair* (1939), a tender and rueful romantic story. He won an Academy Award for his direction of *Going My Way* (1944). McCarey produced and wrote some of the films he directed, such as *My Son John* (1952) and *Rally Round the Flag, Boys!* (1958).

NORMAN Z. McLEOD (1898–1964)
Beginning as an animator and screenwriter, Norman Z. McLeod became one of the most active directors of comedy films. He directed two of the Marx Brothers' earliest films, *Monkey Business* (1931) and *Horse Feathers* (1932), and *It's a Gift* (1934), one of W. C. Fields' funniest movies. Although he directed the original *Topper* in 1937, his other thirties comedies were derivative: *Merrily We Live* (1938) was very similar to *My Man Godfrey* (1936) and *There Goes My Heart* (1938) had virtually the same heiress-reporter plot as *It Happened One Night* (1934). His forties and fifties comedies were variably amusing, ranging from two Danny Kaye films *(The Kid From Brooklyn*, 1946; *The Secret Life of Walter Mitty*, 1947) to farces with Bob Hope *(The Paleface*, 1948; *My Favorite Spy*, 1951; *Casanova's Big Night*, 1954). His last film, *Alias Jesse James* (1959), also starred Bob Hope.

ELLIOTT NUGENT (1900–   )
A stage actor who also played in several early sound films, Elliott Nugent directed a number of films in the thirties and forties, mostly comedies such as *Three Cornered Moon* (1933), *It's All Yours* (1938), *The Cat and the Canary* (1939), and *Up in Arms* (1944), Danny Kaye's feature film debut. He also directed the film version of his stage play, *The Male Animal* (1942), which he wrote with James Thurber.

GREGORY RATOFF (1897–1961)
As an actor, Gregory Ratoff appeared in scores of thirties films (and some films afterwards), usually as a volatile, heavy-accented Russian entrepreneur. He was perhaps most memorable as film producer Herman Glogauer in *Once in a Lifetime* (1932), and as stage producer Max Fabian in *All About Eve* (1950). As a director, his films were competent, sometimes amusing, but seldom inspired. He directed Ingrid Bergman in her first and second English-language films, *Intermezzo* (1939) and *Adam Had Four Sons* (1941). Apart from the intermittently clever *Where Do We Go From Here?* (1945), his musicals were strictly routine or worse (*Something to Shout About*, 1943; *Carnival in Costa Rica*, 1947, etc.). Among his comedy films: *Wife, Husband and Friend* (1939), *Daytime Wife* (1939), and *Public Deb No. 1* (1940).

STEPHEN ROBERTS (1895–   )
In the early thirties, Stephen Roberts directed several films for Paramount, including one episode of the multipart *If I Had a Million* (1932), *The Story of Temple Drake* (1933)—the first version of William Faulkner's novel, *Sanctuary*—and *One Sunday Afternoon* (1933), a film adaptation of James Hagan's play, later filmed by Warner Brothers as *The Strawberry Blonde* (1941). His two comedy-mysteries, *Star of Midnight* (1935) and *The Ex-Mrs. Bradford* (1936), both starring William Powell, were enjoyable variations on *The Thin Man* (1934).

WESLEY RUGGLES (1889–1972)
Originally one of Mack Sennett's Keystone Kops and then a silent film director, comedian Charlie Ruggles' older brother worked at Paramount in the thirties and at Columbia and MGM in the forties. In his first years at Paramount, his credits included *No Man of Her Own* (1932), the only film in which Clark Gable and Carole Lombard (later Mrs. Gable) appeared together; *College Humor* (1933), a Bing Crosby musical ("Down the Old Ox Road"); *I'm No Angel* (1933), with Mae West cavorting as Tira the lion tamer; and *Bolero* (1934), which had George Raft dancing his way into a fatal heart attack. His string of thirties comedies were pleasant (*The Gilded Lily*, 1935), vacuous (*I Met Him in Paris*, 1937), or hilarious (*True Confession*, 1937). At Columbia, he directed three films: the inept *Too Many Husbands* (1940), a sluggish but occasionally effective Western, *Arizona* (1941), and the moder-

ately amusing *You Belong to Me* (1941). His few films for MGM included *See Here, Private Hargrove* (1944).

WILLIAM A. SEITER (1891–1964)

William A. Seiter's credits go back to the silent years, when he directed such films as *The Teaser* (1925), *Dangerous Innocence* (1925), and *Out All Night* (1927). From 1930 to 1939 he directed over forty films, mostly comedies and farces (an episode of *If I Had a Million,* 1932; *Sons of the Desert,* 1934, one of the best Laurel and Hardy farces; *We're Rich Again,* 1934; etc.). Among his best thirties films were: *Roberta* (1935), a glittering version of the Jerome Kern musical; *If You Could Only Cook* (1935), an "incognito" comedy with Jean Arthur and Herbert Marshall; *The Moon's Our Home* (1936), with Margaret Sullavan and Henry Fonda; and *Three Blind Mice* (1938), one of Fox's first variations on the "three-girls-in-search-of-rich-husbands" theme.

GEORGE STEVENS (1904–   )

A skillful director with a sometimes heavy touch, George Stevens started his official career on a frivolous note—his first two films after some years of working in Hollywood were *The Cohens and Kellys in Trouble* (1933) and *Kentucky Kernels* (1934), with Bert Wheeler and Robert Woolsey. He progressed to more serious endeavors afterwards, directing Katharine Hepburn in one of her best roles as the tremulous, socially ambitious *Alice Adams* (1935) and putting Cary Grant and Irene Dunne through the emotional wringer in *Penny Serenade* (1941). Despite the grandiose nature of his recent films (*The Greatest Story Ever Told,* 1965, etc.), his best efforts have been such popular entertainments as *Swing Time* (1936), *Gunga Din* (1939), and a string of brightly scripted, enjoyable comedies: *Woman of the Year* (1942), *The Talk of the Town* (1942), *The More the Merrier* (1943), etc. He won an Academy Award for his direction of *A Place in the Sun* (1951).

PRESTON STURGES (1898–1959)

Preston Sturges' career has been covered in Chapter Nine. He was one of the few original writers and directors to emerge from the studio system: a brilliantly talented creator of a body of riotous if uneven comedies that poked fun at America's most revered ideals and institutions, from heroism to motherhood. The Sturges "stock" company created a marvelous gallery of cartoon-like characters: fussy (Franklin Pangborn), crochety (Eugene Pallette, William Demarest), bombastically stupid (Raymond Walburn), and pathetic (Eddie Bracken). On balance his best film is probably *Hail the Conquering Hero* (1944) but there are many who would cast their votes for *Sullivan's Travels* (1942).

318

NORMAN TAUROG (1899–   )
Amazingly prolific director Norman Taurog spanned the period from the
silent era to the late sixties, turning out dozens of pleasurable movies. He
handled every genre, every kind of performer, with aplomb and without
pretension. In 1931, he won an Academy Award for directing *Skippy*, and
in the early thirties, he directed entertainers as varied as George M. Cohan
(*The Phantom President*, 1932), Maurice Chevalier (*A Bedtime Story*, 1933),
Gracie Allen (*The Big Broadcast of 1936*, 1935), and Eddie Cantor (*Strike Me
Pink*, 1936). From 1938 to 1951, he directed many films at MGM, beginning
with that sentiment-soaked drama, *Boys Town* (1938), and continuing with
Young Tom Edison (1940), *A Yank at Eton* (1942), and *Girl Crazy* (1943), all
with Mickey Rooney. His comedies included *Design for Scandal* (1942), *The
Bride Goes Wild* (1948), and one side excursion to Paramount, *Are Husbands
Necessary?* (1942). In the fifties, he directed six films starring Dean Martin
and Jerry Lewis, and in the sixties, eight films with Elvis Presley.

RICHARD THORPE (1896–   )
Richard Thorpe directed an extraordinary number of films for MGM from
the mid-thirties to the sixties, including *Night Must Fall* (1937), *Cry Havoc*
(1943), *Three Little Words* (1950), *The Great Caruso* (1951), and *Ivanhoe* (1952).
He also directed four of the studio's *Tarzan* films and one in the *Thin Man*
series, *The Thin Man Goes Home* (1945). His busy schedule over the years
included a batch of unexceptional comedies: *Double Wedding* (1937), *Man-
Proof* (1938), *Three Loves Has Nancy* (1938), *Three Hearts for Julia* (1943), etc.

W. S. VAN DYKE (1889–1944)
W. S. Van Dyke directed films at MGM from the late twenties until 1942.
He brought no special style to his movies, but they were often solidly
entertaining and in several cases, historically important. His *Trader Horn*
(1931) was the first major Hollywood film to go on location in the African
jungle; *Tarzan, the Ape Man* (1932) was the first in MGM's series on the jungle
hero; and *The Thin Man* (1934) started Nick and Nora Charles on their merry
way. (He also directed three of the *Thin Man* sequels.) His credits include
five Jeanette MacDonald–Nelson Eddy musicals. Among his many comedies
were: *Love on the Run* (1936), with Clark Gable and Joan Crawford; *It's a
Wonderful World* (1939), a comedy-mystery with Claudette Colbert and James
Stewart; *I Love You Again* (1940), with William Powell and Myrna Loy; and
The Feminine Touch (1941), with Rosalind Russell and Don Ameche. Van
Dyke's most lavish films were *San Francisco* (1936), with its famous earth-
quake sequence, and *Marie Antoinette* (1938), with Norma Shearer as the
ill-fated queen. His last movie, *Journey for Margaret* (1942), introduced little
Margaret O'Brien to the screen.

RICHARD WALLACE (1894–1951)

Starting as a cutter for Mack Sennett, Richard Wallace learned his trade with a number of silent films, then went on to direct many movies in the thirties and forties. They included costume romance (*The Little Minister*, 1934), adventure stories (*Captain Caution*, 1940; *Sinbad the Sailor*, 1947), and a group of comedies ranging from superior (*The Young in Heart*, 1938) to mediocre or misguided (*She Knew All the Answers*, 1941; *A Night to Remember*, 1942).

THE WRITERS

Following is an annotated listing of the screenwriters who appear most regularly in the pages of this book.

GRAHAM BAKER (–   )
Collaborating with Gene Towne—their madcap antics are part of Hollywood lore—Graham Baker wrote a number of good and competent screenplays, the best being Fritz Lang's *You Only Live Once* (1937) and *History is Made at Night* (1937). Their comedy scripts included *Stand-In* (1937), a Hollywood spoof with Leslie Howard and Joan Blondell, and *Eternally Yours* (1939), with Loretta Young and David Niven. At RKO, they joined with other writers for the screenplay of *Joy of Living* (1938) and adaptations of two popular children's classics, *Swiss Family Robinson* (1940) and *Tom Brown's School Days* (1940).

CLAUDE BINYON (1905–   )
Claude Binyon was a busy, prolific writer at Columbia and Paramount in the thirties and forties, and at Fox in the fifties, where he also directed. His comedies were occasionally emaciated (*The Bride Comes Home* (1935), or heavy-handed (*Too Many Husbands* (1940), but a number of them were sprightly: *The Gilded Lily* (1935), *True Confession* (1937), and *Take a Letter, Darling* (1942). His scenarios for Fox included *Dreamboat* (1952), *A Woman's World* (1954), and *Rally 'Round the Flag, Boys!* (1958).

CHARLES BRACKETT (1892–1969)
From *Bluebeard's Eighth Wife* in 1938 to *Sunset Boulevard* in 1950, Charles Brackett worked with Billy Wilder on the screenplays for some of the best-remembered comedies and dramas of the period, many of them marked by skillful, literate writing. *Midnight* (1939) was a sparkling Cinderella comedy;

Ninotchka (1939) was a glowing triumph for Greta Garbo; and *The Lost Weekend* (1945) stunned audiences with its uncompromising view of alcoholism. Brackett also turned to producing at Paramount in 1943, beginning with the Brackett-Wilder script for *Five Graves to Cairo* (1943) and continuing for a number of years afterwards at Fox. Wilder went on to write, produce, and direct a series of pungent, sharply observant comedies: *The Apartment* (1960), *One, Two, Three* (1961), and *The Fortune Cookie* (1966).

SIDNEY BUCHMAN (1902–   )
In the late thirties and early forties, Sidney Buchman wrote or collaborated on a group of distinctive screenplays for Columbia, including *Theodora Goes Wild* (1936),* *Holiday* (1938, with Donald Ogden Stewart), *Mr. Smith Goes to Washington* (1939), *Here Comes Mr. Jordan* (1941, with Seton I Miller), and *The Talk of the Town* (1942, with Irwin Shaw). Later, he produced and wrote the screenplays for *A Song to Remember* (1945) and *Jolson Sings Again* (1949), also for Columbia.

KEN ENGLUND (1914–   )
Ken Englund worked at Columbia on a number of comedy scenarios, including *There's That Woman Again* (1939), *Good Girls Go to Paris* (1939), *The Doctor Takes a Wife* (1940), and *This Thing Called Love* (1941). His later credits included the screenplay for Samuel Goldwyn's *The Secret Life of Walter Mitty* (1947), for which he recorded some amusing and revealing notes on his relationship with Goldwyn and James Thurber.

JULIUS J. EPSTEIN (1909–   ) and PHILIP G. EPSTEIN (1912–1952)
The Epstein brothers had their most prolific period at Warner Brothers from the late thirties to the mid-forties. They were frequently assigned to adapt successful stage plays, including *The Man Who Came to Dinner* (1942), *The Male Animal* (1942), and *Arsenic and Old Lace* (1944). They also wrote the now-legendary screenplay for *Casablanca* (1942) with Howard Koch. Before becoming a team, they had worked with other writers, Julius mainly with Jerry Wald *(Living on Velvet,* 1935; *In Caliente,* 1935, etc.) and Philip with various collaborators *(The Bride Walks Out,* 1936, *There's That Woman Again,* 1939, etc.)

JOSEPH FIELDS (–1966)
When Joseph Fields joined with Jerome Chodorov to adapt Ruth McKenney's stories of *My Sister Eileen* (1942) into a play, he created one of the durable theatrical properties of the last few decades. It was filmed by Columbia in 1942, with Fields and Chodorov writing the screenplay; trans-

---

*This film was based on a story by Mary McCarthy. Thirty years later, Buchman produced and wrote the script for the film adaptation of Miss McCarthy's novel, *The Group.*

formed into the stage musical *Wonderful Town* in 1953, with Rosalind Russell repeating her film role; and made into a film musical in 1955, using an entirely different score from *Wonderful Town*'s and starring Betty Garrett in the Russell role. It was even a television series with Elaine Stritch. Fields also wrote a number of other screenplays, including *Fools for Scandal* (Warners, 1938, with Herbert Fields) and *Rich Man, Poor Girl* (MGM, 1938, with Jerome Chodorov). In 1959 he worked with Chodorov on adapting their play *Anniversary Waltz* to the screen as *Happy Anniversary*.

FRANCES GOODRICH (–   )
In a long, fruitful association with MGM, Frances Goodrich worked with her husband Albert Hackett on many first-rate screenplays. Most notably, they collaborated on the screenplays for the first three *Thin Man* films, *The Thin Man* (1934), *After the Thin Man* (1936), and *Another Thin Man* (1939). They also wrote the scripts for many of MGM's most popular musical films, including *Naughty Marietta* (1935, with John Lee Mahin), *Rose Marie* (1936, with Alice Duer Miller), *The Pirate* (1948), *Easter Parade* (1948), and *Seven Brides for Seven Brothers* (1954, with Dorothy Kingsley). In 1959, they adapted their own stage play of *The Diary of Anne Frank* for Fox.

ALBERT HACKETT (1900–   )
See Frances Goodrich.

FELIX JACKSON (1902–   )
A writer and producer at Universal in the forties, Felix Jackson collaborated with Bruce Manning on the scripts for *The Rage of Paris* (1938), *Three Smart Girls Grow Up* (1939), and *Appointment for Love* (1941). With Gertrude Purcell and Henry Myers, he wrote the screenplay for *Destry Rides Again* (1939), still the best version of the Max Brand novel.

JACK JEVNE (–   )
Jack Jevne's principal credit is as the author (with Eric Hatch and Eddie Moran) of the screenplay for *Topper* (MGM, 1937). With Eddie Moran he also wrote the scripts for two freewheeling 1938 comedies, *Merrily We Live* and *There Goes My Heart.* They also collaborated with Corey Ford on a sequel to *Topper*, *Topper Takes a Trip* (1938).

NUNNALLY JOHNSON (1897–   )
Nunnally Johnson was associated for many years with Twentieth Century–Fox as a writer and producer, except for a brief association with International Pictures (released by RKO) from 1944 to 1946. His most famous screenplay was for *The Grapes of Wrath* in 1940, but he also wrote many of the studio's most popular and entertaining films, including *Jesse James* (1939), *Wife, Husband and Friend* (1939), *Holy Matrimony* (1943), *How to Marry a Millionaire* (1953), and *The Three Faces of Eve* (1957).

CHARLES KENYON (1880–1961)
Charles Kenyon wrote the scenario for John Ford's epic silent film, *The Iron Horse* (1924), but his later credits were not as auspicious. He wrote the screenplays for several minor Warners comedies, including *The Girl from Tenth Avenue* (1935), with Bette Davis, and *The Goose and the Gander* (1935), with Kay Francis, and he collaborated on the script for *100 Men and a Girl* (Universal, 1937), Deanna Durbin's second feature film.

NORMAN KRASNA (1909–   )
Playwright, screenwriter, and producer, Norman Krasna has written a number of diverting scripts over the years, including *Hands Across the Table* (Paramount, 1935), *Bachelor Mother* (RKO, 1939), *Mr. and Mrs. Smith* (RKO, 1941), and *The Devil and Miss Jones* (RKO, 1941). He adapted several of his plays for the screen—*Who Was That Lady?* (Columbia, 1960) and *Sunday in New York* (MGM, 1964)—but other of his plays, most notably *Dear Ruth* (Paramount, 1947), were turned over to other writers. Surprisingly, Krasna also wrote the original story for *Fury* (1936), MGM's powerful study of mob violence.

HARRY KURNITZ (1909–1968)
A well-loved Hollywood wit, Harry Kurnitz wrote the screenplays for two of the three Joel and Garda Sloane comedy mysteries, *Fast and Loose* (1939) and *Fast and Furious* (1939). He also collaborated on two of MGM's *Thin Man* films, *Shadow of the Thin Man* (1941) and *The Thin Man Goes Home* (1944). His script for *I Love You Again* (MGM, 1940, with George Oppenheimer and Charles Lederer) was called "a surefire screwball for the corner pocket" by the *New York Times*. His important later credits include *The Inspector General* (Warners, 1949, with Philip Rapp), *Witness for the Prosecution* (United Artists, 1958, with Billy Wilder), and *How to Steal a Million* (Fox, 1966).

CHARLES LEDERER (c. 1906–   )
Charles Lederer, a prolific and versatile writer since the early thirties, collaborated on many comedy films, notably the two William Powell–Myrna Loy farces, *I Love You Again* (1940) and *Love Crazy* (1941). He has also worked on melodramas (*Kiss of Death*, Fox, 1947), musicals (*Kismet*, MGM, 1955), and adventure stories (*Mutiny on the Bounty*, MGM, 1962). He has directed a few films as well.

GLADYS LEHMAN (–   )
At Fox in the thirties, Gladys Lehman collaborated on the screenplays for two Shirley Temple vehicles, *Captain January* (1936) and *The Poor Little Rich Girl* (1936), and on two for Will Rogers, *The County Chairman* (1935) and *In Old Kentucky* (1935). Later, she wrote the screenplays for *There's Always a Woman* (Columbia, 1938), *Good Girls Go to Paris* (Columbia, 1939, with Ken Englund), and *Hired Wife* (Universal, 1940, with Richard Connell).

SETON I. MILLER (1902–   )
After a number of years at Warner Brothers, where he worked on a great
many screenplays, including *G Men* (1935), *Kid Galahad* (1937), and *The
Adventures of Robin Hood* (1938), Seton I. Miller went to Columbia to collabo-
rate with Sidney Buchman on the script for *Here Comes Mr. Jordan* (1941), for
which they won an Academy Award. His later work was heavily geographical:
Calcutta (1947), *Singapore* (1947) *The Shanghai Story* (1954) and *Istanbul*
(1957).

GEORGE OPPENHEIMER (1900–   )
With a variety of collaborators, George Oppenheimer was responsible for
some of MGM's brightest films of the thirties and forties, including *Libeled
Lady* (1936), *A Day at the Races* (1937), *Three Loves Has Nancy* (1938), and
I Love You Again (1940). He also collaborated on the screenplay for Greta
Garbo's ill-advised last film, *Two-Faced Woman* (1942).

ROBERT RISKIN (1897–1955)
Robert Riskin's most famous screenplay was Frank Capra's *Mr. Deeds Goes
to Town* (Columbia, 1936), which was edged out for the year's writing award
by Warners' *The Story of Louis Pasteur*. As Capra's favorite scenarist, he also
wrote *Lost Horizon* (Columbia, 1937), *You Can't Take It With You* (Columbia,
1938), *Meet John Doe* (1941), and others. He directed one film for Columbia
—*When You're in Love* (1937)—and also wrote the screenplay for this Grace
Moore musical.

KATHRYN SCOLA (–   )
Kathryn Scola worked largely on the writing staff of Twentieth Century–Fox
in the thirties and forties, collaborating on such films as *Wife, Doctor and Nurse*
(1937), *Second Honeymoon* (1937), and *The Baroness and the Butler* (1938).
Earlier, with Gene Markey, she wrote the original story for Warners' *Baby
Face* (1933), the film responsible for Darryl F. Zanuck's departure as production head of the studio under Jack Warner.

ALLAN SCOTT (–   )
Allan Scott is best remembered for his collaborations on the screenplays for
five of the best Ginger Rogers–Fred Astaire musicals. Later, at RKO and at
Paramount, he wrote or collaborated on the screenplays for a batch of
comedies, including *Fifth Avenue Girl* (1939), *Lucky Partners* (1940),
and *Skylark* (1941). His later credits ranged from Bing Crosby musicals
such as *Blue Skies* (1946) to the 1959 remake of *Imitation of Life*, with Lana
Turner.

GEORGE SEATON (1911–   )

Writer, producer, and director George Seaton's first major credit was the story and screenplay (with Robert Pirosh and George Oppenheimer) for MGM's *A Day at the Races* (1937), with the Marx Brothers. Several years later at Columbia, he wrote the screenplays for two fairly amusing marital comedies, *The Doctor Takes a Wife* (1940, with Ken Englund) and *This Thing Called Love* (1941, with Ken Englund and P. J. Wolfson). Through the forties, he worked for Twentieth Century–Fox as one of their busiest writers and directors, turning out such enjoyable films as *Miracle on 34th Street* (1947) and *Apartment for Peggy* (1948). In the fifties and early sixties, he worked for Paramount as a producer as well as a writer and director.

LYNN STARLING (–1955)

Lynn Starling collaborated on screenplays for several studios, but none more curious than her first, written single-handedly, for *The President Vanishes* (Paramount, 1934), a political mystery story based on an anonymous novel generally credited to Rex Stout. Her comedy scripts include *More Than a Secretary* (Columbia, 1936, with Dale Van Every), *Three Blind Mice* (Fox, 1938, with Brown Holmes),* and two Paramount films for Bob Hope, *Thanks for the Memory* (1938) and *The Cat and the Canary* (1939, with Walter De Leon).

DONALD OGDEN STEWART (1894–   )

Humorist, playwright, and actor, Donald Ogden Stewart joined Sidney Buchman in writing the screenplay for Philip Barry's *Holiday* (1938), in which he had appeared on Broadway. He also wrote the script for *Love Affair* (RKO, 1939), a moving romantic drama with Irene Dunne and Charles Boyer, and for MGM's *Keeper of the Flame* (1943), one of the few dramatic efforts by the team of Katharine Hepburn and Spencer Tracy. His comedy screenplays include two other Hepburn films: *The Philadelphia Story* (MGM, 1940) and *Without Love* (MGM, 1945), both from plays by Philip Barry.

PRESTON STURGES (1898–1959)

The career of Preston Sturges as a director and writer is discussed fully in Chapter Nine. He was one of the screen's great originals, an innovative and gifted man who reached his peak in the early forties with *The Lady Eve* (1941), *Sullivan's Travels* (1942), *The Miracle of Morgan's Creek* (1944), and *Hail the Conquering Hero* (1944). Earlier he wrote the screenplays for the diverting *Easy Living* (1937) and for *Remember the Night* (1940), a charming comedy-drama with Barbara Stanwyck. His work declined after *Hail the*

---

*Fox was never a studio to let a serviceable idea rest. The three-girls-seeking-rich-husbands concept of this script was repeated in *Moon Over Miami* (1941) and *Three Little Girls in Blue* (1946). Miss Starling worked on the screenplays for both films.

Conquering Hero, but even the later films had moments in which Sturges' sense of human foibles and eccentricities shone through.

Jo Swerling (1894–)

Jo Swerling wrote or collaborated on the screenplays of some notable films of the thirties and forties, including *The Whole Town's Talking* (Columbia, 1935, with Robert Riskin), *Love Me Forever* (Columbia, 1935, with Sidney Buchman), *Made for Each Other* (Selznick International, 1939), *The Westerner* (Goldwyn, 1940, with Niven Busch), and *Pride of the Yankees* (Goldwyn, 1942, with Herman Mankiewicz). He wrote the script for MGM's *Double Wedding* (1937) and the original story of Paramount's *New York Town* (1941). He collaborated with Abe Burrows on the book for the stage musical, *Guys and Dolls*.

Gene Towne (1904–)
See Graham Baker.

Virginia Van Upp (c. 1913–)

In the forties, Virginia Van Upp was kept busy turning out frothy screenplays for Paramount, including *Cafe Society* (1939), *Honeymoon in Bali* (1939), and *One Night in Lisbon* (1941). Later, at Columbia, she wrote and produced such films as *Together Again* (1944), with Irene Dunne and Charles Boyer, and *She Wouldn't Say Yes* (1946), with Rosalind Russell.

Darrell Ware (–)

Darrell Ware worked mostly for Fox during the thirties and early forties, collaborating on such comedy scenarios as *Wife, Doctor and Nurse* (1937), *Second Honeymoon* (1937), *He Married His Wife* (1940), and *Tall, Dark and Handsome* (1941), as well as a number of musicals. He later worked on screenplays at Paramount.

Billy Wilder (1906–)
See Charles Brackett.

P. J. Wolfson (–)

P. J. Wolfson contributed to the screenplays of a cluster of thirties and forties comedies, including *The Bride Walks Out* (RKO, 1936), *Vivacious Lady* (RKO, 1938), *He Stayed for Breakfast* (Columbia, 1940), and *This Thing Called Love* (Columbia, 1941). He also collaborated with John Balderston on the script for *Mad Love* (MGM, 1935), Peter Lorre's first American film.

FILMOGRAPHY

Covering the years 1932 to 1944, this Filmography lists all the film comedies discussed in this book, as well as some related films. The director's name (D) follows the name of the producing company, (Sp) refers to the screenplay, and (b/o) indicates that the screenplay was based on another work.

1932

THE ANIMAL KINGDOM. RKO. D: Edward H. Griffith. Sp: Horace Jackson, b/o play by Philip Barry. Cast: Leslie Howard, Ann Harding, Myrna Loy, Neil Hamilton, Ilka Chase. Married man still loves old girlfriend. Remade by Warners in 1946 as *One More Tomorrow.*

LADIES OF THE JURY. RKO. D: Lowell Sherman. Sp: Salisbury Field and Marion Dix, b/o play by Frederick Ballard. Cast: Edna May Oliver, Ken Murray, Roscoe Ates, Guinn Williams. Society woman disrupts jury. Remade in 1937 as *We're on the Jury.*

MAKE ME A STAR. Paramount. D: William Beaudine. Sp: Sam Mintz, Walter De Leon, and Arthur Kober, b/o play by George S. Kaufman and Marc Connolly and novel by Harry Leon Wilson. Cast: Stuart Erwin, Joan Blondell, ZaSu Pitts, Ben Turpin. First sound version of *Merton of the Movies.* Remade in 1947 under original title.

THE MISLEADING LADY. Paramount. D: Stuart Walker. Sp: Lois Zellner, b/o play by Charles W. Goddard and Paul Dickey. Cast: Claudette Colbert, Edmund Lowe, Stuart Erwin, George Meeker, Selena Royle. Actress tries to get marriage proposal from well-known misogynist.

ONCE IN A LIFETIME. Universal. D: Russell Mack. Sp: Seton I. Miller, b/o play by George S. Kaufman and Moss Hart. Cast: Aline MacMahon, Jack Oakie,

Sidney Fox, Gregory Ratoff, Louise Fazenda, Russell Hopton. Hollywood spoof.

THE TENDERFOOT. Warners. D: Ray Enright. Sp: Earl Baldwin, Monty Banks, and Arthur Caesar, b/o play by George S. Kaufman. Cast: Joe E. Brown, Ginger Rogers, Lew Cody, Vivian Oakland. Comic cowboy becomes involved with gangsters. Remade in 1937 as *Dance Charlie Dance* and in 1940 as *An Angel from Texas* (All versions of Kaufman's *The Butter-and-Egg Man*).

1933
BOMBSHELL. MGM. D: Victor Fleming. Sp: John Lee Mahin and Jules Furthman, b/o play by Caroline Francke and Mack Crane. Cast: Jean Harlow, Lee Tracy, Franchot Tone, Frank Morgan, Una Merkel, Pat O'Brien. Hollywood star gets in all kinds of trouble.

CLEAR ALL WIRES. MGM. D: George Hill. Sp: Bella and Samuel Spewack, b/o their play. Cast: Lee Tracy, Benita Hume, Una Merkel, James Gleason. Comedy about head of newspaper foreign service.

DESIGN FOR LIVING. Paramount. D: Ernst Lubitsch. Sp: Ben Hecht, b/o play by Noël Coward. Cast: Miriam Hopkins, Gary Cooper, Fredric March, Edward Everett Horton. Woman loves two men.

DINNER AT EIGHT. MGM. D: George Cukor. Sp: Frances Marion and Herman J. Mankiewicz, b/o play by George S. Kaufman and Edna Ferber. Cast: John Barrymore, Jean Harlow, Marie Dressler, Wallace Beery, Lionel Barrymore, Lee Tracy, Billie Burke, Madge Evans. About the changing lives of a group of dinner guests.

ELMER THE GREAT. Warners. D: Mervyn LeRoy. Sp: Tom Geraghty, b/o play by Ring Lardner and George M. Cohan. Cast: Joe E. Brown, Patricia Ellis, Frank McHugh, Claire Dodd, Preston Foster. Baseball comedy.

ONE SUNDAY AFTERNOON. Paramount. D: Stephen Roberts. Sp: Grover Jones and William Slavens McNutt, b/o play by James Hagan. Cast: Gary Cooper, Fay Wray, Neil Hamilton, Frances Fuller, Roscoe Karns. Tribulations of a turn-of-the-century dentist. Remade by Warners in 1941 as *The Strawberry Blonde* and also in 1948 under original title.

OUR BETTERS. RKO. D: George Cukor. Sp: Jane Murfin and Harry Wagstaff Gribble, b/o play by W. Somerset Maugham. Cast: Constance Bennett, Gilbert Roland, Anita Louise, Charles Starrett, Alan Mowbray. Scandalous doings in London society.

REUNION IN VIENNA. MGM. D: Sidney Franklin. Sp: Ernest Vajda and Claudine West, b/o play by Robert E. Sherwood. Cast: John Barrymore, Diana Wynyard, Frank Morgan, May Robson, Una Merkel. Amorous archduke is reunited with former mistress.

THREE-CORNERED MOON. Paramount. D: Elliott Nugent. Sp: S. K. Lauren and Ray Harris, b/o play by Gertrude Tonkonogy. Cast: Claudette Colbert, Mary Boland, Wallace Ford, Richard Arlen, Tom Brown. Adventures of eccentric family.

TONIGHT IS OURS. Paramount. D: Stuart Walker. Sp: Edwin Justus Mayer, b/o play by Noël Coward. Cast: Claudette Colbert, Fredric March, Alison Skipworth, Paul Cavanagh. Royal romance.

WHEN LADIES MEET. MGM. D: Harry Beaumont. Sp: John Meehan and Leon Gordon, b/o play by Rachel Crothers. Cast: Ann Harding, Robert Montgomery, Myrna Loy, Alice Brady, Frank Morgan. Lady novelist has complicated love life. Remade in 1941.

WHISTLING IN THE DARK. MGM. D: Elliott Nugent. Sp: Elliott Nugent, b/o play by Laurence Gross and Edward Childs Carpenter. Cast: Ernest Truex, Una Merkel, Edward Arnold, John Miljan, Nat Pendleton. Comedy melodrama. Remade in 1941.

1934

BLIND DATE. Columbia. D: Roy William Neill. Sp: Ethel Hill, b/o story by Vida Hurst. Cast: Ann Sothern, Neil Hamilton, Paul Kelly, Mickey Rooney, Jane Darwell. Daughter of eccentric family has romantic problems.

BROADWAY BILL. Columbia. D: Frank Capra. Sp: Robert Riskin, b/o story by Mark Hellinger. Cast: Warner Baxter, Myrna Loy, Helen Vinson, Douglas Dumbrille, Raymond Walburn, Lynne Overman. Racetrack comedy. Remade in 1956 as *Riding High.*

THE CAT'S PAW. Fox. D: Samuel Taylor. Sp: Samuel Taylor, b/o story by Clarence Budington Kelland. Cast: Harold Lloyd, Una Merkel, George Barbier, Alan Dinehart, Nat Pendleton, Grant Mitchell. Young man routs crooked politicians in his hometown.

DOWN TO THEIR LAST YACHT. RKO. D: Paul Sloane. Sp: Marion Dix and Lynn Starling, b/o story by Herbert Fields and Lou Brock. Cast: Mary Boland, Polly Moran, Ned Sparks, Sidney Fox, Sterling Holloway. Socialite family turns their yacht into a chartered boat.

FORSAKING ALL OTHERS. MGM. D: W. S. Van Dyke. Sp: Joseph L. Mankiewicz, b/o play by Edward Barry Roberts and Frank Morgan Cavett. Cast: Joan Crawford, Clark Gable, Robert Montgomery, Charles Butterworth, Billie Burke, Rosalind Russell. Triangle of three old friends.

HIDE-OUT. MGM. D: W. S. Van Dyke. Sp: Frances Goodrich and Albert Hackett, b/o story by Mauri Grashin. Cast: Robert Montgomery, Maureen O'Sullivan, Edward Arnold, Elizabeth Patterson, Mickey Rooney. Gangster hides out on farm, finds love.

IT HAPPENED ONE NIGHT. Columbia. D: Frank Capra. Sp: Robert Riskin, b/o story by Samuel Hopkins Adams. Cast: Claudette Colbert, Clark Gable, Walter Connolly, Roscoe Karns, Alan Hale. Runaway heiress and reporter fall in love. Remade in 1956 as *You Can't Run Away From It.*

THE PURSUIT OF HAPPINESS. Paramount. D: Alexander Hall. Sp: J. P. McEvoy and Virginia Van Upp, b/o play by Lawrence Langner and Armina Marshall. Cast: Francis Lederer, Joan Bennett, Mary Boland, Minor Watson, Charlie Ruggles. Hessian deserter in Revolutionary days learns colonial custom of bundling.

THE RICHEST GIRL IN THE WORLD. RKO. D: William A. Seiter. Sp: Norman Krasna. Cast: Miriam Hopkins, Joel McCrea, Fay Wray, Henry Stephenson, Reginald Denny. Wealthy girl sets trap for her suitor to determine his sincerity.

SERVANTS' ENTRANCE. Fox. D: Frank Lloyd. Sp: Samson Raphaelson, b/o novel by Sigrid Boo. Cast: Janet Gaynor, Lew Ayres, Walter Connolly, Ned Sparks, Astrid Allwyn. Wealthy girl about to lose her fortune hires out as servant.

THE SHOW-OFF. MGM. D: Charles F. Riesner. Sp: Herman J. Mankiewicz, b/o play by George Kelly. Cast: Spencer Tracy, Madge Evans, Henry Wadsworth, Clara Blandick. Bombastic show-off gets his comeuppance. Remade in 1947.

THE THIN MAN. MGM. D: W. S. Van Dyke. Sp: Albert Hackett and Frances Goodrich, b/o novel by Dashiell Hammett. Cast: William Powell, Myrna Loy, Maureen O'Sullivan, Nat Pendleton, Minna Gombell, Porter Hall, Cesar Romero. First adventure of Nick and Nora Charles.

THIRTY DAY PRINCESS. Paramount. D: Marion Gering. Sp: Preston Sturges and Frank Partos, adapted by Sam Hellman and Edwin Justus Mayer from story by Clarence Budington Kelland. Cast: Sylvia Sidney, Cary Grant, Edward Arnold, Vince Barnett, Henry Stephenson. New York girl poses as princess.

20TH CENTURY. Columbia. D: Howard Hawks. Sp: Ben Hecht and Charles MacArthur, b/o their play. Cast: John Barrymore, Carole Lombard, Walter Connolly, Roscoe Karns. Eccentric stage producer and his temperamental star clash aboard a train.

WE'RE RICH AGAIN. RKO. D: William A. Seiter. Sp: Ray Harris, b/o play by Alden Nash. Cast: Edna May Oliver, Billie Burke, Marian Nixon, Buster Crabbe. Once-affluent family wants to marry daughter to wealthy man.

1935
ACCENT ON YOUTH. Paramount. D: Wesley Ruggles. Sp: Herbert Fields and Claude Binyon, b/o play by Samson Raphaelson. Cast: Sylvia Sidney, Herbert Marshall, Philip Reed, Holmes Herbert, Donald Meek, Lon Chaney, Jr. Comedy of middle-aged love. Remade in 1950 as *Mr. Music* and in 1959 as *But Not For Me.*

AFTER OFFICE HOURS. MGM. D: Robert Z. Leonard. Sp: Herman J. Mankiewicz, b/o story by Laurence Stallings and Dale Van Every. Cast: Constance Bennett, Clark Gable, Stuart Erwin, Billie Burke. Newspaper editor and music critic squabble, fall in love.

ALIBI IKE. Warners. D: Ray Enright. Sp: William Wister Haines, b/o story by Ring Lardner. Cast: Joe E. Brown, Olivia de Havilland, Ruth Donnelly, Roscoe Karns, William Frawley. Baseball player has excuse for everything.

BABY FACE HARRINGTON. MGM. D: Raoul Walsh. Sp: Nunnally Johnson and Edwin H. Knopf. Cast: Charles Butterworth, Una Merkel, Nat Pendleton. Meek man gets involved with the underworld.

BIOGRAPHY OF A BACHELOR GIRL. MGM. D: Edward H. Griffith. Sp: Anita Loos, with additional dialogue by Horace Jackson, b/o play by S. N. Behrman. Cast: Ann Harding, Robert Montgomery, Edward Arnold, Edward Everett Horton, Una Merkel. Wise lady artist meets venomous radical editor.

THE BRIDE COMES HOME. Paramount. D: Wesley Ruggles. Sp: Claude Binyon, b/o story by Elisabeth Sanxay Holding. Cast: Claudette Colbert, Fred MacMurray, Robert Young, William Collier, Sr., Donald Meek. Girl made penniless in the Crash has two suitors.

THE GAY DECEPTION. Fox. D: William Wyler. Sp: Stephen Avery and Don Hartman, with additional dialogue by Jesse L. Lasky. Cast: Francis Lederer, Frances Dee, Benita Hume, Alan Mowbray, Akim Tamiroff. Prince pretending to be bellhop meets girl who has won a lottery.

THE GILDED LILY. Paramount. D: Wesley Ruggles. Sp: Claude Binyon, b/o story by Melville Baker and Jack Kirkland. Cast: Claudette Colbert, Fred MacMurray, Ray Milland, C. Aubrey Smith, Luis Alberni. Girl becomes famous by rejecting titled suitor.

THE GIRL FROM 10TH AVENUE. First National. D: Alfred E. Green. Sp: Charles Kenyon, b/o play by Hubert Henry Davies. Cast: Bette Davis, Ian Hunter, Colin Clive, Alison Skipworth, Philip Reed. Slum girl enters high society.

THE GOOD FAIRY. Universal. D: William Wyler. Sp: Preston Sturges, b/o play by Ferenc Molnar. Cast: Margaret Sullavan, Herbert Marshall, Frank Morgan, Reginald Owen, Alan Hale, Cesar Romero, Beulah Bondi. Innocent young girl attracts three admirers. Remade in 1947 as *I'll Be Yours.*

HANDS ACROSS THE TABLE. Paramount. D: Mitchell Leisen. Sp: Norman Krasna, Vincent Lawrence, and Herbert Fields, b/o story by Vina Delmar. Cast: Carole Lombard, Fred MacMurray, Ralph Bellamy, Astrid Allwyn, Ruth Donnelly, William Demarest. Manicurist searches for rich husband.

IF YOU COULD ONLY COOK. Columbia. D: William A. Seiter. Sp: Howard J. Green and Gertrude Purcell, b/o story by F. Hugh Herbert. Cast: Jean Arthur, Herbert Marshall, Leo Carrillo, Lionel Stander, Frieda Inescort. Homeless girl and secret millionaire go into domestic service in gangster's home.

IN PERSON. RKO. D: William A. Seiter. Sp: Allan Scott, b/o story by Samuel Hopkins Adams. Cast: Ginger Rogers, George Brent, Alan Mowbray, Grant Mitchell. Film star flees to country to escape public.

NO MORE LADIES. MGM. D: Edward H. Griffith. Sp: Donald Ogden Stewart and Horace Jackson, b/o play by A. E. Thomas. Cast: Joan Crawford, Robert Montgomery, Franchot Tone, Charlie Ruggles, Edna May Oliver, Gail Patrick, Arthur Treacher. Wife decides to teach her wandering husband a lesson.

PAGE MISS GLORY. Warners. D: Mervyn LeRoy. Sp: Delmer Daves and Robert Lord, b/o play by Joseph Schrank and Philip Dunning. Cast: Marion Davies, Pat O'Brien, Dick Powell, Mary Astor, Frank McHugh, Patsy Kelly, Lyle Talbot. Chambermaid becomes America's sweetheart.

REMEMBER LAST NIGHT? Universal. D: James Whale. Sp: Doris Malloy, Harry Clork, and Louise Henry, b/o novel by Adam Hobhouse. Cast: Edward Arnold, Constance Cummings, Robert Young, Sally Eilers, Reginald Denny, Robert Armstrong. Comedy murder mystery.

RUGGLES OF RED GAP. Paramount. D: Leo McCarey. Sp: Walter De Leon and Harlan Thompson, adapted by Humphrey Pearson from novel by Harry Leon Wilson. Cast: Charles Laughton, Mary Boland, Charlie Ruggles, ZaSu Pitts, Roland Young. Perfect English butler comes to American West. Remade in 1950 as *Fancy Pants.*

SHE COULDN'T TAKE IT. Columbia. D: Tay Garnett. Sp: Oliver H. P. Garrett, b/o story by Gene Towne and Graham Baker. Cast: George Raft, Joan Bennett, Walter Connolly, Billie Burke, Lloyd Nolan, Wallace Ford. Irresponsible rich girl is tamed by gunman.

SHE MARRIED HER BOSS. Columbia. D: Gregory La Cava. Sp: Sidney Buchman, b/o story by Thyra Samter Winslow. Cast: Claudette Colbert, Melvyn Douglas, Michael Bartlett, Raymond Walburn, Jean Dixon. Secretary enters into a "business" marriage with her employer.

STAR OF MIDNIGHT. RKO. D: Stephen Roberts. Sp: Howard J. Green, Anthony Veiller, and Edward Kaufman, b/o novel by Arthur Somers Roche. Cast: William Powell, Ginger Rogers, Paul Kelly, Gene Lockhart, Ralph Morgan. Debonair lawyer-sleuth solves mystery.

TIMES SQUARE LADY. MGM. D: George B. Seitz. Sp: Albert Cohen, Robert Shannon. Cast: Robert Taylor, Virginia Bruce, Helen Twelvetrees, Isabel Jewell, Nat Pendleton, Pinky Tomlin. Girl inherits fortune, comes to New York.

THE WHOLE TOWN'S TALKING. Columbia. D: John Ford. Sp: Jo Swerling and Robert Riskin, b/o story by W. R. Burnett. Cast: Edward G. Robinson, Jean Arthur, Arthur Hohl, Wallace Ford, Donald Meek. Timid clerk is mistaken for escaped killer.

1936

ADVENTURE IN MANHATTAN. Columbia. D: Edward Ludwig. Sp: Sidney Buchman, Harry Sauber, and Jack Kirkland, b/o story by Joseph Krumgold, suggested by "Purple and Fine Linen," by May Edington. Cast: Joel McCrea, Jean Arthur, Reginald Owen, Thomas Mitchell. Newspaper man cracks jewel theft with help of actress.

AFTER THE THIN MAN. MGM. D: W. S. Van Dyke. Sp: Frances Goodrich and Albert Hackett, b/o story by Dashiell Hammett. Cast: Myrna Loy, William

Powell, James Stewart, Elissa Landi, Joseph Calleia, Sam Levene, Teddy Hart. Nick and Nora Charles solve another murder.

THE EX-MRS. BRADFORD. RKO. D: Stephen Roberts. Sp: Anthony Veiller, b/o story by James Edward Grant. Cast: William Powell, Jean Arthur, James Gleason, Eric Blore, Robert Armstrong, Erin O'Brien Moore. Comedy mystery.

THE GOLDEN ARROW. Warners. D: Alfred E. Green. Sp: Charles Kenyon, b/o play by Michael Arlen. Cast: Bette Davis, George Brent, Eugene Pallette, Dick Foran, Carol Hughes. Fake heiress weds reporter.

LIBELED LADY. MGM. D: Jack Conway. Sp: Maurine Watkins, Howard Emmett Rogers and George Oppenheimer, b/o story by Wallace Sullivan. Cast: Spencer Tracy, William Powell, Myrna Loy, Jean Harlow, Walter Connolly. Heiress sues paper for libel. Remade in 1946 as *Easy to Wed.*

LOVE BEFORE BREAKFAST. Universal. D: Walter Lang. Sp: Herbert Fields, b/o novel by Faith Baldwin. Cast: Carole Lombard, Preston Foster, Cesar Romero, Janet Beecher. Wealthy young man woos girl.

LOVE ON THE RUN. MGM. D: W. S. Van Dyke. Sp: John Lee Mahin, Manuel Seff, and Gladys Hurlburt, b/o story by Alan Green and Julian Breen. Cast: Joan Crawford, Clark Gable, Franchot Tone, Reginald Owen, Mona Barrie, Donald Meek. Romance of heiress and foreign correspondent.

THE MILKY WAY. Paramount. D: Leo McCarey. Sp: Grover Jones, Frank Butler, and Richard Connell, b/o play by Lynn Root and Harry Clork. Cast: Harold Lloyd, Adolphe Menjou, Verree Teasdale, Lionel Stander. Milkman becomes prizefighter. Remade in 1946 as *The Kid from Brooklyn.*

MR. DEEDS GOES TO TOWN. Columbia. D: Frank Capra. Sp: Robert Riskin, b/o story by Clarence Budington Kelland. Cast: Gary Cooper, Jean Arthur, George Bancroft, Lionel Stander, Raymond Walburn. H. B. Warner. Small-town poet and tuba-player inherits millions.

THE MOON'S OUR HOME. Paramount. D: William A. Seiter. Sp: Isabel Dawn and Boyce DeGaw, b/o novel by Faith Baldwin. Additional dialogue by Dorothy Parker and Alan Campbell. Cast: Margaret Sullavan, Henry Fonda, Charles Butterworth, Beulah Bondi, Margaret Hamilton, Walter Brennan. Hollywood star marries travel writer.

MORE THAN A SECRETARY. Columbia. D: Alfred E. Green. Sp: Dale Van Every and Lynn Starling, b/o story by Ethel Hill and Aben Kandel, which was based on Matt Taylor's "Safari in Manhattan." Cast: Jean Arthur, George Brent, Lionel Stander, Ruth Donnelly, Dorothea Kent, Reginald Denny. Girl loves editor of health magazine.

MY MAN GODFREY. Universal. D: Gregory La Cava. Sp: Morrie Ryskind and Eric Hatch, b/o novel by Eric Hatch. Caet: Carole Lombard, William Powell, Alice Brady, Eugene Pallette, Gail Patrick, Mischa Auer. Wealthy Harvard man, down on his luck, joins a madcap family as their butler. Remade in 1957.

PETTICOAT FEVER. MGM. D: George Fitzmaurice. Sp: Harold Goldman, b/o play by Mark Reed. Cast: Robert Montgomery, Myrna Loy, Reginald Owen. Romance in Labrador.

THE PRINCESS COMES ACROSS. Paramount. D: William K. Howard. Sp: Walter De Leon, Frances Martin, Frank Butler, and Don Hartman, b/o story by Philip MacDonald, as adapted from novel by Louis Lucien Rogger. Cast: Carole Lombard, Fred MacMurray, Alison Skipworth, Douglas Dumbrille, Porter Hall, Mischa Auer. Brooklyn girl posing as Swedish princess gets involved with murder.

THEODORA GOES WILD. Columbia. D: Richard Boleslawski. Sp: Sidney Buchman, b/o story by Mary McCarthy. Cast: Irene Dunne, Melvyn Douglas, Thomas Mitchell, Thurston Hall, Spring Byington. Prim New England spinster writes sexy novel under pseudonym.

THREE MEN ON A HORSE. Warners. D: Mervyn LeRoy. Sp: Laird Doyle, b/o play by John Cecil Holm and George Abbott. Cast: Frank McHugh, Joan Blondell, Guy Kibbee, Allen Jenkins, Sam Levene, Teddy Hart. Timid writer of greeting-card verse gets involved with racing gamblers.

1937
THE AWFUL TRUTH. Columbia. D: Leo McCarey. Sp: Viña Delmar, b/o play by Arthur Richman. Cast: Irene Dunne, Cary Grant, Ralph Bellamy, Alexander D'Arcy, Cecil Cunningham, Esther Dale. Couple get divorce but are still in love. Remade in 1953 as *Let's Do It Again.*

BREAKFAST FOR TWO. RKO. D: Alfred Santell. Sp: Charles Kaufman, Paul Yawitz, and Viola Brothers Shore. Cast: Barbara Stanwyck, Herbert Marshall, Glenda Farrell, Eric Blore, Donald Meek. Heiress-and-playboy romance.

CALL IT A DAY. Warners. D: Archie Mayo. Sp: Casey Robinson, b/o play by Dodie Smith. Stars Olivia de Havilland, Ian Hunter, Anita Louise, Alice

Brady, Roland Young, Frieda Inescort, Bonita Granville, Peggy Wood. Mix-ups of an eccentric family.

DANGER—LOVE AT WORK. Fox. D: Otto Preminger. Sp: James Edward Grant and Ben Markson, b/o story by James Edward Grant. Cast: Ann Sothern, Jack Haley, Mary Boland, Edward Everett Horton, John Carradine. Lawyer tangles with crackpot family.

DOUBLE WEDDING. MGM. D: Richard Thorpe. Sp: Jo Swerling, b/o play by Ferenc Molnar. Cast: Myrna Loy, William Powell, Florence Rice, John Beal, Jessie Ralph. Vagabond painter romances rich girl.

EASY LIVING. Paramount. D: Mitchell Leisen. Sp: Preston Sturges, b/o story by Vera Caspary. Cast: Jean Arthur, Ray Milland, Edward Arnold, Mary Nash, Luis Alberni, Franklin Pangborn. A girl, a millionaire banker—and a sable coat. Result: confusion.

EVER SINCE EVE. Warners. D: Lloyd Bacon. Sp: Lawrence Riley, Earl Baldwin, Lillie Hayward, b/o story by Margaret Lee and Gene Baker. Cast: Marion Davies, Robert Montgomery, Patsy Kelly, Frank McHugh, Allen Jenkins, Louise Fazenda. Blonde stenographer involved in romantic mixup with novelist.

FIRST LADY. Warners. D: Stanley Logan. Sp: Rowland Leigh, b/o play by George S. Kaufman and Katharine Dayton. Cast: Kay Francis, Preston Foster, Anita Louise, Walter Connolly, Verree Teasdale, Victor Jory, Marjorie Rambeau. Distaff activities in Washington.

I MET HIM IN PARIS. Paramount. D: Wesley Ruggles. Sp: Claude Binyon, b/o story by Helen Meinardi. Cast: Claudette Colbert, Melvyn Douglas, Robert Young, Lee Bowman, Mona Barrie. Girl on Paris fling is pursued by two men.

IT'S LOVE I'M AFTER. Warners. D: Archie Mayo. Sp: Casey Robinson, b/o story by Maurice Hanline. Cast: Leslie Howard, Bette Davis, Olivia de Havilland, Eric Blore, Bonita Granville, Patric Knowles. Squabbling theatre couple are involved with dizzy heiress.

LIVE, LOVE AND LEARN. MGM. D: George Fitzmaurice. Sp: Charles Brackett, Cyril Hume, and Richard Maibaum, b/o story by Marion Parsonnet; suggested by story by Helen Grace Carlisle. Cast: Rosalind Russell, Robert Montgomery, Robert Benchley, Helen Vinson, Monty Woolley, Mickey Rooney. Rich girl marries Greenwich Village artist.

LOVE IS NEWS. Fox. D: Tay Garnett. Sp: Harry Tugend and Jack Yellen b/o story by William R. Lipman and Frederick Stephani. Cast: Loretta Young, Tyrone Power, Don Ameche, Slim Summerville, George Sanders, Dudley Digges, Jane Darwell. Heiress feuds with, loves reporter. Remade as *That Wonderful Urge* in 1948.

NOTHING SACRED. Selznick International. D: William Wellman. Sp: Ben Hecht. Cast: Carole Lombard, Fredric March, Charles Winninger, Walter Connolly, Sig Rumann, Frank Fay, Margaret Hamilton, Hattie McDaniel. Girl mistakenly thought to be dying causes uproar. Remade as *Living It Up* in 1954.

SECOND HONEYMOON. Fox. D: Walter Lang. Sp: Kathryn Scola and Darrell Ware, b/o story by Philip Wylie. Cast Tyrone Power, Loretta Young, Stuart Erwin, Claire Trevor, Marjorie Weaver, J. Edward Bromberg. Husband tries to win back his ex-wife.

SUPER-SLEUTH. RKO. D: Ben Stoloff. Sp: Gertrude Purcell and Ernest Pagano, b/o play by Harry Segall. Cast: Jack Oakie, Ann Sothern, Eduardo Ciannelli, Edgar Kennedy. Inept movie detective tries to solve mystery.

TOPPER. MGM. D: Norman Z. McLeod. Sp: Jack Jevne, Eric Hatch, and Eddie Moran, b/o novel by Thorne Smith. Cast: Constance Bennett, Cary Grant, Roland Young, Billie Burke, Alan Mowbray, Hedda Hopper. Adventures of Cosmo Topper and his ghostly friends.

TOVARICH. Warners. D: Anatole Litvak. Sp: Casey Robinson, b/o play by Jacques Deval. Cast: Claudette Colbert, Charles Boyer, Basil Rathbone, Anita Louise, Melville Cooper, Isabel Jeans. Impoverished Russian couple in Paris take jobs as maid and butler.

TRUE CONFESSION. Paramount. D: Wesley Ruggles. Sp: Claude Binyon, b/o play by Louis Verneuil and Georges Berr. Cast: Carole Lombard, Fred MacMurray, John Barrymore, Una Merkel, Lynne Overman, Porter Hall, Edgar Kennedy. Attorney's wife with a penchant for lying gets involved with a murder. Remade in 1946 as *Cross My Heart.*

WIFE, DOCTOR AND NURSE. Fox. D: Walter Lang. Sp: Kathryn Scola, Darrell Ware, and Lamar Trotti. Cast: Loretta Young, Warner Baxter, Virginia Bruce, Jane Darwell, Sidney Blackmer. Marital triangle.

WISE GIRL. RKO. D: Leigh Jason. Sp: Allan Scott, b/o story by Allan Scott and Charles Norman. Cast: Miriam Hopkins, Ray Milland, Walter Abel, Henry Stephenson. Romance of incognito heiress and Greenwich Village artist.

WOMAN CHASES MAN. Goldwyn. D: John Blystone. Sp: Dorothy Parker, Alan Campbell, Joe Bigelow, b/o story by Lynn Root and Frank Fenton. Cast: Miriam Hopkins, Joel McCrea, Charles Winninger, Erik Rhodes, Ella Logan, Broderick Crawford. Girl architect sets her cap for wealthy young man.

1938

THE AMAZING DR. CLITTERHOUSE. Warners. D: Anatole Litvak. Sp: John Wexley and John Huston, b/o play by Barre Lyndon. Cast: Edward G. Robinson, Claire Trevor, Humphrey Bogart, Donald Crisp, Gale Page. Doctor takes up life of crime for "research" purposes.

BLUEBEARD'S EIGHTH WIFE. Paramount. D: Ernst Lubitsch. Sp: Charles Brackett and Billy Wilder, b/o play by Alfred Savoir as adapted by Charlton Andrews. Cast: Claudette Colbert, Gary Cooper, Edward Everett Horton, David Niven, Franklin Pangborn. Much-married young tycoon takes wife No. 8.

BOY MEETS GIRL. Warners. D: Lloyd Bacon. Sp: Bella and Samuel Spewack, b/o their play. Cast: James Cagney, Pat O'Brien, Marie Wilson, Ralph Bellamy, Frank McHugh, Dick Foran. Screwball antics of two Hollywood writers.

BRINGING UP BABY. RKO. D: Howard Hawks. Sp: Dudley Nichols and Hagar Wilde, b/o story by Hagar Wilde. Cast: Katharine Hepburn, Cary Grant, May Robson, Barry Fitzgerald, Charlie Ruggles. Antics involving an anthropologist, a madcap heiress, her pet leopard, a wire-haired terrier, and a dinosaur bone.

BROTHER RAT. Warners. D: William Keighley. Sp: Richard Macaulay and Jerry Wald, b/o play by John Monks, Jr. and Fred F. Finklehoffe. Cast: Wayne Morris, Ronald Reagan, Priscilla Lane, Eddie Albert, Jane Wyman, Johnnie Davis. Comic doings at Virginia Military Institute. Remade in 1952 as *About Face.*

THE COWBOY AND THE LADY. Goldwyn. D: H. C. Potter. Sp: S. N. Behrman and Sonya Levien, b/o story by Leo McCarey and Frank R. Adams. Cast: Gary Cooper, Merle Oberon, Patsy Kelly, Walter Brennan, Mabel Todd, Fuzzy Knight. Daughter of presidential candidate elopes with rodeo cowboy.

FAST COMPANY. MGM. D: Edward Buzzell. Sp: Marco Page and Harold Tarshis, b/o novel by Marco Page. Cast: Melvyn Douglas, Florence Rice, Claire Dodd, Louis Calhern. First mystery adventure of Joel and Garda Sloane.

HARD TO GET. Warners. D: Ray Enright. Sp: Jerry Wald, Maurice Leo and Richard Macauley, b/o story by Wally Klein and Joseph Schrank. Cast: Dick Powell, Olivia de Havilland, Charles Winninger, Allen Jenkins, Bonita Granville, Melville Cooper, Isabel Jeans. Wild heiress is tamed into domesticity.

HAVING WONDERFUL TIME. RKO. D: Alfred Santell. Sp: Arthur Kober, b/o his play. Cast: Ginger Rogers, Douglas Fairbanks, Jr., Lucille Ball, Peggy Conklin, Lee Bowman, Eve Arden, Ann Miller, Jack Carson, Donald Meek. Love blossoms in a resort camp.

HOLIDAY. Columbia. D: George Cukor. Sp: Donald Ogden Stewart and Sidney Buchman, b/o play by Philip Barry. Cast: Katharine Hepburn, Cary Grant, Doris Nolan, Lew Ayres, Edward Everett Horton, Binnie Barnes, Jean Dixon. Carefree young man plans to marry rich girl, then meets her sister.

IT'S ALL YOURS. Columbia. D: Elliott Nugent. Sp: Mary C. McCall, Jr., b/o story by Adelaide Heilbron. Cast: Madeleine Carroll, Francis Lederer, Mischa Auer, Grace Bradley. Playboy's uncle wills his fortune to a secretary.

JOY OF LIVING. RKO. D: Tay Garnett. Sp: Gene Towne, Graham Baker, and Allan Scott, b/o story by Dorothy and Herbert Fields. Cast: Irene Dunne, Douglas Fairbanks, Jr., Alice Brady, Guy Kibbee, Jean Dixon, Lucille Ball, Eric Blore. Playboy tries to convert musical comedy star to the joy of living. Songs by Jerome Kern and Dorothy Fields.

THE MAD MISS MANTON. RKO. D: Leigh Jason. Sp: Philip G. Epstein, b/o story by Wilson Collison. Cast: Barbara Stanwyck, Henry Fonda, Sam Levene, Frances Mercer, Stanley Ridges, Penny Singleton. Madcap rich girl and her friends solve several murders.

MAN-PROOF. MGM. D: Richard Thorpe. Sp: Vincent Lawrence, Waldemar Young, George Oppenheimer, b/o book by Fanny Heaslip Lea. Cast: Myrna Loy, Franchot Tone, Rosalind Russell, Walter Pidgeon, Rita Johnson, Ruth Hussey. Girl loves married man.

MERRILY WE LIVE. Hal Roach. D: Norman Z. McLeod. Sp: Eddie Moran and Jack Jevne. Cast: Constance Bennett, Brian Aherne, Billie Burke, Alan Mowbray, Patsy Kelly, Ann Dvorak, Bonita Granville, Tom Brown. Tramp is adopted by eccentric mistress of scatterbrained family.

RICH MAN, POOR GIRL. MGM. D: Reinhold Schunzel. Sp: Joseph Fields and Jerome Chodorov, b/o story by Edgar Franklin. Cast: Robert Young, Lew Ayres, Ruth Hussey, Lana Turner, Rita Johnson, Guy Kibbee. Wealthy young man falls in love with his secretary.

A SLIGHT CASE OF MURDER. Warners. D: Lloyd Bacon. Sp: Earl Baldwin and Joseph Schrank, b/o play by Damon Runyon and Howard Lindsay. Cast: Edward G. Robinson, Ruth Donnelly, Jane Bryan, Allen Jenkins, Bobby Jordan. Retired racketeer has all sorts of troubles. Remade in 1952 as *Stop, You're Killing Me!*

THERE GOES MY HEART. Hal Roach. D: Norman Z. McLeod. Sp: Eddie Moran and Jack Jevne, b/o story by Ed Sullivan. Cast: Fredric March, Virginia Bruce, Patsy Kelly, Alan Mowbray, Nancy Carroll, Arthur Lake. Heiress and reporter romance.

THERE'S ALWAYS A WOMAN. Columbia. D: Alexander Hall. Sp: Gladys Lehman, b/o story by Wilson Collison. Cast: Joan Blondell, Melvyn Douglas, Mary Astor, Frances Drake, Jerome Cowan, Robert Paige. Comedy-mystery involving detective and his wife.

THREE BLIND MICE. Fox. D: William A. Seiter. Sp: Brown Holmes and Lynn Starling, b/o play by Stephen Powys. Cast: Loretta Young, Joel McCrea, David Niven, Stuart Erwin, Marjorie Weaver, Binnie Barnes. Three sisters seek rich husbands. Remade in 1941 as *Moon Over Miami* and in 1946 as *Three Little Girls in Blue.*

THREE LOVES HAS NANCY. MGM. D: Richard Thorpe. Sp: Bella and Samuel Spewack, George Oppenheimer, and David Hertz, b/o story by Lee Loeb and Mortimer Braus. Cast: Janet Gaynor, Robert Montgomery, Franchot Tone, Guy Kibbee, Claire Dodd, Reginald Owen. Girl is romantically involved with two playboy bachelors.

TOPPER TAKES A TRIP. Hal Roach. D: Norman Z. McLeod. Sp: Eddie Moran, Jack Jevne and Corey Ford, b/o novel by Thorne Smith. Cast: Constance Bennett, Roland Young, Billie Burke, Alan Mowbray, Verree Teasdale, Franklin Pangborn. Another adventure of Topper and friends.

VIVACIOUS LADY. RKO. D: George Stevens. Sp: P. J. Wolfson and Ernest Pagano, b/o story by I. A. R. Wylie. Cast: Ginger Rogers, James Stewart, Charles Coburn, Beulah Bondi, James Ellison, Franklin Pangborn, Grady Sutton, Jack Carson. Professor marries nightclub singer.

YOU CAN'T TAKE IT WTH YOU. Columbia. D: Frank Capra. Sp: Robert Riskin, b/o play by George S. Kaufman and Moss Hart. Cast: Jean Arthur, Lionel Barrymore, James Stewart, Edward Arnold, Spring Byington, Ann Miller, Donald Meek. Life with a family of amiable lunatics.

THE YOUNG IN HEART. Selznick International. D: Richard Wallace. Sp: Paul Osborn, as adapted by Charles Bennett from novel by I. A. R. Wylie. Cast:

Janet Gaynor, Douglas Fairbanks, Jr., Paulette Goddard, Roland Young, Billie Burke, Richard Carlson, Minnie Dupree, Lucile Watson, Irvin S. Cobb. Larcenous family takes up with lonely old lady.

1939

ANOTHER THIN MAN. MGM. D: W. S. Van Dyke. Sp: Frances Goodrich and Albert Hackett, b/o story by Dashiell Hammett. Cast: William Powell, Myrna Loy, Otto Kruger, C. Aubrey Smith, Ruth Hussey, Patric Knowles, Virginia Grey. Nick and Nora Charles on the mystery trail again.

BACHELOR MOTHER. RKO. D: Garson Kanin. Sp: Norman Krasna, b/o story by Felix Jackson. Cast: Ginger Rogers, David Niven, Charles Coburn, Frank Albertson. Shopgirl finds baby, is unable to convince anyone she is not the mother. Remade in 1956 as *Bundle of Joy*.

CAFE SOCIETY. Paramount. D: Edward H. Griffith. Sp: Virginia Van Upp. Cast: Madeleine Carroll, Fred MacMurray, Shirley Ross, Jessie Ralph, Claude Gillingwater. Romance of spoiled heiress and reporter.

THE CAT AND THE CANARY. Paramount. D: Elliott Nugent. Sp: Walter De Leon and Lynn Starling, b/o play by John Willard. Cast: Bob Hope, Paulette Goddard, John Beal, Gale Sondergaard. Comedy-mystery set in eerie mansion.

DAYTIME WIFE. Fox. D: Gregory Ratoff. Sp: Art Arthur and Robert Harari, b/o story by Rex Taylor. Cast: Tyrone Power, Linda Darnell, Warren William, Wendy Barrie, Joan Davis, Binnie Barnes. Neglected wife becomes secretary.

ETERNALLY YOURS. Walter Wanger. D: Tay Garnett. Sp: Gene Towne and Graham Baker. Cast: Loretta Young, David Niven, Hugh Herbert, Billie Burke, C. Aubrey Smith, Broderick Crawford, ZaSu Pitts, Eve Arden. Magician and wife have marital difficulties.

FAST AND FURIOUS. MGM. D: Busby Berkeley. Sp: Harry Kurnitz. Cast: Franchot Tone, Ann Sothern, Ruth Hussey, Lee Bowman, Allyn Joslyn. Further adventures of Joel and Garda Sloane.

FAST AND LOOSE. MGM. D: Edwin L. Marin. Sp: Harry Kurnitz. Cast: Robert Montgomery, Rosalind Russell, Reginald Owen, Ralph Morgan. Joel and Garda Sloane involved again in murder.

FIFTH AVENUE GIRL. RKO. D: Gregory La Cava. Sp: Allan Scott. Cast: Ginger Rogers, Walter Connolly, James Ellison, Verree Teasdale, Tim Holt, Franklin Pangborn. Neglected tycoon installs young girl in his house.

GOOD GIRLS GO TO PARIS. Columbia. D: Alexander Hall. Sp: Gladys Lehman and Ken Englund, b/o story by Lenore Coffee and William Joyce Cowan. Cast: Melvyn Douglas, Joan Blondell, Walter Connolly, Alan Curtis. Waitress dreams of snaring rich man's son and living on blackmail.

THE GRACIE ALLEN MURDER CASE. Paramount. D: Alfred E. Green. Sp: Nat Perrin, b/o novel by S. S. Van Dine. Cast: Gracie Allen, Warren William, Ellen Drew, Kent Taylor. Detective Philo Vance gets mixed up in mystery with Gracie.

HONEYMOON IN BALI. Paramount. D: Edward H. Griffith. Sp: Virginia Van Upp, b/o stories by Grace Sartwell Mason and Katharine Brush. Cast: Madeleine Carroll, Fred MacMurray, Allan Jones, Akim Tamiroff, Helen Broderick, Osa Massen. Career girl boasts she rules out love, then meets man from Bali.

THE HOUSEKEEPER'S DAUGHTER. Hal Roach. D: Hal Roach. Sp: Rian James and Gordon Douglas, b/o novel by Donald Henderson Clarke. Cast: Joan Bennett, Adolphe Menjou, John Hubbard, William Gargan, Peggy Wood, Victor Mature, Donald Meek. Mixups in household of young millionaire.

IT'S A WONDERFUL WORLD. MGM. D: W. S. Van Dyke. Sp: Ben Hecht, b/o story by Ben Hecht and Herman J. Mankiewicz. Cast: Claudette Colbert, James Stewart, Guy Kibbee, Nat Pendleton, Edgar Kennedy. Comedy-mystery.

MIDNIGHT. Paramount. D: Mitchell Leisen. Sp: Charles Brackett and Billy Wilder, b/o story by Edwin Justus Mayer and Franz Schulz. Cast: Claudette Colbert, Don Ameche, John Barrymore, Mary Astor, Francis Lederer, Rex O'Malley. Girl is hired by millionaire to break up his wife's romance. Remade in 1945 as *Masquerade in Mexico.*

MR. SMITH GOES TO WASHINGTON. Columbia. D: Frank Capra. Sp: Sidney Buchman, b/o story by Lewis R. Foster. Cast: James Stewart, Jean Arthur, Claude Rains, Thomas Mitchell, Edward Arnold, Eugene Pallette, Ruth Donnelly. Naïve small-town young man is elected to Congress.

NINOTCHKA. MGM. D: Ernst Lubitsch. Sp: Billy Wilder, Charles Brackett, and Walter Reisch, b/o original screen story by Melchior Lengyel. Cast:

Greta Garbo, Melvyn Douglas, Ina Claire, Sig Rumann, Felix Bressart, Alexander Granach, Bela Lugosi. Forbidding Soviet girl finds love in Paris. Remade in 1957 as *Silk Stockings*.

THERE'S THAT WOMAN AGAIN. Columbia. D: Alexander Hall. Sp: Philip G. Epstein, James Edward Grant, and Ken Englund, b/o story by Gladys Lehman and work by Wilson Collison. Cast: Melvyn Douglas, Virginia Bruce, Margaret Lindsay, Stanley Ridges. Detective and scatterbrained wife solve a mystery.

WIFE, HUSBAND AND FRIEND. Fox. D: Gregory Ratoff. Sp: Nunnally Johnson, b/o novel by James M. Cain. Cast: Loretta Young, Warner Baxter, Binnie Barnes, Cesar Romero, Helen Westley, J. Edward Bromberg. Wife and husband both aspire to sing in opera. Remade in 1949 as *Everybody Does It*.

THE WOMEN, MGM. D: George Cukor. Sp: Anita Loos and Jane Murfin. b/o play by Clare Boothe. Cast: Norma Shearer, Joan Crawford, Rosalind Russell, Mary Boland, Paulette Goddard, Joan Fontaine, Virginia Weidler, Lucile Watson. Woman suffers from straying husband and gossipy friends. Remade in 1956 as *The Opposite Sex*.

1940
THE AMAZING MR. WILLIAMS. Columbia. D: Alexander Hall. Sp: Dwight Taylor, Sy Bartlett, and Richard Maibum, b/o story by Sy Bartlett, Cast: Melvyn Douglas, Joan Blondell, Clarence Kolb, Ruth Donnelly, Donald MacBride. Detective solves mystery with girlfriend's help.

CHRISTMAS IN JULY. Paramount. D: Preston Sturges. Sp: Preston Sturges. Cast: Dick Powell, Ellen Drew, Raymond Walburn, Franklin Pangborn, Ernest Truex, William Demarest. Young man thinks he has written prizewinning slogan.

THE DOCTOR TAKES A WIFE. Columbia. D: Alexander Hall. Sp: George Seaton and Ken Englund, b/o story by Aleen Leslie. Cast: Loretta Young, Ray Milland, Reginald Gardiner, Gail Patrick, Edmund Gwenn. Doctor and bachelor girl are mistaken for newlyweds.

DULCY. MGM. D: S. Sylvan Simon. Sp: Albert Mannheimer, Jerome Chodorov, and J. A. Fields, b/o play by George S. Kaufman and Marc Connelly. Cast: Ann Sothern, Ian Hunter, Roland Young, Reginald Gardiner, Billie Burke, Dan Dailey, Hans Conried. Daffy Dulcy gets into hot water.

THE GHOST BREAKERS. Paramount. D: George Marshall. Sp: Walter De Leon, b/o play by Paul Dickey and Charles W. Goddard. Cast: Bob Hope,

Paulette Goddard, Richard Carlson, Paul Lukas, Willie Best, Anthony Quinn. Mysterious and comic occurrences at a Cuban castle. Remade in 1953 as *Scared Stiff.*

THE GOLDEN FLEECING. MGM. D: Leslie Fenton. Sp: S. J. and Laura Perelman and Marion Parsonnet, b/o story by Lynn Root, Frank Fenton, and John Fante. Cast: Lew Ayres, Rita Johnson, Lloyd Nolan, Virginia Grey, Leon Errol, Nat Pendleton. Young insurance broker sells policy to mobster.

THE GREAT McGINTY. Paramount. D: Preston Sturges. Sp: Preston Sturges. Cast: Brian Donlevy, Akim Tamiroff, Muriel Angelus, William Demarest, Allyn Joslyn. Bum rises to top position in politics.

HE MARRIED HIS WIFE. Fox. D: Roy Del Ruth. Sp: Sam Hellman, Darrell Ware, Lynn Starling, and John O'Hara, b/o story by Erna Lazarus and Scott Darling. Cast: Joel McCrea, Nancy Kelly, Roland Young, Mary Boland, Cesar Romero, Mary Healy. Divorced woman faces matrimonial decision.

HE STAYED FOR BREAKFAST. Columbia. D: Alexander Hall. Sp: P. J. Wolfson, Michael Fessier, and Ernest Vajda, b/o Sidney Howard's adaptation of a play by Michel Duran. Cast: Loretta Young, Melvyn Douglas, Alan Marshal, Eugene Pallette, Una O'Connor. Communist seeks refuge in Paris apartment of beautiful woman.

HIRED WIFE. Universal. D: William A. Seiter. Sp: Richard Connell and Gladys Lehman, b/o story by George Beck. Cast: Rosalind Russell, Brian Aherne, Virginia Bruce, Robert Benchley, John Carroll. Secretary marries her boss—but only as a legal maneuver.

HIS GIRL FRIDAY. Columbia. D: Howard Hawks. Sp: Charles Lederer, b/o play by Ben Hecht and Charles MacArthur. Cast: Rosalind Russell, Cary Grant, Ralph Bellamy, Gene Lockhart, Helen Mack, Porter Hall, John Qualen. Film version of newspaper comedy, *The Front Page.*

I LOVE YOU AGAIN. MGM. D: W. S. Van Dyke. Sp: Charles Lederer, George Oppenheimer, and Harry Kurnitz, b/o story by Leon Gordon and Maurine Watkins and on novel by Octavus Roy Cohen. Cast: William Powell, Myrna Loy, Frank McHugh, Edmund Lowe. Man has dual identity—but only one wife.

LUCKY PARTNERS. RKO. D: Lewis Milestone. Sp: Allan Scott and John Van Druten, b/o story by Sacha Guitry. Cast: Ronald Colman, Ginger Rogers, Jack Carson, Spring Byington, Harry Davenport. Artist and bookstore clerk share a sweepstake ticket.

My Favorite Wife. RKO. D: Garson Kanin. Sp: Samuel and Bella Spewack, b/o their story. Cast: Irene Dunne, Cary Grant, Randolph Scott, Gail Patrick, Ann Shoemaker, Granville Bates, Donald MacBride. Wife thought to be dead returns to her newly married husband. Remade in 1963 as *Move Over, Darling.*

My Love Came Back. Warners. D: Curtis Bernhardt. Sp: Ivan Goff, Robert Buckner, and Earl Baldwin, b/o story by Walter Reisch. Cast: Olivia de Havilland, Charles Winninger, Eddie Albert, Spring Byington, Jane Wyman, S. Z. Sakall. Girl violinist has secret benefactor.

No Time for Comedy. Warners. D: William Keighley. Sp: Julius J. and Philip G. Epstein, b/o play by S. N. Behrman. Cast: Rosalind Russell, James Stewart, Charlie Ruggles, Genevieve Tobin, Allyn Joslyn, Louise Beavers. About a successful playwright and his actress wife.

The Philadelphia Story. MGM. D: George Cukor. Sp: Donald Ogden Stewart, b/o play by Philip Barry. Cast: Katharine Hepburn, Cary Grant, James Stewart, Roland Young, Ruth Hussey, John Howard, John Halliday, Virginia Weidler. Spoiled wealthy girl finds her humanity. Remade in 1956 as *High Society.*

Primrose Path. RKO. D: Gregory La Cava. Sp: Allan Scott and Gregory La Cava, b/o play by Robert Buckner and Walter Hart. Cast: Ginger Rogers, Joel McCrea, Marjorie Rambeau, Henry Travers, Joan Carroll. Daughter of disreputable family falls in love.

Private Affairs. Universal. D: Albert S. Rogell. Sp: Charles Grayson, Leonard Spigelgass, and Peter Milne, b/o story by Walton Green. Cast: Nancy Kelly, Hugh Herbert, Roland Young, Robert Cummings. Zany doings among some Boston Brahmins.

Public Deb No. 1. Fox. D: Gregory Ratoff. Sp: Karl Tunberg and Darrell Ware. Cast: George Murphy, Brenda Joyce, Elsa Maxwell, Mischa Auer, Charlie Ruggles, Maxie Rosenbloom. Wealthy debutante embraces communism.

Remember the Night. Paramount. D: Mitchell Leisen. Sp: Preston Sturges. Cast: Barbara Stanwyck, Fred MacMurray, Beulah Bondi, Elizabeth Patterson, Sterling Holloway. Assistant district attorney falls for pretty thief he is prosecuting.

Susan and God. MGM. D: George Cukor. Sp: Anita Loos, b/o play by Rachel Crothers. Cast: Joan Crawford, Fredric March, Ruth Hussey, John

Carroll, Rita Hayworth, Nigel Bruce. Woman discovers new "religious" movement.

THIRD FINGER, LEFT HAND. MGM. D: Robert Z. Leonard. Sp: Lionel Houser. Cast: Myrna Loy, Melvyn Douglas, Raymond Walburn, Lee Bowman, Bonita Granville, Felix Bressart. Magazine editor pretends to be married.

TOO MANY HUSBANDS. Columbia. D: Wesley Ruggles. Sp: Claude Binyon, b/o play by W. Somerset Maugham. Cast: Jean Arthur, Fred MacMurray, Melvyn Douglas, Harry Davenport, Melville Cooper. Remarried woman discovers first husband is alive. Remade in 1955 as *Three for the Show.*

TURNABOUT. Hal Roach. D: Hal Roach. Sp: Mickell Novak, Berne Giler, and John McClain, b/o novel by Thorne Smith. Cast: Carole Landis, John Hubbard, Adolphe Menjou, Mary Astor, William Gargan, Verree Teasdale, Franklin Pangborn, Marjorie Main. Husband and wife reverse their biological status.

1941

APPOINTMENT FOR LOVE. Universal. D: William A. Seiter. Sp: Bruce Manning and Felix Jackson, b/o story by Ladislaus Bus-Fekete. Cast: Charles Boyer, Margaret Sullavan, Rita Johnson, Eugene Pallette, Ruth Terry, Reginald Denny. Playwright marries lady doctor.

BALL OF FIRE. Goldwyn. D: Howard Hawks. Sp: Charles Brackett and Billy Wilder, b/o story by Billy Wilder and Thomas Monroe. Cast: Gary Cooper, Barbara Stanwyck, Oscar Homolka, Henry Travers, S.Z. Sakall, Dana Andrews, Dan Duryea. Nightclub singer joins *ménage* of prim professors. Remade in 1948 as *A Song Is Born.*

THE BRIDE CAME C.O.D. Warners. D: William Keighley. Sp: Julius J. and Philip G. Epstein. Cast: James Cagney, Bette Davis, Stuart Erwin, Jack Carson, Harry Davenport, George Tobias. Runaway heiress is taken in hand by pilot.

THE DEVIL AND MISS JONES. RKO. D: Sam Wood. Sp: Norman Krasna. Cast: Jean Arthur, Charles Coburn, Robert Cummings, Edmund Gwenn, Spring Byington, S. Z. Sakall, William Demarest. Department-store owner takes job incognito in his store to find out why he is hated.

THE FEMININE TOUCH. MGM. D: W. S. Van Dyke. Sp: George Oppenheimer, Edmund L. Hartmann, and Ogden Nash. Cast: Rosalind Russell, Don Ameche, Kay Francis, Van Heflin, Donald Meek. Professor comes to New York with his wife—and a book on jealousy.

A GIRL, A GUY AND A GOB. RKO. D: Richard Wallace. Sp: Frank Ryan and Bert Granet, b/o story by Grover Jones. Cast: Lucille Ball, George Murphy, Edmond O'Brien, Henry Travers, Franklin Pangborn, Marguerite Chapman. Rich young man and sailor vie for affection of a girl with an eccentric family.

HERE COMES MR. JORDAN. Columbia. D: Alexander Hall. Sp: Sidney Buchman and Seton I. Miller, b/o play by Harry Segall. Cast: Robert Montgomery, Claude Rains, Evelyn Keyes, Rita Johnson, James Gleason, Edward Everett Horton. Prematurely dead boxer is given another body to inhabit.

THE LADY EVE. Paramount. D: Preston Sturges. Sp: Preston Sturges, b/o story by Monckton Hoffe. Cast: Barbara Stanwyck, Henry Fonda, Charles Coburn, Eugene Pallette, Eric Blore, William Demarest. Father and daughter cardsharps set their sights on gullible young millionaire. Remade in 1956 as *The Birds and the Bees*.

LOVE CRAZY. MGM. D: Jack Conway. Sp: William Ludwig, Charles Lederer, and David Hertz, b/o story by William Ludwig and David Hertz. Cast: William Powell, Myrna Loy, Gail Patrick, Jack Carson, Florence Bates, Sidney Blackmer. Man tries to prevent wife from divorcing him by faking insanity.

MARRIED BACHELOR. MGM. D: Edward Buzzell. Sp: Dore Schary, b/o story by Manuel Seff. Cast: Robert Young, Ruth Hussey, Felix Bressart, Lee Bowman, Sam Levene. Married man pretends to be unmarried author of book on marital advice.

MODEL WIFE. Universal. D: Leigh Jason. Sp: Charles Kaufman, Horace Jackson, and Grant Garrett, b/o story by Leigh Jason. Cast: Joan Blondell, Dick Powell, Charlie Ruggles, Lee Bowman, Lucile Watson, Ruth Donnelly, Billy Gilbert. Wife and husband work secretly for same company.

MR. AND MRS. SMITH. RKO. D: Alfred Hitchcock. Sp: Norman Krasna. Cast: Carole Lombard, Robert Montgomery, Gene Raymond, Jack Carson, Lucile Watson. Couple discovers their marriage is not legal.

NEW YORK TOWN. Paramount. D: Charles Vidor. Sp: Lewis Meltzer, b/o story by Jo Swerling. Cast: Mary Martin, Fred MacMurray, Robert Preston, Akim Tamiroff, Lynne Overman, Eric Blore. Sidewalk photographer befriends homeless girl.

OUR WIFE. Columbia. D: John M. Stahl. Sp: P. J. Wolfson, b/o play by Lillian Day and Lyon Mearson. Cast: Melvyn Douglas, Ruth Hussey, Ellen Drew,

Drew, Charles Coburn, John Hubbard. Man falls for lady scientist, until his estranged wife appears.

SHADOW OF THE THIN MAN. MGM. D: W. S. Van Dyke. Sp: Irving Brecher and Harry Kurnitz, b/o story by Harry Kurnitz and characters created by Dashiell Hammett. Cast: William Powell, Myrna Loy, Barry Nelson, Donna Reed, Sam Levene, Alan Baxter. Nick and Nora Charles on the prowl again.

SHE KNEW ALL THE ANSWERS. Columbia. D: Richard Wallace. Sp: Harry Segall, Kenneth Earl, and Curtis Kenyon, b/o story by Jane Allen. Cast: Joan Bennett, Franchot Tone, John Hubbard, Eve Arden. Romance involving playboy, chorus girl, and financier.

SKYLARK. Paramount. D: Mark Sandrich. Sp: Allan Scott, b/o play and novel by Samson Raphaelson. Cast: Claudette Colbert, Ray Milland, Brian Aherne, Binnie Barnes, Walter Abel. Wife has romantic fling with another man.

THAT UNCERTAIN FEELING. United Artists. D: Ernst Lubitsch. Sp: Donald Ogden Stewart, adapted by Walter Reisch. Cast: Merle Oberon, Melvyn Douglas, Burgess Meredith, Alan Mowbray, Harry Davenport, Eve Arden. Wife develops hiccups after six years of married life.

THIS THING CALLED LOVE. Columbia. D: Alexander Hall. Sp: George Seaton, Ken Englund, and P. J. Wolfson, b/o play by Edwin Burke. Cast: Rosalind Russell, Melvyn Douglas, Binnie Barnes, Allyn Joslyn, Lee J. Cobb. Bride insists on remaining "kissless."

TOM, DICK AND HARRY. RKO. D: Garson Kanin. Sp: Paul Jarrico. Cast: Ginger Rogers, Burgess Meredith, George Murphy, Alan Marshal, Lenore Lonergan, Phil Silvers. Girl must choose between three ardent suitors. Remade in 1957 as *The Girl Most Likely*.

UNFINISHED BUSINESS. Universal. D: Gregory La Cava. Sp: Eugene Thackrey. Cast: Irene Dunne, Robert Montgomery, Preston Foster, Dick Foran, Eugene Pallette. Girl marries the brother of the man she really loves.

WHEN LADIES MEET. MGM. D: Robert Z. Leonard. Sp: S. K. Lauren and Anita Loos, b/o play by Rachel Crothers. Cast: Joan Crawford, Robert Taylor, Greer Garson, Herbert Marshall, Spring Byington. Lady novelist is loved by journalist, but loves her publisher.

WHISTLING IN THE DARK. MGM. D: S. Sylvan Simon. Sp: Robert MacGunigle, Harry Clork, and Albert Mannheimer, b/o play by Laurence Gross and Edward Childs Carpenter. Cast: Red Skelton, Conrad Veidt, Ann Rutherford, Rags Ragland, Eve Arden. Adventures of radio detective, "The Fox."

YOU BELONG TO ME. Columbia. D: Wesley Ruggles. Sp: Claude Binyon, b/o story by Dalton Trumbo. Cast: Barbara Stanwyck, Henry Fonda, Edgar Buchanan, Ruth Donnelly, Roger Clark. Man is jealous of his doctor-wife. Remade in 1950 as *Emergency Wedding*.

1942
ARE HUSBANDS NECESSARY? Paramount. D: Norman Taurog. Sp: Tess Slesinger and Frank Davis, b/o novel by Isabel Scott Rorick. Cast: Ray Milland, Betty Field, Patricia Morison, Eugene Pallette, Flighty wife manages to set things right.

BEDTIME STORY. Columbia. D: Alexander Hall. Sp: Richard Flournoy, b/o story by Horace Jackson and Grant Garrett. Cast: Fredric March, Loretta Young, Robert Benchley, Allyn Joslyn, Eve Arden, Helen Westley. Actress wife leaves her husband.

DESIGN FOR SCANDAL. MGM. D: Norman Taurog. Sp: Lionel Houser. Cast: Rosalind Russell, Walter Pidgeon, Edward Arnold, Lee Bowman, Jean Rogers, Mary Beth Hughes, Guy Kibbee. Lady judge in hot water.

GEORGE WASHINGTON SLEPT HERE. Warners. D: William Keighley. Sp: Everett Freeman, b/o play by George S. Kaufman and Moss Hart. Cast: Jack Benny, Ann Sheridan, Charles Coburn, Percy Kilbride, Hattie McDaniel, Charles Dingle, Joyce Reynolds. Couple buys ramshackle Bucks County house.

I MARRIED A WITCH. United Artists. D: René Clair. Sp: Robert Pirosh and Marc Connolly, b/o story by Thorne Smith completed by Norman Matson. Cast: Fredric March, Veronica Lake, Susan Hayward, Robert Benchley, Cecil Kellaway. A blonde witch enters the life of a smug New Englander.

THE MAGNIFICENT DOPE. Fox. D: Walter Lang. Sp: George Seaton, b/o story by Joseph Schrank. Cast: Henry Fonda, Don Ameche, Lynn Bari, Edward Everett Horton, George Barbier. Country bumpkin confounds city slickers.

THE MAJOR AND THE MINOR. Paramount. D: Billy Wilder. Sp: Charles Brackett and Billy Wilder, b/o play by Edward Childs Carpenter and story by Fannie Kilbourne. Cast: Ginger Rogers, Ray Milland, Diana Lynn, Rita

Johnson, Robert Benchley. Girl disguises herself as twelve-year-old at military academy. Remade in 1955 as *You're Never Too Young.*

THE MALE ANIMAL. Warners. D: Elliott Nugent. Sp: Julius J. and Philip G. Epstein and Stephen Morehouse Avery, b/o play by James Thurber and Elliott Nugent. Cast: Henry Fonda, Olivia de Havilland, Jack Carson, Joan Leslie, Eugene Pallette, Don DeFore, Hattie McDaniel. College professor gets into trouble by wanting to read Vanzetti letter to his class. Remade in 1952 as *She's Working Her Way Through College.*

THE MAN WHO CAME TO DINNER. Warners. D: William Keighley. Sp: Julius J. and Philip G. Epstein, b/o play by George S. Kaufman and Moss Hart. Cast: Monty Woolley, Bette Davis, Ann Sheridan, Jimmy Durante, Reginald Gardiner, Billie Burke, Mary Wickes, Grant Mitchell. Famous writer descends on Ohio household.

MY SISTER EILEEN. Columbia. D: Alexander Hall. Sp: Joseph Fields and Jerome Chodorov, b/o their play. Cast: Rosalind Russell, Brian Aherne, Janet Blair, George Tobias, Allyn Joslyn, June Havoc, Gordon Jones, Jeff Donnell. Two sisters seek their fortune in Greenwich Village. Remade in 1955.

A NIGHT TO REMEMBER. Columbia. D: Richard Wallace. Sp: Richard Flournoy and Jack Henley, b/o story by Kelley Roos. Cast: Loretta Young, Brian Aherne, Jeff Donnell, Sidney Toler, Gale Sondergaard, Donald MacBride. Couple get involved in Greenwich Village murder.

THE PALM BEACH STORY. Paramount. D: Preston Sturges. Sp: Preston Sturges. Cast: Claudette Colbert, Joel McCrea, Rudy Vallee, Mary Astor, William Demarest, Franklin Pangborn. Wife leaves husband for Florida.

THE REMARKABLE ANDREW. Paramount. D: Stuart Heisler. Sp: Dalton Trumbo, b/o his novel. Cast: William Holden, Brian Donlevy, Ellen Drew, Montagu Love. General Andrew Jackson returns to help small-town man in trouble.

SULLIVAN'S TRAVELS. Paramount. D: Preston Sturges. Sp: Preston Sturges. Cast: Joel McCrea, Veronica Lake, Robert Warwick, William Demarest, Franklin Pangborn, Porter Hall, Eric Blore. Sheltered film director decides to "see life" as a tramp.

TAKE A LETTER, DARLING. Paramount. D: Mitchell Leisen. Sp: Claude Binyon, b/o story by George Beck. Cast: Rosalind Russell, Fred MacMurray, Constance Moore, Macdonald Carey, Robert Benchley. "Boss-lady" hires man to pose as her fiancé.

THE TALK OF THE TOWN. Columbia. D: George Stevens. Sp: Irwin Shaw and Sidney Buchman. Cast: Ronald Colman, Jean Arthur, Cary Grant, Edgar Buchanan, Charles Dingle, Glenda Farrell. Law professor becomes involved with anarchist.

THEY ALL KISSED THE BRIDE. Columbia. D: Alexander Hall. Sp: P. J. Wolfson, adapted by Andrew P. Solt and Henry Altimus from story by Gina Kaus and Andrew P. Solt. Cast: Joan Crawford, Melvyn Douglas, Roland Young, Billie Burke, Allen Jenkins. Lady executive discovers love.

TWO-FACED WOMAN. MGM. D: George Cukor. Sp: S. N. Behrman, Salka Viertel, and George Oppenheimer, b/o play by Ludwig Fulda. Cast: Greta Garbo, Melvyn Douglas, Constance Bennett, Robert Sterling, Roland Young, Ruth Gordon. Wife pretends to be her own twin sister.

THE WIFE TAKES A FLYER. Columbia. D: Richard Wallace. Sp: Gina Kaus and Jay Dratler, b/o story by Gina Kaus, with additional dialogue by Harry Segall. Cast: Joan Bennett, Franchot Tone, Allyn Joslyn, Cecil Cunningham, Lloyd Corrigan. British flier poses as lady's husband in occupied Holland.

WOMAN OF THE YEAR. MGM. D: George Stevens. Sp: Ring Lardner, Jr. and Michael Kanin. Cast: Katharine Hepburn, Spencer Tracy, Fay Bainter, Reginald Owen, Minor Watson, William Bendix. Sports writer and columnist marry after a whirlwind romance. Remade in 1957 as *Designing Woman*.

1943

CLAUDIA. Fox. D: Edmund Goulding. Sp: Morrie Ryskind, b/o play by Rose Franken. Cast: Dorothy McGuire, Robert Young, Ina Claire, Reginald Gardiner, Olga Baclanova. Emotional problems of young wife.

HEAVEN CAN WAIT. Fox. D: Ernst Lubitsch. Sp: Samson Raphaelson, b/o play by Ladislaus Bus-Fekete. Cast: Don Ameche, Gene Tierney, Charles Coburn, Marjorie Main, Laird Cregar, Eugene Pallette, Spring Byington, Allyn Joslyn. Elderly rake relives his past.

A LADY TAKES A CHANCE. RKO. D: William A. Seiter. Sp: Robert Ardrey, b/o story by Jo Swerling. Cast: Jean Arthur, John Wayne, Charles Winninger, Phil Silvers. Girl on bus tour finds romance with cowboy.

MARGIN FOR ERROR. Fox. D: Otto Preminger. Sp: Lillie Hayward, b/o play by Clare Boothe. Cast: Joan Bennett, Milton Berle, Otto Preminger, Carl Esmond. Murder and skulduggery at a Nazi consulate.

THE MORE THE MERRIER. Columbia. D: George Stevens. Sp: Richard Flournoy, Lewis R. Foster, Robert Russell, and Frank Ross, b/o story by Robert

Russell and Frank Ross. Cast: Jean Arthur, Joel McCrea, Charles Coburn, Richard Gaines. Elderly gentleman acts as Cupid in crowded wartime Washington. Remade in 1966 as *Walk, Don't Run.*

OLD ACQUAINTANCE. Warners. D: Vincent Sherman. Sp: John Van Druten and Lenore Coffee, b/o play by John Van Druten. Cast: Bette Davis, Miriam Hopkins, Gig Young, John Loder, Dolores Moran, Philip Reed. Two women have a lifelong but stormy friendship.

THREE HEARTS FOR JULIA. MGM. D: Richard Thorpe. Sp: Lionel Houser, b/o his story. Cast: Melvyn Douglas, Ann Sothern, Lee Bowman, Richard Ainley, Felix Bressart. Foreign correspondent has marital problems.

TRUE TO LIFE. Paramount. D: George Marshall. Sp: Don Hartman and Harry Tugend, b/o story by Ben Barzman, Bess Taffel, and Sol Barzman. Cast: Mary Martin, Franchot Tone, Dick Powell, Victor Moore, William Demarest. Radio writer moves in with family to get authentic material.

WHAT A WOMAN. Columbia. D: Irving Cummings. Sp: Therese Lewis and Barry Trivers, b/o story by Erik Charell. Cast: Rosalind Russell, Brian Aherne, Willard Parker, Alan Dinehart, Ann Savage. Authors' agent has romantic and business troubles.

1944

ARSENIC AND OLD LACE. Warners. D: Frank Capra. Sp: Julius J. and Philip G. Epstein, b/o play by Joseph Kesselring. Cast: Cary Grant, Josephine Hull, Priscilla Lane, Raymond Massey, Peter Lorre, Jean Adair, Jack Carson. Drama critic must deal with his two sweet but homicidal aunts.

THE CANTERVILLE GHOST. MGM. D: Jules Dassin. Sp: Edwin Harvey Blum, b/o story by Oscar Wilde. Cast: Charles Laughton, Robert Young, Margaret O'Brien, William Gargan, Reginald Owen. Ghost haunts castle occupied by American Rangers.

THE DOUGHGIRLS. Warners. D: James V. Kern. Sp: James V. Kern and Sam Hellman, with additional dialogue by Wilkie Mahoney, b/o play by Joseph A. Fields. Cast: Ann Sheridan, Alexis Smith, Jane Wyman, Eve Arden, Charlie Ruggles, Irene Manning. Lunacy in a Washington hotel room.

GOVERNMENT GIRL. RKO. D: Dudley Nichols. Sp: Dudley Nichols, b/o story by Adela Rogers St. John. Cast: Olivia de Havilland, Sonny Tufts, Anne Shirley, James Dunn, Agnes Moorehead, Harry Davenport. Secretary loves her boss in crowded Washington.

THE GREAT MOMENT. Paramount. D: Preston Sturges. Sp: Preston Sturges, from book by Rene Fulop-Miller. Cast: Joel McCrea, Betty Field, Harry Carey, William Demarest, Porter Hall, Franklin Pangborn. Dentist in 1840s wants to use ether as an anesthetic.

HAIL THE CONQUERING HERO. Paramount. D: Preston Sturges. Sp: Preston Sturges. Cast: Eddie Bracken, Ella Raines, Raymond Walburn, William Demarest, Franklin Pangborn, Freddie Steele, Georgia Caine. Young 4–F is acclaimed as hero by his hometown.

THE IMPATIENT YEARS. Columbia. D: Irving Cummings. Sp: Virginia Van Upp. Cast: Jean Arthur, Charles Coburn, Lee Bowman, Edgar Buchanan, Charley Grapewin. Young couple is reunited after year-and-a-half separation.

JANIE. Warners. D: Michael Curtiz. Sp: Agnes Christine Johnston and Charles Hoffman, b/o play by Josephine Bentham and Herschel V. Williams, Jr. Cast: Joyce Reynolds, Edward Arnold, Robert Hutton, Ann Harding, Robert Benchley, Alan Hale. Teenage girl disrupts her family.

LADY IN THE DARK. Paramount. D: Mitchell Leisen. Sp: Frances Goodrich and Albert Hackett, b/o play by Moss Hart. Cast: Ginger Rogers, Ray Milland, Jon Hall, Warner Baxter, Mischa Auer. Editor of fashion magazine has unhappy past.

THE MIRACLE OF MORGAN'S CREEK. Paramount. D: Preston Sturges. Sp: Preston Sturges. Cast: Betty Hutton, Eddie Bracken, William Demarest, Diana Lynn, Porter Hall, Alan Bridge. Small-town girl becomes pregnant by unknown soldier.

ONCE UPON A TIME. Columbia. D: Alexander Hall. Sp: Lewis Meltzer and Oscar Paul, adapted by Irving Fineman from story by Norman Corwin and Lucille Fletcher Herrmann. Cast: Cary Grant, Janet Blair, James Gleason, Ted Donaldson. Theatre impresario discovers boy and his dancing caterpillar.

THE THIN MAN GOES HOME. MGM. D: Richard Thorpe. Sp: Robert Riskin and Dwight Taylor, b/o story by Robert Riskin and Harry Kurnitz and characters created by Dashiell Hammett. Cast: William Powell, Myrna Loy, Gloria DeHaven, Lucile Watson, Anne Revere, Leon Ames. The Charleses visit Nick's parents and get involved in a murder.

3 IS A FAMILY. United Artists. D: Edward Ludwig. Sp: Harry Chandlee and Marjorie L. Pfailzer, b/o play by Phoebe and Henry Ephron. Cast: Marjorie

Reynolds, Charlie Ruggles, Fay Bainter, Helen Broderick, Arthur Lake, Hattie McDaniel. Many frantic people are crowded into one small New York apartment.

TOGETHER AGAIN. Columbia. D: Charles Vidor. Sp: Virginia Van Upp and F. Hugh Herbert, b/o story by Stanley Russell and Herbert Biberman. Cast: Irene Dunne, Charles Boyer, Charles Coburn, Mona Freeman, Jerome Courtland. Romance grows between lady mayor and sculptor.

WHISTLING IN BROOKLYN. MGM. D: S. Sylvan Simon. Sp: Nat Perrin, with additional dialogue by Wilkie Mahoney. Cast: Red Skelton, Ann Rutherford, Jean Rogers, Rags Ragland, Sam Levene. More adventures of radio detective.

BIBLIOGRAPHY

Agee, James. *Agee on Film*. New York: McDowell, Oblensky, 1958.

Baxter, John. *Hollywood in the Thirties*. New York: A. S. Barnes, 1968.

Bergman, Andrew. *We're in the Money*. New York: New York University Press, 1971.

Capra, Frank. *The Name Above the Title*. New York: Macmillan, 1971.

Dickens, Homer. "Carole Lombard." *Films in Review*, February, 1961.

_____. *The Films of Gary Cooper*. New York: Citadel Press, 1970.

_____. *The Films of Katharine Hepburn*. New York: Citadel Press, 1971.

Durgnat, Raymond. *The Crazy Mirror: Hollywood Comedy and the American Image*. London: Faber, 1969.

Editors of *American Heritage*. *The American Heritage History of the 20's and 30's*. New York: American Heritage Publishing Co. (a Subsidiary of McGraw-Hill Book Company), 1970.

Farber, Manny. *Negative Space*. New York: Praeger, 1971.

Ferguson, Otis. *The Film Criticism of Otis Ferguson*. Edited by Robert Wilson. Philadelphia: Temple University Press, 1971.

Griffith, Richard, and Mayer, Arthur. *The Movies*. New York: Bonanza Books, 1957.

Hagen, Ray. "The Day of the Runaway Heiress." *Films and Filming*, April, 1966.

Halliwell, Leslie. *The Filmgoer's Companion*. 2d ed. New York: Hill and Wang, 1967.

Higham, Charles, and Greenberg, Joel. *Hollywood in the Forties*. New York: A. S. Barnes, 1968.

Kael, Pauline. *The Citizen Kane Book*. Boston: Atlantic Monthly Press/Little, Brown and Company, 1971.

Lambert, Gavin. *On Cukor*. New York: G. P. Putnam's Sons, 1972.

Michael, Paul, ed. *The American Movies Reference Book*. Englewood Cliffs: Prentice-Hall, 1969.

The New York Times Directory of the Film. New York: Arno Press/Random House, 1971.

The New York Times Film Reviews, 1932–1948. New York: New York Times and Arno Press, 1970.

Ott, Frederick W. *The Films of Carole Lombard.* Secaucus, N.J.: Citadel Press, 1972.

Pechter, William S. *Twenty-Four Times a Second: Films and Film-makers.* New York: Harper & Row, 1971.

Thomaier, William. "Early Sound Comedy." *Films in Review,* May, 1959.

Ursini, James. *Preston Sturges: An American Dreamer.* New York: Curtis Books, 1973.

Zinman, David. *50 Classic Motion Pictures.* New York: Crown Publishers, 1970.

———. *Saturday Afternoon at the Bijou.* New Rochelle: Arlington House, 1973.

INDEX

Abbott, Bud, 190
Abbott, George, 275
Abel, Walter, 81
Adair, Jean, 287
Adam's Rib, 221, 223
Adams, Samuel Hopkins, 16
Adler, Stella, 168
Adventure in Manhattan, 180, 182
After All, 256
After the Thin Man, 166
Ah, Wilderness!, 267
Aherne, Brian, 69, 81, 158, 182, 202, 215, 257, 268
Alberni, Luis, 27, 33
Albert, Eddie, 45, 275
Albertson, Frank, 40, 277
Albright, Hardie, 143
Alexander, John, 287
Alexander, Katharine, 26, 203
Alibi Ike, 125
Allen, Gracie, 184
Allwyn, Astrid, 28
Allyson, June, 94
Along Came Jones, 138
Amazing Dr. Clitterhouse, The, 277, 280
Amazing Mr. Williams, The, 184
Ameche, Don, 36, 73, 96, 135, 195
American Madness, 15
Ames, Leon, 168
Ames, Robert, 52, 105
Anderson, Eddie "Rochester," 190
Anderson, Maxwell, 267
Andrews, Ann, 226
Andrews, Dana, 138
Angel On My Shoulder, 196
Angelus, Muriel, 230
Animal Kingdom, The, 257
Anne of Windy Poplars, 161

Another Language, 257
Another Thin Man, 166, 168
Appointment for Love, 76, 80, 89
Arden, Eve, 18, 89, 267, 285
Are Husbands Necessary?, 88
Arlen, Richard, 143
Arno, Sig, 242
Arnold, Edward, 33, 48, 128, 146, 171, 217, 285
Arrowsmith, 163
Arsenic and Old Lace, 285, 287
Arthur, Art, 61
Arthur, Jean, 17, 23, 33, 48, 51, 63, 65, 101, 103, 117, 118, 120, 128, 129, 131, 133, 135, 146, 171, 172, 180, 204, 227
As Husbands Go, 257
Astaire, Fred, 40
Astor, Mary, 27, 36, 38, 39, 68, 105, 175, 242, 244
Ates, Roscoe, 242
Auer, Mischa, 36, 147, 154, 156
Avery, Stephen, 27, 282
Awful Truth, The, 16, 17, 18, 52, 53–54, 56, 58, 89, 112, 189
Ayres, Lew, 101, 107, 133, 150

Baby Face Harrington, 124
Bachelor Mother, 40–41, 45, 47
Back Street, 17, 54
Bacon, Lloyd, 280
Bainter, Fay, 86, 150
Baker, Melville, 24
Bakewell, William, 143
Baldwin, Earl, 280
Baldwin, Faith, 104
Ball, Lucille, 81, 267
Ball of Fire, 138
Ballard, Frederick, 259

Bancroft, George, 259
Bankhead, Tallulah, 54, 257
Barbier, George, 282
Bari, Lynn, 135
Barnes, Binnie, 61, 73, 81
Barrie, James, 257
Barrie, Wendy, 61, 111
Barry, Philip, 52, 83, 105, 288
Barry, Phyllis, 52
Barrymore, John, 17, 36, 38, 39, 178, 190, 256, 262, 263, 288
Barrymore, Lionel, 142, 146, 262
Bartlett, Bennie, 144
Bartlett, Sy, 184
Bates, Barbara, 213
Bates, Granville, 66
Battle of the Century, 16
Baxter, Alan, 168
Baxter, Anne, 196
Baxter, Warner, 58, 61, 213
Beau Geste, 163
Beautiful Blonde from Bashful Bend, The, 252
Bedtime Story, 88–89
Beery, Wallace, 262, 263, 288
Behrman, S. N., 68, 83, 257, 280
Bellamy, Ralph, 56, 277
Belle of the Nineties, 54
Benchley, Robert, 18, 60, 69, 88, 192, 203
Bendix, William, 86
Bennett, Charles, 159
Bennett, Constance, 83, 84, 158, 187, 189, 190, 257
Bennett, Joan, 21, 45, 105, 266
Bennett, Marjorie, 213
Benny, Jack, 195, 285
Bentham, Josephine, 285
Bercovici, Leonardo, 195
Berkeley, Busby, 175
Bernhardt, Curtis, 45
Berr, Georges, 178
Best, Willie, 185
Beware of Widows, 16
Biberman, Herbert, 221
Bickford, Charles, 94
Big Pond, The, 23
Bing, Herman, 61, 182
Binyon, Claude, 16, 24, 30, 31, 63, 80, 178, 203
Biography, 257
Biography of a Bachelor Girl, 257
Birds and the Bees, The, 237
Bishop's Wife, The, 195
Bitter Tea of General Yen, The, 15
Blackmer, Sidney, 175
Blair, Janet, 267
Blessed Event, 259
Blind Date, 143–144
Blonde Venus, 54
Blondell, Joan, 75, 175, 177, 184, 190, 275

Blore, Eric, 45, 172, 235, 237
Bluebeard's Eighth Wife, 60–61
Blum, Edwin Harvey, 190
Blystone, John, 156
Bob and Carol and Ted and Alice, 89
Bogart, Humphrey, 51, 280
Boland, Mary, 63, 122, 124, 143, 144, 259, 266, 273, 274, 288
Boles, John, 226
Bombshell, 259, 262
Bondi, Beulah, 104, 227
Booth, Shirley, 267
Boothe, Clare, 271
Bought, 21
Bowman, Lee, 31, 175, 200, 217
Boy Meets Girl, 277, 288
Boyer, Charles, 76, 80, 221, 275
Bracken, Eddie, 244, 248
Brackett, Charles, 16, 36, 61, 138
Brady, Alice, 154, 156, 158
Brecher, Irving, 168
Brent, George, 21, 104, 204
Breslow, Lou, 152
Bressart, Felix, 184
Bride Came C.O.D., The, 90, 111
Bride Comes Home, The, 30
Bride of Frankenstein, The, 171
Bridge, Alan, 248, 251, 252, 254
Bringing Up Baby, 17, 111–112, 114–115, 266
Broderick, Helen, 18, 199, 200
Brophy, Edward, 120, 122, 165, 171, 184
Brother Rat, 277
Brown, Clarence, 75
Brown, Joe E., 125, 259
Brown, Tom, 158
Bruce, Nigel, 269
Bruce, Virginia, 58, 69, 96, 125, 175, 177, 190
Brush, Katharine, 200
Bryan, Jane, 277, 280
Buchanan, Edgar, 135
Buchanan, Jack, 254
Buchman, Sidney, 107, 128, 133, 135, 182, 192
Buckner, Robert L., 150
Burke, Billie, 143, 158, 159, 187, 190, 202, 262, 271, 282
Burke, Edwin, 69, 187, 190
Burnett, W. R., 122
Burns, George, 184
Bus-Fekete, Ladislaus, 195
Butler, Frank, 125, 178
Butterworth, Charles, 124
Buzzell, Edward, 168, 172
Byington, Spring, 45, 133, 146, 149, 150
Byron, Walter, 21

Cafe Society, 90, 96–97
Cagney, James, 13, 90, 111, 122, 275, 277
Caine, Georgia, 254

Calhern, Louis, 172
Call it a Day, 158
Calleia, Joseph, 166
Campbell, Alan, 104
Canterville Ghost, The, 190
Capra, Frank, 15–16, 23, 91, 111, 117, 120,
    127, 128, 129, 131, 140, 144, 147, 149,
    193, 233, 248, 287, 289
Carey, Harry, 131
Carey, Macdonald, 203
Carlson, Richard, 159, 185
Carminati, Tullio, 226
Carol, Martine, 254
Caron, Leslie, 51
Carradine, John, 144
Carrillo, Leo, 103
Carroll, Joan, 150
Carroll, John, 69, 269
Carroll, Leo G., 288
Carroll, Madeleine, 18, 36, 90, 96, 199
Carroll, Nancy, 226
Carson, Jack, 44, 111, 267, 283, 285, 287
Cat and the Canary, The, 185, 187
Cat Creeps, The, 185
Catlett, Walter, 114, 118, 144
Cat's Paw, The, 119
Cavett, Frank Morgan, 257
Ceiling Zero, 275
Champion, Gower, 65
Champion, Marge, 65
Charters, Spencer, 144
Chatterton, Ruth, 14, 21, 52
Chevalier, Maurice, 23
Child of Manhattan, 226
Chodorov, Jerome, 150, 267, 269
Christmas in Connecticut, 213
Christmas in July, 232–233, 244
Ciannelli, Eduardo, 185
Citizen Kane, 227
Clair, René, 187, 192
Claire, Ina, 53, 271
Claudia, 271
Clear All Wires, 259
Cleopatra, 24
Clive, Colin, 26
Clive, E. E., 100
Clork, Harry, 125
Cobb, Irvin S., 159
Cobb, Lee J., 72
Coburn, Charles, 41, 48, 51, 76, 133, 195,
    217, 234, 237, 285
Cockeyed Miracle, The, 195
Coffee, Lenore, 211
Cohan, George M., 259
Cohen, Octavus Roy, 68
Cohn, Harry, 15, 54
Colbert, Claudette, 16, 17, 18, 20, 23, 24, 26,
    30, 31, 36, 51, 60, 81, 90, 91, 94, 143,
    182, 203, 211, 241, 257, 275

Collier, Constance, 269
Collier, Sr., William, 30
Collison, Wilson, 175, 182
Colman, Ronald, 44, 45, 52, 135, 138, 288
Come Live With Me, 75
Compromised, 21
Compton, Joyce, 56
Conlin, Jimmy, 249, 254
Connell, Richard, 69, 125
Connelly, Marc, 192, 259, 269, 275
Connolly, Walter, 24, 43, 94, 105, 127, 265,
    266, 275
Conway, Jack, 76, 98
Cooper, Gary, 60, 61, 101, 116, 117, 138,
    257, 266
Cooper, Gladys, 195
Cooper, Melville, 65, 80
Cornell, Katharine, 68, 280
Cortez, Ricardo, 21
Costello, Lou, 190
Cotten, Joseph, 109, 110
Courtland, Jerome, 221
Cowan, Jerome, 175, 184, 277
Coward, Noël, 226, 283
Cowboy and the Lady, The, 81
Cowl, Jane, 275
Crabbe, Buster, 143
Crane, Harry, 168
Crane, Mack, 259
Crawford, Broderick, 63, 156, 280
Crawford, Joan, 96, 197, 200, 202, 211, 257,
    269, 271, 273, 274
Cregar, Laird, 195
Croft, Douglas, 285
Crosland, Alan, 104
Cross Country Romance, 111
Cross My Heart, 178
Crothers, Rachel, 211, 257, 269
Crouse, Russel, 288
Crowd Roars, The, 263
Cukor, George, 83, 107, 223, 262, 269, 271
Culver, Ronald, 193
Cummings, Constance, 171
Cummings, Irving, 215
Cummings, Robert, 133, 195, 217
Cunningham, Cecil, 56, 58
Curtiz, Michael, 285
Cynara, 52

Dailey, Dan, 271
Danger—Love At Work, 144
Daninos, Pierre, 254
D'Arcy, Alexander, 54
Darnell, Linda, 61, 252
Darwell, Jane, 144
Dassin, Jules, 190
Davenport, Harry, 44, 63, 65, 101, 168, 217,
    275
Daves, Delmer, 27

Davies, Marion, 27
Davis, Bette, 26, 90, 111, 211, 213, 282
Davis, Owen, 184
Dawn, Isabel, 104
Daytime Wife, 61
Dayton, Katharine, 275
Dear Ruth, 288
Dee, Frances, 27
DeGaw, Boyce, 104
de Havilland, Olivia, 45, 48, 158, 283
De Leon, Walter, 178, 185
Delmar, Viña, 54
Del Ruth, Roy, 63, 140, 190
Demarest, William, 28, 138, 230, 232, 234,
    237, 241, 242, 244, 248, 249, 252
DeMille, Cecil B., 23
Dempsey (Desti), Mary, 226
Design for Living, 257
Design for Scandal, 217
Deval, Jacques, 275
Devil and Miss Jones, The, 133
Devil and the Deep, 54
De Wolf, Karen, 195
Diamond Jim, 227
Dickey, Paul, 185
Dietrich, Marlene, 18, 54
Digges, Dudley, 96
Dinehart, Alan, 119
Dingle, Charles, 137, 285
Dinner at Eight, 262–263
Divorce American Style, 89
Dix, Richard, 16
Dixon, Jean, 107, 109, 154, 285
Dr. Jekyll and Mr. Hyde, 84
Doctor Takes a Wife, The, 209, 211
Dodd, Claire, 172
Don Juan, 104
Donaldson, Ted, 140
Donat, Robert, 131, 187
Donlevy, Brian, 193, 195, 225, 229, 230, 244
Donnell, Jeff, 268
Donnelly, Ruth, 75, 80, 206, 280
Doughgirls, The, 285
Douglas, Melvyn, 18, 31, 63, 65, 72, 73, 76,
    83, 84, 172, 175, 184, 197, 200, 202,
    203, 207, 226
Douglas, Paul, 61
Down to Earth, 193
Down to Their Last Yacht, 143
Doyle, Laird, 275
Dressler, Marie, 262, 263
Drew, Ellen, 76, 184, 232
Duck Soup, 16, 54
Dudley, Robert, 241
Dulcy, 269, 271
Dumbrille, Douglas, 117, 172, 180, 226
Dunne, Irene, 17, 52, 54, 58, 66, 68, 197, 206,
    217
Dunning, Philip, 27

Dupree, Minnie, 159, 161
Durante, Jimmy, 283
Durbin, Deanna, 24
Duryea, Dan, 138

Earthworn Tractors, 125
Easy Living, 31, 33–34, 36, 227
Easy to Wed, 100
Eburne, Maude, 124
Eggar, Samantha, 51
Ellis, Edward, 165
Elmer and Elsie, 259
Elmer the Great, 125, 259
Elser, Frank B., 266
Emerson, Hope, 223
Emery, John, 192
Emma, 163
Englund, Ken, 177, 209
Epstein, Julius, 16, 68, 111, 274, 282, 283,
    285
Epstein, Philip, 16, 68, 111, 177, 182, 275,
    282, 283, 285
Erwin, Stuart, 58
Eternally Yours, 61, 63
Evans, Madge, 262
Everybody Does It, 61
Ewell, Tom, 223
Ex-Mrs. Bradford, The, 171–172

Fairbanks, Jr., Douglas, 40, 159, 267
Fancy Pants, 124
Farmer Takes a Wife, The, 266
Farrell, Glenda, 15, 23, 137, 226
Fast and Furious, 175
Fast and Loose, 172, 174
Fast Company, 172
Fazenda, Louise, 259, 275
Feel My Pulse, 163
Fellows, Edith, 203
Feminine Touch, The, 69, 73, 89
Fenton, Leslie, 133
Ferber, Edna, 262
Ferrer, Jose, 277
Fessier, Michael, 195
Field, Betty, 88
Fields, Dorothy, 104
Fields, Herbert, 28
Fields, Joseph A., 150, 267, 269, 285
Fields, W. C., 14, 124
Fifth Avenue Girl, 41, 43–44, 45, 96, 150, 155
Finklehoffe, Fred F., 277
First Lady, 275
Fisher, Steve, 168
Fitzgerald, Barry, 114
Fitzmaurice, George, 58
Flournoy, Richard, 48, 88, 182
Fonda, Henry, 80, 104, 105, 135, 182, 234,
    237, 267, 283
Fontaine, Joan, 101, 273

Fontanne, Lynn, 271
Foran, Dick, 277
Forbes, Ralph, 265
Ford, John, 119
Ford, Wallace, 143
Forsaking All Others, 257
Foster, Lewis R., 48
Foster, Norman, 217
Four Feathers, The, 163
Fourflusher, The, 16
Fox, Sidney, 143, 259
Francis, Arlene, 285
Francis, Kay, 21, 53, 73, 163, 275
Francke, Caroline, 259
Franken, Rose, 257, 271
Frankenstein, 171
Freeman, Devery, 217
Freeman, Mona, 221
French They Are a Funny Race, The, 254
Front Page, The, 257
Fuller, Frances, 259
Furthman, Jules, 262

Gable, Clark, 16, 17, 90, 91, 94, 96, 163, 257
Gaines, Richard, 50
Gale, Joan, 144
Garbo, Greta, 83, 84
Gardiner, Reginald, 211, 213, 271, 283
Garfield, John, 267
Garnett, Tay, 61, 105
Garrett, Betty, 269
Garrett, Oliver H. P., 105
Garson, Greer, 211
Gay Deception, The, 27
Gaynor, Janet, 36, 101, 159, 161
Gaynor, Mitzi, 237
George Washington Slept Here, 283, 285
Gershwin, Ira, 213
Ghost and Mrs. Muir, The, 190, 192
Ghost Breaker, The, 185
Ghost Breakers, The, 185
Ghost Goes West, The, 187
Gibbons, Cedric, 165, 271
Gilded Lily, The, 16, 24, 26
Gillingwater, Claude, 90, 96
Girardot, Etienne, 120, 122, 144, 175, 265, 266
Glass Slipper, The, 51
Gleason, James, 172, 193, 195
Gobel, George, 237
Goddard, Charles W., 185
Goddard, Paulette, 48, 159, 185, 273, 274
Godfrey, Peter, 213
Gold Diggers of 1937, 23
Golden Fleecing, The, 133
Goldwyn, Samuel, 52, 101, 125, 138, 156
Gombell, Minna, 165
Gone With the Wind, 133
Good Fairy, The, 24, 227

Goodbye, Mr. Chips, 131
Goodrich, Frances, 165, 166
Gordon, Ruth, 84, 143, 221
Gorog, Laslo, 217
Gottschalk, Ferdinand, 27
Government Girl, 48
Grable, Betty, 65, 252
Gracie Allen Murder Case, The, 184
Grant, Cary, 17–18, 51, 54, 58, 66, 68, 105, 107, 109, 110, 112, 115, 135, 187, 189, 195, 287
Grant, James Edward, 144, 172, 177
Granville, Bonita, 158
Great McGinty, The, 225, 229–230
Great Moment, The (Great Without Glory), 252
Greeks Had a Word For It, The, 23
Green, Alfred E., 26, 140, 184
Green, Howard J., 101, 171
Green Pastures, The, 275
Greenstreet, Sydney, 213
Grey, Virginia, 168
Grieg, Robert, 237, 242
Griffith, Edward H., 199
Gwenn, Edmund, 211

Hackett, Albert, 165, 166
Hagan, James, 266
Hagen, Jean, 223
Hail the Conquering Hero, 225, 248–249, 251–252, 254, 255
Haley, Jack, 144
Hall, Alexander, 88, 175, 184, 193, 200, 209, 217, 266, 267
Hall, Dickie, 168
Hall, Dorothy, 226
Hall, Jon, 213
Hall, Porter, 152, 165, 178, 180, 241, 245, 252
Halliday, John, 110
Halton, Charles, 206
Hamilton, Margaret, 105, 127
Hamilton, Neil, 144
Hammett, Dashiell, 163, 168
Hands Across the Table, 20, 27–28, 30, 36, 54
Harari, Robert, 61
Harding, Ann, 52, 53, 105, 211, 257, 285
Hardwicke, Cedric, 280
Hardy, Oliver, 16
Harlow, Jean, 15, 18, 21, 54, 98, 100, 101, 262, 263, 288
Harris, Ray, 143
Harrison, Rex, 190, 252
Hart, Moss, 144, 146, 213, 259, 282, 283
Hart, Teddy, 275
Hart, Walter, 150
Hartman, Don, 27, 178
Hartmann, Edmund L., 73
Harvey, Paul, 120
Hatch, Eric, 105, 152, 187

Having Wonderful Time, 40, 267
Havoc, June, 268
Hawks, Howard, 112, 138, 263, 266, 275
Hayes, Helen, 257
Hayward, Susan, 192
Hayworth, Rita, 193, 269
He Married His Wife, 63
Heather, Jean, 152
Heaven Can Wait, 195–196
Heaven Only Knows, 195
Hecht, Ben, 125, 127, 182, 257, 263, 266
Heflin, Van, 73, 109, 110
Heisler, Stuart, 138, 193
Hellman, Sam, 63, 285
Henley, Jack, 182
Henry, William, 165
Hepburn, Audrey, 51
Hepburn, Katharine, 17, 18, 19, 83, 86, 88,
    105, 107, 109, 110, 112, 115, 221, 223,
    288
Herbert, F. Hugh, 101, 221
Here Comes Mr. Jordan, 18, 192–193
Hertz, David, 36, 76
Hinds, Samuel S., 146
Hired Wife, 69, 76, 202
Hitchcock, Alfred, 73
Hobart, Rose, 185
Hobbes, Halliwell, 147
Holden, William, 193
Holiday, 17, 105, 107, 109, 112
Holliday, Judy, 223, 224
Holloway, Sterling, 143, 227, 252
Holm, Celeste, 61
Holm, John Cecil, 275
Holt, Tim, 43
Honeymoon in Bali, 96, 199–200
Hope, Bob, 124, 185, 187
Hopkins, Miriam, 156, 211, 257
Hopper, Hedda, 38
Hopton, Russell, 259
Horn Blows at Midnight, The, 195
Horton, Edward Everett, 18, 60, 61, 107, 109,
    192, 193, 287
Houser, Lionel, 200, 217
Howard, Esther, 238
Howard, John, 110
Howard, Leslie, 257
Howard, William K., 178
Hubbard, John, 45, 68
Hughes, Mary Beth, 175
Hull, Josephine, 287
Hume, Benita, 27
Hunter, Ian, 26, 158, 271
Hussey, Ruth, 76, 111, 150, 168, 175, 269
Huston, John, 277
Huston, Walter, 15, 259
Hutton, Betty, 178, 244, 246
Hutton, Jim, 51
Hutton, Robert, 285

Hymer, Warren, 61

I Am a Fugitive From a Chain Gang, 13
I Love You Again, 66, 68, 69
I Married a Witch, 192
I Met Him in Paris, 31
I Remember Mama, 288
I Take This Woman, 23
If I Were Free, 54
If I Were King, 227
If You Could Only Cook, 76, 101, 103–104
I'll Be Yours, 24
I'm No Angel, 54
Imitation of Life, 24
In Person, 104
Inescort, Frieda, 158
Invisible Man, The, 171, 190
Invisible Woman, The, 190
It Happened in New York, 104
It Happened on Fifth Avenue, 140
It Happened One Night, 16, 23, 90–91, 93–94,
    96, 111, 143
It's a Wonderful World, 182
It's All Yours, 36

Jackson, Felix, 76
Jacoby, John, 217
Janie, 285, 287
Janie Gets Married, 285
Jarrico, Paul, 47
Jason, Leigh, 182
Jazz Singer, The, 104
Jenkins, Allen, 27, 202
Jevne, Jack, 158, 187
Jewell, Isabel, 125
Jezebel, 150
John Loves Mary, 288
Johnson, Nunnally, 124, 138
Johnson, Rita, 80, 133, 192
Johnson, Van, 101
Jones, Allan, 199
Jones, Gordon, 268
Jones, Grover, 125
Jordan, Bobby, 280
Jory, Victor, 275
Joslyn, Allyn, 72, 89, 96, 175, 196, 268, 277,
    282
Joyce, Brenda, 105
June Bride, 213
Junior Miss, 287, 288

Kanin, Garson, 40, 41, 47, 66, 221, 277
Kanin, Michael, 84
Karloff, Boris, 287
Karns, Roscoe, 86, 93, 264, 266
Kaufman, Edward, 171
Kaufman, George S., 144, 146, 259, 262, 269,
    282, 283
Kaye, Danny, 125, 133, 138

Keeler, Ruby, 277
Keighley, William, 277, 283, 285
Kelland, Clarence Budington, 119
Kellaway, Cecil, 192
Kelly, Nancy, 63
Kelly, Patsy, 27, 158
Kelly, Paul, 144, 171, 184
Kennedy, Edgar, 30, 178, 185
Kent, Dorothea, 206
Kenyon, Charles, 26
Kern, James V., 285
Kern, Jerome, 54
Kesselring, Joseph, 285
Keyes, Evelyn, 193
Kibbee, Guy, 15, 128, 150
Kibbee, Roland, 196
Kid From Brooklyn, The, 125
Kilbride, Percy, 285
King, Walter Woolf, 158
Kingsford, Walter, 266
Kinskey, Leonid, 26
Kirkland, Jack, 24, 182
Kirkland, Muriel, 226
Kirkwood, James, 21
Kiss and Tell, 287
Knoph, Edwin H., 124
Knowles, Patric, 168
Kober, Arthur, 40, 267
Kolb, Clarence, 158, 184
Kolker, Henry, 107, 125, 209
Krasna, Norman, 16, 28, 40, 41, 73, 133
Kurnitz, Harry, 68, 168, 172, 175

La Cava, Gregory, 16, 41, 150, 152, 155, 203
Ladies in Retirement, 45
Ladies of the Jury, 259
Lady Eve, The, 233–235, 237, 244
Lady for a Day, 15
Lady in the Dark, 211, 213
Lake, Veronica, 192, 238, 241
Lamarr, Hedy, 75
Lamont, Charles, 195
Lanchester, Elsa, 195
Landi, Elissa, 166´
Landis, Carole, 68, 190
Lane, Priscilla, 277, 287
Lang, Walter, 58, 135
Langdon, Harry, 15
Langner, Lawrence, 266
Lardner, Jr., Ring, 84
Late George Apley, The, 288
Laughton, Charles, 122, 124, 190
Laurel, Stan, 16
Lauren, S. K., 143, 184, 211
Lawrence, Gertrude, 81, 269, 283
Lawrence, Vincent, 28
Le Baron, William, 229
Lederer, Charles, 68, 76
Lederer, Francis, 27, 36, 266

Lee, Carolyn, 199
Lehman, Gladys, 69, 175
Leigh, Rowland, 275
Leisen, Mitchell, 27, 28, 36, 203, 227
Lemmon, Jack, 65, 94
Leonard, Robert Z., 200, 211
Leonard, Sheldon, 76, 168
LeRoy, Mervyn, 275
Levant, Oscar, 104
Levene, Sam, 76, 166, 182, 275
Levison, Charles, 266
Lewis, Therese, 215
Libeled Lady, 96, 98, 100–101
Life With Father, 288
Lindsay, Howard, 280, 288
Lindsay, Margaret, 177
Little Caesar, 119, 277
Little Man, What Now?, 24
Litvak, Anatole, 277
Live, Love and Learn, 58, 60
Lloyd, Harold, 119, 125, 252
Lockhart, Gene, 171, 195
Lockridge, Frances, 184
Lockridge, Richard, 184
Logan, Ella, 156
Lombard, Carole, 17, 20, 21, 23, 27–28, 30,
    73, 75, 125, 127, 154, 156, 158, 177,
    178, 263, 288
Lonergan, Lenore, 47
Loos, Anita, 211, 269, 271
Lord, Robert, 27
Lorimer, Graeme, 213
Lorre, Peter, 287
Louise, Anita, 158
Love Crazy, 76
Love in the Afternoon, 61
Love Is News, 96
Love Me Tonight, 163
Love on the Run, 96
Lowe, Edmund, 262
Loy, Myrna, 17, 18, 53, 66, 68, 76, 96, 98,
    100, 101, 163, 165, 200, 211, 256, 257
Lubitsch, Ernst, 27, 28, 60, 61, 75, 83, 195
Lucky Partners, 44–45
Ludwig, Edward, 182
Ludwig, William, 76
Lukas, Paul, 52, 185
Lyndon, Barre, 280
Lynn, Betty, 213
Lynn, Diana, 244, 248

MacArthur, Charles, 257, 263, 266
MacBride, Donald, 66, 184, 190
MacDonald, Marie, 217
MacDougall, Ranald, 213
Mack, Russell, 259
MacLane, Barton, 27
MacMahon, Aline, 259
MacMurray, Fred, 18, 24, 26, 27–28, 30, 45,

48, 63, 65, 96, 152, 177, 178, 179, 199, 200, 202, 203, 215, 227
Mad Miss Manton, The, 182
Mad Wednesday (The Sin of Harold Diddlebock), 252, 254
Magnificent Dope, The, 133–134
Magnificent Obsession, 17
Mahin, John Lee, 262
Maibaum, Richard, 184
Maid's Night Out, 101
Main, Marjorie, 68, 152, 168, 195, 269, 273
Make Way For Tomorrow, 54
Male Animal, The, 88, 283
Maltese Falcon, The, 175
Man From the Diner's Club, The, 133
Man Who Came to Dinner, The, 282
Mander, Miles, 150
Manhattan Melodrama, 163
Mankiewicz, Herman J., 182, 262
Mankiewicz, Joseph L., 192
Manners, David, 21
Mannheimer, Albert, 269
Manning, Bruce, 76
March, Fredric, 88, 89, 96, 125, 127, 192, 257, 269
Maricle, Leona, 209
Marin, Edwin L., 172
Marion, Frances, 262
Maris, Mona, 259
Markson, Ben, 144
Married Bachelor, 76
Marshal, Alan, 47
Marshall, George, 152, 185
Marshall, Herbert, 24, 101, 103, 211
Martin, Francis, 178
Martin, Mary, 45, 47
Marx Brothers, The, 14, 89, 124
Marx, Harpo, 283
Mask of Fu Manchu, The, 163
Mason, Grace Sartwell, 200
Massen, Osa, 200
Massey, Raymond, 287
Maugham, W. Somerset, 63, 257
Mayer, Edwin Justus, 36
Mayer, Louis B., 163
Mayo, Archie, 158, 196
McCarey, Leo, 16, 54, 58, 124, 125
McCarthy, Justin Huntly, 227
McCrea, Joel, 48, 51, 63, 150, 156, 180, 225, 241, 252
McDaniel, Hattie, 182
McGuire, Dorothy, 271
McHugh, Frank, 27, 275, 277
McLeod, Norman Z., 158, 189
McNulty, Dorothy (Penny Singleton), 166
Meek, Donald, 31, 68, 73, 120, 146, 149, 200
Meltzer, Lewis, 45
Men in White, 163
Menjou, Adolphe, 68, 125, 257

Meredith, Burgess, 47, 76
Merivale, Philip, 75
Merkel, Una, 119, 124
Merrily We Live, 158
Michael, Gertrude, 104
Midnight, 20, 36, 38–39, 61, 282
Midnight Mary, 21, 23
Milestone, Lewis, 45, 257
Milky Way, The, 125
Milland, Ray, 18, 24, 81, 88, 209, 213
Miller, Ann, 146
Miller, Seton I., 192, 259
Miracle of Morgan's Creek, The, 244–246, 248, 254, 255
Mr. and Mrs. North, 184–185
Mr. and Mrs. Smith, 73, 75
Mr. Deeds Goes to Town, 17, 116–119, 125, 149, 150
Mr. Smith Goes to Washington, 128–129, 131, 133
Mr. Winkle Goes to War, 138
Mitchell, Grant, 119, 268, 282
Mitchell, Thomas, 125, 131, 182, 207
Model Wife, 75
Modern Times, 159
Molnar, Ferenc, 24, 227
Monks, Jr., John, 277
Monroe, Marilyn, 51
Montgomery, Robert, 18, 36, 58, 73, 75, 172, 192, 193, 211, 213, 257
Moon's Our Home, The, 104–105
Moore, Constance, 203
Moore, Victor, 23, 140
Moorhead, Natalie, 165
Moran, Eddie, 158, 187
Moran, Polly, 143
More Than a Secretary, 204, 206
More the Merrier, The, 16, 19, 48, 50–51
Morgan, Dennis, 213
Morgan, Frank, 24, 195, 211
Morgan, Ralph, 171, 175
Morison, Patricia, 88
Morris, Chester, 21
Morris, Wayne, 277
Mowbray, Alan, 27, 154, 158, 187, 190
Muni, Paul, 196
Murder, He Says, 152
Murfin, Jane, 271
Murphy, George, 47, 105
My Favorite Wife, 47, 66, 68
My Love Came Back, 45
My Man Godfrey, 16, 41, 142, 152, 154–156, 158
My Sister Eileen, 256, 267–269, 288

Nash, Florence, 273
Nash, Mary, 110
Nash, Ogden, 73
Nathan, Robert, 195

Neill, Roy William, 144
Nelson, Barry, 168
New Adventures of Fu Manchu, The, 23
New Morals for Old, 256
New York Town, 45, 46
Nichols, Dudley, 112
Night at the Opera, A, 89
Night Must Fall, 18
Night to Remember, A, 182, 184
Ninotchka, 61, 83
Niven, David, 18, 40, 61, 63, 195
Nixon, Marian, 143
No Man of Her Own, 23
No Time for Comedy, 68, 280, 282
Nolan, Doris, 105, 107
Nolan, Lloyd, 266
Norton, Jack, 80, 242, 244, 254
Notebooks of Major Thompson, The, 254
Nothing Sacred, 125, 127
Nugent, Elliott, 36, 88, 143, 185, 187, 283

Oakie, Jack, 185, 195, 259
Oberon, Merle, 76, 101
O'Brien, Margaret, 190
O'Brien, Pat, 27, 257, 275, 277
O'Connor, Una, 213
O'Hanlon, James, 168
O'Hara, John, 63
Old Acquaintance, 211
Oliver, Edna May, 143, 257
Oliver, Gordon, 177
Olivier, Laurence, 51, 280
O'Malley, Rex, 36, 38
Once in a Lifetime, 259
One More Tomorrow, 257
One Sunday Afternoon, 266
One Way Passage, 163
O'Neill, Eugene, 267
Oppenheimer, George, 36, 68, 73, 83, 98
Osborn, Paul, 159
O'Sullivan, Maureen, 165
Our Betters, 257
Our Wife, 76
Overman, Lynne, 45, 178
Owen, Reginald, 24, 175, 180, 226

Padden, Sarah, 150
Pagano, Ernest, 195
Page, Marco, 172
Page Miss Glory, 27
Paige, Mabel, 152
Pallette, Eugene, 18, 80, 111, 142, 154, 156,
    158, 189, 195, 235, 237, 283
Palm Beach Story, The, 241–242, 244
Pangborn, Franklin, 18, 33, 68, 232, 241, 249,
    252, 254
Parker, Dorothy, 28, 104
Parker, Willard, 215, 217, 280
Parks, Larry, 81

Parrish, Helen, 202
Parsonnet, Marion, 133
Paterson, Pat, 105
Patrick, Gail, 66, 154, 156, 209, 211
Patterson, Elizabeth, 61, 227, 268
Paulsen, William A., 166
Pendleton, Nat, 124, 125
Perelman, Laura, 133
Perelman, S. J., 133
Perrin, Nat, 168, 217
Philadelphia Story, The, 17, 83, 84, 109–111
Pidgeon, Walter, 217
Pinza, Ezio, 226
Pirosh, Robert, 192
Pitts, ZaSu, 122, 259
Platinum Blonde, 15
Port of Seven Seas, 227
Porter, Cole, 224
Post, Jr., William, 184
Potter, H. C., 101
Povah, Phyllis, 273
Powell, Dick, 27, 75, 94, 232, 252, 277
Powell, William, 17, 18, 53, 66, 68, 76, 98,
    100, 101, 154, 156, 158, 163, 165, 171,
    172
Power and the Glory, The, 227
Power, Tyrone, 58, 61, 96
Preminger, Otto, 144
Preston, Robert, 45
Primrose Path, 150, 152
Prince and the Showgirl, The, 51
Princess Comes Across, The, 178, 180
Private Lives, 226, 256
Public Deb No. 1, 105
Purcell, Gertrude, 101
Pursuit of Happiness, The, 266

Queen Was in the Parlor, The, 257
Quine, Richard, 268
Quinn, Anthony, 185

Raft, George, 105
Raines, Ella, 249
Rains, Claude, 128, 192, 193, 196, 267
Ralph, Jessie, 166, 226
Ralston, Marcia, 158
Rambeau, Marjorie, 150, 275
Raphaelson, Samson, 81, 195
Ratoff, Gregory, 61, 259
Raymond, Gene, 75, 111
Reagan, Ronald, 277
Recapture, 226
Red-Headed Woman, 21
Reed, Donna, 168
Remarkable Andrew, The, 193
Remember Last Night?, 171
Remember the Night, 227, 229
Revere, Anne, 168
Reynolds, Joyce, 285

Reynolds, Marjorie, 190
Rice, Florence, 172
Rich Man, Poor Girl, 150
Richman, Arthur, 53
Ridges, Stanley, 177, 182
Risdon, Elizabeth, 209
Riskin, Robert, 16, 91, 117, 120, 144, 146, 149, 168
Roach, Hal, 15, 16, 68, 96, 158
Roberts, Edward Barry, 257
Roberts, Stanley, 168
Roberts, Stephen, 171
Robinson, Casey, 158, 275
Robinson, Dewey, 242
Robinson, Edward G., 119, 120, 122, 140, 277, 280
Robson, May, 15, 112, 115
Roche, Arthur Somers, 171
Rogell, Albert S., 195
Rogers, Ginger, 39, 40, 41, 43, 44, 45, 47, 104, 150, 171, 213, 267
Rogers, Howard Emmett, 98
Rogger, Louis Lucien, 178
Roland, Gilbert, 257
Romero, Cesar, 63, 165
Rooney, Mickey, 60, 144
Roos, Kelley, 182
Rosenbloom, Maxie, 127
Ross, Frank, 48
Ross, Shirley, 96
Ruggles, Charles, 68, 75, 114, 115, 122, 124, 140, 266, 280, 282, 285
Ruggles of Red Gap, 16, 54, 122, 124
Ruggles, Wesley, 16, 26, 30, 31, 63, 80, 178
Rumann, Sig, 127, 180
Runyon, Damon, 15, 280
Russell, Robert, 48
Russell, Rosalind, 18, 58, 68, 69, 72, 73, 172, 199, 202, 203, 213, 215, 217, 256, 267, 269, 271, 273, 274, 280, 282, 288
Russell, Stanley, 221
Rutherford, Ann, 187
Ryan, Peggy, 195
Ryskind, Morrie, 152, 271

Sabrina, 51
Sakall, S. Z., 45, 213
Sanders, George, 96
Santell, Alfred, 267
Saturday's Children, 267
Sauber, Harry, 182
Say It Again, 16
Scarface, 263
Schary, Dore, 76
Schilling, Gus, 80
Schrank, Joseph, 27, 135, 280
Schulberg, B. P., 117, 118
Schulz, Franz, 36
Schunzel, Reinhold, 150

Scola, Kathryn, 58
Scott, Allan, 41, 44, 81, 150
Scott, Randolph, 66
Seaton, George, 16, 135, 195, 209
Second Honeymoon, 58
Seff, Manuel, 76, 259
Segall, Harry, 192, 196
Seiter, William A., 76, 101
Seitz, George B., 125
Sennett, Mack, 15, 16, 17, 23
Servants' Entrance, 101
Sessions, Almira, 238
Shadow of the Thin Man, 168
Shaw, Irwin, 135
She Couldn't Take It, 105
She Done Him Wrong, 54
She Knew All the Answers, 45
She Married Her Boss, 203–204
She Wanted a Millionaire, 21
She Wouldn't Say Yes, 217
Shearer, Norma, 257, 271
Sheridan, Ann, 283, 285
Sherman, Vincent, 211, 267
Sherwood, Robert, 195, 275
She's a Sheik, 163
Shirley, Anne, 267
Shopworn, 21
Show Boat, 17, 54, 226
Show of Shows, 163
Sign of the Cross, The, 23
Silvers, Phil, 47
Simon, S. Sylvan, 185, 187, 195, 271
Sinclair, Robert B., 185
Singleton, Penny (Dorothy McNulty), 166
Sinners in the Sun, 21
Skelton, Red, 185, 187, 267
Skipworth, Alison, 26, 178
Skylark, 81, 83, 215
Slight Case of Murder, A, 277, 280
Sloane, Paul, 143
Smith, C. Aubrey, 168
Smith, Dodie, 158
Smith, Thorne, 68, 187, 192
So This is College, 18
Song Is Born, A, 138
Song of the Thin Man, 168
Sothern, Ann, 144, 175, 185, 269
Spendthrift, 105
Spewack, Bella, 36, 66, 259, 277
Spewack, Samuel, 36, 66, 259, 277
Stahl, John, 76
Stander, Lionel, 103, 118, 125, 206
Standing Room Only, 48
Stanwyck, Barbara, 14, 21, 80, 138, 182, 213, 227, 234, 237
Star of Midnight, 171
Starling, Lynn, 63, 185
State of the Union, 288
Steele, Freddie, 248

Stephenson, Henry, 161
Stevens, George, 16, 48, 138
Stevens, Onslow, 259
Stewart, Donald Ogden, 75, 107, 262
Stewart, James, 40, 68, 75, 110, 111, 128, 131, 146, 166, 182, 280, 282
Stockwell, Dean, 168
Stoloff, Ben, 185
Stone, Ezra, 277
Stone, Lewis, 256
Stop! You're Killing Me!, 280
Strictly Dishonorable, 226
Stritch, Elaine, 269
Strudwick, Shepperd, 172
Sturges, Preston, 15, 24, 31, 225–255
Sturges, Solomon, 226
Sullavan, Margaret, 24, 76, 80, 104, 105
Sullivan's Travels, 15, 225, 237–239, 241, 244
Summerville, Slim, 96
Super-Sleuth, 185
Susan and God, 269
Sutton, Grady, 154
Suzy, 54
Swerling, Jo, 45, 122

Take a Letter, Darling, 202, 215
Talbot, Lyle, 27, 58, 63, 104
Talk of the Town, The, 16, 135, 137–138
Tamiroff, Akim, 27, 45, 200, 225, 229, 230
Tarshis, Harold, 172
Taurog, Norman, 88, 217
Taylor, Dub, 146
Taylor, Dwight, 54, 168, 184
Taylor, Kent, 184
Taylor, Robert, 125
Taylor, Sam, 119
Teasdale, Verree, 44, 68, 275
Tell It to the Judge, 217
Temple, Shirley, 14
Terris, Norma, 226
Tevis, Carol, 259
That Uncertain Feeling, 75–76
That's the Spirit, 193–194
Theodora Goes Wild, 17, 54, 197, 206–207, 209
There Goes My Heart, 96
There's Always a Woman, 175, 177
There's That Woman Again, 175, 177
They All Kissed the Bride, 197, 201, 202
They Call It Sin, 21
Thiele, William, 217
Thin Man, The, 17, 52, 163, 165–166, 171, 172, 175, 185
Thin Man Goes Home, The, 168
Third Finger, Left Hand, 200
This is the Night, 17
This Thing Called Love, 69, 72–73
Thomas, Jameson, 91
Thorpe, Richard, 36, 168
Three Blind Mice, 76

Three-Cornered Moon, 143, 259
Three for the Show, 65
Three Loves Has Nancy, 36
Three Men on a Horse, 275
Thurber, James, 88, 283
Tierney, Gene, 190, 195
Tighe, Eileen, 213
Time of Their Lives, The, 190
Times Square Lady, 125
To the Ladies, 259
Tobias, George, 268
Tobias, Sarett, 217
Tobin, Genevieve, 68, 280
Todd, Thelma, 17
Together Again, 217, 221
Tom, Dick and Harry, 45, 47
Tomlin, Pinky, 125
Tomorrow and Tomorrow, 52
Tone, Franchot, 18, 21, 36, 45, 175, 262
Tonight Is Ours, 257
Tonkonogy, Gertrude, 143, 259
Too Many Husbands, 63, 65, 89
Topper, 18, 163, 187, 189, 190
Topper Returns, 190
Topper Takes a Trip, 189
Tovarich, 275, 277
Tracy, Lee, 259
Tracy, Spencer, 19, 21, 84, 86, 96, 98, 100, 101, 111, 221, 223, 262, 288
Tracy, William, 277
Travis, Richard, 282
Trevor, Claire, 58, 280
Trivers, Barry, 215
Trotti, Lamar, 58
True Confession, 16, 177–178
Truex, Ernest, 187, 283
Trumbo, Dalton, 80, 193
Tufts, Sonny, 48
Tugend, Harry, 178
Tully, Tom, 213
Turnabout, 68
Turner, Lana, 150
20th Century, 17, 27, 256, 263, 265–266, 288
Two-Faced Woman, 83–84

Unfaithfully Yours, 252

Vallee, Rudy, 242, 244, 252
Van Druten, John, 44, 211, 256
Van Dyke, W. S., 66, 73, 96, 163, 165, 166, 182
Van Upp, Virginia, 16, 200, 217, 221
Vassar, Queenie, 150
Veiller, Anthony, 171, 172
Verneuil, Louis, 178
Vidor, Charles, 45, 221
Vidor, King, 13, 52
Viertel, Salka, 83
Vinson, Helen, 168

Virtuous Husband, The, 23
Vivacious Lady, 40
Vivian, Ruth, 282
Von Sternberg, Josef, 117, 118

Walburn, Raymond, 118, 200, 204, 204, 232,
    233, 248, 254
Walk, Don't Run, 51
Walker, Helen, 152
Wallace, Richard, 45
Walsh, Raoul, 105, 195
Wanger, Walter, 61
Ware, Darrell, 58, 63
Warner, H. B., 149
Warrick, Ruth, 140
Warwick, Robert, 241
Watkins, Maurine, 98
Watson, Lucile, 75, 159, 168, 273
Watson, Minor, 86
Wayne, David, 223
Wayne, John, 211
Wead, Frank, 275
Weaver, Marjorie, 58
Weidler, Virginia, 111, 274
Weill, Kurt, 213
Well of Romance, The, 226
Wellman, William, 127
Wells, H. G., 190
We're Rich Again, 143
West, Mae, 14, 18, 54
Wexley, John, 277
Whale, James, 171
What a Woman, 215, 217
What Every Woman Knows, 257
When Ladies Meet (1933), 257
When Ladies Meet (1941), 211
Whistling in Brooklyn, 187
Whistling in Dixie, 187
Whistling in the Dark, 185, 187
Whitney, Peter, 152
Whole Town's Talking, The, 17, 119–120, 122,
    140
Wickes, Mary, 282
Wife, Doctor and Nurse, 58

Wife, Husband and Friend, 61
Wilde, Hagar, 112
Wilder, Billy, 16, 36, 61, 138
Willard, John, 185
Willes, Peter, 158
William, Warren, 15, 61, 184
Williams, Esther, 101
Williams, Jr., Herschel V., 285
Wilson, Forrest, 259
Wilson, Harry Leon, 122
Wilson, Marie, 277
Windust, Bretaigne, 213
Winninger, Charles, 45, 156, 217
Without Love, 288
Without Reservations, 211
Woman Chases Man, 156
Woman of the Year, 16, 84, 86, 88, 89
Womanhandled, 16
Women, The, 271, 273–274
Wonderful Town, 269
Wood, Peggy, 158
Wood, Sam, 133
Woollcott, Alexander, 282
Woolley, Monty, 39, 60, 127, 195, 282, 288
Wray, John, 119
Wyler, William, 24, 27
Wylie, I. A. R., 159
Wyman, Jane, 45, 277, 285
Wynn, Keenan, 101, 195

You Belong to Me, 80–81, 89
You Can't Run Away From It, 94
You Can't Take It With You, 142, 144, 146–147,
    149–150, 152, 158
Young, Gig, 75, 217
Young in Heart, The, 158–159, 161
Young, Loretta, 21, 58, 61, 63, 88, 96, 138,
    182, 184, 195, 209, 271
Young, Robert, 30, 31, 53, 76, 150, 171, 190,
    256, 271
Young, Roland, 48, 63, 84, 111, 124, 158,
    159, 161, 163, 187, 189, 202

Zucco, George, 172